Industrial Cities

Clemens Zimmermann is Professor of Cultural- and Media History in Saarbrücken.

Clemens Zimmermann (ed.)

Industrial Cities

History and Future

Campus Verlag
Frankfurt/New York

Bibliographic Information published by the Deutsche Nationalbibliothek.
The Deutsche Nationalbibliothek lists this publication in the Deutsche Nationalbibliografie; detailed bibliographic data are available in the Internet at http://dnb.d-nb.de
ISBN 978-3-593-39914-0

Cover design: Campus Verlag, Frankfurt-on-Main
Cover illustration: © Glasgow Clyde Auditorium, © PantherMedia GmbH, photo: Manuel Lesch; Völklinger Hütte, Archiv des Saarlandes, photo: Erich Isenhuth
Typeset: Campus Verlag GmbH, Frankfurt-on-Main
Printing office and bookbinder: CPI buchbuecher.de, Birkach
Printed on acid free paper.
Printed in Germany

This book is also available as an E-Book.
www.campus.de
www.press.uchicago.edu

Contents

Part II
Crisis and Recovery

Part III
Cultural and Sociological Concepts

Part IV
The Mediated Industrial City

Foreword

This volume is based on a conference that took place on 21st and 22nd September 2012 at Villa Lessing in Saarbrücken, organized by the Chair for Cultural and Media History of the University of the Saarland. The generous support of the Fritz-Thyssen-Foundation, the Saarland Ministry of Economy and Education, the Chamber of Industry and Commerce, and the Friends of the University of the Saarland made the realization of the conference and the production of this volume possible. For the planning and organization of the conference, the Saarbrücken team – Susanne Dengel, Melanie Manusch, Michael Röhrig, Martin Schreiber and Heike Werner – once more proved invaluable. I very much thank them all for their great engagement. Further thanks are due to Oliver Groll of the Chamber of Industry and Commerce, Wolfgang Bach of the State Chancellery of the Saarland, and Volker Linneweber, the President of the University of the Saarland for their illustrative and detailed introductory contributions. I would also like to thank our editor Stefanie Evita Schaefer from the publisher Campus Frankfurt/New York for her practical support and her many valuable ideas. Of great importance and indispensable was the work undertaken by Aline Maldener and Michael Röhrig from the Chair of Cultural and Media History who not only standardized the manuscripts with great care and indefatigable attention, but also offered editorial suggestions. Special thanks are due to Anna Richter, a translator and editor in Berlin, who played a vital role in the production of the volume. She translated the introduction and the volume overall greatly benefited from her editorial experience and numerous linguistic and editorial improvements.

Saarbrücken, May 2013   *Clemens Zimmermann*

Introduction:
'Industrial Cities—History and Future'[1]

Clemens Zimmermann

Preliminary remarks

In 2012 Frankfurt am Main celebrated the jubilee of its Eastern harbor, which—a hundred years ago—secured the metropolis' ascendancy as industrial city that it remains until today despite the importance of financial services. What was built then were not just port facilities; big plants and workshops settled around it and Riederwald estate, too, is a 'child of the Eastern harbor'. Even today, 8,000 people work there, although the real estate sector "is eager to grab the area" (Riebsamen 2012). Currently, the production of Opel's Astra model in the near-by Rüsselsheim (Zimmermann 2014) looses out and in the long run, the existence of the traditional automobile production is in jeopardy. Yet today, the car city Rüsselsheim is already more dependent on the jobs provided by Frankfurt Airport than on those provided by Opel. Both the Eastern harbor in Frankfurt and Opel as well as the airport imply the dangerous potential of industrial jobs and their situation in cities and regions. Frankfurt itself and its metropolitan region stand par excellence for contemporary urban spaces that feature mixed economic functions. Jobs are not just provided by the financial sector and logistics companies, but also by both traditional and knowledge sector industries. At the same time, the area features individual classic, previously mono-structural industrial cities, such as Rüsselsheim that is drudgingly asserting its position and has to deal with the general structural transition and constant sales slumps of Opel in a globalized automobile market. In the meantime, the structural transition equally progresses for example in the Saar region. Whilst the once determin-

---

1 This introduction is based on Heßler and Zimmermann (2012) and Heßler and Zimmermann (2011), in which the newer literature has been thoroughly revisited and reconsidered in the light of international perspectives. In addition, significant publications are listed individually. For the older research on industrial cities see amongst others: Agulhon (1983), Engeli and Matzerath (1989), Waller (1983) and Reif (1993).

ing coal extraction came to a halt last year, steel production continues and the Saar region has developed into a location of the automotive industry (Freitag 2012). The number of scientific publications on the industry city is great. In the southwestern German library catalogue, there are 422 publications to be found under the entry 'industry city', in the National Union catalogue, the key word 'industrial town' comes up with 526 entries and 'industrial city' with 3,456.[2] And these are only monographs that are categorized under history, social and spatial sciences, to a somewhat lesser degree under literary studies and urban studies and even more rarely under architecture. The fact that there is a certain consensus in all these disciplines over what characterizes 'industry city' is due to three circumstances: Firstly, the development of the industry city was in general tightly related to industrialization and social modernization in general, which presented decisive paradigms of the historical and social sciences disciplines. Secondly, throughout the period of urban boom, the growth of industry cities was a strong focus: 'urban and urbanization history' in Germany, urban history and urban studies in Anglophone contexts. Admittedly we know today that cities such as Brighton and London did not primarily grow from an industrial basis, equally Vienna and Berlin were characterized by a rather mixed structure and strong central and cultural functions. Industrialization and urbanization were tightly interrelated, yet not as tightly as it was conceptualized until recently. Contemporary mega cities such as Lagos, Bangkok and Mexico City are a point in case (Osterhammel 2010, 366–464).

Furthermore, research into industry cities was strongly tied to migration and protest research. Thirdly, common imaginations of industry cities were based upon—and are still based on—contemporary discourses, on works of painters and writers. They passed on to us external and internal imaginations: of dynamic, chaos, apocalyptic insecurity, dirt, dark living conditions, strong and intense protest and desperation of the individual. These highly charged, negative images—especially of cities with heavy industry and regions of coal extraction—had strong impacts and reached deep into the 20th century. The 19th century left us with 'coke town' where 'dangerous classes' seemed to question the *bourgeois* order (Reif 2012). Over the course of the 20th century, new images were created: of disciplined workers at the furnaces, of heroic construction efforts in the socialist industry cities that can also be

---

2 Viewed July 22, 2012.

considered as company towns, of social and council estates of the post war era and the model kindergartens there. The industry cities of the 20th century were in every respect the places of modernity, of rationalization with an abundance of certainty about the future and even utopian optimism, as in Magnitogorsk, Zlín and Wolfsburg. Not much later, however, this posed the questions whether work remains in the cities, what demands it made to people and what new spatial regimes would emerge.[3] Furthermore, it was questioned how a future of industry cities could be envisioned in an increasingly European and globalized economy and in the face of the growing importance of the tertiary sector: is their perspective to develop knowledge industries or should they, albeit as late-comers, subordinate themselves under the trend of a tertiary economy?

Existing research

Until the 1990s, this field of research explained the demographic dynamic of the mutually reinforcing and asynchronous processes of industrialization and urbanization, the emergence of particular industrial types of cities (cities of the textile industry such as Manchester or Mühlhausen) and of a new type of industrial agglomeration. It was also concerned with hygienic and social living conditions, with economic cycles as well as housing construction and housing reform (Reulecke 1997), with processes of class formation, actors of urban reform and with the image and the discourses of 'coke town', Sheffield the 'Steel City' and the major industrial cities. Since the 1990s, the still expanding urban and urbanization research turned to a plethora of themes on the basis of changing methodological approaches. This category is comprised of different non-industrial types of cities such as the rural towns, questions regarding perceptions of the urban, the formation of boroughs and quarters, relationships between formations of citizenship and urban publics and the question concerning the character of the city of the 20th century shaped by mediatization, urbanization and the emergence of a third sector on the one hand and by peripheralization and de-concentration on the other. In particular, the question of planning processes and the characteristics of the 'European city' emerged (Lenger and Tenfelde 2006; Bohn 2008). Social historical

---

3 See the early publication: Stadtbauwelt (1993).

approaches, however, always remained crucial grounds for research into the Western European city and urbanization (Zimmermann 2011).

Classic research on industrial cities that has contributed to the emergence of the discipline urban history and historical urbanization research in countries such as the Federal Republic of Germany, France and Great Britain has begun to recede in recent years. Only in the last ten years has the relevance of an explicitly as such formulated research into industrial cities grown again significantly. The reasons for this development are relatively clear:

1. Urban and urbanization research has undergone processes of Europeanization and internationalization so that increasingly, comparative approaches are found that specifically interrogate the 'delay' of industrial cities in the European urban agglomerations and question the chances and strategies of their realignment (Clark 2009; Power et al. 2010; Gilman 1997),

2. The dramatic processes of shrinking in old industrial agglomerations in the East and West are not only of interest to geographers, sociologists, urban planners and urban developers, but also to historians who are integrated in a new interdisciplinary field (Heßler and Zimmermann 2011, 683–691). "The great manufacturing crisis of the 1970s and 1980s, poorly recognized at the time, badly affected the urban economy, West European cities suffered most of all, and numerous specialist industrial towns found it difficult to adapt and move in new directions" (Clark 2009, 277). Hence we need to bear in mind that the conditions for urban renewal in industry cities include education and the qualification for the work force, the active support of individual motivation for learning and achievement as well as the writing off of communal debt. The competition amongst cities and the bidding for model projects was a flawed practice. State and society together need to build the capacity and bundle their powers in order to support cities with international competitive advantage. We cannot develop places everywhere at the same time, albeit painful for some.

3. Research has also studied the shrinking processes in industrialized small towns and the planned industrial establishments of the GDR and the concept of the 'socialist' industrial city (Bernhardt 2012) as well as capitalist forms of industrial cities, i.e. planning processes, actors and concepts of utopian character.

4. The relationship between industry and city has been newly conceptualized. Specifically, existing research until now has addressed the question

in how far individual industrial plants in different political systems have controlled urban development (Heßler and Zimmermann 2011, 663–673). The history of the industrial city thus is everything but free of politics; and relations of power among urban actors, interventions by governments, and internationally organized capital have to be taken into account. The new research into infrastructures focused on the history of technology is concerned with the fact that industrially produced and organized infrastructures have massively influenced the urban *gestalt* (Hård and Misa 2008; Levin et al. 2010). Another strand studies contemporary media enterprises as forms of urban industrialized economy (Holt and Perren 2009). Ultimately, research is confronted with the question as to how in contrast to earlier post-industrial negative scenarios new service- and technology-oriented industrial cores emerged and still emerge.

5. The important aspect of Car Cities: Today of equally great interest is the car city that by now has become globally present, exhibiting great dynamic in the context of an extremely globalised system of suppliers whilst conversely being intricately related to the highly relevant question of the generation of regimes of mobility (Heßler 2011; Wollen and Kerr 2002; Loubet and Hatzfeld 2001; Siegelbaum 2008; Stein 2012; Schmidtpott 2012). Martina Heßler stresses in particular the global correlation of the car cities. This results from the history of auto-mobilization that is catching up and from the global shifts of sales markets. This brought about severe losses for the existing car cities in Europe, Detroit and Flint (Volkmann and Walther 2012); in Japan, China and India the emergence of newly created car cities that in turn influenced the development of places such as Wolfsburg as the headquarter of Volkswagen. The history of the car cities, the way they were pulled early on 'into the undertow of global developments' led Heßler to demand of urban history to take a global, rather than Eurocentric and comparative perspective. Although this publication is not likely to lead to a global history of industry cities, the endeavor to carry out an interlinking history is extremely important; examples include the linkages between Turin and Togliattigrad or the role model of the River-Rouge Works for the Volkswagen plant (Heßler 2011, 97–98). The new global history or world history focuses on the European and non-European *contour* of different types of industrial cities and their colonial or artificial form (Osterhammel 2010, 366–464), as for instance Shanghai's rise. To be noted is furthermore that the structural transformations in Western Europe, with their susceptible decreases in employ-

ment since the 1960s/70s, correspond with the powerful reconstruction of industrial production in newly industrializing countries that increasingly attempt to build *R&D* (research and development) facilities. Hundreds if not thousands of new industry cities and industrially oriented cities as well as classical company towns have emerged in Asia.

6. Internationally, all disciplines are faced with the question of a reconstruction of previous and present industrial agglomerations and cities. In Great Britain for example, questions around possibilities of a reconstruction of employment in the service and cultural sectors have arisen early—considering the opportunities to visit musealized monuments of industrialism in Manchester and Liverpool. It was not historians, however, who asked the decisive question: the question of the 'rise and fall', not merely the 'fall and rise' of industry cities (Power et al. 2010).

This collection

So this volume aims to address both 'rise and fall', shrinkage and deindustrialization, and 'fall and rise', the newer industrial cores, historical and new structures of urban spaces since the classical age of industrial cities, the 19th century. The first aim is to establish an international research context that builds on the appropriation of earlier research on industry cities in different countries and on the discussion of recent approaches. The volume attempts to introduce into the internationalized horizon the consequences of the cultural turn and the spatial turn that are broadly observable in urban research in many countries as well as the implementation of technological dimensions, e.g. in the context of environmental problems. The book brings together representatives of historical urban research, culturally-oriented history of economics, of urban sociology, spatial sciences, media studies as well as contemporary history, and it is, altogether, orientated on what Simon Gunn called the "Return of the Social in the Scientific Field of History" (Gunn 2009).

In his chapter "Beyond Coketown: The Industrial City in the Twentieth Century", the English urban historian provides a fundamental typology of the development of European and Northern American industrial cities in the 20th Century. He considers as a first type the *classic* industrial cities of the first and second industrial revolution that after their formative beginnings continued to strongly develop further. Company towns and planned industrial cities make up the second type. Like the first, this type can be found across the Western world; many of their characteristics equally hold for the planned socialist industry cities of the Soviet Union. Gunn's third type comprises 'mixed' greater cities and metropolises with strong industrial cores. The author offers suggestions regarding a periodization according to genuinely social history criteria: He distinguishes between a first phase 1880 to 1930 with its specific internationality, a second phase until 1970 with considerable modernization and the then commencing phase of deindustrialization. He reflects further on the contours of a future structural history of industrial cities and stresses that the conventional narrative scheme of 'rise and fall' is entirely inadequate.

Furthermore it is attempted to avoid an unfortunately common trait of urban history, namely to cut short the general *contours* of the economic and social process. The collection addresses the relationship between specific, i.e. localized, urban and industrial processes and general historical processes. This includes a continuous reflection of the spatial dimension.

Taking a long perspective, Christoph Bernhardt considers "The Contested Industrial city. Governing Pollution in France and Germany, 1810–1930". He describes, for the first time via comparative analysis, the challenges facing cities and their inhabitants due to environmental pollution caused by industrial companies. The author retraces the processes some of which, during industrialization, led to a continuation of older strategies of distancing from commercial environmental damage, while others resulted in the emergence of legal instruments that comparatively privileged industrial companies, as demonstrated by Napoleon's decree of 1810. Urban planning strategies of zoning, applied in both structurally mixed cities and actual industrial cities, only emerged after some time and especially so in Germany. This strategy prevailed throughout most of the 20th century and led to increasing social and functional segregation. Bernhardt thus demonstrates that even from the vantage point of an analysis of the environmental and spatial history, industry became a decisive factor for urban development in both countries.

Richard Rodger, in "Echoes of Industrialization: Cities and the Trajectories of Development", discusses the historiography of the process of industrialization as well as its spatial and social variability. Similar to Bernhardt, he identifies relations between industry and tendencies of segregation. The author thus combines economic and urban history, revisits the importance of conjunctures in industrial history, shows that typological approaches are indispensable, and discusses—novel in its kind in research—the concrete and close (here quantified) relationship between industrial boom, industrial development and housing development. As it occurred in waves, the construction of buildings and settlements resulted in strong monotonies regarding their form that mirrored generations, which in turn equally enabled common social experiences among residents. Focusing on spatial and economic history, Rodger's concern is the industry city with its distinct characteristics.

In "Networks and the Industrial Metropolis: Chicago's Calumet district 1870–1940", Robert Lewis demonstrates how this center of industry developed in constant tension between the city and its physical environment, and how "a new set of place-based assets" emerged here that in turn "produced a landscape suitable for production". The author further contends that rather than describing the history of industrial cities in terms of 'contained space', one need to take into account the multiple networks that produced both potential and history in the first place. Calumet grew because of flows of material and monetary, relationships with the city region, the exchange with other centers of production, partly across wide distances. Simultaneously, very specific qualifications concentrated here and produced a specialization in production and skills that existed nowhere else. Similar to Rodger's contribution, Lewis' history of networks and specialization, not least with respect to potential political influence of particular companies, will present a future theoretical reference point for the history of other and older industrial cities.

Also included in this volume is the more classical perspective, that considers how existing locational advantages turned into disadvantages (coal, steel), amongst other reasons because of the emerging cataclysmic mono structures for example in socialist states, in England and in the Rust Belt. The volume however equally addresses the question how supposedly desperate situations in specific places (were) transformed again, be it for employment in the high tech sector or for the establishment of cultural and media economies.

In his contribution "In-Between: The Conversion of Former Iron and Steel Industry Sites and Cities in the Saarland. Uneven and Complex Development Paths", Peter Dörrenbächer traces the successes and failures of conversion policies in the two mono structural industrial cities Völklingen and Neunkirchen, and in Saarbrücken's district Burbach. He identifies varying constellations of actors, the problem of path-dependency, and the potential of industry-culture and industrial heritage for redevelopment, yet also the tendency to remove industrial heritage for such purposes. Success, he argues, depends on the social negotiation processes between different interest groups or actors.

Similarly, Christine Hannemann in "The Industrial City as a Shrinking City and the Special Case of Flint, MI" carves out not only the formerly booming car city's dramatic erosion and the failed attempt to revitalize Flint as a theme park. Despite the economic and demographic losses, it is attempted to maintain the city by way of a 'Land Bank' that has a continued relationship with the main actor General Motors, by way of 'Downtown development', 'Brownfield handling', and the mobilization of neighborhood initiatives. Yet in order to secure its future, it is necessary to fundamentally revise the existing urban planning and profit-oriented growth model for which there is a seemingly limited alternative.

In "Crisis in Automotive Cities: The Ambivalent Role of the Car Industry in the 'Autostadt' Wolfsburg and 'Motor Town' Detroit", Martina Heßler is also concerned with mono structural car cities. Yet while the metropolis Detroit experienced an unparalleled decline, great losses of jobs and residents, the car city Wolfsburg overcame diverse crises. The author analyses the structural causes of decline and threats as well as the social and political forces that projected a productive future. Heßler shows that the conservation of Volkswagen's head quarter in particular and interventions by state and city in cooperation with the company (public private partnerships on the local level) as well as the importance of marketing and entertainment enabled Wolfsburg's stabilization and continuous development.

In the final chapter, "Comeback Cities? Urban Recovery Approaches in European Industrial Cities", Jörg Plöger establishes—on the basis of a conceptually broad overview of mixed industrial cities—the role of political institutions and larger programs to renew and retrain skills and qualifications in the context of their restructuration. These had formerly suffered great, often irreversible demographic losses, showed record high unemployment numbers, lacked labor qualifications fit for the future. Many of these problems remained, as in Leipzig, yet it is possible to discern a process of recovery and diversification. A strong industrial basis of the economy remains structurally the determining force in Germany.

It is generally assumed that the close historical relationship between industrialization and urban history throughout the 20th century is relevant and research-worthy. According to this thesis, the 1970s had proven to present the decisive critical phase, a European turning point, the beginning of the erosion of a Fordist life-course, the watershed of new cultural styles and the end of the promise of permanent growth (Ferguson et al. 2010; Wirsching 2011). How strongly globalization in fact produces new crises of industrial urban development, or whether their chances balance out the disadvantages, is one of the most important aspects here. In this context emerges a concrete link to above mentioned strategies for the (re)construction of great industrial cities, for instance new social policies, land use management and land re-cultivation, establishment of technology-oriented businesses and health enterprises, tourism offers and the accentuation of landmarks (Power et al. 2010; Hannemann 2009). Surely, there are disadvantages and drawbacks to upgrading strategies. New powerful actors in the property sector, households with spending powers desiring greater residential space, equally the development of highly mobile life styles—all this has the tendency of leading to a decrease of affordable housing. This volume did not focus on the debates on gentrification, but it is to keep in mind that urban renewal programs possibly result at least partly in such gentrifying practices. We should therefore remain sensitive to these ambivalences.

The still relatively rare approaches of cultural- and media-historical research on industry cities are prominent in this volume. It is after all aimed to clarify how specific self-images and socio-cultural (as well as specific sociopolitical) strategies have emerged in industry cities.[4]

The three contributions of Adelheid von Saldern, Martin Jemelka and Ondřej Ševeček, and Timo Luks establish utopian aspects and historical potentials resulting from the ability to plan industrial cities. In "Fordist Elements of the Industrial City in Germany and the United States", Adelheid von Saldern is concerned with the question how the industrial model based on assembly line production and connected with Henry Ford's name may transfer to industrially used social space. These considerations lead to the concept of the linear industrial city (*Bandstadt*). In her US-American—German comparison, however, strong divergences appear between such an industrial city model and reality, while these discrepancies were paradoxically only marginal in the early Soviet Union. Those elements that were eventually realized—such as decentralization and 'social engineering' of 'human capital'—were culturally transferable and functioned in other contexts, such as that of 'organic modernity'. When the first decades after 1945 started to be referred to as the 'Fordist city', the term had been stretched to such a degree that it now referred to the generally functionalist and rationalist urban de-

---

4 See Schürmann (2005) about Recklinghausen and Klingan (2009).

velopment of that time—beyond the specific type of an industrial city. The industrial settlement Zlín, charged with strong utopian aspiration, showed equally Fordist elements as it developed into a city in which modernity meets standardization in a unique way.

In "The Utopian Industrial City: The Case of Baťa City of Zlín", Martin Jemelka and Ondřej Ševeček demonstrate how a particular way of life of the *company town's* residents emerged in which modernized labor and leisure time activities, planned housing development and surveillance and information strategies concurred. The 'old' model of paternalism merged with the 'new', the ability to plan.[5]

Conceptually comparable to the preceding one, Timo Luks' chapter "Social Engineering, the Factory and Urban Environment: Cadbury/Bournville and Opel/Rüsselsheim (1878–1960)" illustrates how the industrial settlement Bournville and the trade village Rüsselsheim deliberately regulated the built environment of the work force. The construction of company housing and green spaces modeled after the Garden City Movement in particular were attempts to curtail unwanted dissonances caused by industrialization. He thus goes beyond the conventional concept of 'paternalism', showing that 'social engineering' represented a rational master plan in the aspiration to control the future. Yet an at least partly still existing rural lifestyle equally emerges as an important factor of social control in Rüsselsheim.

Rebecca Madgin's chapter "A Town Without Memory? Inferring the Industrial Past. Clydebank Re-built, 1941–2013" also presents a cultural historical perspective. She analyses how the Scottish industrial city Clydebank avoided the phase of postindustrial urban regeneration due to its destruction in the Second World War and subsequent demolition of industrial buildings. The author shows the constant interaction between the built and the collectively imagined city. Various strategies of conserving and creating spaces of collective memory helped residents to identify with their city anew. The collective memory work, driven by a number of political and cultural actors, resulted in the revaluation of the lived space. 'The incorporation of collective memory in new urban spaces' today, according to this optimistic interpretation, shows signs of becoming a future resource.

By questioning the specific media conventions in the representation of industry cities we are finding ourselves in unchartered waters: Is a specific way of representing people typical in this regard that is in turn combined

---

5 See also Jemelka and Ševeček (2013).

with schemes of industry? Is the contrast between old and new a novel concept, oppositional motives of horror and youth (Manusch 2010)? It can be assumed that such media presences in turn have influenced urban planning and urban policy by historic actors. It is equally probable that media interrelationships of representations of industry cities, for example between films and photograph publications, were considered an important task (Heßler and Zimmermann 2012, 14).

Judith Thissen shows in "Representing the Industrial City: Rotterdam, 1880–1970" that the harbor of Rotterdam—whilst of great economic importance and central in terms of residents' self-image—"was only marginally visible" on common postcards, highly popular photo books, and Iven's famous film 'The Bridge'. Industrial buildings, if at all, were depicted from a romantic perspective. Until around 1920, when photographic modernity and the 'New Objectivity' (*Neue Sachlichkeit*) emerged, film makers and photographers turned their attention to industrial reality, yet largely faded out the social world of the workers. This aesthetic and experiential reality was only acknowledged in the mediatized urban image after 1960.[6]

In his article "Representations of Industrial Cities in Photo Books and Promotional Films of the 1950s and 1960s", Rolf Sachsse considers on the basis of broad sources the two genres from a media historical perspective. He discusses the genre of illustrated city monographs and analyses their image repertoires in correlation with representation on film. Here, an arcane realm comes into view as well: the inner side of works (privately owned and locked away) and the reality of the working day that was rarely shown. Even images of the 'guest workers' of the 1960s in the car city Wolfsburg were difficult to publish.

In his chapter "Tradition and Contrast: Industrial Cities and Industrial Work in the Documentaries of Michael Glawogger: From 'Megacities' (1998) to 'Working Man's Death' (2005)", Henry Keazor finds the distortions of modern industrialized city and agglomeration explicitly discussed in the present, namely in the film works of Michael Glawogger (1998/2005). Initially, industry is presented positively in poetry and documentary at the beginning of the 20th century, as an element of a new ideal type, as a part of a new social reality. Keazor identifies the urban qualities of the industrial city, its progressive function regarding social policy, its cleanliness, its role as friendly environment for leisure activities, and its positive position between

---

6 Similar findings in Guckes (2011, 199, 256, 415, 421).

tradition and modernity in the documentary urban (commercial) film of 1972, 'Sheffield: City on the Move'. Yet following the era of deindustrialization, Glawogger's work takes on a paradigmatic quality in that it turns to industrial work and the deprivations it causes. Showing megacities outside Europe, the film illustrates the—still existing—industrial work after deindustrialization in the West.

Overall and in conclusion: This collection is built on previous research into industry regions and cities, concentrates not only on shrinkage, but also on the fact that industry cities do not just disappear and that cultural aspects and potentials belong essentially to their history. It is not to remain with a problematic history, but to focus on abilities and possibilities for development and survival.

Works Cited

Agulhon, M. (ed.). (1983). *La ville de l'âge industriel: Le cycle haussmannien*. Paris: Seuil.

Bernhardt, C. (2012). Zur Spezifik und historischen Verortung sozialistischer Industriestädte. *Informationen zur modernen Stadtgeschichte*, (1), 45–54.

Bohn, T. M. (2008). *Minsk—Musterstadt des Sozialismus: Stadtplanung und Urbanisierung in der Sowjetunion nach 1945*. Köln, Weimar and Wien: Böhlau.

Clark, P. (2009). *European Cities and Towns: 400–2000*, Oxford: Oxford University Press.

Engeli, C., and H. Matzerath (eds.). (1989). *Moderne Stadtgeschichtsforschung in Europa, USA und Japan*. Stuttgart: Kohlhammer.

Ferguson, N., et al. (eds.). (2010). *The Shock of the Global: The 1970s in Perspective*, Cambridge, Mass. and London: Belknap Press of Harvard University Press.

Freitag, B. (2012). Hoffnungsfunken über der Saar. *Frankfurter Allgemeine Zeitung*, 1/21/2012, 12.

Gilman, T. J. (1997). Urban Redevelopment in Omuta, Japan, and Flint, Michigan: A Comparison. In P. P. Karan and K. Stapleton (eds.). *The Japanese City*, 176–220. Lexington, Kentucky: University Press of Kentucky.

Guckes, J. (2011). *Konstruktionen bürgerlicher Identität. Städtische Selbstbilder in Freiburg, Dresden und Dortmund 1900–1960*. Paderborn: Ferdinand Schöningh.

Gunn, S. (2009). *After the Cultural Turn: History and the Return of the Social*. Unpublished Paper, Symposium Bridging the Divide, Vienna, February 5–6, 2009. (Will be published in German in *Eine neue Sozialgeschichte für Wien? Brückenschläge zwischen Kultur- und Gesellschaftsgeschichte* (1867–1919), edited by W. Fischer and G. Meißl, Wien: Studienverlag 2013).

Hannemann, C. (2009). Saint-Étienne: Stadtpolitik in einer schrumpfenden Stadt. *Revue d'Allemagne et des pays de langue allemande*, 41 (3), 359–378.

Hård, M., and T. J. Misa (eds.). (2008). *Urban Machinery: Inside modern European cities*. Cambridge, Mass. and London: MIT Press.

Heßler, M. (2011). Die Geschichte von Autostädten in globaler Perspektive: Plädoyer für eine global orientierte Zeitgeschichtsschreibung. *Informationen zur modernen Stadtgeschichte*, (1), 91–100.

Heßler, M., and C. Zimmermann (2011). Perspektiven historischer Industriestadtforschung: Neubetrachtungen eines etablierten Forschungsfeldes. *Archiv für Sozialgeschichte*, 51, 661–694.

Heßler, M., and C. Zimmermann (2012). Einleitung: Neue Potenziale historischer Industriestadtforschung. *Informationen zur modernen Stadtgeschichte*, (1), 6–14.

Holt, J., and A. Perren (eds.). (2009). *Media Industries: History, Theory, and Method*. Malden: Wiley-Blackwell.

Jemelka, M., and O. Ševeček (eds.). (2013). *Company Towns of the Bat'a Concern. An Anthology*. Stuttgart: Steiner.

Klingan, K. (ed.). (2009). *A Utopia of Modernity: Zlín*. Berlin: Jovis.

Lenger, F., and K. Tenfelde (eds.). (2006). *Die europäische Stadt im 20. Jahrhundert: Wahrnehmung, Entwicklung, Erosion*. Köln, Weimar and Wien: Böhlau.

Levin, M. R., et al. (eds.). (2010). *Urban Modernity: Cultural Innovation in the Second Industrial Revolution*, Cambridge, Mass. and London: MIT Press.

Loubet, J.-L., and N. Hatzfeld (2001). *Les sept vies de Poissy*. Boulogne: ETAI.

Manusch, M. (2010). *Die Selbstrepräsentation von Städten in Bildbänden*, Working Paper, Chair for Cultural and Media History, Saarbrücken.

Osterhammel, J. (2010). *Die Verwandlung der Welt: Eine Geschichte des 19. Jahrhunderts*. München: Beck.

Power, A., J. Plöger, and A. Winkler (2010). *Phoenix Cities: The Fall and Rise of Great Industrial Cities*, Bristol: Policy Press.

Reif, H. (1993). *Die verspätete Stadt: Industrialisierung, städtischer Raum und Politik in Oberhausen 1846–1929*. Köln: Rheinland-Verlag.

Reif, H. (2012). Städte und Städteagglomerationen der Montanindustrie in Deutschland, 1850–1914. *Informationen zur modernen Stadtgeschichte*, (1), 15–28.

Reulecke, J. (ed.). (1997). *Geschichte des Wohnens, Vol. 3: 1800–1918: Das bürgerliche Zeitalter*. Stuttgart: Deutsche Verlags-Anstalt.

Riebsamen, H. (2012). Das Herz der Industriestadt. *Frankfurter Allgemeine Zeitung*, 5/24/2012, 37.

Schmidtpott, K. (2012). Neue Perspektiven der historischen Industriestadtforschung in Japan. *Informationen zur modernen Stadtgeschichte*, (1), 87–103.

Schürmann, S. (2005). *Dornröschen und König Bergbau: Kulturelle Urbanisierung und bürgerliche Repräsentationen am Beispiel der Stadt Recklinghausen (1930–1960)*. Paderborn: Schöningh.

Siegelbaum, L. H. (2008). *Cars for Comrades: The Life of the Soviet Automobile*. Ithaca, New York: Cornell University Press.

Stadtbauwelt, 120 (1993).

Stein, S. (2012). Ein Wald rauchender Fabrikschornsteine. Rückblicke auf die chinesische 'Produktionsstadt' der 1950er Jahre. *Informationen zur modernen Stadtgeschichte*, (1), 69–86.

Volkmann, A., and U.-J. Walther (2012). Aufstieg und Fall der Stadt Flint, Michigan ... end of story? *Informationen zur modernen Stadtgeschichte*, (1), 29–44.

Waller, P. J. (1983). *Town, City and Nation: England 1850–1914*. Oxford: Oxford University Press.

Wirsching, A. (ed.). (2011). The 1970s and 1980s as a Turning Point in European History? *Journal of Modern History*, 9, 8–26.

Wollen, P., and J. Kerr (eds.). (2002). *Autopia: Cars and Culture*. London: Reaktion Books.

Zimmermann, C. (2011). Zurück zum Sozialen? Stadtgeschichtsforschung zwischen den Kategorien Gesellschaft, Kultur und Medien. In I. C. Becker (ed.). *Die Stadt als Kommunikationsraum: Reden, Schreiben und Schauen in Großstädten des Mittelalters und der Neuzeit*, 15–28. Ostfildern: Thorbecke.

Zimmermann, C. (2014). Autostadt Rüsselsheim: Räume, Akteure und Selbstbilder zwischen Lokalität und Globalität. In M. Heßler and G. Riederer (eds.) Autostädte. Wachstums- und Schrumpfprozesse in globaler Perspektive. Stuttgart: Steiner (forthcoming, probable title).

Part I
Research Perspectives and Historical Developments

Beyond Coketown: The Industrial City in the Twentieth Century

Simon Gunn

What do we mean when we speak of the "industrial city" in the context of 20th-century Europe and North America? We might variously refer to the steel towns of Ohio or the Urals or the automotive cities of Detroit or Wolfsburg. But current views of the industrial city remain dominated by the experience of the 19th century, rather than the 20th; we have, for example, few literary representations of industrial urbanism as powerful as Dickens' Coketown or the French mining towns described by Emile Zola in *Germinal*. In much of modern historiography, too, the industrial city is seen as the product of the first and second industrial revolutions between 1800 and 1900 that spawned new metropolises such as Manchester and Birmingham, Turin and Chicago, and whole urban regions such as Wallonia and the Ruhr. In the 19th century urbanization was the sister of industrialization and the morphology of industrial cities was understood as shaped by the requirements of capitalist industrial production, which might produce—paradoxically—a highly rational spatial ordering even under conditions of laissez-faire, as Engels was among the first to note of 1840s Manchester (Engels 1892, 48–53; Marcus 1974). More than a hundred years later the great urbanist Lewis Mumford followed Engels in describing the 19th-century industrial city in epochal terms as the outgrowth and nemesis of the palaeotechnic age, "leaving deep wounds on the urban environment" that would not be healed in the course of the 20th century (Mumford 1966, 545).

In *Technics and Civilization* (1934) Mumford borrowed the term "palaeotechnic" from Patrick Geddes to designate an epoch defined by "carboniferous capitalism" which reached its highpoint in the 19th century. It was replaced in the 20th by a "neotechnic" civilization based on new sources of energy, such as oil and electricity, and new materials like nylon and plastic. For Mumford, however, the form of the industrial city was set by a mixture of laissez-faire capitalism, productivism and utilitarianism in the course of the 19th century. His later work, *The City in History* (1961), provides both a detailed description and a critique of the tendencies to environmental degradation, social squalor and visual ugliness epitomized by "Coketown", which are depicted in terms of path dependence: the 19th century programmed the industrial city in a format which its 20th-century successors struggled to amend. While Mumford's direct influence on the generation of urban and social historians who followed him was limited, his prognosis has proved enduring. 20th-century industrial cities are thus described in much recent urban history as the mirror-image of their 19th-century predecessors. They provided precisely what the latter were seen to lack: town planning, welfare provision, state regulation. But even in this mirror-image the 19th-century inheritance still looms large.

One effect of this powerful legacy of the early industrial city has been to obscure other later visions of industrialism. Put crudely, it is by no means clear what form the industrial city was to take in the mid- and later 20th century, and whether such a city could be envisaged in generic terms of equivalent power and coherence to those attributed to its 19th-century predecessor. There is, of course, a degree of Anglo-centrism implicit here, since in many parts of Europe, not to mention the rest of the world, industrial cities were only to emerge in the course of the 20th century and were to take forms other than those seen in the classic industrial revolution. The differential timing of and paths to the industrial world in East and West influenced not only matters such as the entry-point into technological development but also the related question of the urban form that industrialism might take (Gershenkron 1962; Pomeranz 2001). So to begin to analyze industrial urbanism in the 20th century it is necessary to recognize the extent to which a number of powerful inherited ideas are already installed as conceptual parameters; such ideas over-determine the ways in which industrial cities in the 20th century have been viewed.

Types of Industrial Urbanism

At the outset, then, we have to pull apart the idea of a single type; Engels may have described the Lancashire textile towns as so many "little Manchesters" but in the 20th century there was no *ur*-city of which others were merely smaller or larger variants. Instead, we might think of at least three broad types of industrial-urban formation that were characteristic of much of Europe and North America, at least before wide-scale deindustrialization from the 1970s.

In the first place there were the classic cities of the first and second industrial revolutions, the former associated with textiles and metals, such as Manchester, Birmingham, Lowell and Lyon, the latter identified primarily with the expansion of iron and steel production between 1880 and 1920: Essen, Pittsburgh, Lille, Bilbao. Collectively, such cities often developed as centers of larger industrial regions, the "conurbations" which Patrick Geddes presented in 1915 as a new urban phenomenon (Geddes 1915). By contrast with this urban expansion, such cities also witnessed the emergence of new varieties of urban-industrial concentration with the creation of industrial "parks" or "estates". Manchester's Trafford Park claimed to be the world's first such estate, developed alongside the recently opened Ship Canal in 1896 with over forty firms on its site by the early 1900s, dominated by large-scale works such as grain silos and flour mills. Trafford Park continued to expand in the 1920s and 1930s with the addition of Rolls Royce engines and the European headquarters of the American food giant, Kellogg; by the Second World War some 75,000 workers were employed on the estate (Parkinson-Bailey 2000, 128–129).

As this implies, the older industrial cities often became the locus of new industries after 1918, such as chemicals and electrical engineering. From the 1920s a marked feature of these old-established industrial metropolises was the prevalence of the motor industry as the engine of industrial and urban renewal: the examples are not only the obvious ones of Detroit, headquarters of the Ford Motor Company and Turin, home to Fiat, but also of Birmingham (Austin), Clermont-Ferrand (Michelin tires), Cologne (Ford Europe and others) and Gothenburg (Volvo). In some cases, such as Cologne and Birmingham, their transformation from old industrial centers to new "motor cities" was completed after 1945 with the insertion of state-of-the-art networks of urban motorways, creating new, ultra-modern landscapes such as Spaghetti Junction and the Cologne Ring (Moran 2008; Diefendorf 1989). Cities produced by the first and second industrial revolutions were thus not merely able to demonstrate considerable economic adaptability over time, benefitting from technology transfer and accumulated industrial infrastructure; they were also to prove innovative in the organization of urban space and the generation of new architectural and engineering forms.

The second type of industrial urbanism was the company town, itself more often the product of the 20th century than the 19th. Company towns were to be found across the West, sometimes single-firm centers like Wolfs-burg in Germany, emerging from 1938 as the home of Volkswagen or Gary, Indiana, developed by the United States Steel Corporation from 1906. In new growths such as these any larger sense of the *urbs* as a cultural or politi-cal entity was subordinated to the industry whose works dominated both landscape and housing (Weber 1962; Honhart 1990; Lane 1978). In Fin-land, the town of Nokia grew from the early 1900s near the older industrial hub of Tampere. Nokia expanded rapidly as the site for two large industrial firms, the Nokia Company, producing electrical power, and the rubber firm Suomen Gummitehdas; between them, these two firms employed roughly two-thirds of the town's workforce by the 1930s (Lähteenmäki 2007). Pur-pose-built industrial towns were especially characteristic of the Soviet Union under Stalin. A well-known example was the iron and steel town of Mag-nitogorsk in the Urals, designed from 1929 by the German Ernst May and based on the form of Gary, Indiana but becoming a closed town from 1937 following Stalin's terror. Imported Western models were frequently promi-nent in Russia's industrial cities of the 1930s, as at Stalingrad where Ford and Austin were involved (Kotkin 1992; Scott 1942). The planned character of such towns was also typical, encompassing industrial works, great tracts of workers' housing and, in some cases, cultural and leisure facilities. In Britain, new industrial growths were relatively rare but included new towns like coal-mining Peterlee and the steel town of Corby after 1945 (Bulmer 1978; Harp-er 2013). Such places generally lacked the population size or politico-cultural power to be designated cities, but they nevertheless formed an essential com-ponent of the urban and industrial landscape throughout the 20th century.

Finally, it is important not to overlook a third category, cities where in-dustry was a substantial part of the urban economy but which were not defined as industrial *per se*. Foremost among these were Europe's capitals: Edinburgh, Berlin, Paris, Rome, Moscow—and one could make a similar point for major North American cities like Montreal and New York. Recent historians have argued that London's industrial dynamism has been persis-tently underestimated by both contemporaries and scholars, since it does not correspond with London's role as a capital city, an imperial centre, a global port and a site of conspicuous consumption. Yet London was consistently one of the most innovative centers of manufacturing industry in Europe, playing host to a major concentration of consumer goods and food process-ing firms in West London during the inter-war years: the Great West Road was known as the "Golden Mile" for the number of new, frequently American, manufacturing firms located along it in the 1930s (Lee 1981, 451–452; Porter 2000, 400–404; Darley 2003, 175–181). Another factor obscuring the presence of manufacturing in these cities was the frequent small scale of production. In Berlin and Paris in 1914 94 percent of industrial workshops employed fewer than 20 people; only in Moscow and St Petersburg of major European cities did the large factory predominate in the early 20th century (Lawrence et al. 1992; Smith 1985, 8–11, 27). Similarly New York's garment industry was a business of sweated "shops" and domestic outwork. In 1920 the manufacture of women's clothing alone employed 165,000 workers, the great majority recent migrants in the form of East European Jews and Italians (Waldinger 1981).

The general point here is that industrial activity was very widespread in urban terms; any sizeable city of the early and mid-20th century would have such activity, even if it was geared primarily to local consumption. Yet just as commentators in the 19th century saw the industrial town or metropolis as a particular urban species, so in the 20th there was little doubt as to what urban places qualified as "industrial" even if they had long ceased to exert the fascination over visitors reported by de Tocqueville and Kohl in the 1830s and 1840s (Lees 1985). George Orwell's *The Road to Wigan Pier* (1937) opens with the sound of clogs on cobbled streets and the text is pervaded by tropes that evoke a long tradition of writing about Coketown and industrial place: "the monstrous scenery of slag-heaps, chimneys, piled scrap-iron, foul canals, paths of cindery mud [...]" (Orwell 1989, 3, 10). So while the various types of industrial place served importantly as bearers of new, modern urban forms, they also continued to be viewed by writers, journalists and policy-makers as a social landscape that harked back to the 19th century, not least where the labor process and technology themselves remained little changed, as in coal-mining. This dichotomy between past and future, utopianism and realism, also marked key areas of governmental practice such as city planning.

Planning the Industrial City

If there was no single type of industrial city in the 20th century, the relationship of industry to the city was likewise less direct or clear-cut than it had been in the classic phase of the industrial revolution. Production and productivity were the overt purpose of the planned industrial town or city, yet industry itself was a less marked feature of industrial cities during the 20th century than it had in the 19th. Even in Soviet Magnitogorsk the productivist ethos competed with—and was to extent qualified by—the demands of collectivism, of communal barracks and socialist education (Jerram 2011, 346–349). Here, as elsewhere in the Soviet bloc, economic and urban planning dovetailed, mediated by the priorities of the omnipresent Communist Party (Kotkin 1992; French and Hamilton 1979).

In the liberal capitalist cities of the West, city authorities were unable to intervene directly in local manufacturing industry. This was largely a consequence of the distrust of private companies towards local and central state intervention; private owners jealously upheld the rights of capital to absolute control of their firms, at least outside wartime and the "nationalized" industries. In the United States as well as elsewhere, industrial policy was considered primarily the responsibility of the central (or federal) state, not the city or locality. Consequently, while industry and manufacturing formed an integral part of the town planning process undertaken by local authorities with increasing alacrity from the First World War onwards, they only featured tangentially in the plans themselves, even in industrial regions. Chicago was something of an exception in witnessing the early birth of an industrial policy involving business and civic leaders, yet this was concerned with zoning, embodied in the 1923 Chicago Zoning Ordinance, which it was argued would help the city's boost industrial competitiveness by concentrating infrastructure, information and expertise (Lewis 2013). After 1945 in the West generally, planning powers continued to be limited to determining the *location* of industry and regulating its most obvious environmental effects, such as air pollution, and did not extend to methods of production, levels of productivity or employment (Hall et al. 1973; Graham 1990).

Within planning circles, the fundamental long-term relationship between industry and city was taken as axiomatic. Where doubts were raised about the economic sustainability of a particular sector, such as textile manufacture or shipbuilding, planners, politicians and industrialists rarely envisaged that the lifespan of the sector might be finite, or that industry itself might be prone to dissolve. In an important article on Patrick Abercrombie and town planning in inter-war Britain, David Matless has argued that planners like Abercrombie were inspired by an idea of "appropriate geography", or "what belongs where". Town and country were to be kept separate (hence the "green belt"), agriculture was to be protected and industry contained within its "natural" setting, which was to say in the depressed areas of Scotland, Wales and the north of England where manufacturing had been concentrated since the industrial revolution (Matless 1993; 1998). The idea that industry was natural to certain urban regions and would continue there in perpetuity was a cornerstone of regional policy in Britain. Even after electrification reduced or eliminated industry's dependence on its proximity to coalfields as a source of power, for half a century after 1930 governments and local authorities consistently sought to return industrial activity to the heartlands of the industrial revolution. While the rationale for regional policy varied across Western Europe, including that pursued by the European Community before the 1980s, it often followed a similar path, seeking to maintain industrial production in its old heartlands and taking as given the historical relationship between particular urban regions and particular industries (Vanhove and Klaassen 1999).

Rather than industry, from the 1920s town planning in industrial centers tended to focus on welfare priorities connected to matters of health and hygiene, such as the clearance of insanitary "slums". Across older cities in Europe especially, housing tended to be the top priority for urban planners, connected to a range of biological, economic and broadly social ends. In Sweden the *Folkhemmet* (the People's Home) concept that dominated social democracy between the 1930s and 1970s naturally placed popular housing at its heart, reaching its apogee in the ambitious program to build a million homes (*Miljonprogrammet*) between 1965 and 1974 (Turner 1996). After housing, priority was often allocated to the redesign of the central areas of industrial cities, emphasizing the demands of retail rather than manufacturing. Bradford in northern England, for example, was capital of the Yorkshire wool textile industry, its skyline still dominated by a forest of mill chimneys in the 1950s. Yet the 1952 Bradford Development Plan took as its showpiece the remaking of the city centre as a consumer center for the region. Public planning here conjoined with private property speculation, responsibility for retail and office construction being devolved to national and international property developers such as John Laing, Arndale and John Graham and Co. of Seattle and New York. Developers in turn were used to attract the major multiples, like Boots and Marks and Spencer, to open branch stores in Bradford (Gunn 2010).

All this meant that the image of the industrial city—what precisely characterized it as industrial—became more diffuse between 1920 and 1960, less easy for contemporaries to identify. In the Soviet bloc, socialist realism tended to celebrate the figure of the worker-hero, not the industrial milieu.

Modernism more generally offered certain strong visual cues in the first half of the 20th century, but these were associated with technology and its products—the ball-bearing, the automobile—rather than with the industrial city as an entity; there was no 20th-century equivalent of *Manchestertum* (Houltz 2007). Even in Fritz Lang's *Metropolis* (1927) the most powerful representations of industrialism are associated with the assembly line and automation (the robot) while their relationship to the city is left opaque; the metropolis itself resembles the financial downtown of New York's Manhattan rather than any place of industrial production *per se*. Lang was indeed strongly influenced by his visit to New York in 1924 and based his visual rendering of *Metropolis* upon it (Bachmann 2002, 4–5). Planning itself, intended to redress many of the perceived urban ills induced by unfettered industrial capitalism, worked to weaken the identity of the industrial city. Not only did it foreground social over economic priorities, planners themselves tended to project the city as a universal, abstract space, a blank canvas awaiting remedial intervention, thus diminishing what differentiated types of cities—industrial, port, financial centre, administrative capital, etc.—from one other (Scott 2000).

Working in the same direction, the growing power of the nation-state clipped the independence of industrial cities and their authorities (Lees and Lees 2007). As I have already suggested, state power did not always and everywhere extend to control of industrial production; for much of the 20th century large swathes of manufacturing and industrial activity in Western Europe and North America lay beyond the purview of the state (and, indeed, the nation), helping to demarcate what became known as the "private sector" and the transnational corporation. Yet the state did exert considerable direct and indirect influence on industrial cities in the 20th century, reshaping them in particular ways. The state was the driving force behind the implantation of new industrial cities not just in Russia but in much of Eastern Europe, like Hungary where eleven planned cities were constructed after 1945 (Clark 2009, 238). In Western Europe it was planning systems established at national level that determined the nature and scope of local urban development, especially after 1945. War was a potent catalyst of change in this regard; state control of industries in both World Wars, but especially the Second, paved the way for continuing state intervention once war was over (Judt 2005). Even in liberal Britain the Board of Trade regulated the location of all new firms nationwide from the 1930s, attempting to keep industrial production in its "natural" urban regions for reasons that were economic and military as well as social (Hall et al. 1973; Cullingworth and Nadin 2011). 20th-century Britain, according to David Edgerton, was a "warfare" rather than a "welfare" state, a state that continuously husbanded its industrial resources by means of planning at all levels (Edgerton 2006). All in all, it is possible to suggest that for much of the 20th century it proved difficult for planners or industrial leaders to re-invent the industrial city in the image of the modern. Industry might stand close to the center of modernism as a movement, as the *Congrés Internationale d'Architecture Moderne* recognized in 1933 in its model of the "functional city" (Mumford 2000). But the complex influences of state and economic change meant that the promise of industrial modernity, whether utopian or pragmatic in inspiration, was constantly compromised and diluted in practice.

Periodizing the Industrial City

How then can we make sense of these various points in historical and chronological terms? What is suggested most obviously is that the periodization of industrial cities does not divide neatly between 19th and 20th century. If the industrial revolution in its various phases saw the emergence of the industrial city as a recognizable urban type in north Western Europe, roughly between the 1820s and 1880s, then the period between the 1880s and the 1920s witnessed the further development of a great arc of industrial cities that stretched from Chicago and Montreal in North America to Moscow and St Petersburg in Russia. Indeed, the imperial networks of this arc had already begun to generate new industrial growths outside the West. Between 1875 and 1925 Bombay's textile mills, for instance, tripled in number and the workforce rose from 13,500 to 148,000 (Chandavarkar 1994, 250). The period 1880–1920 has been characterized in various ways; economically as broadly synchronous with the second industrial revolution associated with the heavy industries of iron and steel, and the inception of Fordist methods of mass production; and socially, with the rise of the industrial city as a "stage for social reform", especially in the domains of welfare and labor policy—what turn of the century reformers like Ebenezer Howard termed more loosely as the "social city", the city to be organized around the innate sociability of its citizens (Lees 2002; Rodgers 1998; Howard 1902; Meller 2001; Joyce 2003, 171–178). Planning was part of the "social city" of course, but it was only from the inter-war decades that the industrial city itself came to be transformed through the sequestration of manufacturing activity in specially defined industrial zones; that mass housing programs were conjoined in older cities with schemes of slum clearance; and—increasingly important after 1950—that new highway systems were constructed in line with the onset of mass motorization. Writing in 1961, Lewis Mumford shrewdly observed that in environmental and other terms, the motorized cities of the mid-20th century were the natural successors to the industrial cities of the 19th (Mumford 1966, 545–546). Whatever one makes of Mumford's claim, the period between 1930 and 1970 can be described as a further distinctive phase when major efforts were made to construct planned industrial cities in the East and to modernize their older counterparts in the West.

Perhaps the most tricky phase to periodize—and, in a sense, to analyze— is that associated with "deindustrialization". This is in part because, although it appears as an inexorable process engulfing all parts of Europe and North America from the 1970s, the roots of industrial decline go back much further, to the inter-war depression or even to the depression that affected the most industrialized economies at the end of the 19th century. In other words, there is a question of how to periodize deindustrialization as an historical process. Since 1970, though, the decline of manufacturing across the West has been a clear trend, contrasting with the rise of the "tiger economies" in the East. One careful economic analysis estimates that between 1970 and 1994 the employment share of manufacturing in the advanced Western economies fell by 8.7 percent (Rowthorn and Coutts 2004, 5). In certain industries and regions, though, the effects were much more sudden and dramatic. In the five years between 1979 and 1984 40 percent of jobs in the American steel industry were lost; similarly, 300,000 car workers in the US were made redundant between 1978 and 1982. "In some areas of the [American industrial] heartland", Steven High observes of these years, "entire industries disappeared. Steel production ceased in Pittsburgh, tire production ended in Akron, and the auto industry shifted much of its production out of Detroit. Few industrial towns and cities were spared" (High 2003, 6). Deindustrialization also had wider societal consequences; the numbers of workers employed in manufacturing in the UK almost halved, from eight million to 4.5 million between 1960 and 2004, making it difficult for the world's first industrial nation to consider itself industrial at all (Rowthorn and Coutts 2004, 11). This inevitably had consequences for towns and cities, as research on the North American rustbelt shows. Just as industrialization and urbanization were yoked together in the classic 19th-century phase, so deindustrialization after 1970 brought with it urban fragmentation and even entropy. Detroit became a symbol and exemplar of the new "urban prairies" that opened up in the wake of the collapse of manufacturing industry: dilapidated buildings, weed-strewn borders, desolate factory works, boarded-up houses (Bluestone and Harrison 1984; High 2003; High and Lewis 2007). The examples could of course be multiplied, from the German Ruhr to Spain's Basque Country.

While the phenomenon of deindustrialization offers historians the temptation of a satisfying "rise and fall" narrative to the industrial city, it is one they might do well to avoid. To begin with the story was less one of decline than of relocation with manufacturing processes—and sometimes the old plant—being moved to eastern or southern Europe and to Asia in order to exploit cheaper sources of labor and new markets. Even so, in much of Europe manufacturing industry has remained important. In 2007 manufacturing still accounted for between a quarter and a fifth of GDP in Germany, Sweden, Finland and Hungary. Overall, the European Commission has estimated that within the European Union manufacturing industry accounted for 17.1 percent of GDP and some 22 million jobs in 2007, with the figure for GDP rising to 37 percent if elements like power generation, construction and associated business services are added in. This might appear a relatively low proportion, but the equivalent figure for the world's most rapidly developing industrial economy, that of China, was only a third of GDP (33 percent) in 2007 (World Bank 2011; European Commission 2010, 2). Responses to deindustrialization have likewise been very diverse. While in neo-liberal Britain the Thatcher government's reaction to industrial and economic crisis in the 1980s was the privatization of previously nationalized industries, in republican France it was the reverse; from 1978 the state intervened strongly, first in steel, then in engineering and other major industries, forcing mergers and creating industrial combines (Sutcliffe 1996, 229, 242–244). Deindustrialization also pushed city authorities into a more directly interventionist role in the urban economy from the 1980s, exemplified in cities such as Bilbao and Seattle where culture-led regeneration was used to deflect from if not reverse industrial decline (Landry and Bianchini 1995; Heßler and Zimmerman 2008).

If manufacturing has proved enduring, so has the relationship between industry and the city. The urban morphology of industrial activity in the later 20th century was very different from the 19th, with manufacturing tending to be located in discrete science or business parks. But evidence from urban areas where high-tech industries have taken hold, whether in Cambridge, Munich or California's silicon valley, suggests that such industrial change has profoundly affected the urban form that surrounds it. Indeed, it is precisely the purpose of Allen Scott's *Technopolis* to show that southern California's pattern of urban and residential "dispersion" is predicated on a concomitant decentralization of high-technology firms, occurring since the 1950s, with labor and services following suit. Scott describes the urban-industrial development of southern California in terms of an agglomeration of technological, economic, spatial and infrastructure networks that distinguished the region from Fordist production centers like Pittsburgh and Detroit, while also having certain historical parallels with older industrial districts, based on craft manufacture, like the Birmingham metal trades or Lyon's silk production in the 19th century (Scott 1993, 25–27). Scott's model of late 20th-century "technolopolis" is therefore useful in its ability to identify what is new about such industrial formations, and the kind of 'checkerboard' urbanism that is seen to result from them, while also pointing to longer-term continuities in the relationship between manufacturing production and urban form (Dear 2000).

Overall, this suggests the need for a more fluid periodization of urban industrialism that is not organized, in conventional fashion, either around centuries or major wars. Extrapolating from the arguments I have outlined here, a more plausible history of the modern, Western industrial city might be defined around four distinct phases:

- Urbanization and the first industrial revolution, 1800–1880
- The second industrial revolution and the creation of industrial metropolises, 1880–1920
- Planned cities and industrial renewal, 1920–1970
- Deindustrialization, dispersion and 'checkerboard' urbanism, 1970–2010.

These phases are understood as overlapping. Historical processes are synchronous, not unilinear; just as one technology does not automatically displace another, so urban forms such as "slums" and factory districts persist, are recycled or recombined within and between historical phases. Equally, there is a geographical dimension here, which is to say that Western industrial cities were continuously being reshaped by forces outside the West, by trade patterns, migration flows, and so on from Latin America, Asia and the Middle East. Put crudely, if Manchester's history in the 19th century was interlinked with that of Bombay, so Detroit's history in the mid- and late 20th century was intimately connected to what was happening in other powerful car-producing urban regions such as Nagoya and Yokohama. Empire and the transnational corporation were also part of the story of the industrial city, of course, but one which, to be properly understood, requires the opening out a still more global perspective than has been possible here.

Conclusion: The Future of the Past

How, then, is the history of the industrial city to be written? Looking back to Lewis Mumford can be instructive in this regard. In retrospect Mumford's coruscating critique of the industrial city as the debased urban product of the palaeotechnic age appears in large measure polemic. In the portrait of urban industrialism painted in *The City in History*, the form of the modern industrial city was set by laissez-faire capitalism and utilitarianism in the 19th century; Mumford's was a highly determinist account that saw industrialism in the 20th century as an extension of earlier tendencies to unregulated environmental degradation and ugliness. He presented the industrial city as a flawed ideal type, tending to elide the different historical varieties of industrial urbanism I examined at the start of the chapter. And his sense of periodization was constricted both by his own determinism as well as a binary vision which saw unfettered industrial growth calling forth public or state-led solutions in the form of greater planning, regulation and intervention from above. In Mumford's account, as I suggested earlier, the history of the Western industrial city in the 20th century was the effective mirror-image of its predecessor in the 19th.

In one crucial respect, however, it is necessary to acknowledge the value of Lewis Mumford's account that will be essential for any future history of the topic. This is his point that the ecology of the industrial city is one of the most important determinants of its historical existence and an integral part of its global legacy in the *longue*—or not so *longue*—*durée*. Mumford was a generation in advance of environmental history on this score and his attention to energy and power, to carbon monoxide and noise pollution, to the creation of an "underground city" and its relationship to the threat of nuclear war, was in many ways both salutary and inspirational (Mumford 1966, 545–548). More recently, the postcolonial historian Dipesh Chakrabarty has taken up Mumford's insight, reminding us that industrialization since the later 18th century has combined with escalating urbanization over the same period to create a wholly new environmental condition in our own time. It is a condition of dizzying complexity and danger in which humans themselves have become "geological agents" and urbanized societies a seemingly unstoppable force of nature. "To call ourselves geological agents", Chakrabarty writes, "is to attribute to us a force on the same scale as that released at other times when there has been a mass extinction of species. [...] Our footprint was not always that large. Humans began to acquire this agency only since the Industrial Revolution, but the process really picked up in the second half of the twentieth century" (Chakrabarty 2009, 206–207). From this vantage-point the history of the industrial city is far from a pageant of human progress; it represents in concentrated form the kernel and catalyst of our present, environmentally fragile, predicament. Both Mumford and Chakrabarty vividly convey to us, in short, the scale of what is at stake when we consider the history of the industrial city in the 19th and 20th century. For what they show us is that it is a history whose full significance, and potentially disastrous consequences, are only now beginning to be recognized.

Works Cited

Bachmann, H. (2002). The production and contemporary reception of *Metropolis*. In M. Minden and H. Bachmann (eds.). *Fritz Lang's Metropolis: Cinematic Visions of Technology and Fear*, 3–45. Rochester, New York: Camden House.

Bluestone, B., and B. Harrison (1984). *The Deindustrialization of America: Plant Closings, Community Abandonment and the Dismantling of Basic Industry*. New York: Basic Books.

Bulmer, M. (1978). *Mining and Social Change: Durham County in the Twentieth Century*. London: Croom Helm.

Chakrabarty, D. (2009). The Climate of History: Four Theses. *Critical Inquiry*, 35 (2), 197–222.

Chandavarkar, R. (1994). *The origins of industrial capitalism in India. Business strategies and the working classes in Bombay, 1900–1940*. Cambridge: Cambridge University Press.

Clark, P. (2009). *European Cities and Towns 400–2000*. Oxford: Oxford University Press.

Cullingworth, J., and V. Nadin (eds.). (2011). *Town and Country Planning in the UK*. London: Routledge.

Darley, G. (2003). *Factory*. London: Reaktion Books.

Dear, M. (2000). *The Postmodern Urban Condition*. Oxford: Blackwell.

Diefendorf, J. (1989). Artery: Urban Reconstruction and Traffic Planning in Postwar Germany. *Journal of Urban History*, 15 (2), 131–158.

Edgerton, D. (2006). *Warfare State: Britain 1920–1970*. Cambridge: Cambridge University Press.

Engels, F. (1892 [1845]). *The Condition of the Working Class in England in 1844*. London: Swan Sonnenschein.

European Commission (2010). *EU Manufacturing Industry*. Brussels.

French, R., and F. Hamilton (eds.). (1979). *The Socialist City: Spatial Structure and Urban Policy*. New York: Wiley.

Geddes, P. (1915). *Cities in Evolution: An Introduction to the Town Planning Movement and the Study of Civics*. London: Williams & Norgate.

Gerschenkron, A. (1962). *Economic Backwardness in Historical Perspective*. Cambridge, Mass.: Belknap Press of Harvard University Press.

Graham, A. (ed.). (1990). *Government and Economics in the Postwar World, 1945–1985*. London: Routledge.

Gunn, S. (2010). The rise and fall of British urban modernism: planning Bradford, 1945–1970. *Journal of British Studies*, 49 (3), 849–869.

Hall, P., et al. (1973). *The Containment of Urban England, Vols. 1 and 2*. London: Allen & Unwin.

Harper, M. (2013). "Come to Corby": a Scottish steel town in the heart of England. *Immigrants and Minorities*, 31 (1), 27–47.

Heßler, M., and C. Zimmerman (eds.). (2008). *Creative Urban Milieus: Historical Perspectives on Culture, Economy and the City*. Frankfurt am Main: Campus.

High, S. (2003). *Industrial Sunset: The Making of North America's Rust Belt, 1969–1984*. Toronto: University of Toronto Press.

High, S., and D. Lewis (2007). *Corporate Wasteland: The Landscape and Memory of Deindustrialization*. Ithaca, New York: ILR Press.

Honhart, M. (1990). Company housing as urban planning in Germany, 1870–1940. *Central European History*, 23 (1), 3–21.

Houltz, A. (2007). Industrial flow and national pride: SKF and Volvo, icons of the high-industrial period. In A. Nevanlinna (ed.). *Industry and Modernism: Companies, Architecture and Identity in the Nordic and Baltic Countries during the High-Industrial Period*, 294–310. Helsinki: Finnish Literature Society.

Howard, E. (1902). *Garden Cities of Tomorrow*. London: Swan Sonnenschein.

Jerram, L. (2011). *Streetlife. The Untold History of Europe's Twentieth Century*. Oxford: Oxford University Press.

Joyce, P. (2003). *The Rule of Freedom: Liberalism and the Modern City*. London and New York: Verso.

Judt, T. (2005). *Postwar: A History of Europe since 1945*. London: Penguin Books.

Kotkin, S. (1992). *Steeltown, USSR. Soviet Society in the Gorbachev Era*. Berkeley and Los Angeles, California: University of California Press.

Lähteenmäki, M. (2007). Conflicting Forces in Nokia Town Planning. In A. Nevanlinna (ed.). *Industry and Modernism: Companies, Architecture and Identity in the Nordic and Baltic Countries during the High-Industrial Period*, 122–145. Helsinki: Finnish Literature Society.

Landry, C., and F. Bianchini (1995). *The Creative City*. London: Demos.

Lane, J. (1978). *City of the Century: A History of Gary, Indiana*. Bloomington, Indiana: Indiana University Press.

Lawrence, J., D. Martin, and J.-L. Robert (1992). The outbreak of war and the urban economy: Paris, Berlin and London in 1914. *Economic History Review*, 45 (3), 564–593.

Lee, H. (1981). Regional Growth and Structural Change in Victorian Britain. *Economic History Review*, 34 (3), 438–452.

Lees, A. (1985). *Cities Perceived: Urban Society in European and American Thought, 1820–1940*. Manchester: Manchester University Press.

Lees, A. (2002). *Cities, Sin and Social Reform in Imperial Germany*. Ann Arbor: The University of Michigan Press.

Lees, A., and L. Lees (2007). *Cities and the Making of Modern Europe 1750–1914*. Cambridge: Cambridge University Press.

Lewis, R. (2013). Modern industrial policy and zoning: Chicago, 1910–1930. *Urban History*, 40 (1), 92–113.

Marcus, S. (1974). *Engels, Manchester and the Working Class*. London: Weidenfeld and Nicolson.

Matless, D. (1993). Appropriate Geography: Patrick Abercrombie and the Energy of the World. *Journal of Design History*, 6 (3), 167–178.

Matless, D. (1998). *Landscape and Englishness*, London: Reaktion Books.

Meller, H. (2001). *European Cities 1890–1930s: History, Culture and the Built Environment*. Chichester: Wiley.

Moran, J. (2008). *On Roads: A Hidden History*. London: Profile Books.

Mumford, E. (2000). *The CIAM Discourse on Urbanism 1928–1960*. Cambridge, Mass.: MIT Press.

Mumford, L. (1966 [1961]). *The City in History*. Harmondsworth: Penguin Books.

Orwell, G. (1989 [1937]). *The Road to Wigan Pier*. London: Penguin Books.

Parkinson-Bailey, J. (2000). *Manchester: An Architectural History*. Manchester: Manchester University Press.

Pomeranz, K. (2001). *The Great Divergence: China, Europe and the Making of the Modern World Economy*. Princeton: Princeton University Press.

Porter, R. (2000). *London: A Social History*. London: Penguin Books.

Rodgers, D. (1998). *Atlantic Crossings: Social Politics in a Progressive Age*. Cambridge, Mass.: Belknap Press of Harvard University Press.

Rowthorn, R., and K. Coutts (2004). De-industrialization and the balance of payments in advanced economies. *UNCTAD Discussion Papers*, 170.

Scott, A. (1993). *Technopolis: High Technology Industry and Regional Development in Southern California*. Berkeley and Los Angeles, California: University of California Press.

Scott, J. (1942). *Behind the Urals: An American in Russia's City of Steel*. Bloomington, Indiana: Indiana University Press.

Scott, J. (2000). *Seeing Like a State: How Certain Schemes to Improve the Human Condition Have Failed*. New Haven: Yale University Press.

Smith, S. (1985). *Red Petrograd: Revolution in the Factories, 1917–1918*. Cambridge: Cambridge University Press.

Sutcliffe, A. (1996). *An Economic and Social History of Western Europe since 1945*. Harlow: Longman.

Turner, B. (1996). Sweden. In P. Balchin (ed.). *Housing Policy in Europe*, 99–112. London: Routledge.

Vanhove, N., and L. Klaassen (1999). *Regional Policy: A European Approach*. Aldershot: Ashgate.

Waldinger, R. (1984). Immigrant enterprise in the New York garment industry. *Social Problems*, 32 (1), 60–71.

Weber, M. (1962 [1921]). *The City*. New York: Collier Books.

World Bank (2011). *World Development Indicators*. Washington DC: World Bank.

The Contested Industrial City: Governing Pollution in France and Germany, 1810–1930

Christoph Bernhardt

Introduction

Since the early days of modern industry in the late 18th century conflicts between the use of urban space for industrial production and for other purposes, such as housing or leisure, have fundamentally shaped the European cities. Environmental problems like air pollution and noise were at the very centre of these conflicts of interests.[1] In the long run the struggles became so intense that urban societies and administrations from the local scale up to the central state fiercely discussed the issues and desperately looked for solutions. As a result, a wide range of political strategies and legal instruments was developed. This article demonstrates that in their attempts to regulate the problems of industrial pollution, the French and the German societies and states took different paths: While in France the famous Napoleon decree of 1810 set up a special legal framework for industrial activities (Guillerme, Lefort and Jigaudon 2004), German states in the long run gave priority to town planning as an instrument to deal with these problems.

In order to reconstruct these two pathways in dealing with industrial pollution in urban contexts, this article makes five points: Following some introductory remarks on the modes of regulation of pollution in pre-modern cities, the role of the famous Napoleon decree from 1810 will be discussed. Secondly, the Prussian way to introduce a similar legislation three decades later will be analyzed. In a third step, the article highlights the role of private contracts between urban landowners, which represent a strategy of civic agreement to prevent certain urban areas from being polluted. The fourth section reconstructs the emergence of public zoning as an instrument of town planning by which industrial and other uses of urban space were sepa-

---

1 For an introduction to the general lines of urban development and pollution in France, Great-Britain and Germany see Massard-Guilbaud (2010), Mosley (2001), Brueggemeier (1996), Bernhardt (2004a) and Bernhardt and Massard-Guilbaud (2002).

rated and clearly demarcated from one another. Finally, the growing role of functional segregation by voluntary migration of residents and enterprises in the early 20th century is demonstrated by means of the case of Berlin.

The scope of this article does not allow discussing the wide variety and eminent importance of cultural perceptions of industry on the part of urban citizens that ranged from strong passion to strict opposition. A famous painting of Carl Blechen documenting the origins of the industrial landscape of Berlin-Brandenburg around 1800 suggests an idyllic harmony between early modern industry and nature which completely dissipated in the following hundred years.

Fig. 1: Steelmill Neustadt-Eberswalde (near Berlin). Drawing of Carl Blechen (around 1830)

(Source: Staatliche Museen Preußischer Kulturbesitz, Kupferstichkabinett—Sammlung der Zeichnungen und Druckgraphik, Blechen 310)

Modes of regulating pollution in the pre-industrial city

Pre-industrial urban societies knew three main strategies to deal with the problems that industrial pollution of any kind (such as smoke, water and noise pollution) evoked. One strategy was to externalize pollution by locating harmful activities at the urban periphery. Consequently in most towns polluting industries like tanneries and dyers were located at the urban periphery and/or downstream of the city (Bernhardt 2004b, 9; Konold 1994) if not even, as in the case of charcoal burning sites, far away from urban settlements.

The second strategy was administrative intervention, which considerably differed from one city to another. Around 1810 Vienna, to give only one example, employed a large number of workers who cleaned the open sewers, removed dead animals and discharged garbage from the canals. In contrast, Berlin streets were not cleaned this way and thus much dirtier (Mieck 1989, 223). The different modes of regulation shaped the environmental image and status of cities as perceived by their contemporaries. But in the pre-industrial period compared to rural areas, cities in general were regarded as "graveyards of mankind" due to their poor sanitary conditions.[2] Besides spatial externalization and administrative intervention, civil law offered a third strategy of dealing with pollution in urban contexts. Citizens who wanted to protect themselves against pollution could take legal action by way of civil law (German: 'Nachbarschaftsrecht'). This legislation had been developed since pre-industrial or even Roman times and mainly called for a minimal distance of smell-emitting sources from the neighboring parcel, primarily addressing private domestic practices (Richter 1999, 9). As legal action in the field of 'Nachbarschaftsrecht' was regulated by courts for private law, citizens could hope to legally ban harmful industrial activities and force them to be closed down and relocated elsewhere. Chances to prevent unwanted nuisances with the help of civil lawsuits were not bad. Consequently in the early days of industrialization around 1800, this legislation proved to be increasingly dangerous for industrial activities. This was especially true for the chemical industries that emerged in countries such as France and Prussia at that time.

---

2 This dictum is accredited to Goethe's personal doctor Hufeland. See Bernhardt 2004a, 8.

Napoleon's decree of 1810

It was this context in which Napoleon passed the decree of 15th October 1810. It established a new legal framework for public negotiation and administrative decision regarding industrial production in urban areas (Décret impérial 1810; Massard-Guilbaud 2010, 28–52). The decree implemented three main concepts. It:

1. classified industrial branches into three categories with regard to their polluting potential,
2. separated urban areas for industry from those for housing, and
3. legally established a public discourse on polluting enterprises, the famous "enquêtes commodo et incommodo".

From that time on every industrial enterprise in France that took up production or introduced new technologies had to announce their project in advance to the regional representative of the state (the Préfet of the departement). Those branches of industry that were classified as dangerous due to fire, potential explosions or damage to health were assembled under the first category. Amongst the 32 branches listed in this category, especially chemical industries and technologies used to process dead animals were given much attention (Mieck 1981, 1152). This type of enterprises could legally be forced to locate its production in a certain distance to residential areas. In fact the preindustrial concept of separating conflicting uses of urban land and spatially externalizing pollution was thereby transferred to the industrial age. The second category comprised branches, which caused nuisances but were not regarded as being evidently dangerous. All other industries were categorized into the third group. For enterprises of the first category a permission of the *Conseil d'état* (Supreme Court) was obligatory, while for those of the second category a concession had to be granted from the Préfet. Before making his decision, the prefect who was responsible for all kinds of queries from 1852 onwards, ordered a report on the enterprise to be constructed (Massard-Guilbaud 2004, 70) from the regional board of health (*comité de l'hygiène et de salubrité*). In the following decades the legislation building on Napoleon's decree was expanded into a complex legal system aimed at regulating all kinds of "industrial pollution" in France. Starting with a list of about 70 industrial branches in 1810 mentioned in the 1810 decree, the number of branches that needed a license from public authorities was increased to 307 in 1845 (Mieck 1989, 220). But it is important to note that the 1810 decree exclusively affected newly founded industries while the existing ones were excluded except for some special cases (Mieck 1981, 1153).

The dominance of small scale industries

The implementation of the decree into everyday legal interaction during the following decades provides deep insights into the 19th century urban industries and environmental conflicts. The majority of these conflicts until the late 19th century was still provoked by small scale industrial enterprises and by traditional technologies of production. In her studies on the inquiries (*'enquêtes'*) based on the 1810 decree, Geneviève Massard-Guilbaud found lemonade producers, urban pig farms, skinners and other small-scale businesses amongst the contested enterprises (Massard-Guilbaud 2004, 70, 77). For the mid-sized town of Grenoble, Estelle Barret-Bourgoin has shown that around 1900 tanneries, industries of meat or textile and other workshops still played a dominant role amongst the "etablissements classés" (Barret-Bourgoin 2002, 304).

An evaluation of civil lawsuits at German civil courts confirms this observation and gives an indication of the variety of environmental conflicts of daily urban life. The courts imposed restrictions on the operation of motors in cellars of apartment buildings, which were regarded as a danger for health, on the drying of animals' skins because of strong smells as well as on the keeping of pigs in large numbers within the city. Restrictions were also imposed on the noisy production of steel shells and on the transport of milk cans during the night, on lorries operating without pneumatic tyres and on the storage of bones in large numbers in cellars (because of the flies that were attracted) (Richter 1999, 38). In principle any kind of environmental nuisance caused by industrial production, from the damage of buildings or vegetation, harmful effects on the use of land for housing or production up to dangers for the health of residents could be legally disputed (Richer 1999, 15).

French historians have focussed their analyses on the industries of the second category because the decree of 1810 formally introduced public inquiries for this category. The prefect not only had to task the regional board of health (*'Comité departementale de l'hygiène et salubrité'*) with giving a report on the possible effects on public health. Furthermore he had to advise the

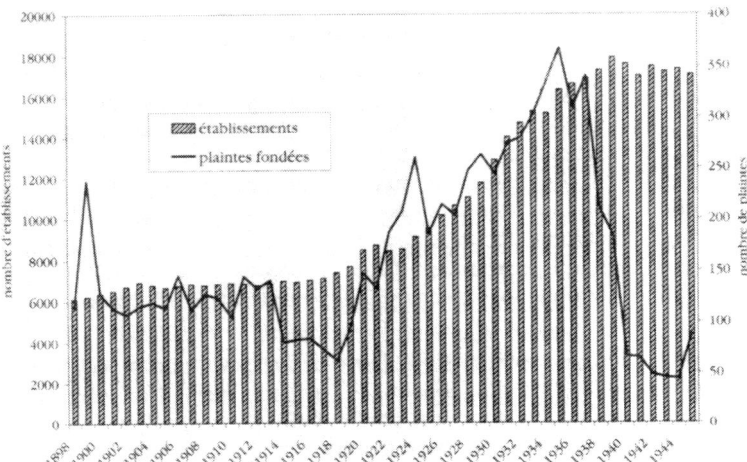

Fig. 2: Environmentally harmful "classified enterprises" and complaints in the banlieue north-west of Paris (1898–1945)

(Source: Jigaudon 2002, 346)

mayors of the municipalities in an area of five square kilometers around the projected plant to start a public inquiry on harmful effects. Every citizen had the right to submit a petition or outline his arguments in a letter (Massard-Guilbaud 2004). Parallel to the rise of industrialisation, this opportunity increasingly motivated the citizens to articulate their perceptions and demands. Gerard Jigaudon has evaluated the number of classified enterprises and the citizens' pleas for the Paris region and found a constantly growing number of public inquiries up to the second Word War (Jigaudon 2004, 346). Christophe Verbruggen has analysed the main arguments of the pleas of citizens of the Belgian city of Genth and found remarkable shifts in the perceptions of nuisances and dangers in the course of the 19th century.

Much scholarly research over the last few years has found a remarkable gap between legislation and real life in at least two regards: Firstly, most of the enterprises only applied for a concession after they had already constructed the plants and started production. As a consequence many of them produced illegally at least for a certain time, but sometimes for years or decades. Secondly, only a minority of the enterprises was formally forced to close down or relocate their production facilities. But the authorities intervened in many ways against harmful industries and imposed a large number of orders to improve technological processes and machinery. Constructing walls, planting

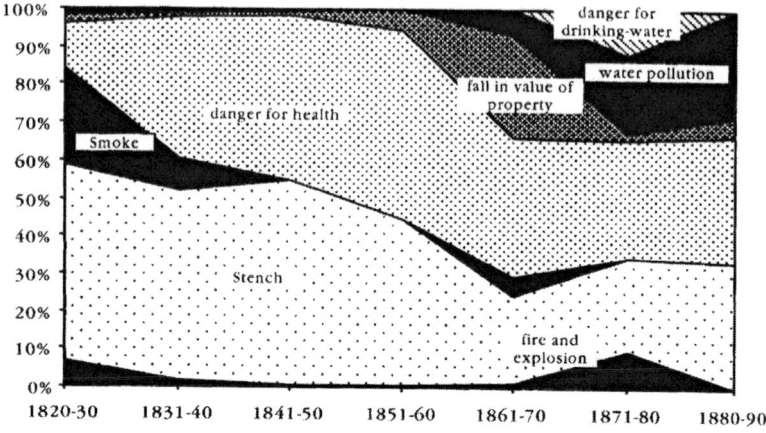

Fig. 3: Evolution of arguments against the concessions to establish a chemical factory in Ghent/Belgium, 1820–1890

(Source: Verbruggen 2002, 383)

trees and isolating waste disposals were among the mainly simple measures of protecting against pollution (Massard-Guilbaud 2004, 72–73).

Scholars have also underlined that beyond limited environmental improvements, the main intention of Napoleon's decree and similar legislation in other European countries was to protect industry (Massard-Guilbaud 2010, 41). Indeed, this type of legal regulation provided industrials with strong protection in at least one regard: when an industrial plant once had obtained public permission, no private legal action was able to ask for production to stop. Or, as the Saxonian High Court put it 1865: Enterprises that had received a public concession worked "under the protection of public law" (Richter 1999, 39). But as a consequence of the Napoleon decree, French industrial enterprises and their noxious effects were publicly discussed earlier than in other countries. Smell, noise, smoke, water pollution, and dust were the main nuisances that citizens criticized in a growing number of public inquiries.

The commodo/incommodo legislation in Prussia

When in the German states similar conflicts arose in the early 19th century, they were regulated according to different types of civil law. While in Prussia's mainland the common law (*Allgemeines Landrecht*) from 1794 set the legal framework, the Prussians provinces westwards of the Rhine still maintained the French legislation and the 1810 decree even after their re-integration into the German Federation in 1815. States in southern and eastern Germany knew yet other types of civil laws. Some Prussian regional authorities used the very general framework of the 1794 common law and other legal rules to direct certain chemical industries to the urban periphery by means of special advice as a part of public concession, as Mieck has demonstrated for the case of the Mattes & Weber plant in Duisburg during the 1840s (Mieck 1981, 1149). In the 1830s some Berlin house owners complained to the police president about bad smells from a sugar producing plant that was subsequently sentenced to elevate its chimneys by 15 feet and change the fuel (ibid. 1169). But these were single cases, which were not backed by a comprehensive legal basis and strong administrative practices. In Germany, steam engines were the first modern industrial technology to become critical. As early as 1831, Prussia passed a decree that called for an obligatory public permission and prescribed technical standards for this type of machinery. Saxony passed similar regulations in 1849. With regard to other legal activities, such as the Prussian legislation on private water bodies (*'Privatflussgesetz'*) from 1843, the 1840s can be considered as a turning point in German environmental legislation (Richter 1999, 11).

In the early 19th century the French 1810 decree step by step turned into a role model for a number of European countries, like Belgium, Italy, Prussia and others. In the Netherlands and the regions that later would become Belgium, the Napoleon decree was adopted in 1824 (Verbruggen 2004, 378). Amongst the German states Prussia was a forerunner in the field of environmental legislation. Here the ground-breaking law on commercial activities (*'Gewerbeordnung'*) from 1845 established a system of classification and concession similar to the French law from 1810. But there were considerable differences to the French role model in several regards. While Napoleon had passed a special law that was exclusively dedicated to environmental problems of industrial production, Prussia merely implemented some paragraphs on environmental issues into the broader framework of a general law on commercial activities (*'Gewerbeordnung'*). This law in fact assembled the various existing rules and by means of clauses 26 and 27 generally introduced the requirement of a public concession for any enterprises that "by its local situation or type of production can cause substantial damages, dangers or nuisances for the owner or the inhabitants of the neighboring parcels or for the public in general."[3] Demands for permissions had to be examined by the regional authorities and made publicly available by the local administrations. Within four weeks every citizen was able to bring forward their arguments before the regional authorities made their decision (Mieck 1981, 1163). Evidently the Prussian law followed a similar logic, but it was very much less complex and rigid than the French decree, as it did not differentiate industries in several categories and was in fact limited to a case-by-case-review (Uekötter 2007, 11). Delegating decision making to the regional authorities was motivated by the expectation that local authorities eventually would be too restrictive against industry. In Saxony, at that time the most industrialized German region, a similar law on commercial activities including paragraphs on environmental problems was passed only 16 years after the Prussian law in 1861 (Richter 1999, 6).

The 1845 Prussian and the 1871 national legislation in operation

A typical conflict to which the new Prussian legislation of 1845 applied developed from 1852 onwards around a cement plant that private investors intended to construct near the royal Park of *Tiergarten* in Berlin. In a lively inter-administrative debate the Berlin police president clearly suggested to reject the petition for a concession with regard to the protection of the upper class residential area nearby and the special legal status of the Royal *Tiergarten*. By contrast, the ministry for commerce strongly argued in favor of the applicant. The investors of the cement plant finally withdrew their peti-

---

3 The original German paragraph declared a concession as necessary for any plant that "by its local situatedness or the condition of its workshop could impact negatively on owners or residents of the neighboring grounds or on the public in general through disadvantage, dangers or disturbance" ("durch die örtliche Lage oder die Beschaffenheit der Betriebsstätte für die Besitzer oder Bewohner der benachbarten Grundstücke oder für das Publikum überhaupt erhebliche Nachteile, Gefahren oder Belästigungen herbeiführen können"); cited after Mieck 1981, 1163.

tion, but in the following years the authorities started to lose control over the demands of investors. They had to accept a number of polluting enterprises for the area, especially those working with steam engines (Brüggemeier 1996, 256–257). The main argument of the ministry of commerce which also proved to be a strong weapon against any legal restrictions for industrial production was the land owners right to ask for financial compensation in cases of legal limitations on the free use of land. In 1871 the national law on commercial activities ('Gewerbeordnung') for the newly founded German Reich implemented a special clause (§ 23) that allowed the authorities to exclude industrial plants from certain urban areas. But the instruments of this legislation continued to prove insufficient in controlling the settling of polluting industries (Brüggemeier 1996, 257).

The federal law of 1871 called for an obligatory public permission for certain branches (§ 16) and gave citizens the right to intervene against demands for the settling of industrial plants (§ 17). But this regulation remained rather general. The law addressed 16 industrial sectors from gunpowder production up to the recycling of animal cadavers and affected 470 out of 1900 industrial plants in Berlin around 1870 (Winklhöfer 2010, 3). With regard to the weak legal instruments and public control the concept commodo/incommodo in Prussia and Germany in the long run never assumed the same importance as it did in France and consequently received less attention in scholarly research.

As a consequence of the implementation of paragraphs on environmental issues into the existing legislation on commercial activities, two legal modes co-existed: public law based on the Napoleon decree and the Prussian law of 1845 were executed by state authorities while civil law ('Nachbarschafts-recht') was practiced at the courts of justice. Whereas public law regulated and partly limited citizens' rights to ban harmful industrial activities, private legal action promised financial compensation and was widely used. This was especially the case with regard to industries that did not need form l public permission. Yet, they could still be questioned by means of civil law and requested to stop any polluting production or sentenced to financially compensate any damaged parties.

Both pieces of legislation fundamentally distinguished between "common" and "extraordinary" nuisances. Common practices of private households like cooking or heating had to be tolerated as well as "common local" nuisances ('ortsübliche Belästigungen') from industrial production. In contrast, it was possible to legally restrict "extraordinary" nuisances that were emitted by special installations for commercial uses. In the course of the 19th century jurisdiction had to interpret key terms of legislation that had been defined only very generally. In consequence, terms such as "common local" nuisances or standards were in fact used as legal instruments for the defense of harmful industries: Lawyers and courts of justice increasingly argued that a certain level of industrial pollution in urbanized areas had to be tolerated as being a "common" nuisance ('ortsüblich'). Another strategy to protect industries from being restricted or even forced to re-locate was the old technique of externalization. German laws like the Saxon decree on steam engines virtually encouraged industrialists to construct high chimneys for the discharge and diversion of smoke. As steam engines were considered an "indispensable means" of industrial production and urban or regional development, the authorities tried to save them and generally called for soft mechanisms of environmental protection (Richter 1999, 11–17).

As the judicial terminology for environmental problems and conflicts remained relatively undefined and objective criteria like critical threshold values for chemical substances had not yet been developed, a wide range of differing judicial decisions emerged. The majority of these decisions tended to privilege industrial entrepreneurs. The broad range of judicial decisions was additionally increased by a strong legal pluralism that characterized German federalism. Thus, Saxonian courts did not see the need to grant permission for paper, ink and sugar plants as well as for forges but called for such a concession for the production of metallic files. In contrast, other German states like Prussia and Bavaria did not regulate these industries (Richter 1999, 36–40).

Water issues

Water issues have received less attention in recent historical research than problems of industrial smoke and noise. This limited interest might be explained by two main arguments. Firstly water-power, which had been the main energy source of the pre-industrial age and had caused innumerous conflicts between mill-owners and other entrepreneurs, seriously lost in importance since around 1800. It was increasingly replaced by coal in the context of the rise of industry in the 19th century. Secondly, towards the end of the century the problem of urban domestic waste water and locally administered projects for central sewerage systems dominated public discourses. In the shadow of these dominant discourses, industrial water pollution was a neglected issue even though it was rapidly becoming more important as increasingly dangerous substances were discharged into the public sewerages and urban water circulation.

From a long term perspective the legislation for water protection in the industrial city shifted from private cooperative associations to public regulation. Studies on water issues in early industrialized regions, such as the west of Cologne, have shown that mill owners in the early 19th century made sophisticated cooperative agreements to distribute the limited regional water resources. But as soon as public concessions for *new* enterprises were formally required, the state entered the scene and tried to moderate these conflicts of interest. As Adelheid von Saldern has shown for cases in the Dueren region west of Cologne, water regulation, as realized in decisions on concessions for mills, was a major political instrument for regional authorities to stimulate and moderate regional development (von Saldern 2009, 175–177).

With the rise of modern industry, water pollution became increasingly critical. State authorities paid special attention to the discharge of industrial waste water and often linked concessions to legal obligations to clean waste water. As Büschenfeld and Winklhöfer have shown, industrial entrepreneurs however had good chances to start lawsuits and limit the public restrictions. In the Berlin region, large chemical and textile plants accumulated upstream of the German capital near Koepenick which was known as "Berlins laundry". They not only polluted the River Spree but also repeatedly caused major hazards, such as the spectacular wave of burning naphtalin that moved down the river several kilometers in 1908. (Winklhöfer 2010, 4–6). While in the late 19th century central sewage systems for domestic waste water became the heart of the modern municipal infrastructure, industrial water pollution remained relatively unregulated and uncontrolled. This was also true for fresh water production, when in the 1920s more than 1000 private commercial water works broke the rigid municipal monopoly of public drinking water provision in the Berlin region (Bernhardt 2009, 107).

Separating uses and eliminating industrial nuisances by private contract

In the long run, German states privileged two strategies in dealing with industrial pollution that were different from the French approach set up by Napoleon. These strategies aimed at separating industrial uses from other uses of urban space by private regulation and town planning. Until now, no systematic analysis of this very important strategy of private regulation has been undertaken. From the early 19th century onwards a growing number of citizens, citizens groups and landowners tried to prevent or exclude from residential areas any installation that emitted noise and smoke. Since that time many contracts on transactions of land in middle and upper class residential areas comprised a clause by which the new owner was legally forced to avoid any noise or smoke emission on his land. This was for example the case in the *Tiergarten* area mentioned above where major restaurants and pubs were not admitted either (Reif 2008, 133–135). Furthermore, these restrictions were also written into the public cadastre, which ensured a certain long term validity beyond individual transactions of land.

This collective strategy had a constantly growing impact on the spatial patterns of segregation in the Berlin agglomeration when new types of land owners and developers became dominant from the 1860s onwards. Pioneering figures like Johann Wilhelm Carstenn who was the first large scale land developer in Berlin bought extended areas of land, which was divided into parcels and sold to the growing number of middle class residents. Carstenn always implemented the paragraph mentioned above in the contracts together with other restrictions, like those on the maximum of height of the new buildings. When from the 1890s onwards large capital companies like Deutsche Bank intervened in the business they, too, took over this kind of paragraph in the contracts and implemented it in the cadastres, and so did some of the first housing cooperatives which emerged at the time. If from that time onward until today the south-western part of the Berlin agglomeration has become a quite homogenous middle and upper class residential area, this strategy of civic legal agreement has very much laid the ground for it (Bernhardt 2004b, 17).

Separating uses and eliminating industrial nuisances by public zoning

During the so-called "Nervous Age" of the German Empire the desire for peaceful leisure time at home and for the protection of health in general became highly estimated collective values. As a consequence the private legal agreements analyzed above were transferred into public zoning legislation. Old local legal rules that for example prescribed a minimal distance from graveyards to wells for drinking water or the concentration of harmful industries in certain suburbs had prepared the ground for a long time. High court decisions also guaranteed special protection for certain public buildings like churches, hospitals, schools. For these places authorities could prohibit or limit the location of noisy industries, large stables for horses and pigs and other industries. In contrast, they permitted extended storage of coal and bones and the concentration of other harmful industries in certain urban districts (Richter 1999, 41).

The forerunner in the field of public zoning in Germany was the city of Dresden, which as early as from the 1840s onwards tried to concentrate industrial plants in certain parts of the urban area. Dresden implemented the first local zoning legislation in 1878, which dedicated a part of the city exclusively to industrial plants. Building law thereby converged with legislation on commercial activities, which equally proposed special districts for industries in Saxony as early as 1861. Dresdens entrepreneurs avidly supported this early type of zoning as they expected immunity from lawsuits of neighbors (Bernhardt 2004b, 17; Richter 1999, 20).

Even if this strategy of public control over the location of industrial plants was not able to completely separate industrial pollution from other land uses, it nevertheless indicates a strong trend in German capital cities: In Dresden the king and his government together with parts of the middle classes decided to protect the famous beautiful scenery of the Saxonian capital against industry, and this argument also dominated public debates in the capital cities of Munich, Karlsruhe, Darmstadt and other European municipalities (Bernhardt 1998, 282). Dieter Schott has shown in detail how for instance the city of Darmstadt/Hessen tried to concentrate and marginalize industry in a "factory district" at the western urban periphery from 1886 onwards (Schott 2002, 315). Here the municipal administration and Merck's large chemical plant came to an agreement to relocate the enterprise in the west of Darmstadt. Similar to those in Darmstadt and Dresden industrialists in other cities also favored the concentration of their plants in special districts. Around 1900 more than 30 major German cities had established an early and simple type of zoning in order to separate industrial districts from areas dominated by housing (Richter 1999, 20).

Migration as a strategy of voluntary functional segregation

In the long run and in the dominant context of liberalism migration was the main strategy to moderate conflicting uses of urban space. It was certainly due to a wide variety of economic and environmental push and pull factors that enterprises and people of different social status moved to the urban periphery, such as prices for land, rents, and public transport. Amongst these motives the attempt to escape from nuisances caused by pollution played a key role. A large number of autobiographic reports, letters—for example by Werner Siemens –, and articles in newspapers discussed the industrial nuisances in the inner city as a push-factor towards suburbanization.

A well-known place in Berlin where such push-factors accumulated around 1850 was the center of the early Berlin machine building industry near today's main station, the so-called "land of fire" ('Feuerland'). In this area some of the most renowned German machine building enterprises, like Borsig, were located just outside the old Berlin wall constructed in the early modern period. In the course of rapid urban growth from the 1850s onwards, this area was densely populated by poorer people. The popular name "land of fire" reflects the fact that the area was often illuminated by industrial production and shaken by the noise and vibrations from the steam hammers, as contemporary reports document (Mieck 1987, 576). Berlin's chemical industry was concentrated only some kilometers north of the "land of fire". Workshops like the "oil-kitchen" of the Cohn chemical plant provided very unhealthy labour conditions and emitted polluting substances into the air and the water system. Some large enterprises, like the chemical plant of W. Spindler, undertook considerable measures to protect their workers from the harmful effects of petrol emissions and at the same time saved this precious substance for the reuse in production. In contrast the chemical plant of Kuhnheim is a prominent example of a polluting enterprise, which as a result of its resistance against the implementation of new technologies was forced to relocate. As early as 1827, police authorities succeeded in implementing a formal interdiction by the ministry for the Interior of Kuhnheim's bone-burning and soap-producing technologies. As a result of long lasting conflicts the plant was moved twice in the following decades, first to the southern periphery of Berlin and then outside of the municipal boundaries (Borgmann 1987, 348–351).

From around 1870 onwards Berlin's most important industrial enterprises relocated their production and migrated to the periphery in order to prevent conflicts with neighboring citizens and the authorities, to comfortably discharge their wastes and to profit from the large availability of rural land. These and other environmental motives for migration have been underestimated by traditional historiography compared to factors like low prices for land, better conditions for production and expansion as well as transport facilities. For Berlin, scholarly research has identified two intense migration waves of large industrial enterprises to the periphery. In the course of the so-called "second migration to the periphery" (*'zweite Randwanderung'*) in Greater Berlin after 1890 large industrial enterprises like Siemens, AEG, and Borsig moved to places as distant as ten to 20 kilometers from the city centre (Erbe 1987, 729).

The pressure of environmental conflicts and motives for migration were very much determined by the nature of industrial production in different branches. The technologies used in the machine building, coal mining and electric industries caused very different kinds of environmental nuisances and public reactions in the surrounding areas. 19th century citizens and authorities were perfectly aware of these different environmental effects of industries. The alkali industries, amongst others, were known as a highly polluting branch, which in the south of Liverpool devastated the landscape and created a real "moon landscape". As a result of public campaigns, English Parliament passed the "Alcali etc. Works Regulation Act" in 1863 which was the most important 19th century environmental law in Britain. The pottash industry was another sector that seriously polluted the water bodies with sulphur, chlorine base and other chemical substances. The mining and smelting industries counted amongst the most polluting industries and with their smoke emissions devastated large areas. Trees and forests showed serious damages so that the phenomenon of "dying woods" (*'Waldsterben'*) was very common as early as in the 19th century, long before becoming an environmental key term in late 20th century Germany (Mieck 1989, 220–224).

In comparison to Borsig's steam hammers in the mid-19th century 'land of fire'-period mentioned above even the large scale electric plants of Siemens in the west of Berlin caused considerably less environmental nuisances. Consequently the enterprise was able to locate its rapidly growing production in relative proximity to the residential areas in the new quarter of "Siemensstadt". Yet the situation of Siemens and of Berlin in general presented a special case in several regards. There was no mining industry and the density of Berlin's surrounding region of Brandenburg was quite low so that the conditions for relocating large scale industries were better than in other areas. As a result Greater Berlin showed a relatively strong social and functional segregation. In the Ruhr valley, by contrast, major mining enterprises and urban centres were located in close proximity to each other in a densely mixed "multipolar" structure (Cordes 1972, 5). A close spatial co-existence of railway areas, large coal fields and industrial "no-go areas" massively disturbed mobility, spatial cohesion and the environmental status of the area.

Conclusion: Towards zoning

Studies on the history of town planning have shown that public zoning as a mode of regulating industrial pollution became very important in the 20th century and culminated in the famous town planning Charta of CIAM. In Berlin, the first zoning legislation for parts of the urban area was introduced in 1892. It was modernized in 1905 and then expanded after the 1918 revolution in the famous Berlin building legislation and zoning plan of 1925/29. From that time on every industrial entrepreneur, landlord, and citizen was eligible to get an overview over the industrial, residential and other uses that are admitted in the urban area be studying the official planning document (the so-called "Flächennutzungsplan"). Surprisingly the role of environmental motives as a trigger within this movement towards zoning has not yet been sufficiently reflected by planning historians up to now.

This article intended to show that from the very beginning of the industrial age in continental Europe, citizens and administrations were engaged in extended public discourses on the nuisances brought about by modern industry. A wide range of private agreements and public interventions from the individual contract regulating the transaction of land up to the national legislation desperately intended to mediate between the conflicting uses of urban space. Other accomplishments that could not be considered here, such as the break-through of fire protection in building legislation, confirm this observation. If city and regional planning in the 20th century placed the concept of functional segregation and zoning center stage in its philosophy, it did so by building on strong old traditions in civil society as well as in municipal administration and national legislation since the early 19th century.

Works Cited

Barret-Bourgoin, E. (2002). Modifications du paysage industriel et esprit industrialiste: les autorités municipales face aus pollutions industrielles à Grenoble au XIXe siècle. In C. Bernhardt and G. Massard-Guilbaud (eds.). *Le démon moderne. La pollution dans les sociétés urbaines et industrielles d'Europe. The modern demon. Pollution in urban and industrial European societies*, 289–310. Clermont-Ferrand: Presses Universitaires Blaise-Pascal Histoire Croisées.

Bernhardt, C. (1998). *Bauplatz Groß-Berlin*. Berlin and New York: Walter de Gruyter.

Bernhardt, C. (ed.) (2004a). *Environmental problems in European Cities in the 19th and 20th century. Umweltprobleme europäischer Städte des 19. und 20. Jahrhunderts*. Münster: Waxmann.

Bernhardt, C. (2004b). Umweltprobleme in der neueren europäischen Stadtgeschichte. In C. Bernhardt (ed.). *Environmental problems in European Cities in the 19th and 20th century. Umweltprobleme europäischer Städte des 19. und 20. Jahrhunderts*, 5–24. Münster: Waxmann.

Bernhardt, C. (2009). Die Grenzen der sanitären Moderne—Aufstieg und Krise der Wasserpolitik in Berlin-Brandenburg 1900–1937. In C. Bernhardt, H. Kilper and T. Moss (eds.). *Im Interesse des Gemeinwohls. Regionale Gemeinschaftsgüter in Geschichte, Politik und Planung*, 85–114. Frankfurt am Main and New York: Campus Verlag.

Bernhardt, C., and G. Massard-Guilbaud (eds.) (2002). *Le démon moderne. La pollution dans les sociétés urbaines et industrielles d'Europe. The modern demon. Pollution in urban and industrial European societies*. Clermont-Ferrand: Presses Universitaires Blaise-Pascal Histoire Croisées.

Borgmann, M. (1987). Die chemische Industrie. In J. Boberg et al. (eds.). *Exerzierfeld der Moderne*, 344–351. München: C.H. Beck.

Brüggemeier, F.-J. (1996). *Das unendliche Meer der Lüfte. Luftverschmutzung, Industrialisierung und Risikodebatten im 19. Jahrhundert*. Essen: Klartext Verlag.

Cordes, G. (1972). *Zechenstillegungen im Ruhrgebiet (1900–1968)*. Essen: Kommunalverband Ruhrgebiet.

Décret impérial relatif au Manufactures et Ateliers qui répandent une Odeur insalubre ou incommode du 15 Octobre 1810. In Recueil des lois, décrets et avis du conseil d'état publiés dans les départements de l'Ems Supérieure, des Bouches-du-Weser, et des Bouches-de-l'Elbe, tom. 4, Paris 1811, 452–461.

Erbe, M. (1987). Berlin im Kaiserreich (1871–1918). In W. Ribbe (ed.). *Geschichte Berlins*, Vol. 2, 691–793. München: C. H. Beck.

Guillerme, A., A.-C. Lefort, and G. Jigaudon (2004). *Dangereux, insalubres et incommodes. Paysages industriels en banlieu Parisienne XIXe–XXe siècle*. Seyssel: Éditions Champs Vallons.

Jigaudon, G. (2002). Un siècle de cohabitation habitat—industrie dans la banlieue nord—ouest de Paris (1860–1960). In C. Bernhardt and G. Massard-Guilbaud (eds.). *Le démon moderne. La pollution dans les sociétés urbaines et industrielles d'Europe. The modern demon. Pollution in urban and industrial European societies*, 333–349. Clermont-Ferrand: Presses Universitaires Blaise-Pascal Histoire Croisées.

Konold, W. (1994). Wassernutzung und Wasserbewirtschaftung in Isny im Allgäu. In W. Konold (ed.). *Historische Wasserwirtschaft im Alpenraum und an der Donau*, 299–342. Stuttgart: Verlag Konrad Wittwer.

Massard-Guilbaud, G. (2004). Einspruch! Stadtbürger und Umweltverschmutzung im Frankreich des 19. Jahrhunderts. In C. Bernhardt (ed.). *Environmental problems in European Cities in the 19th and 20th century. Umweltprobleme europäischer Städte des 19. und 20. Jahrhunderts*, 67–86. Münster: Waxmann.

Massard-Guilbaud, G. (2010). *Histoire de la pollution industrielle. France, 1789–1914*. Paris: Éditions de l'École des hautes études en sciences sociales.

Mieck, I. (1981). Umweltschutz in Preußen zur Zeit der Frühindustrialisierung. In O. Büsch and W. Neugebauer (eds.). *Moderne Preußische Geschichte 1648–1947. Eine Anthologie*. Vol. 2, 1141–1167. Berlin and New York: Walter de Gruyter.

Mieck, I. (1987). Von der Reformzeit zur Revolution. In W. Ribbe (ed.). *Geschichte Berlins*. Vol. 1, 407–602. München: C. H. Beck Verlag.

Mieck, I. (1989). Industrialisierung und Umweltschutz. In J. Calließ, J. Rüsen, and M. Stiegnitz (eds.). *Mensch und Umwelt in der Geschichte*, 205–227. Pfaffenweiler: Centaurus Verlag.

Mosley, S. (2001). *The chimney of the world. A history of smoke pollution in Viktorian and Edwardian Manchester*. Cambridge: The White Horse Press.

Reif, H. (2008). Das Tiergartenviertel. In H. Reif (ed.). *Berliner Villenleben*, 133–162. Berlin: Gebr. Mann Verlag.

Richter, G. (1999). *Aspekte des Umweltschutzes in der Rechtsprechung von 1850 bis 1945*. Dresden: Institut für ökologische Raumentwicklung.

Saldern, A. von (2009). *Netzwerkökonomie im frühen 19. Jahrhundert*. Stuttgart: Franz Steiner Verlag.

Schott, D. (2002). The formation of an urban industrial policy to counter pollution in German cities (1890–1914). In C. Bernhardt and G. Massard-Guilbaud (eds.). *Le démon moderne. La pollution dans les sociétés urbaines et industrielles d'Europe. The modern demon. Pollution in urban and industrial European societies*, 311–332. Clermont-Ferrand: Presses Universitaires Blaise-Pascal Histoire Croisées.

Uekötter, F. (2007). *Umweltgeschichte im 19. und 20. Jahrhundert*. München: Oldenbourg.

Verbruggen, C. (2002). Nineteenth century reactions to industrial pollution in Ghent, the Manchester of the continent. The case of the chemical industry. In C. Bernhardt and G. Massard-Guilbaud (eds.). *Le démon moderne. La pollution dans les sociétés urbaines et industrielles d'Europe. The modern demon. Pollution in urban and industrial European societies*, 377–392. Clermont-Ferrand: Presses Universitaires Blaise-Pascal Histoire Croisées.

Echoes of Industrialization: Cities and the Trajectories of Development

Richard Rodger

The concepts of an industrial 'revolution' and of a 'take-off into self-sustained growth' have long since disappeared. Instead, 'proto-industrialisation' with its emphasis on a rural- and village-based acceleration of the economy has gained ascendancy (Ogilvie and Cerman 1996). Gradualism and pluralism have replaced the drama of abrupt industrial transformation as historians have become increasingly adept at deploying empiricism where previously generalised theories prevailed. This was unsurprising since the industrial state simply did not map on to the 19th century nation state, nor did it fit with the diversity of economic and urban geography, nor with the significance increasingly attached to agricultural productivity in the process of industrialisation (Pollard 1981; Hudson 1989; Lee 1981, 45; Southall 1988, 236). Attention has since been directed to Lancashire and Lanarkshire, to Bohemia and Silesia, the Saar and the Ruhr. Nodes of industrialization and the scale of analysis are crucial to understanding the trajectories of urban development.

This chapter explores three dimensions with an urban perspective uppermost: firstly, the varieties of 19th- and 20th-century industrial experience with their divergent trajectories and typologies in an urban setting; secondly, the consequences of these trajectories and the 'echo effects' that result are considered; and thirdly, alongside the production structure of towns and cities—the scale of business and corporate structures—a long run harmonic is woven into an explanation of the legacies of industrialisation that also influences the timing and nature of urban renewal.

Typologies and trajectories: the production of the industrial town

One point of departure is to focus on typologies of place (Checkland 1983, 464). This is based on a straightforward categorisation of towns and cities using similar characteristics. At one level, such an approach embraces, as a type, Braudel's Mediterranean cities; another, Canadian prairie cities; British industrial or American rust belt cities or cities of North Rhine-Westphalia in Germany; or even Scottish New Towns. A unifying characteristic legitimatises membership of the family of towns and cities; it transcends the national framework when port cities, primate cities, socialist cities and tourist cities, for example, are considered. The family members may share characteristics that are socio-economic, spatial, perceptual and cultural.

To use a different motif, the 'family' genes are the result of fundamental processes associated with urbanisation and industrialisation that in turn are shaped around common or similar features in the form of business structure, capital formation, demography, and crucially, income and class profiles. In short, within the framework of a national economy there are parallel experiences conditioned by the core business or principal economic activity in the group of towns or cities. Individually, and as family members, towns contribute hugely to the national economy, of course, but crucially, the manner in which they do so, and the trajectory of urban expansion and contraction, is conditioned by their core business.

The explanation for sluggish growth, and its relevance to the trajectory of expansion and contraction of towns and cities, can be advanced in terms of the income-elasticity of demand. To over-simplify the urbanisation process considerably, the countryside can be considered as the producer of food and raw materials and the city as the producer of goods and services. However, the income elasticity of demand, that is, the responsiveness of the demand for a good to a change in the income of the people demanding, is much lower in the countryside, while towns and cities generally have a higher income elasticity for their goods and services. It is sometimes presented as a universal law that as an economy becomes more advanced so its service sector expands significantly. In short, with rising incomes there is a limit to the volume of food that can be consumed and proportionately greater scope for increased demand for secondary goods and services. So a sustained rise in real per capita incomes actually results in lower relative demand for primary goods and a shift towards the production of goods and services. In essence this is the basis of the urban transition and the underlying rationale for rural to urban migrations. However, not all industries—and thus the towns where they are concentrated—enjoy the same level of income elasticity and thus are more prone to depressions and ultimately to bankruptcies and closures than others. At a national level, the 'retardation' of the British economy in the late-19th century and the depression in the 1920s had much to do with the composition of the economy. The balance of British industry was skewed towards slow-growing industries with lower income elasticities than was the case amongst its competitors; in other words, there were few high-flying, world-leading industrial sectors in the portfolio of British industry during the inter-war years (Aldcroft and Fearon 1969).

One way of conceptualising the trajectory of urban growth is to consider the specialism of a 'family' group, this time based on products. A typology of towns can be developed in relation to specific industries: brewing, footwear, iron and steel, pottery, shipbuilding, cotton and wool textiles, engineering and tool-making, coal mining, and later, chemicals, automobiles, and air-craft each provided a distinctive character and trajectory to the development of the towns and cities producing them. Indeed, some places and products are almost interchangeable: Stoke-on-Trent is known as 'The Potteries; Li-moges is linked indissolubly with porcelain; Delft with pottery. In America Milwaukee and Pittsburgh sports teams are identified by the terms 'Brewers' and 'Steelers', and in England football teams are affectionately known by the dominant industry of the town: Northampton 'Cobblers', Luton 'Hatters', Walsall 'Saddlers', and Yeovil 'Glovers.' Individually distinctive, these places are in turn members of a family, and if there may not be many members of the hatters or glovers families, some cases of extended families do exist: in Britain the steel 'family' included Middlesbrough, Motherwell, Sheffield, Rotherham, Ebbw Vale, and Wishaw, as well as some junior members. The shipbuilding family dominated world production; in 1913 over 20 percent of merchant shipping in the world was launched from the various Clydeside yards, and another 39 percent was built by other prominent 'family' mem-bers—Birkenhead, Belfast, Barrow and Jarrow (Tyneside) yards to be found on estuaries around Britain (Robertson 1977, 262). The urban typology was not confined to industrial production; county towns, distribution centres, railway hubs, spas, and regional capitals each constituted another family type based on distinctive administrative and service functions.

The focus on typology is highly significant because it produced defining characteristics for the town. For example, in Leicester, the footwear industry expanded so rapidly between 1861 and 1891 that a century later 60 percent of the firms in the boot and shoe industry did so from factory premises constructed in this late-Victorian period (Mounfield 1972, 370). Footwear and knitwear, jointly, underpinned the Leicester economy. In 1881, six out of ten workers in hosiery were women; seven out of ten workers in the shoe trade were men. This was highly significant. In terms of household income Leicester families were heavily insulated against bouts of unemployment. Though not exempt from trade cycles, hosiery and footwear as consumption-based industries were less prone to the periodic and sometimes prolonged depressions and 'lumpy' investment patterns that were characteristic of capital goods industries. The complementarity and continuity of employment in Leicester enabled workers to enjoy a high standard of living as reflected in the quality of the housing stock and the number of persons per room was 20 percent below the average of the larger English boroughs. The quality and durability of the pre-1914 housing stock can also be assessed from the fact that 35 percent of the habitable housing in Leicester in 2011 was built before 1914 compared to the national average of just 25 percent (Rodger 2013).

The gender balance in cities, as determined by the industrial structure and employment opportunities, also affected household incomes and thus defined living standards, including the physical fabric of the home. Leicester contrasted starkly, therefore, with other English boroughs. The 'participation' rate for Leicester women—the proportion of women of working age (13–64) who were active in the labour force—was 54 percent, significantly above the English average of 37 percent in 1911, and above all the major cities nearby (Census of England 1911). In the steel city of Sheffield (32 percent) and railway engineering borough of Derby (35 percent) the much lower female participation rates reflected the influence of a capital goods based industrial structure and the greater dependence of local workers on the wages of the male breadwinner. Masculinity was more dominant in such locations and was reflected in the socio-cultural structures of steel-making and ship-building places.

The nature and composition of industrial employment fundamentally influenced the scale and capital complexity of factories and plant, as well as the affordability and amenity of the housing stock. Where industrialists were heavily involved in politics and voluntary organisations, then public buildings, too, were often gifted as a result of generous donations and legacies.

Each industrial 'family' member had a comparative advantage based on the coincidence of suitable and sustainable power sources and raw materials.

Since agricultural goods have a low elasticity, or are inelastic in relation to income growth, what productivity gains there were in the countryside did not result in significantly increased employment opportunities there; accordingly labourers gravitated towards towns and cities for work. Urban wages reflected the rise in labour productivity, and the rural-urban wage divide widened prompting further labour migrations. Thus the buoyant urban economy was boosted yet again, with employment multipliers that spread into other sectors of the city economy, especially building. The ultimate destination of migrants depended on many factors, including kinship networks and local knowledge, but the magnetic effect of one town or city over another depended ultimately on employment prospects there. If these proved negligible or uncertain, then emigration was the preferred option of thousands.

Building Synchronicity in the City

Critically, not all industries expanded—or contracted—at the same pace, and so the construction of houses and industrial premises experienced divergent time trends from one place to another. There were, of course, common factors—credit, changes in fashion, and most significantly technological advances based on knowledge exchanges within the cities themselves. Indeed, in an emphatic reversal of the conventional view of the role of the city in the growth of commerce and the professions, greater stress has been attached to the role of the educated middle classes in city formation by providing knowledge networks and 'information super-highways of the 19th century' (Reeder and Rodger 2000, 554). Put differently, 'The talk of the bourgeoisie, not the smoke of the factory, was the defining characteristic of the modern city economy' (Clark and Nardinelli 1996, 384).

The correspondence between industrial activity and fluctuations in housebuilding is apparent from an analysis of Bradford investment (Fig. 1). Between 1852 and 1900 a positive correlation of +0.50 existed between fluctuations in industrial and residential construction. When Bradford's woollen industry went progressively into decline from 1900 the correlation coefficient was -0.28, and the recovery of the residential sector depended less upon the woollen sector and more upon incomes generated by other local sources and national factors. This pattern of prosperity and structural decline

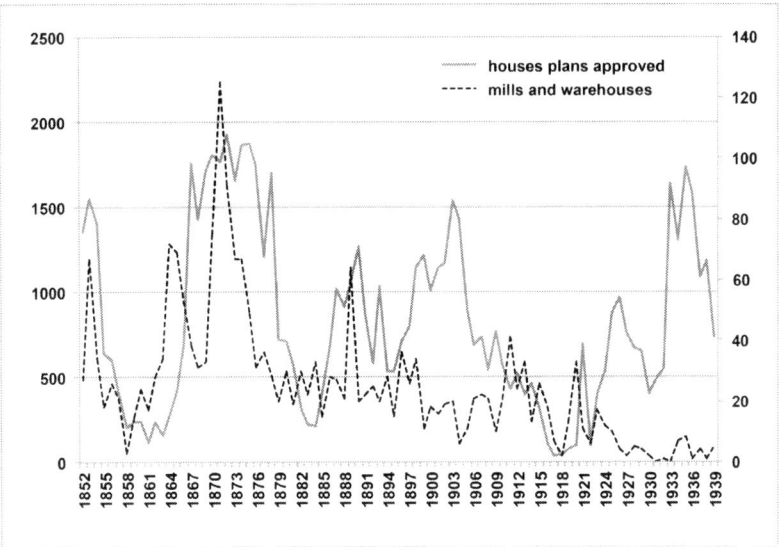

Fig. 1: Bradford Housebuilding and Industrial Building 1852–1939

(Source: Based on data J. P. Lewis, 1965, Appendix 5. See also Appendices 8 and 9 for data on Liverpool and Hull)

Note: the correlation coefficients would be slightly higher with a lagged relationship for the housebuilding series.

in the woollen industry and its impact on the construction sector was mirrored in the woollen towns of the Scottish borders (see Tab. 1 below).

The particular example of Bradford can be extended to explore the synchronicity of housebuilding at a sectoral level. Different families of industrial towns and cities can be identified by industrial sector and long-run fluctuations in housebuilding investment compared, in this case for the largest twenty-five Scottish towns and cities between 1873 and 1914 (Tab. 1). Different types of urban settlement—county or administrative centres, iron steel producing towns, shipbuilding burghs, woollen towns, and a group of urban 'hubs' described as 'lesser burghs'—diverged considerably from the overall pattern of Scottish residential construction, and from each other. As in Bradford, the decline in the woollen towns of the Scottish borders was already steep by the late-19th century and this shows up in Table 1 through weak, and indeed inverse, patterns when compared to Scottish towns overall and, indeed compared to the different family elements in the urban typology. Conversely, where shipbuilding and iron and steel production dominated the incomes and employment of burghs then they closely corresponded with the overall Scottish patterns. In short, and as could even be demonstrated for the four principal cities (Edinburgh, Glasgow, Aberdeen and Dundee), very distinctive 'personalities' existed according to the composition of the local economy (Rodger 1985, 25). Dundee with its jute-based local economy, for example, was susceptible to violent booms and slumps in ways that differed radically to Edinburgh where the complementarity of professional, commercial, and financial service employment produced a steady demand for consumption-based industries such as printing and publishing, furniture and interior fittings, and what would nowadays be termed 'creative industries.' A diverse portfolio of income generation in the capital city spread risks, diminished the impact of the business cycle fluctuations, and produced a more stable trajectory of growth for the local economy as a result.

	County towns[1]	Woollen towns[2]	Ship-building burghs[3]	Iron & Steel burghs[4]	Lesser burghs[5]
Scotland	0.78	0.37	0.83	0.83	0.18
County towns	–	0.75	0.49	0.73	0.42
Woollen towns		–	0.04	0.36	-0.18
Shipbuilding burghs			–	0.60	0.36
Iron and Steel burghs					0.52

Tab. 1: Building Synchronicity: the Correlation of Housebuilding Fluctuations in Scottish Burghs, 1873–1914

(Sources: Dean of Guild Court Registers, Minutes books in the various burghs)

Note: correlation coefficients range ±0-1.0. Coefficient of 1 equivalent to exact correlation of one group with another.

1 County towns: Ayr, Inverness, Perth, Stirling.
2 Woollen towns: Galashiels, Hawick.
3 Shipbuilding: Clydebank, Govan, Port Glasgow, Partick.
4 Iron and Steel: Airdrie, Coatbridge, Falkirk, Motherwell, Wishaw.
5 Lesser burghs: Dunfermline, Irvine, Kirkcaldy, Musselburgh.

Surges in capital formation in Bradford were replicated in other towns and cities in the United Kingdom (Rodger 1983, Table 10.5). Where there was sufficient momentum generated by the coincidence of peaks and troughs in two or three industrial sectors, and especially where these coincided with trade cycles, then spectacular peaks and troughs existed in the building industry regionally and throughout the country (Lewis 1965, 317; Lewis and Richards 1961, 57; Kenwood 1963, 115). An underlying harmonic existed— the building cycle—yet the effect of aggregation into national indices or regional groupings of towns, as with the 36 towns included in the 'Manchester conurbation' or 31 towns in 'South Wales' or even 25 Scottish burghs, homogenised the waves of building activity and diminished the amplitude of fluctuation that affected individual places (Rodger 1986, 178). Even using a regional filter, the towns of north-east England, the profile of iron and steel dominated towns differed to those where mining was dominant. Presented in such a condensed manner the volatility of investment and the local impact at the level of the individual town or city has been understated.

Harmonics and echoes: building rhythms

Interest in the volatility of housebuilding first developed in the 1930s as economists explored the underlying dynamics of the 'Great Depression' (Riggleman 1933, 174; Grebler 1936, 344; Long 1939, 371; Bowen 1940, 110). Business cycle theorists recognised the centrality of domestic fixed capital formation as a determinant of boom and bust and the emergent Chicago School of sociologists applied spatial dimensions to capital formation in their concentric rings of development for residential and other uses.

In Britain, the harmonics of housebuilding generated appeal after World War II for several reasons. First, there was a residual post-war belief in the capacity of the state to manage the modern economy—a Keynesian conviction in which investment, income and employment were immutably linked, and in which housebuilding and construction generally played a critical part as a major component of investment. Connected to this was an academic engagement with the nature of capital accumulation, and a Marxist critique in which residential segregation played an active role in social segregation and thus of class formation. Housing was a potential instrument of control and subordination (Castells 1977, 298; Melling 1980, 9). There was also a wide-ranging debate about whether fluctuations in local economies origi-nated at home or abroad, and thus the focus on the internal structure of cities emerged through the study of urban history (Cairncross 1953, 1; Thomas 1954; Dyos and Reeder 1973, 359; Aspinall, 1982, 75).

For these varied reasons the importance of residential building is difficult to understate (Tab. 2). In Britain it constituted 18–20 percent of gross fixed capital formation between and 1856 and 1910, and within the construction sector itself represented an average of 57.7 percent of all forms of construc-tion over the same period (Feinstein 1972, Tables 88–92). Given this scale of contribution to capital formation, the labour intensity of construction, and the multiplier effects on other industries such as glass, bricks, furniture and internal fixtures and fittings, and gas and water industries, it is not difficult to understand how governments even now are concerned about the perfor-mance of house construction and its role in generating recovery. Further exploration at the level of the city, in this case, Glasgow between 1873 and 1939, reinforces its significance. Over this 65-year period, industrial building constituted 21 percent; public building (schools, halls, churches and civic buildings) 14 percent; small scale jobbing work described as alterations and additions also contributed 14 percent; and residential building represented exactly 50 percent of all construction work after adjustments for price chang-es have been taken into account (Fig. 2).

	Housebuilding as a percent of GDFCF		Housebuilding as a percent of GDFCF
1761–1770	22.4	1841–1850	15.4
1771–1780	19.6	1851–1860	17.7
1781–1790	19.5	1861–1870	16.5
1791–1800	23.4	1871–1880	20.3
1801–1810	27.6	1881–1890	18.1
1811–1820	28.4	1891–1900	19.5
1821–1830	31.5	1901–1911	17.4
1831–1840	26.6		

Tab. 2: Housebuilding Investment in Britain 1760–1913

(Source: Feinstein 1972, Tables 88–89; Feinstein 1978, 40)

Note: GDFCF—Gross Domestic Fixed Capital Formation

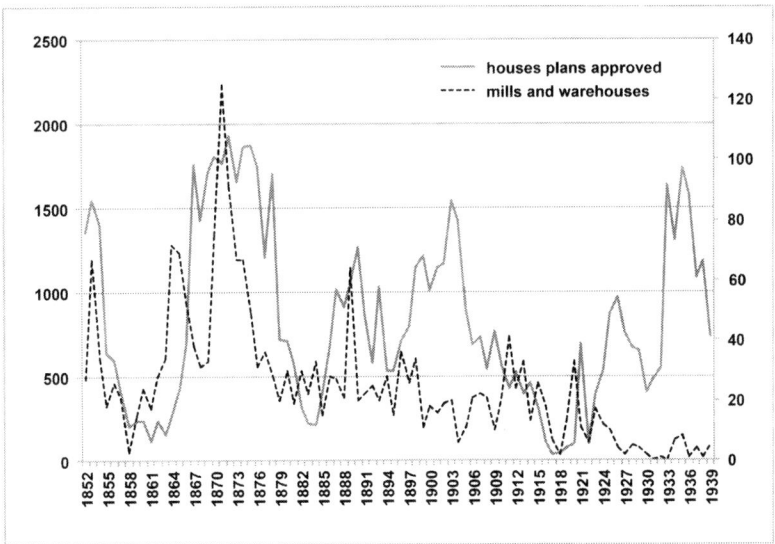

Fig. 2: The Value of Building Construction: Glasgow, 1873–1939 (£ million, adjusted for price changes)

(Source: City of Glasgow, Linings Granted by the Dean of Guild Court, printed by the Office of Public Works (private archive))

Note: important boundary extensions in 1891–92 and 1912–13.

The scale of housebuilding investment had major implications for the future management of urban space. Housebuilding was compressed into a relatively short span of years within a building cycle that was conventionally considered to have a periodicity of about 20 years—that is, the interval from peak to peak or trough to trough. Fields, and even small agricultural estates, on the urban fringe were covered with geometrical precision in parallel brick-built terraces for the working classes. Where gentry homes once were surrounded by generous gardens and orchards their owners, increasingly hemmed in as the urban frontier advanced, liquidated their asset and sold out to developers who built houses for an emerging suburban middle class. Crucially, within a space of a very few years, sometimes as few as five years, entire areas were clothed in accommodation from the same vintage, for the same socio-economic bracket, and in a practical style that cloned the builder's or developer's preference and often his ill-tutored ability (Dyos 1973, 122). Frequently a speculative activity, not only did speculative housebuilding introduce a visual monotony, it also meant that hundreds of houses possessed much the same 'shelf-life—they would all be regarded as obsolete or deficient in relation to some future standards at approximately the same time. City form was cloned by these means. Each English city was notable for its 'byelaw' housing whereby piped water and waste, minimum street widths, and regulated frontages were a requirement which became standard as a result of model building regulations produced as a result of the passage through parliament of the Local Government Act, 1858 (Gaskell 1983, 23). Much the same process applied in Scottish burghs with the difference that the stone-built four-storey tenements had an even longer structural shelf-life and internally suffered from deficient amenities at an earlier stage because of problems associated with the introduction and disposal of water in high-rise properties.

Housebuilding, with its compression in time and space within the city, and its durability—the life expectancy of a house might be century—introduced a problematical legacy in most British cities. Durability and volatility were key features of housebuilding and, as a glance at Figure 2 shows, and for the years before 1919 when market forces were unaffected by state housing provision, dramatic peaks were concentrated into relatively few years. There is considerable evidence that industrial and public construction reinforced the rhythms of residential building (Fig. 2) though there is only limited support for the view that land-extensive public building on the fringe of the city was counter-cyclical (Whitehand 1975, 211). If the British historiography appears most developed in this field, if now a little dated, there is also support from French, Swedish, Canadian and American studies (Lescure 1992, 224; Thomas 1954, 126, 251).

The relationship between vacancies and new construction is a revealing feature of the building industry, and is one that stresses a supply side response. It is a relationship akin to a capital stock adjustment model whereby firms adjust the rate at which they close the gap between desired and actual stocks of capital—in this case, housing. With a preponderance of small firms, no barriers to entry, and a dependence on loans and working credit, small building firms in the 19th century had only the most rudimentary understanding of market analysis until highly visible signs were apparent—unsold houses, rising vacancies, and bankruptcies. In any event, builders needed to complete a house to sell it and repay their loans, and so production overshot the point at which market conditions indicated that retrenchment was necessary, and so adding to the oversupply of accommodation and a rising percentage of vacancies.

	Years																			
%	1	2	3	4	5	6	7	8	9	10	11	12	13	14	15	16	17	18	19	20
empty housing	6																			
population growth	-1	-1	-1	-1	-1	-1	-1	-1	-1	-1	-1	-1	-1	-1	-1	-1	-1	-1	-1	-1
new housebuilding	2	2	3	1	0	0	0	0	0	0	0	0	1	2	2	1	2	2	2	2
end of year empty housing	7	8	10	10	9	8	7	6	5	4	3	2	2	3	4	4	5	6	7	8

Tab. 3: Autonomous Housebuilding: A Schematic Model over a 20-year Cycle

The schematic relationships in Table 3 indicate how a cyclical rhythm could be autonomously generated within the building industry. No structural changes in population growth, household formation, real income changes or demolitions are assumed in Table 3. To do so would introduce an even more exaggerated new dynamic. For example, the rate of increase in population growth and real income changes are likely to diminish in the downswing so that even less new building would be taken up thus leaving yet more empty property. For simplicity, the level of population growth is assumed to be fixed at 1 percent annually over the 20-year cycle and this mops up some of the new housebuilding but also leaves a changing level of empty or unoccupied housing.

In reality, overshooting the volume of new housing required to replace dilapidated or demolished homes and structural changes in demand resulted in a surplus of 10–11 percent in Glasgow in the late-1870s (Fig. 3). This was equivalent to 5 years supply assuming household formation in the form of population changes continued to increase at 1 percent p.a. On this basis it would take about 5 years of zero housebuilding to wipe out the 10.3 percent of surplus housing stock in Glasgow in 1879. Only when this was substantially reduced did housebuilding recommence on any scale and then, as empties fell to 2–3 percent of the total housing, first sluggish then enthusiastic responses from an atomistic building industry resulted in the next round of speculative over-building, before another bout of bankruptcies and stock-adjustment brought the house construction sector to a halt again. To work off a surplus housing stock with a vacancy rate of about 10 percent could take 8 years if builders operated at half the capacity of the peak years; it would take another 4 years at double that capacity to generate a surplus of 10 percent again. Thus without institutional shocks such as the City of Glasgow Bank crash in 1878 which caused one-third of Glasgow builders to go bankrupt, the building cycle could self-generate a cyclical dynamic of about 12 years without any change in demand at all (Cairncross 1953, 31; Rodger 1979, 226).

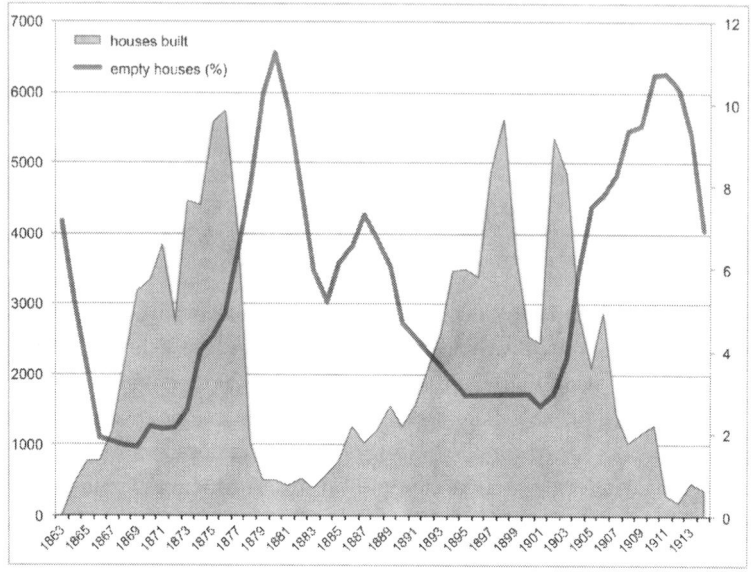

Fig. 3: Vacancies and the Relationship with New Housebuilding: Glasgow, 1864–1914

(*Source: City of Glasgow, Linings Granted by the Dean of Guild Court, printed by the Office of Public Works (private archive)*)

Scale issues: incorporating the corporation

Echo effects have produced, or rather reproduced, waves of capital investment in the residential sector, and are visible in the morphology of towns
and cities. These surges, and their echoes, produced a visually homogenised
and enduring cityscape because building development was frequently compressed into relatively few years of the cycle. As a result, many streets aged
together because entire districts were built at, or about, the same time and so
area renewal tended to deal with the entire neighbourhood, if at all.

It is because of issues of scale and timing, and the complexity of urbanisation itself that inertia reigned for so long as far as urban redevelopment
was concerned. As one commentator explained: "The geographical landscape
which fixed and immobile capital comprises is both a crowning glory of past
capital development and a prison which inhibits further progress of accumulation" (Harvey 1977, 154).

'Fixed and immobile capital' included swathes of residential streets cloned in the course of a building bonanza, and the many 'dark satanic mills', warehouses, and industrial complexes throughout Britain. Development was inhibited because the scale of capital investment—sunk costs—was so high as to prohibit change. 'Fixed and immobile' capital investment in buildings meant it was cheaper and administratively easier to extend a house, or add a wing to a hospital or prison rather than redevelop from cleared land. As 19th century housing became out-moded and factories out-dated so there were acres of silent sites no longer fit for their original purpose.

However, to assume that the endogenous features of the construction industry alone defined the spatial and visual character of industrial cities would be simplistic. Corporate influences were also significant for their intensive capital investment in the built environment, and its redevelopment. In particular, the growth of corporate Britain contributed to periods of intense construction and was prompted by the introduction of joint-stock and limited liability legislation in 1856 and 1862. Indeed the 'divorce' of ownership from control and the rise of a new 'managerial' capitalism was more advanced in Britain by 1914 than in any other country in the world (Foreman-Peck and Hannah, 2012, 1217). Emphatically it was not a 20th-century phenomenon since already by 1914 directors in the largest 337 British companies owned only 3.4 percent of the shares. A shift had taken place before 1914, therefore, from firms substantially owned and managed by local individuals or syndicates to companies in which most directors held positions by virtue of their knowledge and networks, and not because they were majority shareholders. Multi-firm mergers and acquisitions were part of this phase of coroporate consolidation and were a powerful presence in British cities. Some of the major British household names emerged during this period to dominate their sectors: J. & P. Coats controlled 80 percent of the thread market after 1896; United Alkali (1890) and Borax (1899) both controlled 90 percent of their respective segments of the chemical industry; Imperial Tobacco (1901) managed almost 50 percent of their industry; and the eleven firms that merged to form English Sewing Cotton were responsible for 15 percent of their market (Utton 1972, Table 1; Hannah 1974, 1). The process of amalgamation continued during the inter-war period, often assisted by government schemes to moth-ball capacity as part of rationalistion programmes. Well known brands such as Spillers controlled 34 percent of their industry, Crosse and Blackwell (38), British Sugar Corporation (72), United Steel Company (35), London Brick Company (14), Tate and

Lyle (72), Unilever (72), Imperial Chemical Industries (81), Metal Box (45), Fisons (34), Distillers (74), British Match (89), and Michael Nairn (64 percent). Amalgamations proceeded at such a pace that the result was a degree of concentration in British industry that approached the concentration of American 'big business' and, perhaps suprisingly, surpassed that of German corporations (Tables 4 and 5).

Rank	USA	$m	Britain	$m	Germany	$m
1	US Steel	757	J & P Coats	301	Krupp	143
2	Standard Oil	389	Rio Tinto	143	Siemens	122
3	Pullman	200	Imperial Tobacco	111	AEG	113
4	Anaconda Copper	178	Guinness	109	Gelsen-Bergwerks	96
5	General Electric	174	Shell	91	Deutsch-Luxemburgische	68

Tab. 4: Capitalization of Top 5 American, British, and German Manufacturers, 1912 ($m)

(Source: Schmitz 1993, 23)

	1909	1929	1935	1963
USA	22	25	26	33
GB	16	26	23	38
France	12	16	No data	26

Tab. 5: Net Share of Manufacturing Output of Top 100 Firms (percent)

(Source: Hannah 1983, 180)

Though major industrial companies were scattered across Britain the move to multi-branch production with centralised and functionally departmentalised managerial structures and divisions meant that decision-making was often relocated to a distant head office. This 'Footloose Capital' undermined relationships developed over decades with a local workforce, the City Council and, importantly, the social capital of cities where works facilities and teams provided amenities for its employees and the neighbourhood. The centralisation of industrial organisation also meant the retreat of an entrepreneurial class from public and political offices with dire consequences for the regeneration of new businesses.

The trend to larger-scale corporations in the 20th century also resulted from external stimuli. Conscription during World War II, for example, denuded small firms of key workers and the government's Concentration of Industry Scheme required a miminum level of production to qualify for government contracts. For Leicester, 'the city of a thousand trades', where the preponderance of small-scale enterprises cushioned the worst excesses of previous industrial fluctuations, the government policy to encourage corporate consolidation and reap the economies of scale proved disastrous (Beazley 2006, 75). This was because after 1945 many small firms simply did not restart due to the absence or age of family personnel and insufficient capital to invest in new plant. Also, the Board of Trade limited new start-up firms in an effort to protect existing businesses from competition. The effects of wartime and post-war policies were evident: in the Leicester hosiery industry in 1938 over 130,000 people were employed; by 1946 there were just 68,000. Administrative red tape reappeared in 1960 in the form of an Industrial Development Certificate introduced by the Board of Trade as a pre-requisite for factory re-building. A high profile test case involved a nationally well-known Leicester confectionery firm, Fox's Glacier Mints, which wished to relocate within the city as a result of a compulsory order by the City Council to purchase their factory. Despite the willingness of the City Council to agree to the relocation, an arbiter in Birmingham rejected Fox's case. Government agencies, not local government, therefore influenced the production structure of small and medium sized firms—there were 272 firms considering relocation within the city in 1960. Fox's moved out; Whitbread's brewery just moved away.

Exogenous factors compounded the difficulties of urban redevelopment. These included: government decisions on the nationalisation and, subsequently, privatisation of industry; local council strategies for social housing; the imposition of a poll tax and expenditure caps on public spending, and a variety of more specific planning initiatives each of which affected the capacity of cities to reuse city centre land. Legally and fiscally the redevelopment of inner city sites was constrained; inertia prevailed. Furthermore, with a widespread and sluggish economic performance, the scale of urban redevelopment required increasingly complex negotiations with a variety of agencies—city and county councils, Development Corporations, banks, government agencies, housing associations and community organisations. The endogenous logic and legacy of the building cycle coupled with the exogenous impact of public policy decisions complicated the progress of urban renewal in British towns and cities in the second half of the 20th century.

Conclusion

Nineteenth century families of town types drew their common characteristics from the industrial activities with which each place was particularly associated. Sheffield steel and Burton brewing were uniquely associated with those places and provided a distinctive socio-economic character—and sensory experience—as well as influencing the nature and timing of construction activity in the town or city. The composition of the sources of income and employment contributed to the particular pattern of pulses, or rhythms, in the physical expansion of the city. These ryhthms of construction investment had an internal logic, with significant echo effects. To use a metaphor from another arena of scholarship, medical history, these industrial 'family' characteristics were 'predisposing causes' of the condition of towns and cities, superimposed upon which were the particularities of place, as influenced further by corporate structures and local government initiatives. When combined, predisposing factors and direct or immediate causes of ill-health, the urban condition that can be described as de-industrialisation, which despite palliative care in the form of repairs and maintenance, utlimately necessitated surgical interventions—demolitions, clearances, and a multiplicity of redevelopment and renewal programmes—at the level of specific sites, entire areas, and even for entire towns and cities.

In the late-20th century, different 'family' relationships have emerged, defined less by industrial specialisations as in the 19th century, and more by a portfolio of income and employment opportunities. These have resulted in different typologies—new family formations—which are reflected in patterns of population growth (Rodger 1996, 130, 136–37). A study of over 200 towns and cities in Scotland during the 20th century resulted in the identification of numerous new families using cluster analysis (see Appendix 1 for the clusters; Appendix 2 for sample urban trajectories). Like actual families, there are some quite distant relatives but often the stem relationship, a shared legacy of industrial production, is discernible. These 20th century trajectories of the places listed in Appendix 1 provide powerful evidence of the ability of most, though not all, towns and cities, to regenerate their local economy and that their success is contingent, as before, on the continuity, complementarity and composition of employment provided by companies with a strong place-attachment. Then, and only then, is the resurrection of former industrial centres likely.

long run decline (44)	early 20th C expansion (43)	pronounced post-1945 expansion (19)	stagnation/decline then modest recovery (29)	steady expansion (39)	dramatic recent expansion (8)
Brechin	Cove &Kilcreggan	Linlithgow	Newton Stewart	Kintore	Penicuik
Burghead	Dunooon	Tain	Blairgowrie	Forres	Fort William
Campbeltown	Elie & earlsferry	Stewarton	Kirkwall	Carnoustie	Denny and Dunipace
Whithorn	Rothesay	Lochgilphead	Bridge of Allan	Stonehaven	S Queensferry
Maybole	Millport	Banchory	Dollar	Lerwick	Johnstone
Aberchirder	Buckie	Invergordon	Inverbervie	Lossiemouth	Prestonpans
Langholm	Greenock	Irvine	Montrose	Inverness	Bonnyrigg
Tobermory	Portknockie	Dunblane	Dalbeattie	Stranraer	Thurso
Coldstream	Aberlour	Kirkintilloch	Macduff	Dingwall	
Duns	Findochty	Cumnock	Auhterarder	Lanark	
Alva	Cowdenbeath	Milngavie	Kirkcudbright	Barrhead	
Forfar	Lochgelly	Helensburgh	Kelso	Leslie	
Alyth	Glasgow	Nairn	Lockerbie	Haddington	
Arbroath	Clydebank	Alloa	East Linton	Airdrie	
Abernethy	Buckhaven & Methil	Armadale	Kirriemuir	Stirling	
Anstruther	Musselburgh	Elgin	Fortrose	Loanhead	
Cullen	Falkirk	Annan	Biggar	Ardrossan	
Galashiels	Auchtermuchty	Stornoway	Peterhead	Inverkiething	
Wigtown	Gourock	Tillicoultry	Callander	Tranent	
Banff	Kingussie		Eyemouth	Grangemouth	
Wick	Darvel		Jedburgh	Largs	
Portsoy	Fraserburgh		Falkland	Prestwick	
Pittenweem	Melrose		Lochmaben	Bathgate	
Rothes	Kinross		Turriff	Renfrew	
Keith	Bo'ness		Dalkeith	Dumfries	
Hawick	Edinburgh		Cupar	Troon	
Aberfeldy	Newburgh		Dunbar	Inverurie	
Sellkirk	Paisley			Oban	
Innerleiethen	Dundee			St Andrews	
Tayport	Crieff			Dornoch	
Ballater	Burntisland			Kilmarnock	
Newmilns	Peebles			Ayr	
Lafybank	Kirkcaldy			Hamilton	
Dufftown	Markinch			Kilsyth	
Coupar Angus	Sanquhar			North Berwick	
Laurencekirk	Leven			Girvan	
Huntly	Perth			Dunfermline	
Crail	Castle Douglas			Cockenzie and Port Seton	
Moffat	Port Glasgow			Saltcoats	
Lauder	Dumbarton				
Doune	Coatbridge				
Galston	Aberdeen				
Stromness	Newport				
Cromarty					

Appendix 1: The Trajectories of Urban Development in Scotland 1901–81

(Source: Rodger 1996, 130)

Note: The table shoud be read as a continous list from Brechin to Thurso. Each town is most closely related to the ones above and below in this continuum. However, breaks are introduced to indicate a strong degree of clustering amongst groups of towns and cities. Hence there are 44 burghs in what might be described as long run decline, but the first group of 15 experience the steepest decline, while the next group are less affected but still are in a long run trajectory of decline.

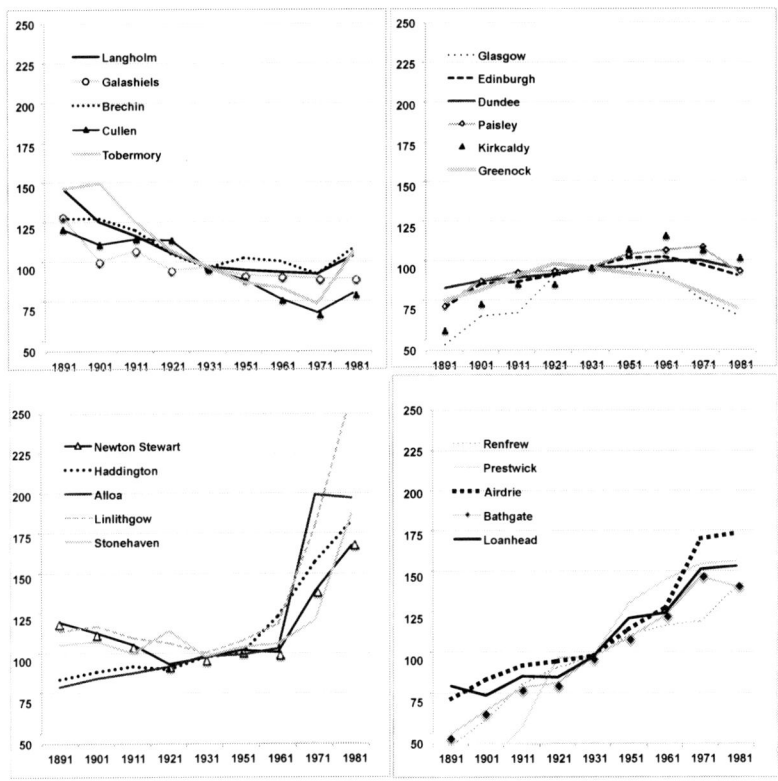

Appendix 2: Population Trajectories and the Redefinition of Urban Typologies: Selected Scottish Towns 1890–1981 (index 1931=100)

(Source: Rodger 1996, 136–137)

Note: Clockwise the urban typology as determined by the cluster analysis includes members of (a) long run decline (44). (b) early 20th centry expansion (43) (c) steady expansion (39) (d) stagnation, decline andmodest recovery (29) Numbers refer to the towns and cities in the 'family.'

Works Cited

Aldcroft, D.H., and P. S. Fearon (1969). *Economic Growth in Twentieth Century Britain.* London: Macmillan.

Aspinall, P. (1982). The internal structure of the housebuilding industry in nineteenth-century Britain. In J. H. Johnson and C. G. Pooley (eds.). *The Internal Structure of Nineteenth Century Cities,* 75–106. London: Croom Helm.

Beazley, B. (2006). *Post War Leicester.* Stroud: Sutton.

Bowen, I. (1940). Building output and the trade cycle, 1924–38. *Oxford Economic Papers,* 3, 110–30.

Cairncross, A. K. (1953). *Home and Foreign Investment 1870–1913.* Cambridge: Cambridge University Press.

Castells, M. (1977). *The Urban Question.* London: Arnold.

Checkland, S. G. (1983). An urban history horoscope. In D. Fraser and A. Sutcliffe (eds.). *The Pursuit of Urban History,* 449–466. London: Edward Arnold.

Dyos, H. J. (1966). *Victorian Suburb: a Study of the Growth of Camberwell.* Leicester: Leicester University Press.

Dyos, H. J., and D. Reeder (1976). Slums and suburbs. In H. J. Dyos and M. Wolff (eds.). *The Victorian City: Images and Reality,* 359–386. London: Routledge and Kegan Paul.

Feinstein, C. H. (1972). *National Income, Expenditure and Output of the United Kingdom 1855–1965.* Cambridge: Cambridge University Press.

Feinstein, C. H. (1978). Capital formation in Great Britain. In P. Mathias and M. M. Postan (eds.). *The Cambridge Economic History of Europe,* Vol. 7, part 1, 28–96. Cambridge: Cambridge University Press.

Feinstein, C. H. (1991). Variety and volatility: some aspects of the labour market in Britain 1880–1913. In C. Holmes and A. Booth (eds.). *Economy and Society: European Industrialisation and its Social Consequences: Essays Presented to Sidney Pollard,* 154–174. Leicester: Leicester University Press.

Foreman-Peck, J., and L. Hannah (2012). Extreme divorce: the managerial revolution in UK companies before 1914. *Economic History Review,* 65 (4), 1217–1238.

Gaskell, S. M. (1983). *Building Control: National Legislation and the Introduction of Local Bye-laws in Victorian England.* London: Bedford Square Press.

Grebler, L. (1936). Housebuilding, the business cycle and state intervention. *International Labour Review,* 33, 344–356, 468–478.

Hannah, L. (1974). Mergers in manufacturing industry, 1880-1919. *Oxford Economic Papers,* 26, 1–20.

Hannah, L. (1983). *The Rise of the Corporate Economy.* London: Methuen.

Harvey, D. (1977). The geography of capitalist accumulation: a reconstruction of the Marxian theory. In R. Peet (ed.). *Radical Geography,* 263–292. Chicago: Maaroufa.

Hudson, P. (1989). Capital and credit in the West Riding wool textile industry c. 1750–1850. In P. Hudson (ed.). *Regions and Industries. A Perspective on the Industrial Revolution in Britain,* 69–102. Cambridge: Cambridge University Press.

Kenwood, A. G. (1963). Residential building activity in north-eastern England 1863–1913. *The Manchester School*, 31, 115–128.

Lee, C. H. (1981). Regional growth and structural change in Victorian Britain. *Economic History Review*, 33, 450–551.

Lescure, M. (1992). France. In C. G. Pooley (ed.). *Housing Strategies in Europe 1880–1930*, 221–239. Leicester: Leicester University Press.

Lewis, J. P. (1965). *Building Cycles and Britain's Growth*. London: Macmillan.

Lewis, J. P., and J. H. Richards (1956). Housebuilding in the South Wales coalfield. *The Manchester School*, 24, 289–302.

Madgin, R., and R. Rodger (2013). Inspiring capital? Deconstructing myths and reconstructing urban environments, Edinburgh 1860-2010. *Urban History*, 40: 3.

Melling, J. (ed.). (1980). *Housing, Social Policy and the State*. London: Croom Helm.

Mounfield, P. R. (1972). The foundations of the modern industrial pattern. In N. Pye (ed.). *Leicester and its Region, 370–373*. Leicester: Leicester University Press.

Ogilvie, S. C., and M. Cerman (eds.). (1996). *European Proto-industrialization*. Cambridge: Cambridge University Press.

Parliamentary Papers (1911). Census of England.

Pollard, S. (1981). *Peaceful Conquest: the Industrialization of Europe 1760–1970*. Oxford: Oxford University Press.

Reeder, D., and R. Rodger (2000). Industrialisation and the city economy. In M. J. Daunton (ed.) *Cambridge Urban History of Britain*, Vol. 3, 553–592. Cambridge: Cambridge University Press.

Riggleman, J. R. (1933). Building cycles in the United States 1875–1932. *Journal of the American Statistical Association*, 28, 174–183.

Robertson, A. J. (1977). Clydeside revisited: a reconsideration of the Clyde shipbuilding industry 1919–38. In W. H Chaloner and B. M. Ratfcliffe (eds.). *Trade and Transport: Essays in Economic history in Honour of T. S. Willan*, 258–278. Manchester: Manchester University Press.

Rodger, R. (1979). Speculative builders and the structure of the Scottish building industry 1860–1914. *Business History*, 21, 226–246.

Rodger, R. (1983). The 'Invisible Hand'—market forces, housing and the urban form in Victorian cities. In D. Fraser and A. Sutcliffe (eds.). *The Pursuit of Urban History*, 190–211. London: Edward Arnold.

Rodger, R. (1985). Wages, employment and poverty in the Scottish cities 1841–1914. In G. Gordon (ed.). *Perspectives of the Scottish City*, 25–63. Aberdeen: Aberdeen University Press.

Rodger, R. (1986). The Victorian building industry and the housing of the Scottish working class. In M. Doughty (ed.) *Building the Industrial City*, 151–206. Leicester: Leicester University Press.

Rodger, R. (1989). *Housing in Urban Britain 1780–1914*. Cambridge: Cambridge University Press.

Rodger, R. (1996). Urbanisation in twentieth century Scotland. In T. M. Devine and R. J. Finlay (eds.). *Scotland in the Twentieth Century*, 122–153. Edinburgh: Edinburgh University Press.

Rodger, R. (2013). Understanding Leicester: independent, radical, tolerant. In R. Rodger and R. Madgin (eds.). *Leicester: A Modern History.* Lancaster: Carnegie Press. (forthcoming)

Schmitz, C. J. (1993). *The Growth of Big Business in the United States and Western Europe 1850–1939.* Cambridge: Cambridge University Press.

Simon, C. J., and C. Nardinelli (1996). The talk of the town: human capital, information, and the growth of English cities, 1861–1961. *Explorations in Economic History*, 33 (3), 384–413.

Southall, H. R. (1988). The origins of the depressed areas: unemployment, growth and regional economic structure before 1914. *Economic History Review*, 41, 236–258.

Thomas, B. (1954). *Migration and Economic Growth.* Oxford: Oxford University Press.

Utton, M. A. (1972). Some features of the early merger movements in British manufacturing industry. *Business History*, 14 (1), 51–60.

Whitehand, J. W. R. (1975). Building activity and the intensity of development at the urban fringe: the case of a London suburb in the nineteenth century, *Journal of Historical Geography*, 1, 211–224.

Networks and the Industrial Metropolis: Chicago's Calumet district, 1870–1940

Robert Lewis

Introduction

In April 1992 the South Works of U.S. Steel was shut down for good. At its peak, the South Works was one of the largest integrated steelmaking facilities in the United States, employing more than 20,000 workers and producing an array of steel products for local and distant customers. It was not the only one. A wide range of other companies that had underpinned the development of Chicago's Calumet district since the 19th century experienced a similar process of job loss and factory closings from the 1950s. Republic Steel operated mills in East Chicago and South Chicago, both of which had been shut down by the turn of the 21st century. Other large companies such as Pullman-Standard and Youngstown Sheet and Tube followed a similar path. By the late 20th century very few manufacturing firms remained in the Calumet. These were not sudden decisions. Chicago's manufacturing sector had experienced severe problems for at least a generation as corporate executives diverted new investment away from the Northeastern metropolitan districts to the American South and overseas. Economic decline and deindustrialization in the Calumet, Chicago and the rest of the 'Rust Belt' was commonplace by the 1960s (Bensman and Lynch 1987; Cowie and Heathcott 2003; High 2003).

This was a great reversal from the preceding 100 years when Chicago and the Calumet developed as mighty industrial districts. The United States moved from a second-tier economic power in the middle of the 19th century to become the industrial powerhouse of the world by the start of World War One. With more than a third of the world's industrial output in 1913, the USA easily out-produced the great industrial nations of Europe—Great Britain, Germany and France (Tomlinson 1999). The dynamic center of America's manufacturing was the country's industrial metropolitan centers, such as Detroit, Philadelphia and Buffalo. With few exceptions, these centers were found in the Manufacturing Belt, America's industrial workshop that covered the northeastern part of the country stretching from New England to the west of the Great Lakes (Meyer 2001; Winder 1999). One of the region's key centers was Chicago. It experienced massive industrial development after the Civil War, growing from a small commercial city hugging the shores of Lake Michigan to the second largest industrial district in the United States by the late 19th century. On the eve of the Great Depression, almost 12,000 firms in metropolitan Chicago employed more than 500,000 manufacturing workers (Lewis 2008).

One of the most important areas within the metropolitan area that contributed to the rise of industrial Chicago was the Calumet. By the 1860s, the indigenous population had been forced out of the area and a smattering of farm houses dotted the otherwise unsettled prairie outside the city's southern boundary that would become the Calumet area. Over the next 60 years, the Calumet developed as the country's premier steelmaking and heavy industry district. This chapter examines the role that the Calumet played in the building of the metropolitan economy and how both the Calumet and the metropolitan economies were built around the development of an intricate web of industrial, financial and institutional networks that stretched across the nation between the Civil War and 1940. No industrial area is an island. A thick skein of multi-scalar relations was necessary for the development of the industrial economy. What I argue is that large industrial districts such as the Calumet that were part of metropolitan areas such as Chicago were deeply embedded in a wideflung set of business networks. The character, scale and success (or not) of these industrial districts and the larger metropolitan economies were created through these networks. This is true of a deindustrializing economy as it is an industrializing one. Chicago and the Calumet have experienced both.

Industrial networks and the metropolis

There are several interpretations of the rise of industrial metropolitan economies from the late 18th century. Two stand out. The first understands industrial places as little more than industrial islands. While firms have links to other firms, they are ultimately separate entities that make rational locational and operational decisions independent of other firms and institutions.

The economy is typically dominated by a large number of small firms held captive by a few large, multi-unit, capital-intensive oligarchic corporations (Chandler 1976). The second views industrial districts as local production systems consisting of both place-based and nonlocal economic and social interdependencies. Writers from this perspective argue that industrial districts have several aspects in common, most notably vertical disintegration, a shared sense of collective purpose, a constant redefining of firm relations, and a host of networks that link small, specialized firms to firms in other places (Scranton 1989).

Chicago does not fit into either of these interpretations. The metropolitan area was not an industrial island, where firms operated as rational, independent entities and functioned separately from other firms. Nor was the metropolitan economy dominated by a large number of small, vertically disintegrated, batch-production firms founded on trust relations. Rather, Chicago was a hybrid place, home to firms operating under varying degrees of trust, interdependencies, specialization, and scale. Nor was Chicago unusual. With few expectations, most notably New York City, the North American metropolis was a hybrid form with firms that ran the gamut from Chandlerian relations of mass production and distribution to Third Italy type specialization rooted in close interfirm relations.

There are five elements common to the building of the metropolitan industrial economy. First, the industrial relations of all firms are boundary spanning. Manufacturing companies, whether they are independent firms or subsidiaries of corporations, have a range of linkages outside of their corporate shell. With few exceptions, firm boundaries are porous and lead to external economies of scale and scope. The scale and character of these relations are heavily dependent upon the material base of industries and the type of commodities that a firm manufactures. To build an airplane requires a fundamentally different set of industrial relations and networks than the making of denim jeans. Second, all firms are arrayed along a production chain, from the extraction of raw materials to the selling of the finished product. In some case, large corporations control a good deal of the chain, while most small firms typically occupy a specialized place. Once again, the specific character of industries matters. The production chain for steel with its dependence on coal and iron ore inputs and the marketing of its products as inputs to a host of other manufacturers is quite different from that of clothing, airplanes and rifles. Regardless, in all cases, the various sequences of the production chain are connective tissue, and ensure that firms are firmly embedded within a tangled web of linkages.

Third, the wide gulf in the scale of industrial units and the resulting differences in economic and political power ensures that most metropolises are big-firm led. Beginning in the middle of the 19th century, the combination of capitalist economic dynamics and collusive-cooperation led to the concentration of industrial power in the hands of a few enormous, multi-unit oligopolies. In the USA, three percent of firms employed 70 percent of the country's workers, while eight financial combines controlled 29 percent of the total nonfinancial and banking assets of the 250 largest corporations in 1940 (Lynch 1946, 111–142). Small and medium-sized firms are tied to large corporations by a range of subordinate relations. Fourth, firms are embedded in local packages of place-bound 'assets' such as land, infrastructures and housing. Local growth machines seek to create an environment appropriate for the reproduction of capitalist productive relations in two ways: discursively by setting out what should be done and by whom, and materially by the building of a production landscape consisting of factories, machines, workers, railroads and so forth.

Finally, the fact that interaction between industrial firms and associated institutions occurs at different scales means that relations are simultaneously local and nonlocal. Industrial districts are centered on both non-proximate and proximate spatial relations. Districts revolve around the ability of firms to construct relationships with other firms and institutional bodies, such as industrial associations, financial institutions, unions and the federal government, that are not dependent on geographic closeness. These relationships span physical distance yet link firms in the connective fabric of the production chain. The industrial economy of a metropolitan district also revolves around the relationships generated within that district. In some cases, firms making similar products or using similar inputs are attracted to the same locale. In other cases, other assets of a place, from cheap land to an accessible location, are the key component. In all cases, these generated a set of multiplier effects in the form of services and facilities within an area. This leads, among other things, to the creation of a specialized labor force, local agencies with contacts for specialized and generic skills, financial institutions which provide industrial credit facilities, and public utilities and infrastructures. In other words, a bundle of spatially differentiated networks emerge that both produce and frame the metropolitan economy.

Industrial firms and the places they inhabit are deeply ensconced in a network of economic and political relations. The ongoing process of capitalist network formation across space created industrial districts that are entangled with other social, political and economic spaces. While capitalist production is driven by the search for profits, a larger market share and so on, the need to coordinate, shape and control, among other things, labor, industrial output, technological development, and locational decisions ensure that capitalists seek out an array of networks in order to facilitate capital accumulation. While many of these decisions are rational from a market perspective and have their intended effects, it is often the case that capitalist production networks have unintended consequences. Moreover, networks can be one time, with few if any lasting consequences; they also can be one time, with longstanding ripple effects on place. On the other hand, they can be routinized and have little effect or have important effects on capitalist industrial space. In the case of the Calumet region between 1870 and 1940, a range of actors created, reproduced, dropped and otherwise took on an array of political, social and economic networks that worked to transform an 'useless' space outside the boundaries of the City of Chicago into one of the leading industrial districts of the world.

Networks and the Calumet, 1870–1945

Starting in the 1870s a range of iron and steel, transportation, chemical and metal-working companies settled in Chicago's Calumet area and turned prairie land on the edge of the city into one of the most important industrial districts in the world. According to the most common definition, the Calumet encompasses the area stretching south from Lake Calumet across the city boundary into the suburban areas on both sides of the Indiana-Illinois state line. It includes areas that would become city neighborhoods after the annexation of 1889, such as South Chicago, Pullman and Hegewisch, as well as independent suburbs bordering Lake Michigan and the Calumet River, including Gary, East Chicago, Chicago Heights, Hammond and, at the western edge, Joliet. By World War One this disparate set of locales strung out along the metropolitan area's southern fringe had developed a common identity and had become the region's major industrial area outside of the downtown core. Over the next 25 years, local, regional and national agents built upon the first flush of industrial development and consolidated the area's manufacturing dominance in the metropolitan district. Despite the problems and stress induced by several rounds of economic downswings, the Calumet continued to expand and had grown to become one of the world's leading industrial areas by World War Two.

Its origins were straightforward for a 19th-century industrial suburban development. By the early 1870s a small cluster of industrial establishments had appeared in what would become South Chicago, and a few steel firms were to be found in the small town of Joliet in the farthest reaches of what would become the Calumet. A succession of industrial firms quickly followed in other parts of the district, including East Chicago, Hammond, Pullman, Chicago Heights and Harvey. The building of several steel mills in Gary by the U.S. Steel Company after 1900 cemented the district's industrial strength and drew an ever larger number of small firms that were dependent on receiving inputs from or serving the large corporations that came to dominate the district from the 1880s (Appleton 1927; Bate 1948; Mohl and Bettten 1986; Moore 1959).

Numerous attractions drew steel firms and an assortment of other industries from Chicago and elsewhere to the rapidly expanding Calumet between 1870 and 1930. Ample areas of flat land next to abundant sources of water were extremely tempting to steel, railroad car, chemical, petroleum and metal-working firms seeking room to build extensive and intricate manufacturing complexes. Working with these resources, the federal government, the Corps of Engineers, the railroads, and local boosters turned the 'natural' attributes of the physical environment into a 'second nature' consisting of industrial property, modern transportation facilities, and working-class residential districts (Cronon 1991). Tens of thousands of acres of industrial land were carved out of the prairie. The building of modern water and rail-based transportation permitted the assembly of relatively cheap raw materials and the marketing of finished products over a wide area with relative ease (Fig. 1). Local boosters, and in some cases, corporations built new housing tracts close to the mills, thus providing manufacturers with a more than adequate labor supply (Buder 1967; Pacyga 1991; Mohl and Betten 1986). The Calumet's location in the southern reaches of the rapidly expanding Chicago metropolitan region provided access to a large market and allowed for the development of a dynamic relationship between the city and the Calumet's industrial firms.

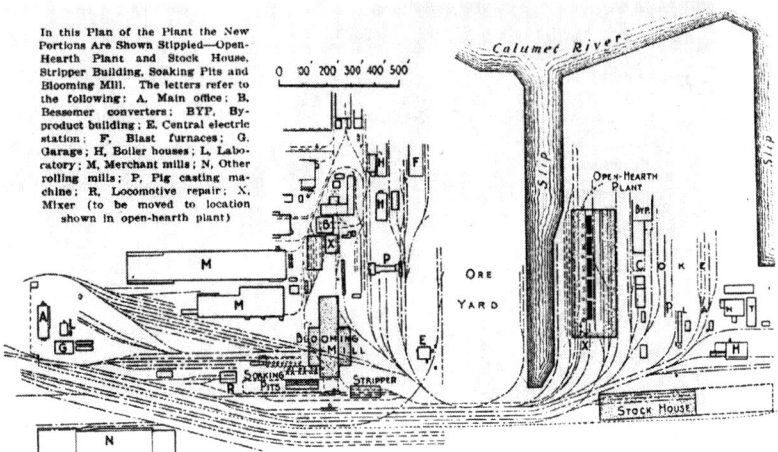

Fig. 1: Wisconsin Mill, 1924

(Source: Iron Age, 05/14/1924, 1421)

By 1924, the district's 341 firms employed close to 160,000 workers and accounted for more than a fifth of the metropolitan area's manufacturing labor force (Tab. 1). Three industrial specializations were particularly prominent: primary metal, railroad equipment and petroleum. Not only were these industries important employers within the Calumet itself, they also accounted for more than 80 percent of employment in metropolitan Chicago's primary metal, railroad equipment and petroleum industries. Large steel companies such as Inland Steel (Chicago Heights), Youngstown Sheet and Tube (South Chicago) and American Steel Foundries (Indiana Harbor) grew up alongside the US Steel plants in South Chicago and Gary. On the western side of Lake Calumet, the Pullman Palace Car complex that had been established in Pullman in the 1880s anchored an extensive set of supplier firms. The chemical industry was kick started when Standard Oil bought land in Whiting in the late 1880s for the building of what would become one of the country's largest petroleum refineries (Appleton 1927; Bate 1948).

The development of the Calumet was built upon a series of relationships which transformed the physical environment, created a new set of place-based assets, and produced a landscape suitable for production. From the 1870s, working under the authority of the federal government, the Army's Corps of Engineers refashioned the river system. Over the next 60 years, substantial expenditures were invested in relocating the Grand Calumet River, dredging the various river systems, filling in marsh lands, building an industrial harbor at the mouth of the Calumet, and connecting the Calumet rivers to the Chicago Sanitary and Ship Canal by way of the Calumet Sag Channel (Colten 1994; Moore 1959, 11–14; Salzmann 2012). A modern second nature was created that linked the Calumet with the rest of the world and provided local firms with a modern transportation system (Fig. 2). The Corps worked with state officials, local municipalities, business associations and property developers to refashion the Calumet and make it ready for industry. As one contemporary noted, the river's "banks are ideal locations for manufacturing plants" (Lee 1908, 71). The refiguring of the area's riverine system was one element in the making of the new industrial space by a local growth alliance working with nonlocal agents.

Industry	Number of workers	Number of firms	Firms by workers		Share of city workers (%)
			> 1,000	1–199	
Primary metal	85,553	46	14	31	81.5
Railroad equipment	26,284	24	5	18	81.8
Fabricated metal	13,976	56	2	49	16.8
Petroleum	7,086	10	2	6	80.0
Automotive	5,752	16	2	10	25.3
Machinery	4,534	23	1	19	12.0
Chemical	4,190	28	1	23	17.6
All firms	159,789	341	28	278	21.9

Tab. 1: Industrial structure of the Calumet, 1924

(Source: Directory of Illinois manufacturers, 1924–1925. Chicago: Illinois Manufacturers' Association, 1924)

Fig. 2: South Chicago Harbor, 1890s

(Source: Library of Congress)

The multi-scalar relationships that reconfigured Calumet's physical environment was dependent upon a layered set of land development practices and property relations. A host of agents worked to transform prairie land into urban private property. One of these agents was the railroad, which opened up land for urban development and linked the Calumet to Chicago and to points further east and west. The first flush of building took place before the end of the Civil War when four lines crossed the district. Another six were built between 1874 and 1902 (Moore 1959, 83–113). A combination of federal and state regulation, financial support and land grants underpinned the ability of railroads such as the Illinois Central to open up unsettled lands in the Calumet. This, along with the laying down of property legislation resting on private ownership, enabled speculative, profit-seeking individuals and companies to turn indigenous and farm land into urban land that was suitable for industrial use. Land speculators, property developers and real estate agents, following the tracks laid out by the railroads, assembled, platted and sold off land for residential, commercial and industrial purposes. In the process of creating a set of land-based networks that connected the Calumet and nonlocal agents, the broad contours of an industrial district in the suburban areas of metropolitan Chicago was put into place.

An early example of the importance of the railroads to the Calumet was the opening of Hammond to industrial development in the 1860s. Hammond's settlement began when the Michigan Central Railroad crossed the region in 1851. The cheap land and the railroad attracted the Hohman family, who bought 39 acres on the north bank of the Grand Calumet River and opened an inn. They were followed by other German families who bought land, built stores, churches and schools. Industry followed. In 1869 a group of investors from the east coast purchased 15 acres from the Hohmans, platted the first subdivision, and built a packing plant. By 1891, the G. H. Hammond and Company, which had been brought out by British interests a year earlier, employed 1,000 workers, was capitalized at 6.4 million Dollar, and distributed packed meat to the east coast by 300 refrigerator cars (Moore 1959, 141–151).

The type of industrial land development taking place in Hammond was found elsewhere across the Calumet. Some of the most important land developers and industrialists in Chicago were interested in the profits to be made out of carving up the Calumet for industry. Land agents working with capital resources, legal practices and both local and nonlocal markets transformed the prairie into private industrial property. One of the first major interventions to turn the prairie into urban land was made by Colonel James Bowen. After making a fortune in Chicago, Bowen turned his attention to the profits to be made from transforming the Calumet area into an industrial and residential one. Working with two large local land holders, Bowen formed the Calumet and Chicago Canal and Dock Company in 1869. The first subdivision was made in 1874. This initial development, which became South Chicago, spurred further residential and industrial growth, including the building of the area's first steel works in 1875 as well as lumber yards, grain elevators and railroad shops (Calumet National Bank 1927). Further west on the other side of Lake Calumet, a group of men from Chicago and the eastern seaboard formed the West Pullman Land Association in 1891. The group quickly established a modern set of infrastructures, including sewers, gas and water mains, a freight station, and railroad spur lines. Attracted by the amenities of the built environment and the large industries within close proximity, an assortment of industries moved into the platted industrial lots before World War One (Roberts 1941; Vlissingen, c. 1910). Networks of finance, land and information created an array of placed-based assets and transformed the prairie into industrial space.

The types of business networks that produced South Chicago and West Pullman were replicated elsewhere. Some of Chicago's leading bourgeoisie was particularly keen on making profits from tying real estate speculation to industrial development in the Calumet. In the Spring of 1909, the Potter Palmer estate purchased 125 acres of factory sites at Indiana Harbor with dockage facilities for 5,000 Dollar to 6,000 Dollar an acre. After building up the Marshall Field department store, Potter Palmer (1826–1902) turned his attention to real estate, converting State Street into Chicago's prime retail street by the end of the century. Flush with surplus capital from his city endeavors, the guardians of the Potter estate looked for new sites where profits could be made through speculation over land, such as that found in the Calumet. Accordingly, the Potter property was turned into industrial land to be used by railway car, shoe and woollen mill concerns. Similarly, the estate of Leander McCormick, a member of one of the city's important industrial family, bought 80 acres at a cost of 500,000 Dollar. Forty acres adjoined the Palmer estate and fronted the river, while another 40 acres were located across from the canal. The prime water-based location was enticing for large companies seeking quick connections outside of the Calumet. The Interstate Iron and Steel Company purchased a site for a large addition to its mill there (Anon. 1909).

The resulting industrial complex was linked to other firms and institutions at a range of scales. Economic and political networks underpinned Calumet's ability to be a home to industry. One scale that sustained the Calumet was the national. Many of the area's steel firms were national corporations that received raw materials and semiprocessed inputs from and sold semifinished products and completed commodities to companies from across the country. The Calumet mills received coal from Appalachia and iron ore from the Mesabi. By 1920 the industry served four major sectors: railroads, construction, electrical and automotive, and agricultural. Even though Calumet producers had to compete with the Pittsburgh and Birmingham districts, low production costs, excellent transportation facilities, and a favorable location ensured that they were able to sell their steel to places across the country (Appleton 1927, 101–107; Bate 1948, 190–211). To successfully obtain and dispose of their materials, steel producers had to generate a range of linkages with local, regional and national agents. The ability to bring iron ore and coal from the Mesabi and Appalachia, for example, rested on creating successful working relations with, among others, mineral and transportation companies, labor unions, and geologists.

Two other important scales that shaped the destiny of Calumet industry were the metropolitan and the district. Metropolitan Chicago was an enormous market for Calumet firms and the supplier of a great deal of provisions and services for the district's firms. Local industrial firms and construction companies bought the steel pouring out of the Calumet's steel mills, while Standard Oil's refinery in Whiting supplied the entire region with petroleum. Utilities such as Commonwealth Edison built power houses made out of locally produced steel to supply the Calumet industrial complex, while the railroads both received cars from local produced such as Pullman-Standard and offered an array of transportation services to local firms. While large industrial corporations sought capital from national and international financial institutions, district banks such as the Calumet National, Interstate National and Hegewish State provided loans to the district's small business and inhabitants. Overseeing the development of the Calumet's industrial neighborhoods, suburbs and towns were a host of interacting business and labor institutions, such as local unions, labor newspapers, the Industrial Club of Chicago Heights and the Chicago Association of Commerce (Keating 1988; Lewis 2008; Pacyga 1991).

Together, the networks generated at the national, metropolitan and district scales created an extensive and intricate web of interactions between Calumet companies, firms in other parts of the metropolis, and nonlocal firms and institutions. These ideas about the linking of multi-scalar network, capitalist social relations and the making of industrial spaces such as the Calumet will be illustrated through two case studies. The first explores one industry. The steel industry was the Calumet's most important industry. The second examines one Calumet company. The Pullman Company, which was one of Chicago's leading firms, created an extensive system of business linkages with local and nonlocal companies.

The Calumet steel mills, corporations, and the greatest center in America

At the end of the 19th century, Theodore Roosevelt, proclaimed that "the Calumet Region is destined to become the greatest center in America" (Vlissingen c. 1910). He wasn't far wrong. With hundreds of manufacturing facilities, the district stretching from Gary to Joliet and encompassing industrial

Company	Location	Established	Facilities
American Brake	Chicago Heights	1899–1900	Foundry
American McKenna	Joliet	1897	Rolling mill
American Steel Foundries	Indiana Harbor	1903	Steel casting
Calumet Steel	Chicago Heights	1907–1908	Rolling mill
Columbia Tool Steel	Chicago Heights	1904–1905	Foundry
Federal Furnace	South Chicago	1905–1907	Blast furnace
Grand Crossing Tack	South Chicago	1902–1903	Steel facilities
Illinois Steel	Joliet	1869–1870	Integrated
Illinois Steel	South Chicago	1880–1881	Integrated
Indiana Steel	Gary	1906	Integrated
Inland Steel	Indiana Harbor	1901	Integrated
Inland Steel	Chicago Heights	1893	Rolling mill
Interstate Iron and Steel	East Chicago	1900	Rolling mill
Iroquois Iron	South Chicago	1890–1891	Blast furnace
Phoenix Horse Shoe	Joliet	1893	Rolling mill
Republic Steel	East Chicago	1889	Blast furnace
Wisconsin Steel	South Chicago	1880–1881	Blast furnace

(Note: Integrated consists of blast furnaces, rolling mills and a foundry)

Tab. 2: The Calumet primary steel industry, 1908

(Source: Directory of Iron and Steel Works of the United States and Canada, 1908. New York: American Iron and Steel Institute, 1908)

areas such as South Chicago, Pullman, East Chicago and Hammond had become a leading, if not the largest, industrial district in the United States by World War One. Although characterized by a relative degree of industrial diversity, the scale and importance of the Calumet was anchored in the rapid growth of the steel industry after 1870. From the establishment of Joliet Iron and Steel in 1869 and the subsequent development of several other primary steel mills and associated secondary metal-working firms, the Calumet industrial district formed around a steelmaking complex centered on a number of large corporate plants. By 1908 at least 17 large primary steel mills belonging to a handful of multi-unit corporations with headquarters elsewhere were located in the Calumet (Tab. 2). The Calumet mills were deeply embedded in a set of oligarchic networks that stretched across the nation (Warren 1973).

The Calumet's corporate steel world emerged very early. In 1889, the country's first major steel consolidation formed the Illinois Steel Company. Forged from the merger of three local firms—North Chicago Rolling Mills, Union Steel and Joliet Steel—the new corporation consisted of, among other productive facilities, 14 blast furnaces, four Bessemer steel mills, an iron-making mill, various coal and ore holdings, and 10,000 workers (Cutcliffe 1994). It was not the last corporate merger to shape the Calumet. The most important consolidation was the creation of US Steel. Created in 1901 out of the merger of several metal-making, iron mine, and transportation companies, including Federal Steel, Carnegie, America Steel and Wire, Lake Superior Consolidated Iron Mines, and Bessemer Steamship, it was the country's largest corporation and the world's first billion dollar corporation. Its 80 blast furnaces, 149 steel mills and plants produced more than 50 percent of the nation's steel in the first decades of the 20th century (Seely 1994). With some of the company's largest mills and a host of dependent local customers, Chicago, along with Pittsburgh, was the center of US Steel's manufacturing empire. Linked by an array of company firms along the production chain and to a range of suppliers and customers across the country, the corporation's Chicago plants were deeply embedded in a range of boundary-spanning business networks.

The rise of the Calumet corporate steel world took place at the expense of the industry in central Chicago. Small foundries were first established along the waterways in the central city before the Civil War to melt down iron bars to make consumer products such as stoves for the local market. At the same time, iron producing companies such as the North Chicago Rolling Mills and the Union Rolling Mill opened up to manufacture rails. The combined effect was that by 1870 the metal-working industries were concentrated along the Chicago river a mile or two downstream from it mouth at Lake Michigan. In the post war period, however, the networks that had made the central city the prime focus of iron and steel manufacture by the Civil War were no longer as strong as they had previously been and the central city's prominence as an iron and steel center was on the wane. Seeking to make connections with the country's leading steelmaking districts, several firms moved their entire operations to the Calumet or opened another branch in the Calumet and slowly divested from the more central plant (Appleton 1927, 27–28; Bensman and Wilson 2004; Warren 1973).

One such case was Acme Steel, which opened in the Chicago district of Bridgeport in 1884 to manufacture cold rolled strip steel and miscellaneous products. In 1918, attracted by a burgeoning and ever increasingly busy steelmaking area with all the advantages that could afford in terms of suppliers, industry know-how, and customers, the company built a new plant in Riverdale, just west of Lake Calumet. As one trade journal writer noted, the move was done on account of "its business had grown to such proportions that the need for a more dependable and reliable source of raw materials led to the purchase of a large acreage at Riverdale" (Lacher 1924, 353). The new plant gave Acme larger premises which allowed for better economies of scale and cheaper rolled steel for fabrication.

Although the shift of production facilities from Chicago to the Calumet took time, the end result was that the company's new spatial division of labor made up of finishing departments in the city and primary steel production in the Calumet was gradually put into place. By 1924 a good deal of the equipment at the Bridgeport plant had been transferred to Riverdale. The aim was to move all of the cold rolled strip equipment to the Calumet and to convert the central-city plant entirely to the fabrication of manufactured products. This was firmly in place by 1940 when the Chicago plant was home to the punch press and specialities manufacturing departments while the Calumet plant manufactured all types of hot and cold strip steel (Anon. 1941). The development of Acme's specialized division of labor within the Chicago metropolitan area rested on the company's ability to create a strong set of interfirm linkages between the two plants and on the Calumet's place within the national world of steel making.

By the early 20th century the Calumet was a key node in the steel industry's division of labor and had become, along with the Pittsburgh area, the nation's leading steel producer. This was made possible through corporate

Fig. 3: Illinois Steel Works, Joliet, 1890s
(*Source: Library of Congress*)

control over the circulation of steel-related information, capital, people and products within the United States. Control over new work processes and machinery was captured, among other things, by patent control and mergers with other firms. In this way, technological information created in the workplace at North Chicago Rolling Mills, Illinois Steel or Inland Steel remained in the hands of the corporation. Skilled managers, executives and workers moved from firm to firm, oftentimes with the locality but sometimes across regional lines. Products made in the Calumet were sent to be manufactured into finished products. Large companies and their place-based allies were able to channel federal appropriations into the refashioning of the built environment, and in the process made the landscape ready for industrial investment. The large Congressional appropriations which remade the Calumet's riverine system or facilitated the expansion of the railroad network, for example, established the basis for the building of the large industrial complexes that dominated South Chicago, East Chicago, Pullman, Gary and Joliet (Fig. 3).

The circulation of information underpinned the changing corporate structure of the Calumet. From the very beginning of industrial development when local elites began to shift capital from projects elsewhere to the Calumet, the flow of information about market share, corporate structure, manufacturing facilities, mill location and so on ensured that corporate executives were ever vigilant in scanning the national and international work of steel manufacture while assessing the character of their Calumet plants. This was apparent in the ongoing consolidation of the steel mills. While the Illinois Steel merger was the first, and the US Steel one was the largest, a series of other mergers consolidated the dominant role of the steel industry in the Calumet. This was made possible by the circulation of information within the industry itself.

Even when mergers were unsuccessful, the need for steel executives to mobilize information to build up capacity, to expand market share, and to rationalize their internal division of labor was ever present. The attempted merger of Youngstown Sheet and Tube and Inland Steel in 1928, for example, would have made the new company the nation's third largest steel company after US Steel and Bethlehem Steel. The two companies were seeking to rationalize their spatial division of labor and to intensify the Calumet's place as the major steel-producing district in America. Youngstown's production of pipe and tin plate in the Calumet would have complemented Inland's manufacture of an assortment of rails, light and heavy structural shapes, bars, rods, plates and sheets. For a variety of reasons the merger did not materialize, but the attempt speaks to the fact that the making of a steel landscape in the Calumet relied on the steel corporations' ability to be plugged into local, regional, national and international circuits of information (Anon. 1928; Sypolt and Seely 1994).

The rise of the Calumet as America's leading steelmaking district relied to a large extent on servicing local demand for the wide range of products that the large corporate steel companies produced in their sprawling production complexes. The growth of Chicago's office, commercial and retail districts were predicated on the "heavy consumption of structural steel" from the Calumet (Backert 1907, 49). In 1906, for example, downtown banks, hotels, department stores and office buildings required huge amounts of steel for their construction. This was true of the city's industrial districts as well. Large amounts of steel flowed from the Calumet mills to the new U.S. Steel complex being built in Gary, as well as additions to South Works, the Montgomery Ward warehouse, Western Electric, and the car wheel foundry of Griffin Wheel Co. One of the largest demands for local steel came from the district's railroads. At its peak in the opening decades of the 20th century, local railroad manufacturers were the single largest market for Calumet steel (Bate 1948, 83–86).

A range of local, specialized services was available to the Calumet steel mills. Water-based transportation companies loaded and unloaded materials at the Calumet River harbor. Warehousing companies offered space on long and short-term options for firms that had to store finished products or supplies. As the railroads penetrated the region, they established a set of shipping stations along their routes. Railroad tracks linked the firms to the Calumet River harbor, which was a key articulation node to the outside world. A profusion of switch spurs servicing individual firms allowed manufacturers to connect to the main railroads and from there to the rest of the United States. Large switch yards were opened at various parts of the district. Wholesalers provided a range of equipment and part supplies. Industrial real estate companies such as J. H. Van Vlissingen offered manufacturers looking to expand their premises with expert advice about the local property markets.

In some cases, a few manufacturers themselves offered specific services to the steel industry. Machine shops and foundries presented specialized manufacturing services. One such company was the Hubbard Steel Foundry of East Chicago. Its normal trade was the production of a variety of castings for iron, steel and alloy steel rolls, steel parts for rock crushing machinery, large steel gears, steel locomotive and car parts. Much of this went to the local mills. A new machine shop in 1925 was equipped with machinery "large enough to handle the heaviest class of work required in the steel mills of the Chicago district" (Fiske 1926, 899). Along with this, the company did a jobbing business in repairs for local steel mills to supplement its regular work. Hubbard was just one of the hundreds of local firms that was directly linked to the Calumet steel mills. Taking advantage of a broad set of place-based assets, the steel corporations created an extensive set of boundary-spanning relationship that linked the Calumet with the rest of metropolitan Chicago and with other parts of the United States.

The Pullman Company, business networks and place

Between January and April 1880 James Bowen, the creator of the Calumet and Chicago Canal and Dock company, secretly bought 4,000 acres of prairie land just west of Lake Calumet. He was doing it for his friend and business partner, George Pullman. The two men were part of a long-standing set of business alliances that Pullman had established over the years with industrialists such as Andrew Carnegie, politicians such as New York senator, Benjamin Field, and financiers such as the London-based Morgan family. From the late 1850s, Pullman, who was an expert at nurturing productive business connections, was heavily involved in an array of affairs across the country. Leaving Albion, New York, he started a contractor business in Chicago in 1859, and quickly branched out into railroad sleeping cars, wire rope and banking. In 1870 he bought out the factory of Detroit Car and Manufacturing Company and went into full-scale production of railroad cars in Detroit. Itching to get back to Chicago, ten years later, Pullman had Bowen purchased the large swath of land in the Calumet so that Pullman could begin manufacturing railroad cars in a large production facility in a new town that would be named after the company's owner. The plant quickly grew, with employment growing from 5,000 in 1893 to more than 20,000 in the 1920s (Buder 1967; Leyendecker 1992).

Pullman's success rested on the ability to create, mobilize and maintain a viable set of industrial networks that extended from small supplier firms within a stone's throw from its large complex next to Lake Calumet to a host of other businesses across the country. Its major customers were the country's leading railroad companies with headquarters in various parts of the country. Pullman's success lay in building, consolidating and maintaining workable leases for the use of its sleeper cars with the country's railroad industry. In some case, such as Illinois Central and the Atchison, Topeka and Santa Fe railroads, the headquarters were in Chicago. In others, decisions about contracts and other issues were made, among other places, in Baltimore (Baltimore and Ohio), New York City (New York Central), San Francisco (Southern Pacific), and Omaha (Union Pacific). By 1880, when Pullman built a new manufacturing plant on 4,000 acres in the undeveloped area west of Lake Calumet, the company had contracts to lease its sleeper cars to most of the country's railroad companies (Buder 1967; Leyendecker 1992).

Pullman established a far-flung empire of industrial networks that was centered in the Chicago metropolitan area but extended across the country. Pullman's growing national prominence relied on the rationalization and concentration of the industry by financiers and railroad speculators such as J. P. Morgan, Jay Gould and Cornelius Vanderbilt. This was centered on the sprawling works close to Lake Calumet (Fig. 4). Paralleling the company's wide set of national customer networks, Pullman also opened manufacturing facilities in St. Louis, Detroit, Elmira, and Wilmington, Delaware as well as several repair shops in various other places. Company executives working

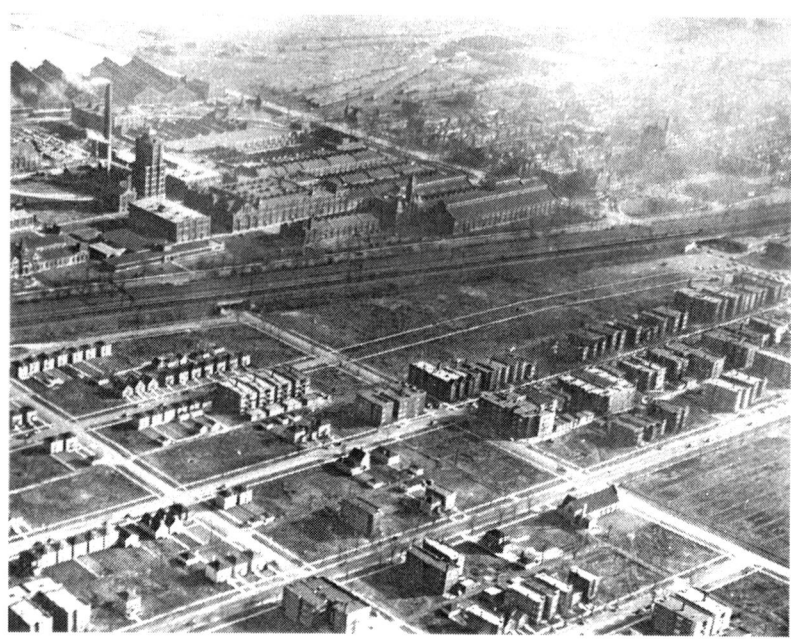

Fig. 4: Pullman factory complex, 1920

(Source: Pullman State Historical Society)

out of the main office in the Loop and the Chicago shop in Pullman would have made financial, operational and manufacturing decisions about and in concert with their counterparts in St. Louis, Detroit and elsewhere (Chandler 1977, 79–187; Buder 1967; Leyendecker 1992). It grew rapidly and by the 1920s its shops close to Lake Calumet were one of the largest production complexes in the metropolitan area and employed thousands of unskilled and skilled workers in a variety of work environments (Fig. 5).

From the 1880s the company became the anchor firm of a metropolitan complex of local manufacturing and transportation companies. Many of its clients were located here. Just as importantly, it built up a thick web of supplier relations with hundreds of local firms. Some sense of this can be obtained from a 1923 survey of the Chicago railroad equipment industries. According to the report, "a large proportion of the rails, spikes, bolts, angle bars, fillers, axles and wheels for the American railroads are manufactured in the Chicago district." There were 559 producers of equipment in the metropolitan area. The metropolitan supply chain consisted of a vast array of steps

Fig. 5: Building a Pullman Car

(Source: Pullman Historical Society)

in the production of railway cars and hundreds of products "from the apparently significant, the all-important spike and washer to the glistening steel rail and palatial Pullman coach" (Anon. 1924, 15).

The Calumet itself was also a key element in Pullman Company's development. The steel mills, foundries, machine shops and specialized railroad equipment factories produced a profusion of steel, machine, lumber and assorted other products. Calumet steel mills supplied an enormous amount of steel plate. Specialized firms such as the Boulton factory were built to serve the Pullman shops. In the late 19th century Boulton was Pullman's major supplier of castings and car wheels. The large sleeper car manufacture had both routinized and specific relations with many other Calumet firms. Harvey's Buda Engine Company manufactured a range of railway products and diesel engines. Along with the railroad companies, the Morden Frog and Crossing Works of Chicago Heights supplied Pullman with a variety of products including railway switches, frogs, guard rails, compromise joints, and rail braces.

The emergence of an extensive regional industrial complex linked to the Pullman company after 1880 appealed to a range of other firms that sought out the place-based attractions generated by Pullman but which had no direct connection with the large railroad car manufacturer. The Niagara Radiator and Boiler Company is a case in point. The North Tonawanda New York company opened a modern new foundry just north of the Pullman shops in September 1922. The company anticipated using the entire factory for molding operations, while the machining and assembly operations were to be done elsewhere in the area. The reason it was built in the Chicago region was to meet the region's growing demand for radiators. A Pullman area address gave the firm many advantages, including proximity to major transportation lines that stretched through the Calumet and connected the firm to the wider metropolitan area and the rest of the Midwest region; the ability to acquire all forms of steel from the nearby mills; and easy access to the massive and rapidly growing market for household and office radiators in the region. Finally, the ample supply of land in the area allowed the firm to build a modern plant consisting of a one-story layout that provided an uninterrupted movement of materials throughout the plant and to plan for future expansion with minimal disturbance and cost (Lacher 1923).

Niagara Radiator exemplifies the spillover effects of place-based locational assets centered on the industrial networks generated by one large anchor firm. The Pullman company was the center of a range of local, regional and national manufacturing and financial ties that built up the industrial facilities of the firm, provided profits for a widespread group of shareholders, and promoted the building of an extensive industrial district on the western side of Lake Calumet. Pullman's ability to build a broad set of networks underpinned the development of an industrial area that others found suitable for their own, unrelated manufacturing needs. Wishing to take advantage of the local locational assets, Niagara Radiator sought out the area. It was not alone. By 1924 more than 50 firms producing, among other things, pharmaceuticals, animal feed, radio units, washing machines, ice cream and barrels sought out the advantages of the Pullman area, and in the process, helped to generate an extensive industrial area within the broader world of the industrial Calumet.

Conclusion

By the late 19th century, the Calumet district was one of the world's leading industrial areas. The district's collection of steel, railroad equipment, petroleum and metal-working companies produced a cornucopia of capitalist commodities that were consumed across the nation. At its peak between 1920 and 1950, Calumet manufacturers provided more than a hundred thousand industrial jobs and countless more in ancillary industrial and service sectors. The Calumet was home to some of the largest industrial concerns of the day. Huge, sprawling complexes such as those operated by US Steel in South Chicago and Gary, or Pullman-Standard in Pullman, or Acme Steel in Riverdale anchored an extensive manufacturing system. A steelmaking, heavy industry district dominated by large capital-intensive, multi-unit corporations, the Calumet was also home to a range of smaller proprietary firms from a variety of industries.

The origins, scale, composition and character of the Calumet resulted from the development of a set of industrial networks that linked the prairie south of the city to metropolitan, regional and national circuits of knowledge, capital, and products. Boundary-spanning industrial relations allowed firms to link up in productive ways and to build up external economies of scale and scope within the district and beyond. The district's ability to capture significant parts of and to specialize in certain production chains enabled manufacturers to build up an extensive place-based industrial competency. The dominance of the district by a handful of large corporations rested on a bewildering set of interfirm and intersectoral networks between large companies such as Pullman and the hundreds of small firms that crowded the area. Similarly, all firms were dependent upon the networks they created with institutions that provided place-based assets, such as land, infrastructures and housing. Finally, district firms were firmly embedded in a wide-range set of multi-scale spatial relations that operated at the local through to the international levels. The development of a sectorally and spatially differentiated package of industrial networks from the 1860s underpinned the rise of the Calumet as one of the world's leading industrial districts.

The unraveling of these networks and the inability of corporate executives to create new, more workable ones underpinned the deindustrialization of the district. The running down of plants, the absence of technological innovation, the search for more modern place-based assets, and the reworking of boundary-spanning relations, all contributed to the rusting of the Calumet. The district's deindustrialization was part of a larger process of the development, consolidation and reproduction of industrial networks that favored districts other than the Calumet, Chicago and the Manufacturing Belt. The transformation of the Manufacturing Belt from the industrial workshop of the world to an ailing, deindustrialized region revolved around the decisions of corporate executives located in a range of cities. Seeking an assortment of advantages such as cheaper and more pliable labor and more friendly environmental legislation available in the American South, Mexico and elsewhere, executives created a new set of networks that would both develop other areas while driving the Manufacturing Belt into industrial ruin. Deindustrialization and disinvestment just like industrialization and investment are rooted in the networks created out of the capitalist relations of production.

Works Cited

Anon. (1909). Activity in factory sites at Indiana Harbor. *Iron Age,* 04/18/1909, 1141.

Anon. (1924). Chicago leads in rail appliance sales. *Chicago Commerce,* 01/15/1924, 15–16.

Anon. (1928). Youngstown-Inland Steel merger. *Iron Age,* 02/02/1928, 342–43, 369.

Anon. (1941). Acme Steel Company. *Commerce,* 03/1941, 89–91.

Appleton, J. (1927). *The iron and steel industry of the Calumet district: a study in economic geography.* Urbana: University of Illinois Press.

Backert, A. (1907). The Chicago iron trade in 1906. *Iron Age,* 01/03/1907, 48–51.

Bate, P. (1948). *The development of the iron and steel industry of the Chicago area, 1900–1920.* PhD diss., University of Chicago.

Bensman, D., and R. Lynch (1987). *Rusted dreams: hard times in a steel community.* New York: McGraw-Hill.

Bensman, D., and M. Wilson (2004). Iron and steel. In J. Grossman, A. D. Keating and J. Reiff (eds.). *The Encyclopedia of Chicago,* 424–27. Chicago: University of Chicago Press.

Buder, S. (1967). *Pullman: an experiment in industrial order and community planning, 1880–1930.* New York: Oxford University Press.

Calumet National Bank (1927). *South Chicago: its history and progress.* Chicago: Calumet National Bank.

Chandler, A. (1977). *The visible hand: the managerial revolution in American business.* Cambridge: Belknap Press.

Colten, C. (1994). Chicago's waste lands refuse disposal and urban growth, 1840–1900. *Journal of Historical Geography*, 20, 124–142.

Cowie, J., and J. Heathcott (eds.). (2003). *Beyond the ruins: the meanings of deindustrialization*. Ithaca: Cornell University Press.

Cronon, W. (1991). *Nature's metropolis; Chicago and the Great West*. New York: Norton.

Cutcliff, S. (1994). Illinois Steel Company. In B. Seely (ed.). *Iron and steel in the twentieth century*, 217–218. New York: Facts on File.

Fiske, R. (1926). Equipment machines for large works. *Iron Age*, 04/01/1926, 899–902.

High, S. (2003). *Industrial sunset: the making of North America's rust belt, 1969–1984*. Toronto: University Of Toronto Press.

Keating, A. D. (1988). *Building Chicago: suburbs developers and the creation of a divided metropolis*. Columbus: Ohio State University Press.

Lacher, G. (1923). Making radiators under new conditions. *Iron Age*, 03/22/1923, 805–809.

Lacher, G. (1924). Acme Steel expands cold strip capacity. *Iron Age*, 01/31/1924, 353–358.

Lee, H. (1908). The Calumet region as an industrial center. *Chicago, the Great Central Market Magazine*, July, 68–71, 74–76.

Lewis, R. (2008). *Chicago made: factory networks in the industrial metropolis*. Chicago: University of Chicago Press.

Leyendecker, L. (1992). *Palace car prince: a biography of George Mortimer Pullman*. Niwat: University Press of Colorado.

Lynch, D. (1946). *The concentration of economic power*. New York: Columbia University Press.

Meyer, D. (2001). The national integration of regional economies. In T. McIlwraith and E. Muller (eds.). *North America: The historical geography of a changing continent*, 307–331. Totowa, NJ: Rowman and Littlefield.

Mohl, R., and N. Betten (1986). *Steel city: urban and ethic patterns in Gary, Indiana, 1905–1950*. New York: Holmes and Meier.

Moore, P. (1959). *The Calumet region: Indiana's last frontier*. Indianapolis: Indiana Historical Bureau.

Pacyga, D. (1991). *Polish immigrants and industrial change: workers on the South Side, 1880–1920*. Columbus: Ohio State University Press.

Roberts, G. (1941). *History of West Pullman*. Typescript. Chicago Public Library, Special Collections, Calumet Regional Community Collection, Box 6, File 7.

Salzmann, J. (2012). The creative destruction of the Chicago River Harbor: spatial and environmental dimensions of industrial capitalism, 1881–1909. *Enterprise and Society*, 13, 235–275.

Scranton, P. (1989). *Figured tapestry: production, markets, and power in Philadelphia textiles, 1885–1941*. Cambridge: Cambridge University Press.

Seely, B. (1994). United States Steel Corporation. In B. Seely (ed.). *Iron and steel in the twentieth century*, 438–446. New York: Facts on File.

Sypolt, L., and B. Seely (1994). Youngstown Sheet and Tube Company. In B. Seely (ed.). *Iron and steel in the twentieth century*, 499–503. New York: Facts on File.

Tomlinson, B. (1999). Economics and empire: the periphery and the imperial economy. In Andrew Porter (ed.). *The Oxford History of the British Empire, volume III: the nineteenth century*, 53–74. Oxford: Oxford University Press.

Vlissingen, A. van (c. 1910). *Why the Calumet district draws manufacturers*. Typescript. Chicago Public Library, Special Collections, Calumet Regional Community Collection, Box 4, File 18.

Warren, K. (1973). *The American steel industry, 1850–1970: a geographical interpretation*. Pittsburgh: University of Pittsburgh Press.

Winder, G. (1999). The North American Manufacturing Belt in 1880: a cluster of regional industrial systems or one large industrial district? *Economic Geography*, 75, 71–91.

Part II
Crisis and Recovery

In-Between: The Conversion of Former Iron and Steel Industry Sites and Cities in the Saarland–Uneven and Complex Development Paths[1]

Peter Dörrenbächer

Introduction: Former Iron and Steel Production Sites as Focal Points for Urban Renewal

As in other old industrial regions such as the Ruhr, coal mines, iron and steelworks in the Saar have equally been focal points of urban renewal processes. As long as these installations were operating they were accessible only to employees of the works. Even after their closure most of these sites have been inaccessible to the public. The closure of iron and steelworks as a result of the steel crisis and economic restructuration in the 1970s and 1980s has led not only to tremendous losses of employment but also to the emergence of large brownfield areas. In addition, their environments were often contaminated and polluted. These exhausted (spatial) centers reflected the urban depletion process provoked by the steel crisis, and led to a further acceleration of industrial decline.

Because of their central location many brownfield areas of the former iron and steel industry imposed a severe burden on urban development. At the same time they bore the potential to become focal points of urban renewal: They have been transformed into new town centers (e.g. Neue Mitte Oberhausen)[2] or into extensions of existing town centers (e.g. the city center of Castrop-Rauxel), into business, science or industry cultural parks (e.g.

---

1 I would like to thank Erich Müller (em-luftbilder) for the permission to use the aerial photo of Saarterrassen (Fig. 4) for this publication.

2 With regard to the revitalization and renewal of iron and steel industry brownfields, one of the most prominent projects in Europe is the so called *Neue Mitte Oberhausen* which combines a large shopping mall, a recreation park, sports and other leisure facilities, to the new town centre of the city of Oberhausen on the site of a former iron and steelworks of the *GHH* corporation, later *Thyssen* (Basten 1998).

Wissenschaftspark Rheinelbe in Gelsenkirchen and Landschaftspark Duisburg–Nord).[3]

Within just seven years and as a consequence of the steel crisis in the 1970s and 1980s, three integrated iron and steelworks have been completely or partly closed in the Saarland. Although these three sites are located not more than five to 20 km apart from each other, their transformation has been considerably different. The following paper reconstructs and analyzes these different transition processes with respect to their complex development paths.

Restructuration of the Saarland Iron and Steel Industry during the Steel Crisis of the 1970s and 1980s

The Saar iron and steel industry which employed more than 40,000 persons in the early 1960s, has dramatically reduced employment during the steel crisis from the mid 1970s to the early 1990s. From 1970 to 1995 29,000 jobs were lost. In the short period between 1975 and 1988 employment fell by 22,000 (Rentmeister 2006, 7). The strong contraction was the result of excess production capacities on the steel world market, overlapping production programs, low product prices, poor cost calculations and diverting interests of former plant owners (Zwick 2012, 16). By the late 1970s, it became clear that a change of the dispersed ownership structure, as well as the closure of production facilities, would be unavoidable.

In February 1978 the ARBED Corporation,[4] which at that time controlled 50 percent of the combined Völklingen and Burbach iron and steelworks (*Stahlwerke Röchling-Burbach GmbH*) opted for a rationalization concept. On December 18, 1978 the *Stahlwerke Röchling-Burbach GmbH* and

---

3 In the 1990s, in the Ruhr area alone, around 100 innovative conversion and renewal projects have been implemented in the framework of the *Internationale Bauausstellung EmscherPark (IBA) (International Building Exhibition)*. The Escher Zone in the northern part of the Ruhr was exceptionally affected by economic, social and ecological problems resulting from the decline of the combined mining, iron and steel industries. The IBA projects—many of them dealing with the conversion of former brownfield areas into new town centers—became models for a number of conversion projects elsewhere.

4 Aciéries Réunies de Burbach-Eich-Dudelange (United Ironworks of Burbach, Eich and Dudellange)

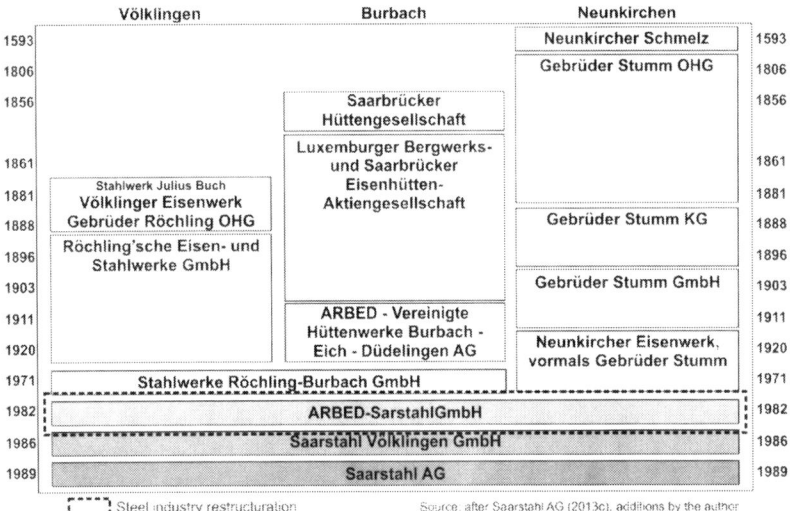

Fig. 1: Development of Saarstahl Corporation

(Source: Saarstahl 2013c, additions by the author)

the *Neunkircher Eisenwerk AG*, with the assistance of the Federal Government, the Government of the Saarland and the trade unions, adopted a restructuration program. This program was revisited in May 1982 and resulted in the fusion of the *Stahlwerke Röchling-Burbach GmbH* with the *Neunkircher Eisenwerk AG* to the *ARBED-Saarstahl GmbH* (Fig. 1). Of greater importance for the population was the fact that at the end of the restructuration process only the integrated iron and steelworks in Dillingen remained. In contrast, the other integrated plants in Neunkirchen, Saarbrücken-Burbach and Völklingen were dismantled (Fig. 2).

In the course of the restructuration process a new steelwork was to be constructed in Völklingen. At the same time the outdated blast furnaces ceased to operate. Pig iron production in Neunkrichen and Saarbrücken-Burbach came to a halt. Iron smelting and related activities such as coke production concentrated in Dillingen. In Völklingen the converters of the new steel mill, an electro oven, some rolling mills and a newly constructed foundry continued to operate. In contrast, in Neunkirchen and Saarbrücken-Burbach all production facilities with the exception of one or two rolling mills closed down (Fig. 2). The reduction of the production capacity by nearly 40 percent combined with this restructuration process provoked not only the loss of around 22,000 jobs but also the need for public financial support

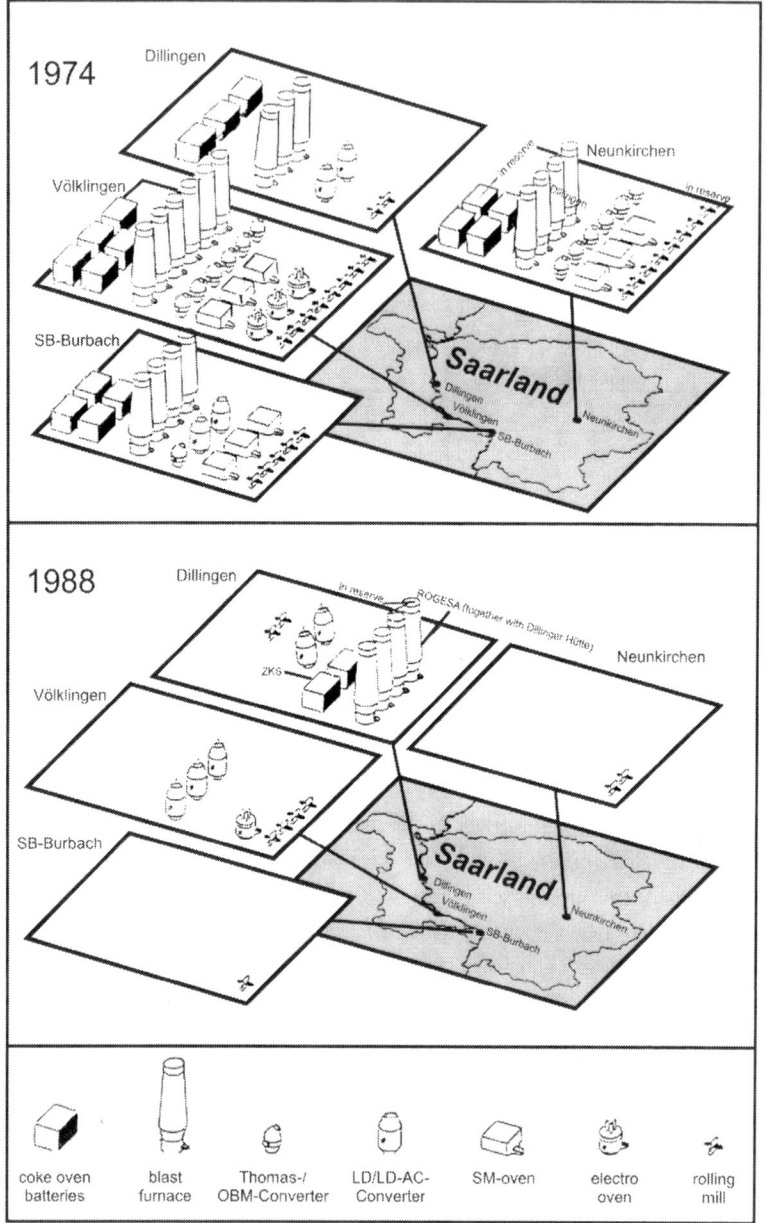

Fig. 2: Restructuration of the Saarland Iron and Steel Industry

(Source: Private archive of the author)

of around a half billion Deutsche Mark[5]. All three affected steel cities were faced with brownfield areas in their centers that were largely polluted.

Similarities and Dissimilarities of the Development of Former Steel Cities in the Saarland–An Overview

All steel cities in the Saarland affected by the steel crisis had similar characteristics as other industrial cities in different regions: The industrial decline led to tremendous job losses, resulting in very high rates of unemployment and long term unemployment. This decline was accompanied by a range of other problems such as: high outmigration especially of the young and better qualified population, which resulted in a decrease (Tab. 1) and aging of the remaining population. At the same time it led to the immigration of ethnic minorities and rising social problems such as high school drop-out rates, drug problems, crime and family violence, high vacancy rates, depleted areas, instances of urban blight, low tax revenues, and an overall poorly developed civil society. The low local participation rates of engagement with the restructuration process and the preservation of industrial heritage demonstrate this. In combination, these factors created a negative image of the cities and the steel industry districts; the emergence of a vicious circle.

	Neunkirchen		Völklingen		Saarbrücken-Burbach*		Saarbrücken (SB)*	
1974	56.818	100,0	48.412	100,0	18.380	100,0	209.104	100,0
2012*	46.704	82,2	39.509	81,6	14.581	79,3	178.951	85,6

*Saarbrücken: 2011

Tab. 1: Population Development in Saarland Iron and Steel Cities (Kreisstadt Neunkirchen (2013); Stadt Völklingen (2012); Landeshauptstadt Saarbrücken (1976; 2012))

However, urban renewing and rehabilitation programs and projects commenced at all steel production sites starting from the late 1970s onwards. In recent years innovative projects have been initiated and implemented un-

---

5 Around 250 million Euros.

Fig. 3: From the Neunkrichen Eisenwerk to the Saarpark Center
(Sources: left: private archive of the author; right: Dörrenbächer, 2012)

der the Federal Programs *Soziale Stadt* and *Stadtumbau West* in all affected cities. Apart from these, another development project was implemented in Saarbrücken-Burbach. This project was part of the framework of the EU sponsored *URBAN* initiative. All these projects combined urban rehabilitation measures, such as the dismantling of vacant and depleted buildings, with social initiatives and aim at including the local population in the urban recovery process. The national award winning *BID Burbach, (Bündnis für Investition und Dienstleistung/Business Improvement District Partnership for Investment and Service)* is one of the most recent projects seeking to strengthen economic self-sufficiency of the former steel industry district of Saarbrücken-Burbach in a civic bottom-up project (BID-Burbach 2013; Lorenz 2013).

In spite of these similarities and the fact that the complete or partial closure of iron and steel production at all three sites took place within a period of less than ten years and within a distance of only some twenty kilometers from one another, there were strong dissimilarities with regards to the transformation of the three cities in general, and the brownfield areas in particular.

In 1989, the *Saarpark Center* in Neunkirchen has been inaugurated on the site of the former ironworks that had been closed in 1982 (Fig. 3). The Saarpark Center is a large shopping mall with 33,500 square meters of retail facilities, 130 stores, including one warehouse and three large textile stores, service providers, restaurants, 1,600 parking lots on-site and 800 parking lots in the vicinity (ECE 2013). A few years later the leisure and recreation Park *Neunkircher Wasserturm* opened adjacent to the mall (Neunkirchen Water Tower). Today, the converted water tower of the former ironworks comprises a multiplex cine-tower, a fitness-center, event restaurants, a micro brewery, a disco, and other entertainment facilities. It is the gateway to a leisure and

Fig. 4: Saarterrassen

(Source: Photo: Erich Müller, em-luftbilder)

recreation park of 40 hectares called the *Neunkircher Hüttenweg* (Neunkirchen Ironworks Trail) (Kreisstadt Neunkirchen 2012).

The blast furnaces complex of the Völklingen ironworks shut down in 1986. In contrast to the complex in Neunkirchen, Völklingen took a completely different path of transition. The blast furnaces in Völklingen were nominated as the first UNESCO industrial *World Heritage* worldwide in 1994. The so-called *Europäisches Zentrum für Kunst und Industriekultur* (European Centre for Arts and Industry Culture) opened in 1999. Today it attracts about 100,000 visitors per year not only from the Saar region but from across Germany and other countries.

The transition of the brownfield area of the former *Burbacher Hütte* (Burbach ironworks) in the district of Burbach (city of Saarbrücken) again differed distinctly from the two other sites. The Burbacher Hütte shut down between 1978 and 1983. After a relatively long period of no obvious rehabilitation, a development company founded and controlled by the City of Saarbrücken developed the so-called *Saarterrassen* (Saar Terraces), a mixed business park and residential area. The focus of the park lies on services, new media, telecommunications, warehouse stores, and craft workshops (Fig. 4).

It comprises 169 enterprises and organizations with around 2,000 employees (Netfutura 2013).

When comparing the transformation and transition processes of these three former iron and steel production sites, strong differences can be discerned not only with regard to their outcomes but also to the processes and actors involved. This deserves a closer conceptual analysis and empirical investigation.

Restructuration as a Path-Dependent and Emerging Process

The uneven development of the three former steel industry sites and cities cannot be explained through either exclusive use of nomothetic neo-classical industrial location theories, or the application of exclusively ideographic small-scale behavioral as well as large-scale institutional approaches of human geography (and history). This is due to the fact that the restructuration and transformation of iron and steel production sites are complex and contingent socio-economic structuration processes that mediate between large and small levels of spatial, social and temporal scales (Fig. 5). With respect to time, Storper (1988) differentiates between *big structure, large processes* and *small events*. Referring to conceptions of *Evolutionary Economic Geography* (Boschma and Franken 2006; 2008; Boschma and Martin 2007; 2010), we can state that restructuration processes are in fact *evolutionary* and at the same time *path-dependent*. According to the standard path dependence model in Regional Economics and Economic Geography, development paths are characterized by the "convergence to a stable, self-reproducing form with the reinforcement of existing technology; little or no innovation; and little, if any, endogenous change in effect, continuity and stasis" (Martin 2010, 21). But as Martin (2010, 20) points out, "path dependence need not lead to or involve lock-in, or indeed lead to any form or equilibrium or stable state or trajectory." While they are *contingent*, restructuration processes are simultaneously *path-evolving* and exhibit a trajectory, which is more prone to change and evolution by layering, conversion, and recombination of place and time specific institutional configurations (Martin 2010, 22; MacKinnon et al. 2009).

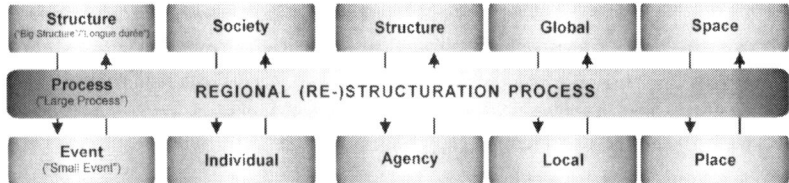

Fig. 5: The Regional (Re-)Structuration Process

(Source: Dörrenbächer, 2013)

The Uneven Conversion of Former Iron and Steel Industry Cities in the Saarland

In what follows, the paper analyses the three distinctive approaches to conversion of the iron and steel brownfield areas and the resulting uneven urban developments in the Saarland. Furthermore, the section reconstructs these processes by linking various spatial, temporal, and social levels of scale. Restructuration is conceived as being path-dependent and constrained, as well as path-evolving and contingent. The analysis is confined to the transformation and conversion of the three iron and steel industry brownfields. That is to say it concentrates on the period *between* the loss of the old function and the acquisition of new functions sustained by the former industrial sites and cities. The analysis refers to the stage with a spatial (scene) as well as a temporal connotation as the period *In-Between*.

Neunkirchen In-Between: From Iron and Steel to Shopping and Leisure

Between December 1978 and summer 1982, the restructuration program of the iron and steel city of Neunkirchen by the *Stahlwerke Röchling-Burbach GmbH* (Steelworks Röchling-Burbach Ltd.) and the *Neunkircher Eisenwerk AG* (Neunkirchen Ironworks Corporation)[6] has resulted in the loss of around 8,400 jobs. Moreover, the city center included 93 hectares of brown-

---

6 Both companies later amalgamated into ARBED-Saarstahl.

field area. With the exception of only two rolling mills, which are still in use, all iron and steel production facilities (blast furnaces, power station, sintering, charging and coking plants, iron ore storage and steelworks) have been closed (Saarstahl AG 2013b; Isoplan 1991, 371; Fig. 2).

The initial position of the city of Neunkirchen at the time of the announcement of the steel restructuration program was very different from that of the two other iron and steel cities, which were also affected by the program in the Saarland. In the period between 1960 and 1968, all five coal mines located within the territory of the city have been closed down resulting in the loss of around 12,000 jobs and the emergence of more than 300 hectares brownfield areas (Isoplan 1991, 371; Dörrenbächer 1989; 2007). Due to these developments, the Government of the Saarland and the City of Neunkirchen had initiated and implemented various regional and urban restructuration programs and measures even before the adoption of the steel restructuration program: In 1973 the Government of the Saarland had launched a Priority Program for the Neunkirchen region (*Schwerpunktprogramm für den Raum Neunkirchen*) (Saarland 1973), and in 1976 the regional Government adopted a Framework Program for Regional Planning (*Landesplanerisches Rahmenprogramm*) requesting a development concept for the town center of Neunkirchen as a medium size central place following the German regional planning regulation (*Raumordnung*). Corresponding with the Framework Program and as a reaction to the restructuration program of the Saar steel industry in February 1978, the City of Neunkirchen decided to launch an urban development concept (Kreisstadt Neunkirchen 1981a; 1981b). The then recently elected Lord-Mayor of the City of Neunkirchen, Peter Neuber (1975–1990), has played a key role in the restructuration process as he had excellent personal contacts to and experiences with the federal administration from his former position as a senior civil servant in the Federal Government.[7] As early as February 1977, in view of past (mining) and expected job losses in the iron and steel industry, he requested a special support program for his city (Neunkirchen 1979, 43–51). In the same year, i.e. one year before the steel restructuration program has been adopted, the City

---

7 With regard to the importance of the Lord-Mayor Neuber for the restructuration process the publication *Neunkirchen wandelt sich. Reden und Rufe 1975–1979* (*Neunkirchen changes. Speeches given by the Lord-Mayor between 1975 and 1979*) (Kreisstadt Neunkirchen 1979) is very revealing as the addresses give some very interesting background information about the restructuration measures initiated and implemented by the Lord-Mayor and the City in the second half of the seventies.

Council drew on the experiences made in North Rhine–Westphalia with regard to the conversion of former steel industry sites and decided to commission *Preparatory studies* for the conversion of the still working ironworks located adjacent to the Neunkirchen Central Business District (CBD). In December 1978, i.e. in the same month that the restructuration program had been adopted, the City Council and the city administration have decided to commission *Preparatory Studies* for the conversion of 83 hectares of the Neunkirchen Ironworks (*Neunkircher Eisenwerk*) area according to the Federal Urban Development Promotion Act (*Städtebauförderungsgesetz (StBauFG)*). These early measures taken by the City of Neunkirchen to convert the city center together with the area of the ironworks which were planned to be closed in the years to come can be explained as the result of another development: the coal crisis of the 1960s. This is documented by the statement given by Lord-Mayor Neuber in the context of the adoption of these preliminary studies and measures in December 1978:

"Resulting from the decision taken by the City Council […] no single stone will be removed, no furnace extinguished, no smoke stake torn down immediately. But what we do need is a vision and we need this conception earlier than in the last crisis—the coal crisis of the last fifteen years, a crisis which we have not yet overcome" (Neunkirchen 1979, 79, translation by the author)[8].

However, from the very beginning it was clear that the City did not seek the preservation of the closed production installations. Instead it strove for their removal as they were considered not only as *the* serious deficit in the field of urban planning but were also hampering the urban economic development, a priority of the City administration.[9] Corresponding with this priority, the development concept for the city center (Kreisstadt Neunkirchen 1981b, 3) sought the restructuration *from an old industrial to a service city* by means of a spatial concentration of retail activities and public services, i.e. the recovery of central place functions that had been lost in the recent past.

---

8 "Als Folge des heutigen Beschlusses wird […] zunächst kein einziger Stein bewegt, kein Hochofen gelöscht und kein Schornstein geschleift. Aber ein Konzept, das müssen wir haben, und zwar rechtzeitiger, als wir es in der letzten Krise hatten, die den Namen Kohle trug vor 15 Jahren—einer Krise, die wir kommunal und städte- sowie landschaftsbaulich heute noch nicht bewältigt haben."

9 This objective is emphasised by the Lord-Mayor's address to the City-Council in the context of the adoption of these preliminary studies and measures in December 1978 (Neunkirchen 1979, 78).

Thanks to the early preliminary studies for the conversion of the iron-works area during the phasing-out period of industrial production parallel to the closing of the ironworks, the City was able to bring forward the conversion very quickly.[10] Even before the iron and steel production had stopped, the City Council passed a so-called *Strukturplan* (structure plan), which was similar to a *Bebauungsplan*, i.e. the official detailed urban district master plan. This plan was the basis on which the formal specification for the future conversion of the ironworks area and the Neunkirchen city center were formulated according to the Federal Urban Development Promotion Act (*Städtebauförderungsgesetz (StBauFG)*). The City had calculated the financial value of the production facilities previously. These calculations resulted in the finding that preserving the facilities would have been more expensive than their demolition. However, before the formal specification of the conversion could be implemented, the City had to acquire the area of the former ironworks and to remove the obsolete production facilities. Following one year of negotiations with the Government of the Saarland, the City acquired the specified urban renewal area comprising 22 hectares of brownfield area at book value, which was only a fractional amount of the current market price. Immediately after the purchase of the real estate, the City started to demolish the former production facilities. In contrast to the ironworks in Völklingen, which were closed a few years later (1986, see below), in Neunkirchen the Landesdenkmalamt Saarland (heritage authority of the Saarland) became interested in preserving *some* relevant parts of the blast furnaces as the core of a future industrial museum only some weeks before the shut-down of the blast furnaces. However, the time was not ripe yet for initiatives willing to preserve the complete ensemble of iron and steel production.

The already quite advanced conversion process was clearly persuing a different direction. Apart from that, the market price for scrap metal had almost tripled between 1981 and 1985. This provided additional grounds to demolish the works. In 1987, a legally binding *Bebauungsplan* (detailed urban district master plan) was passed that sought to renew the area of the former ironworks, including a completely new urban traffic infrastructure and the extension of the existing city center with a focus on services (especially retail services).

---

10 The following description is primarily referring to the thorough documentation by Isoplan (1991, 371–374).

The City made revenues amounting to around 1.6 million DM from selling the scrap iron. Meanwhile, costs for the acquisition of the real estate added up to around 5.5 million DM, and the costs for the decontamination and rehabilitation of the coking plant area were estimated to be around 28 million DM (Isoplan 1991, 381, 386). Conversely, between 1985 and 1989, the Federal Republic had spent more than 22 million DM in accordance with the Federal Urban Development Promotion Act (*Städtebauförderungsgesetz (StBauFG)*). Moreover, between 1986 and 1989 the City received 16.5 million DM from the European Community (Isoplan 1991, 386) originating from a special and follow-up program of the *RESIDER* Community Initiative to assist in the economic conversion and redevelopment of areas that were formerly heavily dependent upon the steel industry (European Community 1999, 100). In addition, the City received millions of DM from other federal and regional sources to bring forward the conversion.

Resulting from the specific development path of industrialization and deindustrialization in Neunkirchen, including place-specific political and personal constellations, conversion measures were implemented very early. This enabled the City of Neunkirchen to attract the *ECE Group*[11] that has established and now runs the *Saarpark Center* (Shopping mall) as the leading investor for the renewal of downtown Neunkirchen and the adjacent brownfield areas.

On the one hand, the *Saarpark Center* has helped the city center and the city in general to change its image and attract further investment, as the leisure facilities mentioned earlier indicate. On the other hand, the new city center also contributed to further drain away purchasing power from other urban areas, which will now need further support in order to stop urban blight.

---

11 "ECE is the European market leader in the field of inner city shopping centers. Moreover, ECE also develops and builds transport complexes, logistics centers, company headquarters, office complexes, hotels, industrial buildings, as well as other special-purpose properties" (ECE 2013).

Völklingen In-Between: From Iron and Steel Industry to Steel Industry and Industry Culture

The restructuration program adopted by the *Stahlwerke Röchling-Burbach GmbH* (Steelworks Röchling-Burbach Ltd.) and the *Neunkircher Eisenwerk AG* (Neunkirchen Ironworks Corporation) in December 1978 and the first adaptation of this program to the deteriorated market conditions in 1981 resulted in the loss of thousands of jobs. After the closure of the Völklingen blast furnaces in 1986 pig iron production was concentrated in Dillingen (Fig. 2) around twenty kilometers away from Völklingen. This relocation alone had led to the loss of around 10,000 jobs (Trapp 1991, 144). The closure of six blast furnaces, of related facilities (blowers house, coking, sintering and charging plants etc.) and of the old *OBM* steel converters (*Oxygen-Bodenblasen-Maxhütte* technique) and the *SM* (*Siemens-Martin*) ovens[12] has resulted in the emergence of brownfield areas of more than 60 hectares (Trapp 1991, 144; Isoplan and FIRU 1992).

Although the former ironworks of Völklingen is located adjacent to the city center, similar to the Neunkirchen works, the conversion of the former ironworks and the development of the city center in Völklingen were very different. This difference is especially poignant with regard to the course of action and consequently led to very different results. Let alone the (un)usual technical, procedural, financial, political and other difficulties connected with the conversion of old industrial areas, the conversion of the Völklingen ironworks area, in particular, and the conversion of the city, in general, were particularly difficult. This was especially due to some place- and time-specific peculiarities of the Völklingen case.

The group of six blast furnaces including the related facilities, among others, a large blowers house, coking, sintering and charging plants, were constructed between 1882 and 1913 and represented the state of the art at that time. The combined operation of the six furnaces with their related supply facilities allowed integrated and therefore extremely efficient pig iron

---

12 The OBM steel converters and the SM ovens were replaced by a new steelworks using the basic oxygen process (BOP). In Völklingen ARBED-Saarstahl implemented the techniques *LD* and *LD/AC*. *LD* stands for the *Linz-Donawitz* steel production technique, whereas *LD/AC* stands for the *Linz-Donawitz Arbed and Centre National de Recherches Métallurgique*, a technique which has been further developed by the Luxembourg *ARBED* Corporation and the Belgian *Centre National de Recherches Métallurgique* (Knebeler 2011, 36–37).

production. This advantage later turned into a disadvantage as the individual elements of this integrated system could not be changed separately without destructing the whole system. Because of this path-dependent lock-in situation the ironworks turned into a unique living industrial fossil that continued production in its original form until its complete closure in 1986. Due to this, only half a year after the closure of the ironworks, the *Initiative Völklinger Hütte* (IVH) was founded. This civil society movement advocated the conservation of the complete old ironworks complex (Kesternich 1990). It is noteworthy that the majority of its members did not originate from Völklingen and the iron and steel workers milieu but from the *bourgeois* and academic milieus of the capital of the Saarland. Some of these activists had already campaigned for the preservation of the Neunkirchen ironworks. These activists as well as the representatives of the Landesdenkmalamt Saarland (heritage authority of the Saarland) have learned from their defeat in the Neunkirchen case (Lüth 1998, 25). Although it was on the agenda from the very beginning[13], it took until 1992 before the Government of the Saarland officially declared the Völklingen ironworks the *heritage of pig iron production* (Lüth 1998, 26).

In the first years, the conversion of the brownfield area was characterized by classic land-use conflicts as the ironworks with its related facilities was situated between factories still working (the new steelworks, the rolling mills and the foundry) on the one side, and the city center and the district of Wehrden, on the other: The preservation of the ironworks as an industrial heritage was in conflict with the still working production facilities whose transmission lines and media traces for gases, electricity and other materials continued to use the area of the former ironworks[14] and with the objective to better connect the district of Wehrden with the city center (Glaser 1997, 6; Isoplan 1991, 403).

---

13 Already before the closure of the ironworks some important parts of the complex (e.g. blowers house) have been declared industrial heritage (Voermanek 1995, 1970; Isoplan 1991, 402), and in early 1988 the *Planungsgemeinschaft* (Planning association) of the IVH has developed an urban vision of an "Industry and Culture Park" (Otto 1990, 33–34). In 1987, the *Landtag des Saarlandes* (Saarland Parliament) has decided to establish a so-called *Industriestraße Saar* (Route of Industrial Culture Saarland) as a part of an *Industriestraße SaarLorLux* (Isoplan 1991, 402). This project has not been implemented until today.

14 It was only in 1990 that the City was able to sign a sales agreement to gain control over the surface of the brownfield that was owned by *Saarstahl* Corporation until 1988 (Isoplan 1991, 403).

In contrast to the City of Neunkirchen, the City of Völklingen reacted only after the closure of the ironworks to the problems caused by this closure. In accordance with the Federal Building Code (*Baugesetzbuch (BauGB)*), from mid-1987 until the end of 1988 the City commissioned *Preliminary Studies* on the territory of the former ironworks, including an inventory of contaminated areas and the designation of an urban renewal zone. In order to implement these measures, the City received, among other monies, 11 million DM from the European Community Initiative *RESIDER* for the period between 1987 and 1990. Not only because of this short deadline, but also because of the complexity of the conversion of this inner-city brownfield area in particular, and other uncertainties with regard to the future urban planning in general (e.g. current canalization of the river Saar and other major regional infrastructure projects in the territory of the city), the city administration, together with the *Landesentwicklungsgesellschaft* (LEG) (Regional Development Corporation) and various governmental taskforce groups applied a completely new planning approach. With the support of the Federal Government, they commissioned the research and consulting company for regional and environmental planning *FIRU (Forschungs- und Informations-Gesellschaft für Fach- und Rechtsfragen der Raum- und Umweltplanung)* to initiate a so-called *Open Urban Expert Planning Process* (*Offenes Städtebauliches Gutachterverfahren (OSGA)*) (Mittelstadt Völklingen 1990). The objective of *OSGA* was to develop an Urban Framework Plan (*Städtebaulicher Rahmenplan*) for the revitalization of the Völklingen ironworks.

The explicitly expressed intention of *OSGA* was to gain a broad consensus as early as possible for the projected path to the revitalization of the urban brownfield area. This approach allowed to account for and to integrate the objections and opposition that often accompany large-scale projects into the reconstruction process instead of settling disputes later on. In this respect *OSGA* was characterized by

- the mutual exchange of knowledge, evaluations and results as a central part of a common planning process
- the willingness to proceed in mutual agreement and in a cooperative way with the aim of formulating comprehensive perspectives for the future
- the willingness to discuss and balance, in a comprehensive way, the differing and conflicting use(s) with regard to issues of urban planning, environmental protection, regional development, and the design of the environment, and

– the wholehearted consideration of suggestions expressed by the public, the affected population, experts and professionals as well as other stakeholders (Isoplan 1991, 408–409).

This approach is reflected by the organization structure of *OSGA,* which consists of a steering committee (*Lenkungsgruppe*), an urban planning expert team (*Städtebauliches Gutachterteam*), a coordination group (*Zentraleinheit und Koordination*), and special experts (*Sonderfachleute*).

At the end of the *OSGA* process in September 1989, there were six draft outlines of an urban framework plan developed by six nationally and internationally recognized planning firms. In a participatory consultation process two of these draft outlines were selected for further development (Mittelstadt Völklingen 1990; Marx 1989; Isoplan 1991, 404–418). The main characteristics of these OSGA urban framework plans were

– the development of a new town district on the area of the former ironworks, which connects the city center with the Wehrden district
– the economic revitalization as a central element of a comprehensive urban development strategy
– a distinct position in favor of the conservation of the blast furnace group, whereas
– all developments and measures had to be oriented to this monumental [i.e. the old ironworks ensemble] location factor (Isoplan 1991, 441).

From the very beginning, the preservation of the extraordinary blast furnace complex and its related facilities was a key issue of the discourse on the development of the Völklingen brownfield area in particular, and the city development in general. However, it was only in the context of the two following processes that this issue received the critical momentum: by the *OSGA* and the resulting framework plans and by the cultural event *Steelopolis.* This took place in August and September 1990 on the site of the closed ironworks (Kesternich 1990, 26) and made the area accessible to the larger public for the first time. Following the event, the cultural magazine *Saarbrücker Hefte* devoted a special issue to the Völklingen ironworks commemorating *Steelopolis* in 1990.

As mentioned before, the Saarland Government declared the ironworks to become heritage of the pig iron production in summer 1992, and in 1993 one of the six blast furnaces was made accessible to the public. But it was not the appreciation of the former industrial complex alone that has motivated the Government to take this position. This was due to the fact that a technical study commissioned earlier by *Saarstahl* Corporation found out that, in contrast to the Neunkirchen case, the demolition of the complex and the recovery of the contaminated brownfield area would have been more expensive than its preservation. However, that meant in fact to leave the complex as it was and to do hardly anything. This situation only changed partially after the old ironworks had been nominated the first industrial *World Heritage* by UNESCO in December 1994 and the Foundation for Industry Culture (*Stiftung Industriekultur*) had been set up. The mission of the foundation was to take care of the industrial heritage of the Saarland, and particularly to contribute to the preservation of the Völklingen ironworks as UNESCO world heritage of industry culture and to make the ensemble accessible to the public. Nevertheless, advocates of the industrial heritage complained that a coherent development concept complying with the objectives expressed by the statute of the foundation did not develop during the first half decade after its nomination (Glaser 1997, 7). With the establishment of the European Center for Arts and Industry Culture (*Europäisches Zentrum für Kunst und Industriekultur*) in 1999 the development of the Völklingen old ironworks gained momentum. Today, with only a few exceptions, all facilities of the ensemble are not only accessible, but also documented. Furthermore, the facilities are used to house prominent exhibitions that attract several thousands of national and international visitors every year.

Unfortunately, the city itself does not gain from the attraction of its UNESCO world heritage. The visitors tend to just visit the heritage site without paying any attention to the city or visiting Völklingen itself. The old ironworks as a world heritage site can be considered as an alien body situated between the modern working facilities of the remaining (and successful) steel industry on the one hand and the city, which is severely marked by the wounds of a declining old industry on the other hand.

Saarbrücken-Burbach In-Between: From Iron and Steel Production to Service Industries and New Technologies

The blast furnaces and related facilities of the integrated iron and steelworks in the Saarbrücken district of Burbach, which belonged to the *Stahlwerke Röchling-Burbach GmbH* had already been shut down before the adoption of the restructuration program of December 1978. With the exception of a new rolling mill, all facilities, including the less than ten year old *LD/AC* steelworks, had been closed until 1983. These measures led to thousands of job loses and the evolution of 80 hectares of partially severely polluted brownfield.

Neither during the closing phase nor after the closure did the City of Saarbrücken make use of the legal instruments of urban renewal according to the Federal Urban Development Promotion Act (*Städtebauförderungsgesetz (StBauFG)*) or the Federal Building Code (*Baugesetzbuch (BauGB)*) that have been adopted in Neunkirchen and Völklingen. Beyond that, there was no documentation of probable contaminations and the hidden location of media traces during the late working phase of the iron and steelworks (Trapp 1991, 154). When the Government of the Saarland had acquired the brownfield area in 1984/85 and handed it over to the City of Saarbrücken, a considerable part of important information regarding the contamination of the area had been lost. Although the City of Saarbrücken commissioned the first soil contamination probing in 1986/87, there was no remarkable progress on the Burbach brownfield area until the early 1990s. The responsibility for the project had changed repeatedly from one department of the City administration to another. The City administration, which neither had the necessary experience to manage the project, nor a vision for the conversion of its recently acquired real estate justified the slow progress with the uncertain costs connected with the probably necessary soil recovery (Saarbrücker Hefte 1991, 63; Koch and Klein 2001, 32). Even after the City participated in the Program of Federal Department of Research and Technology (*Bundesministerium für Forschung und Technologie (BMFT)*) *Model decontamination of contaminated sites* (*Modellhafte Sanierung von Altlasten*) and launched a workshop with eight academic institutes for urbanism to bring forward ideas for an urban framework plan, progress did not improve: The objectives of the large-scale research and technology program and the ideas developed by the city planners were too ambitious and utopian. The costs of the large-scale technology and cleaning model that sought to return the soil to near-natural conditions were estimated at 130–200 million DM (Koch 1997, 45; Koch and Klein 2001, 36).

In the middle of the 1990s it became clear that the large-scale, ambitious and at the same time inflexible approaches hitherto applied would not succeed. It was necessary to re-orient the development strategy and approach for the conversion and development of the Burbach brownfield area. The so-called incremental planning approaches that have been adopted in the course of the *Internationale Bauausstellung EmscherPark (IBA)* in the Ruhr since the late 1980s/early 1990s (see footnote 3) as well as more pragmatic approaches adopted to master the conversion in the New Länder of Eastern Germany after the Reunification opened up new perspectives on the complex conversion of the Burbach brownfield area.

In 1994 the City of Saarbrücken completely changed its strategy by adopting an innovative Public-Private-Partnership approach. The City surrendered the Burbach iron and steelworks brownfield area to the *GIU Flächenmanagement GmbH & Co. KG*. *GIU Flächenmangement* is a subsidiary of the urban development company *GIU GmbH* (*Gesellschaft für Innovation und Unternehmensförderung*). This company had been created some years earlier to manage the conversion of another brownfield area in Saarbrücken-Burbach[15] and brought in its extensive expertise and experience in converting, developing and marketing urban brownfield areas.

GIU adopted an incremental decontamination strategy by adapting the rehabilitation of the soil according to the user objectives (Koch 1997, 46; Brück and Heinrich 1993, 672). At the same time, the company adopted an innovative marketing strategy. By re-labeling the brownfield area into *Saarterrassen*, the former function and the bad image of an old industrial production site dissipated (Koch and Klein 2001, 39–42). This combined approach on the part of *GIU*, which included the development, marketing and management of this extremely problematic brownfield area proved to be very successful: Within just five years, a new mixed business park with a focus on services, new media, telecommunications, warehouse stores, and craft ateliers (169 enterprises and organizations and around 2,000 employees), and a residential area were developed (Fig. 4). This Burbach-approach has only been feasible in the context of processes that took place elsewhere in the early 1990s and thanks to the initiatives taken by creative actors at the local level.

---

15 The first conversion project of GIU was the very successful Saarbrücken Innovation and Technology Center (*Saarbrücker Innovations- und Technologie-Zentrum (SITZ)*), which was later renamed IT Park Saar.

Conclusion

Looking back at the different conversion paths of the former integrated iron and steel production sites and cities in the Saarland, we can summarize as follows:

The conversion of the Neunkirchen brownfield to an extended city center with a focus on retail services, leisure, and recreation was considerably influenced by the experiences made in the course of the coal crisis that had severely affected the city in the 1960s. Apart from this learning process, the place-specific constellation of actors played a decisive role. Without the city's Mayor with his experiences of and contacts to the federal level of administration and government and to economic actors outside of the Saarland, the top-down approach applied in Neunkirchen would not have been successful. Around five years later, in the case of the Völklingen ironworks ensemble, the conversion process has been influenced from the very beginning by the awareness of the cultural importance of the old ironworks, which has been articulated particularly outside of the city itself. The conversion process was strongly influenced by the following constellation of problems:

- a weak local awareness and a lack of vision, material and human resources in the city of Völklingen with regard to the conversion of the ironworks,
- the extreme difficulty to reconcile the preservation of the ironworks as an industrial heritage with the economic interests and exigencies of the still active steel industry and the urban development aspirations.

This combination paradoxically led to the adoption of an innovative discourse on the urban development strategy. While focusing very successfully on the preservation and development of the ironworks as a monument of industry culture, the regional and local actors involved succeeded in generating a prospective development perspective for the city. The Völklingen case can be best conceived as a result of path-dependency and a *lock-in* situation. The once efficient industrial blast furnaces ensemble later became a living fossil, which as UNESCO world heritage site, on the one hand contributed to regional tourism but at the same time complicated urban development. The Burbach case in turn demonstrates that early inertias may take a positive turn. The conversion of the Burbach brownfield area that had been hitherto stagnant turned out to be particularly successful thanks to

- changed political and regulatory conditions at the national and supranational scale,
- newly developed approaches to implement and manage complex planning processes in the early 1990s in combination with
- the presence of very active and creative actors at the local level.

The aim of this paper was to show that the conversion of former iron and steel industry sites and cities in the Saarland were processes that did not derive from strategies in a narrow sense, let alone from any common strategy. Instead, these conversions were the results of social negotiation processes under conditions of path-dependencies as much as they were the result of a combination of structural and singular conditions at various levels of social, spatial and temporal scales. These processes are institutionalized and directed. At the same time, they are evolutionary, and therefore emergent, open and contingent. Last but not least the studied case studies exhibit a tendency of shifting from top-down to more participatory and to incremental approaches to industrial and urban restructuration.

Works Cited

Basten, L. (1998). *Die Neue Mitte Oberhausen. Ein Grossprojekt der Stadtentwicklung im Spannungsfeld von Politik und Planung.* Basel, Boston and Berlin: Birkhäuser.

BID-Burbach (2013)—Bündnis für Investition und Dienstleistung Burbach (2013). *Erstes Bündnis für Investition und Dienstleistung im Saarland.* 02/27/2013, http://bid-burbach.de/.

Boschma, R. A, and K. Frenken (2006). Why is economic geography not an evolutionary science? Towards an Evolutionary Economic Geography. *Journal of Economic Geography,* 6, 273–302.

Boschma, R. A., and K. Frenken (2008). Some Notes on Institutions in Evolutionary Economic Geography. *Economic Geography,* 85 (2), 151–158.

Boschma, R. A., and R. Martin (2007). Editorial: Constructing an evolutionary economic geography. *Journal of Economic Geography,* 7, 537–458.

Boschma, R. A., and R. Martin (2010). The aims and scope of evolutionary economic geography. In R. A. Boschma and R. Martin (eds.). *The Handbook of Evolutionary Economic Geography,* 3–39, Cheltenham: Edward Elgar.

Brück, W., and F. Heinrich (1993). Modellhafte Sanierung des Burbacher Hüttengeländes. In Gesellschaft für Umweltkompatible Prozeßtechnik mbH (ed.). *Contaminated sites—Les sites contaminés.* 2. Euro-Forum Altlasten, Saarbrücken, 663–685, Saarbrücken.

Dörrenbächer, H. P. (1989). Entwicklung und räumliche Organisation der Saarberg-werke AG. In D. Soyez et al. (eds.). *Das Saarland. Bd. 1: Beharrung und Wandel in einem peripheren Grenzraum*, 203–226, Saarbrücken: Geographisches Institut.

Dörrenbächer, H. P. (2007). 50 Jahre Saarland—50 Jahre Kohlekrise. In H. P. Dörrenbächer et al. (eds.). *50 Jahre Saarland im Wandel*, 101–112, Saarbrücken: Institut für Landeskunde im Saarland.

ECE (2013). *Saarpark-Center Neunkirchen*. 02/27/2013, http://www.ece.com/de/geschaeftsfelder/projektuebersicht/center/spn/

European Communities, Statistical Survey of the European Union (1999). *The European Union Encyclopedia and Directory*. London: Europa Publications Ltd.

Glaser, H. (1997). Industriekultur. Zum möglichen Sinn einer Beschäftigung mit der Hinterlassenschaft der Industriegesellschaft und über Schwierigkeiten im konkreten Fall. *Eckstein, Journal für Geschichte*, 7, 4–9.

Isoplan, Institut für Entwicklungsforschung, Wirtschafts- und Sozialplanung GmbH (1991). *Montanregionen im Wandel—Konzepte, Erfahrungen, Perspektiven*. Saarbrücken: Isoplan.

Isoplan, Institut für Entwicklungsforschung, Wirtschafts- und Sozialplanung GmbH, and FIRU, Forschungs- und Informations-Gesellschaft für Fach- und Rechtsfragen der Raum- und Umweltplanung (1992). *Wirtschaftsstruktur-Gutachten für die Mittelstadt Völklingen 1992*. Völklingen.

Jürgenhake, U., et al. (1988). *Fallstudie „Saarstahl/Völklingen"*. Dortmund: Sozialforschungsstelle Dortmund Landesinstitut.

Kesternich, H. (1990). Die Initiative Völklinger Hütte. *Saarbrücker Hefte*, 64, 26–27.

Knebeler, C. (2011). Wichtige technische Beiträge der ARBED zur Stahlherstellung. *Forum für Politik, Gesellschaft und Kultur in Luxemburg*, 304. 36–38.

Koch, M. (1997). Vom ehemaligen Burbacher Hüttengelände zu den Saarbrücker „Saarterrassen". Der Weg von der Industriebrache zu dem dynamischsten Stadtquartier. *Brachflächenrecycling*, 3, 44–49.

Koch, M., and H. P Klein (2001). Gewerbebrachflächenrecycling in der Praxis: das Fallbeispiel der „Saarterrassen". In H. Job and M. Koch (eds.). *Gewerbebrachflächenrecycling. Ein Beitrag zur nachhaltigen Stadt- und Regionalentwicklung*, 31–47. Kallmünz and Regensburg: Verlag Michael Lassleben.

Kreisstadt Neunkirchen (1979). *Neunkirchen wandelt sich. Reden und Rufe 1975–1979*. Neunkirchen.

Kreisstadt Neunkirchen (1981a). *Innenstadtkonzept. Teil 1: Verkehr*. Neunkirchen.

Kreisstadt Neunkirchen (1981b). *Innenstadtkonzept. Teil 2: Städtebaulicher Rahmenplan*. Neunkirchen.

Kreisstadt Neunkirchen (2012). *Neunkircher Hüttenweg*. Neunkirchen.

Kreisstadt Neunkirchen (2013). *Strukturdaten—Bevölkerung*. 02/27/2013, http://www.neunkirchen.de/bevoelkerung-neunkirchen-saar/

Landeshauptstadt Saarbrücken, Amt für Entwicklungsplanung, Statistik und Wahlen (2012). *Die Bevölkerung Saarbrückens im Jahr 2011*. 02/27/2013, http://www.saarbruecken.de/assets/2012_5/1336992288_statinfo_1_12.pdf

Landeshauptstadt Saarbrücken, Amt für Statistik und Stadtforschung (1976). *Beiträge zur Statistik der Stadt Saarbrücken*, Vol. 11. Saarbrücken.

Lorenz, L. P. (2013). *Business Improvement Districts an vom Strukturwandel betroffenen Standorten. Das Beispiel Saarbrücken-Burbach.* Diplomarbeit, Universität des Saarlandes, Historisch orientierte Kulturwissenschaften. Saarbrücken.

Lüth, J. P. (1998). Alte Völklinger Hütte. Anmerkungen eines Denkmalpflegers zum künftigen Gebrauch der Hütte und zum Umgang mit einem Weltkulturerbe. *Metalla: Forschungsberichte des Deutschen Bergbau-Museums*, 5 (1), 25–37.

MacKinnon, D., et al. (2009). Evolution in Economic Geography: Institutions, Political Economy and Adaptation. *Economic Geography*, 85 (2), 129–150.

Martin, R. (2010). Roepke lecture in economic geography. Rethinking regional path dependence: beyond lock-in to evolution. *Economic Geography*, 86 (1), 1–27.

Marx, E. (1989). Revitalisierung Völklinger Hütte. *Bauwelt*, 48, 2290–2297.

Mittelstadt Völklingen (1990). *Modell Völklingen. Revitalisierung einer Industriebrache. Offenes Städtebauliches Gutachterverfahren Völklinger Hütte. Dokumentation und Ergebnisse.* Völklingen and Kaiserslautern.

Netfutura GmbH & Co. KG, Gesellschaft für Informationsmanagement (2013). *Saarterrassen. Firmenverzeichnis.* 02/27/2013, http://www.saarterrassen.de/runtime/cms.run/doc/Deutsch/17/Firmenverzeichnis.html

Otto, M. (1990). Der Niedergang der Stahlstadt Völklingen oder vom "schöpferischen Sinn der Krise". *Saarbrücker Hefte*, 64, 33–34.

Reif, H. (1993). *Die verspätete Stadt.* Bonn: Habelt.

Rentmeister, U. (2006). *Montanindustrie im Saarland. IHK Saarland, Branchenreport.* 02/26/2013, http://www.saarland.ihk.de/ihk/branchenreport/branchenreport-juli2006.pdf

Saarbrücker Hefte (1991). Künstliche Intelligenz und Technologietransfer im Saarland. Gespräch mit Thomas Schuck, Geschäftsführer der GIU. *Saarbrücker Hefte*, 65, 63–69.

Saarbrücker Zeitung (1978). ARBED-Rationalisierungs-Konzept: Bis 1983 Abbau von 8800 Arbeitsplätzen im Saarland. *Saarbrücker Zeitung, Ausgabe B*, 02/14/1978.

Saarland, Minister für Wirtschaft, Verkehr und Landwirtschaft (1973). *Schwerpunktprogramm für den Raum Neunkirchen.* Saarbrücken.

Saarstahl AG (2013a). *Unser Unternehmen. Stationen der Entwicklung des Völklinger Eisen- und Stahlwerkes von den Anfängen bis zur Gegenwart.* 02/26/2013, http://www.saarstahl.com/geschichte_voelklingen.html

Saarstahl AG (2013b). *Unser Unternehmen. Stationen der Entwicklung des Neunkircher Eisenwerkes von den Anfängen bis zur Fusion mit der Stahlwerke Röchling-Burbach GmbH im Jahre 1982.* 02/26/2013, http://www.saarstahl.com/geschichte_neunkirchen.html

Saarstahl AG (2013c). *Unser Unternehmen. Geschichte.* 02/26/2013, http://www.saarstahl.com/geschichte.html

Stadt Völklingen (2013). *Statistik.* 02/27/2013, http://www.voelklingen.de/index.php?id=244

Storper, M. (1988). Big Structures, Small Events, and Large Processes in Economic Geography. *Environment and Planning A,* 20, 165–185.

Trapp, H.-W. (1991). Revitalisierung Völklinger Hütte. *Mitteilungen der Deutschen Akademie für Städtebau und Landesplanung, 35,* 144–154.

Voermanek, K. (1995). Völklinger Hütte. *StadtBauwelt,* 86, 1968–1970.

Zwick, M. (2012). *Die regionalwirtschaftliche Bedeutung der Stahlindustrie für das Saarland.* Saarbrücken and Berlin: Isoplan-Marktforschung.

The Industrial City as a Shrinking City and the Special Case of Flint, MI

Christine Hannemann

Introducing shrinking worldwide

"The gaps between buildings downtown turn into fruit, vegetable and flower gardens; the orphaned industrial estates become plantations for Christmas trees and timber, or preserves for domestic animals and wild deer; the sites of ruined investment develop into carp ponds; the vacant pre-fab concrete buildings turn into greenhouses or mushroom farms."[1] (Touché et al. 2005, 44) This scenario is a very serious proposal for the use of empty pre-fab buildings in the future. In fact, this idea was implemented in the East German city of Gera (Free State of Thuringia). One of the many shrinking cities in East Germany, this city is a very good example of a typical reunification case (Hannemann 2003): In GDR-times Gera had developed from a regular middle-sized industrial town into a socialist city. Based on economic-political decisions, the city was developed as county town and an industrial centre —mechanical and electrical engineering as well as textile industries were established, and uranium mines rounded up the economic structure. Furthermore, large housing estates built for employees of the nationally owned enterprises and *Kombinate*[2] reshaped the structure of Gera. These developments formed Gera's self-image beyond reunification: Gera, the leading and most prosperous town of East Thuringia. Today this structure is absent. The city has lost its administrative status as county seat, and there are only a few leftovers of the former industrial basis. It is suffering from a high rate of unemployment, continuing out-migration, and demographical aging. The decline of the number of inhabitants in particular demonstrates the severity of the situation: the city had 130,000 inhabitants in 1990; today there

---

1 Translation by Christine Hannemann.

2 *Kombinat* was the German term for a large-scale enterprise under the central control of the East German government, which combined several groups of state-owned business concerns with similar production profiles into a single entity.

are only 105,494 left although several small villages have been incorporated. Something similar took place in the vast majority of East German cities as well as to a number of cities in West Germany—e.g. in the Rhine Valley, at the North Sea, in Lower Bavaria as well as in the Saarland—whose industrial structure had been formed by old industries such as mining, steel, shipping or garment. (Hannemann 2005a, 9)

This situation can be observed in most countries of the "First World". Many industrialized countries face shrinkage of their once-industrial cities on a regional scale as in the United Kingdom—Glasgow, Liverpool and New Castle. In Russia and its one-time socialist satellites there are de-industrialized large cities and rural areas as well as in Japan and even more so in South Korea.[3]

Regardless of location, size, economic basis, history, and administrative status, the economic and social repercussions of the end of communism are particularly evident in the profound shrinking processes of East German cities and regions. This is a course of development that had already been apparent at the time of reunification, but has been ignored politically and academically until a short while ago. A report published in 2000 by the Federal Commission "Structural Changes of the Housing Market in East Germany" stated that "the new challenge is called handling shrinkage" (BMVBW 2000, 66). The Commission worked under the instructions of the Federal Ministry of Transport, Building and Urban Affairs of Germany. Since then, a wider social debate developed over the prospects of urban degeneration processes, and the necessity of tackling them. Attempts on the part of urban researchers to address shrinkage as a social reality met with severe resistance of ministerial bureaucracy, science policy, and municipal policy. Only recently has it become politically beneficial to put "shrinking" on the agenda as a new, momentous path of urban development.

This paper analyses recent processes of urban development currently subsumed under the term "shrinking cities" (*schrumpfende Städte*). This term has been adopted into the mainstream discourse particularly as a description for developments that were occurring on a massive scale after reunification in East German cities. Tight budgets, de-industrialization, decreasing population, and sub-urbanization were the most prominent characteristics of urban shrinkage. Since then the topic "shrinking" has become one of the most controversially discussed new urban questions. In German academic discussions,

---

3 For a more detailed discussion of shrinking cities worldwide see: Oswalt (2005).

however, the term "shrinking cities" had already been used before. The German term "*Stadtumbau,*" does not have the negative connotation of shrinking. In Great Britain and France, for instance, this subject matter is discussed in terms of "urban regeneration", in Denmark as "alteration of cities" and in Sweden as "work of rearrangement". In the United States and Canada a lot of literature refers to the term "urban decline". During the postwar decades, the term "decline" was highly en vogue. Since the 1990s the term "shrinkage" is used to describe loss of urban population. "Shrinkage, though, strikes me as an optimistic version of decline. It is less freighted with racial conflict, fiscal crises, slums, poverty, and crime and so better fits the Zeitgeist of the current era of urban resurgence." (Beauregard 2009, 518)

On the one hand, these differentiations in terminology refer to varied analyses and conditions of the problem and, on the other hand to different strategies of coping with "shrinking". The awareness that urban development is more (and less) than spatial allocation and growth has sparked a worldwide discussion and initiated projects in many industrialized countries. An awareness of the need to shape urban retrogression is an important task for urban developers and has been breaking through in the last few years. In Germany, this breakthrough was linked to the transformation of urban policy since the reunification. The processes of economic globalization and political Europeanization were equally important for this development.

Urban decline or urban shrinkage due to demographic and economic changes is not a new phenomenon in the USA or Germany. For several decades, numerous cities and regions in both countries have faced shrinking populations. A declining economy and the abandonment of buildings have accompanied the departure of people, leaving behind poor and desolate neighborhoods as well as social problems. From a broad historical perspective, "shrinkage" is not new. We all know innumerable cities around the globe, which are either: rising, shrinking, or disappearing completely. The rise and fall of cities can be explained by way of different phenomena: natural disasters, globalization, and suburbanization, but the most striking reason is deindustrialization.

How, under these circumstances, can city mothers and fathers develop their cities? What is to be done with a community that reproduces itself neither through influx nor through offspring of its own, which is hence de facto condemned to die out? What will the citizens do once the majority of them become older and increasingly burdened with physical hardship and without financial resources? These are issues of relevance in nearly every East German city, and increasingly in old industrialized cities in West Germany, France, the USA, and Great Britain etc.

Since the mid-1990s I conducted several studies on shrinking cities in different regions badly affected by decline (Hannemann 2006; 2005b; 2004) in East Germany. My interest led me abroad to learn more about how urban policy makers in other countries deal with shrinkage. The conditions under which every urban policy actors operate are unique, yet such studies provide lessons and knowledge for understanding "coping with shrinking" worldwide. One of these studies investigated Saint-Etienne in France (Hannemann 2007; 2009) and the most recent one Flint, Michigan[4]. According to academic literature and newspaper articles, urban political leaders and residents in Flint adopted a new policy to cope with "urban shrinking" (Boardman 2008; Anon. 2011; Streitfeld 2009). It is described as "smart decline". "Smart decline means leaving behind assumptions of growth and finding alternatives to it. In particular, smart decline requires thinking about who and what remains. It may entail recognizing or eliminating some services and providing different ones. It may involve promoting certain land uses and landmarks more as sources of growth." (Popper and Popper 2002, 21–22)

The Flint case study provides insights into the US-American way of dealing with shrinkage. In this teaching-research project we examined documents and published data on Flint and the Saginaw region. Additionally, in-depth interviews with community administrative, economic and civil society engaged actors were conducted. Using all the gathered research materials a more 'objective' process of the development can be discerned. To turn the dramatic change of Flint into a more 'subjective' documentation, I am drawing on quotations about the urban development of Flint as displayed in the exhibition presented in the Alfred P. Sloan Museum. This exhibition is a meaningful presentation of how a shrinking city is presenting its past and present. It is advertised as follows:

---

4 This was a one-year student research project entitled "From Growth to Shrinkage: Urban Redevelopment Policy in the United States" conducted at Humboldt University. It comprised a field trip to Flint, Michigan from September 19th to 30th 2010. An excursion of German students and their professor to the United States would not have been possible without the financial support of various organizations and people. Therefore my thanks go to the DAAD—the German Academic Exchange Service, the Department of International Relations at Humboldt University and especially to Mr. Thomas Pilz (Hannemann 2011, 4).

"Flint's dramatic history as the birthplace of General Motors comes to life at the Alfred P. Sloan Museum. Flint and the American Dream takes visitors on a fascinating journey through Flint in the 20th century—from the birth of the auto industry to the present. Here visitors encounter the ups and downs of General Motors, the birth of the UAW [United Auto Workers], Flint's role as the 'Arsenal of Democracy' and what life was like during the [fifties], [sixties] and [seventies]. The gallery is packed with over 600 artifacts and photographs, including rare antique automobiles, colorful neon signs, period clothing, household furnishings and commercial goods." (Sloan-Museum 2013)

Flint is located about 70 miles northwest of Detroit in Genesee County. It boomed as the well-known city in which General Motors (GM) was founded in 1908. This city is one of the US cities most affected by shrinkage, though once home of General Motors, it is now one of its most problematic cities. Flint, however, seems to be at the cutting-edge when it comes to dealing with shrinking cities. Urban researchers as well as local and regional politicians are all looking for new approaches to the current challenges of shrinking. New ways of understanding the situation may lead to a new paradigm of shrinking rather than continuing the path of believing in growth only.

Flint—A former one-company town steadily eroding[5]

Settlement in Flint started as a fur-trading outpost in 1818. The population increased steadily as the place became a center for lumber trade. Due to its expansion "The City of Flint" was founded in 1855. Flint used to be a 'normal' city with a diversified economic basis and good infrastructure; mainly based on the timber industry (Crow 1945, 20). Until the great "cut" Flint "not only epitomized American history in the way it grew from a river ford to a city, but also in the way it grew up and came of age through its all-out effort in producing the good and tools for war" (Crow 1945, 206). Tanks, armory, and cartridge cases produced in Flint were an important material basic for the United States to win the World War II. As the car production boomed after World War II the city grew rapidly. "In the 1950s it was the second largest city in the state of Michigan and as late as 1978 General Motors employed 76,900 people in the city surrounding Genesee County." (High-

---

5 In a former study I analyzed four types of shrinking cities: 1. consolidated cities, 2. stabilized cities, 3. stagnant cities, 4. eroding cities (Hannemann 2004, 213–217).

smith as in Ryan 2012, 4) The booming car production after 1945 made the city famous as a place of wellbeing where the American Dream could be pursued. "For much of the twentieth century, observers from around the world looked to the partnership between Flint, the UAW, and GM as a microcosm of the American Dream of progress, prosperity, and democracy." (Highsmith 2009, 9–10) The booming years were accompanied by racial segregation:

"Northern Migration. After World War II, Flint's booming automotive industry once again required more workers than the area could provide. Attracted by high wages, workers from the Deep South streamed into Flint. These newcomers tended to settle along racial lines. The majority of white newcomers chose to live in the townships surrounding the city, while African American newcomers settled inside the city limits." (Sloan-Museum n.d.)

Therefore the shock was even worse when General Motors decided to close nearly all plants. Starting in 1978, Flint turned into an urban area that experienced a significant demolition of its industrial employment roots. Today, the decline of General Motors and the job losses are accompanied by extreme vacancy rates. More than a third of all real estate properties are abandoned and more than one quarter of Flint's inhabitants live below the poverty line.

The prolonged process of economic and population decline as well as a rise of local unemployment rates were highlighted in Michael Moore's (in) famous documentary "Roger & Me" (1989). Flint is one of many cities in the US rustbelt that includes Buffalo, Cleveland, Detroit, Pittsburgh, Rochester and Youngstown. "Many of the rustbelt's cities were single industry towns. Some were single company towns, like Kodak in New York's Rochester or GM in Flint." (Anon. 2011) General Motors as the main actor in Flint's development was involved in establishing a College and Cultural Center, the Flint Institute of Music, the Flint Institute of Arts, a planetarium, a museum, a theatre, a gallery, and a research Center.

"Official Ties—Company and Community. Flint's automobile executives were the most powerful and prominent members of the community, and their active participation in city government and community affairs was expected. As a result, most of the social, cultural and civic institutions in Flint were either established or chaired by company leaders. The involvement, however, blurred the distinction between city and company interests and, at least in function, the motto was, 'What's good for GM is good for Flint'." (Sloan-Museum, n.d.)

The UAW is also a very important part of the history of General Motors. It has "more than one million active and retired members. Over 390,000 active members in 2009, and some 600,000 retirees. One of America's most diverse unions, with members in auto and heavy trucks, aerospace, agricultural implements and heavy equipment, as well as health care, higher education, gaming, public service and other technical, office and professional occupations. The UAW also has played a vital role in passing such landmark legislation as Medicare and Medicaid, the Occupational Safety and Health Act, the Employee Retirement Act and the Family and Medical Leave Act. In Washington and state capitols, the UAW is fighting for better schools for kids, secure health care and pensions for retirees, clean air and water, tougher workplace health and safety standards, stronger worker's compensation and unemployment insurance laws and fairer taxes" (UAW 2012).[6]

After a 44 day sit-down-strike 1936/7 the new founded UAW became the most important and most powerful union in the USA. Today, some experts believe that it was not only the effects of globalization which drained jobs out of Flint, but also the power and inflexibility of the UAW. The auto workers at GM factories earned three times more than the average salary in the United States (Roberts 1999). The high level of salaries made car production a very expensive industry in the 1980s. However, the main reason for the decline was the mismanagement and the incapability to modernize cars. In his cheeky yet critical manner the famous documentary filmmaker Michael Moore commented on this course as followed:

GM stubbornly fought environmental and safety regulations. Its executives arrogantly ignored the 'inferior' Japanese and German cars, cars which would become the gold standard for automobile buyers. And it was hell-bent on punishing its unionized workforce, lopping off thousands of workers for no good reason other than to 'improve' the short-term bottom line of the corporation. Beginning in the 1980s, when GM was posting record profits, it moved countless jobs to Mexico and elsewhere, thus destroying the lives of tens of thousands of hard-working Americans." (Moore 2009)

The decline of GM brought about the decline of the city:

"Downsizing. To complete in a global market, GM completely reorganized its auto production process. During the 1980s, the company increased its utilization of independent parts suppliers and introduced robotics and high tech automation to its assembly operations. These measures cut costs, improved quality and increased productivity, but they also resulted in dramatic cuts in the workforce (up to 30 [percent]) and the closing of several Flint plants by decade's end." (Sloan-Museum n.d.)

---

6 See the contributions of Adelheid von Saldern and Martina Heßler in this volume.

"Hard Times. A stunned Flint workforce reacted slowly to the layoffs and plants closings of the seventies and eighties. At first workers reacted as they always had, by sitting tight and waiting for a call back to work. Ironically, the existence of 'safety net' provisions, including supplemental pay and federal rebates, made sitting tigh preferable to retaining and job search programs. When it became obvious that many of the layoffs would be permanent, many area workers returned to school or participated in retaining programs. Workers who were uncomfortable with going back to school and unwilling to accept low pay, service sector jobs, moved to the southern states." (Sloan-Museum n.d.)

In shrinking cities, population always decreases with economic decline: "Flint's population fell by almost one-third in the past half century, declining from 163,143 in 1950 to 112,524 in 2000." (Hollander 2010, 139) In 2008, General Motors organized a big parade to celebrate the 100th anniversary of GM in Flint. That seems strange because there is only one car factory left in Flint. As I know from personal experience it is really only a 'show-production' for tourists fascinated by cars from around the world. The car industry continues to influence local "car culture" in Flint. One indication is the road infrastructure: As Figure 1 shows, three important interstates surround Flint: Interstate 75 passes through the town from north to south, Interstate 69 enters the town from the southwest, and Interstate 475 crosses the town. On the one hand, this kind of infrastructure influences the development of the suburbs, which are still growing. On the other hand, there is no properly developed public transport system in Flint, so that cars remain the main means of transport, which is celebrated once a year by a big car show (Sloan-Museum Auto Fair 2010).

The number of vacant houses grew steadily over time. It is interesting to see that this process affected the suburbs as well as the housing structure within the city limits of Flint. This indicates that more houses were built in the suburbs than were purchased. Flint is badly affected by the problem of vacant housing.

"In 2012, Flint, its population barely above 100,000, was extremely uncertain about its future. Apart from a record high unemployment level, the city was confronting not only near bankruptcy but an ongoing wave of housing abandonment. The 2010 national census indicated that Flint had about 10,000 vacant housing units. In a city that had only 55,000 housing units in 2000 this was a recipe for crisis." (Ryan 2012, 5)

More than one third of the housing units in Flint are renter occupied. This number has been relatively stable over the course of time, while the percentage of owner occupied buildings has decreased due to increasing vacancy.

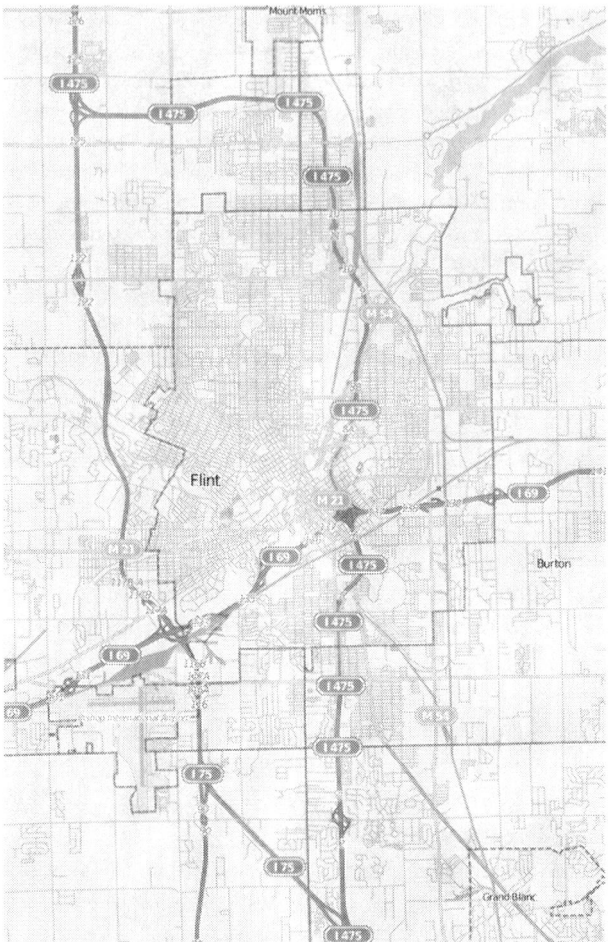

Fig. 1: Interstates in Flint, MI

(Source: © OpenStreetMap 2013. 04/25/2013, http://www.openstreetmap.org/)

The high numbers of renters is rather unusual for a city in the United States and causes problems in the case of foreclosure. The city's unemployment problems suggest that its labor market has been very tight: The rates tripled from 6 percent in 1970 to around 18 percent in 1980 and 1990. In 2000 there was a short period of recovery, when the rate receded to 12.9 percent (SOCDS 2013).

Strategies to cope with Urban Shrinkage

"In some places of the city, the rapid departure of people has resulted in a new pastoral landscape where houses were once packed tightly together. In others, the derelict structures that once housed people now serve as a deterrent to investment and a haven for criminals. In each neighborhood, a certain percentage (often larger) of the population has no place else to go. Together, the desperately poor huddle together and are stuck in an economic ghetto." (Hollander 2010, 140)

In this part of the paper I will shortly illustrate the main strategies for coping with the shrinking process in Flint. Most of this part is taken from the final report on the research teaching project conducted in 2010 (Hannemann 2011). Where necessary and possible, the numbers have been updated.

Land Banking[7]

When the first jobs left and people moved out of Flint the housing market suffered. No one came to replace those residents who had left; vacant houses found no buyers and property values dwindled. Racial segregation and poor housing stock compounded the situation. While these problems are not unique and can be observed in many other industrial cities in northeast of the United States, Flint's approach to dealing with them has long been exceptional: A county-wide land bank authority with extensive powers has been established.

Although the city of Flint has been shrinking for the past 40 years until 1999, there was no instrument to deal with the property, which was left behind. The Charles Mott Foundation, a private Flint based non-profit organization, donated money—200,000 dollars —to a non-profit research institute to develop the framework for this Act (Richards 2006, 5). In that year, Michigan passed the Public Act (PA) 123, which handed over primary responsibility for the administration of the tax foreclosure process to the foreclosing governmental units. These units are defined as the County Treasurer, or—if the county refuses to handle the tax foreclosure—the state authorities. Counties could either choose to "opt in" and become the foreclosing unit or to "opt out" and leave the responsibility with the state. Genesee County opted in (Bassett et al. 2006, 9).

---

7 This part of the paper is a strongly reduced, revised and updated version of Rogge 2011.

In Flint, where roughly one third of all properties—about 18,000 out of 57,000 parcels—were abandoned, the pool became bigger than ever imagined. Firstly, the economic crisis increased the number of home owners threatened by insolvency, thus enlarging the amount of money generated from interest and late fees. Secondly, it increased the number of people who failed to pay their mortgages and had to leave their property, thus enlarging the property inventory of the Land Bank. As of September 2010, the Genesee County Land Bank (GLCB) had an inventory of approximately 5,700 parcels in Genesee County. Though abandonment is most evident in the Northern part of the city, abandoned properties can be found everywhere. Therefore, the Land Bank is confronted with two challenges: (1) a growing number of properties ending up in their ownership, accompanied by (2) the difficulty of managing their widespread inventory.

In response to the increasing number of properties in the pool, the Land Bank launched various responses to the different needs and conditions. In 2010, the Land Bank had ten re-use programs: Planning and Outreach, Brownfield Redevelopment, Development, Adopt-a-Lot, Clean and Green, Demolition, Housing Renovation, Sales, Side Lot Transfer and Foreclosure Prevention. According to the former Genesee County Treasurer, the three most important powers of the Land Bank are (1) the acquisition of tax-foreclosed properties, (2) the ability to sell those properties "on any terms that it deems to be in the community's interest" and (3) to help finance redevelopment activity.

The Genesee County Land Bank is an innovative way of dealing with urban decline. The Land Bank can certainly be described as an improvement as it allows a community-oriented approach to tax-foreclosed properties. It provides local authorities with a tool to individually react to a family's hardship and to take care of the abandoned land. This is on probable reason why it is applauded on a national level. The Genesee County Land Bank was the first and for a while the only Land Bank under the new law in Michigan. The key people of the Genesee County Land Bank also founded a non-profit organization in 2005 called the Genesee Institute to provide technical assistance and planning support to jurisdictions that were interested in the creation of land banks (Gillotti and Kildee 2009, 139). "Flint's policy challenge could thus be compared to other shrinking cities nationwide. The Genesee County Land Bank was held up as a model precisely because so many cities faced the challenge of obtaining ownership and then redeveloping vacant tracts of residential land." (Ryan 2012, 12)

Downtown development[8]

Crossing the River Flint driving down south on Saginaw Street one cannot help noticing the changes surrounding the city. Flint's North Side shows abandonment, deteriorated roads, blight and blocks with just one or two houses left. In contrast, the downtown area shows signs of life with a steady flow of cars driving down the red brick road—S Saginaw Street— and some people walking on the sidewalks. Although Flint is still perceived as being number 2 of the dead cities in the United States (McIntyre 2010), this picture does not match the reality of Flint's downtown. The red brick area of Flint clearly appears to be a separate region of the city. It is an island with restored bloom resembling glorious times that have passed long ago. Many shrinking cities have declared their downtowns as central sites of their prospective redevelopment efforts for their cities as a whole (Pallagst et al. 2009, 8). In the case of Flint there is a long history of attempts to revitalize the downtown.

Suburbanization of local downtown retailers and a flight of residents to the suburbs had dried out the life of downtown Flint by the early 1960s. What once used to be the proud parade ground for the Vehicle City had become a dead downtown. In order to tackle this situation the city of Flint in concert with a private foundation—Charles Stewart Mott Foundation (CSMF)—designed a plan to redevelop the downtown area by encouraging the tourist industry. The basic idea was to create a special theme park as a tribute to the automobile, the so-called AutoWorld. "Elements of this plan included a luxury hotel, an urban theme park (AutoWorld), and two upscale enclosed marketplaces." (Lord and Price 1992, 159) The investment targeted growth policies and was supposed to get Flint's economic engine running again. The projects were initiated, planned and financed by a small private sector elite. Finance was provided through federal grant money, private investors and Charles Stewart Mott Foundation grants. The Foundation was the central figure in the process. It pioneered the idea of an automobile theme park and provided massive financial resources for demolition and reconstruction of the site. All these investments failed, however. The Hyatt Regency Hotel for example never reached full occupancy and closed down in the same decade it had opened. At the beginning of the new century Downtown Flint was the scene for a series of new revitalization efforts, this

---

8 This part of the paper is a strongly reduced, revised and updated version of Tesch 2011.

time focusing on smaller businesses. The projects can be categorized under architecture, arts and education, residency, and culture and events.

Increase Downtown Residency

Currently about 1,000 people are living within the downtown area. Yet most of these people are visible on Saginaw while the smaller side roads remain rather empty. About 700 of the residents are students. Two dormitories exist in the downtown area. One is on Kearsely Street and the other is located in the former Hyatt Regency Hotel familiar from the first failed attempt of downtown revitalization. Both were redeveloped with the help of CSMF. The Hyatt Regency Hotel has been one of the biggest projects for the Uptown Reinvestment Corporation. The massive building provides the capacity for 540 students with about 300 of them living there today. It also includes a gym, Dolby surround movie theatre and other amenities. In September 2010, the Land Bank opened the fully remodeled Durant Hotel. While the Land Bank is mostly concerned with vacated properties outside of the city center, it opened the Durant as its downtown signature project. The Durant—which stood vacant for over 40 years—provides reasonable loft housing for students and other residents. More lofts are available in the First Street Lofts building, which was redeveloped by the Uptown Reinvestment Corporation in partnership with private developer companies. The First Street Lofts with their luxurious interior target rather high-income customers. With the addition of Witherbee's to the local scene, the first grocery store opened in Downtown Flint in over 35 years.

Extend Higher Education Sector

The University of Michigan in Flint is the fastest growing University in the State of Michigan. Many of the current redevelopment efforts focus on the extension of the University of Michigan campus. After AutoWorld had been demolished, the University of Michigan was able to acquire the territory that formerly inhabited the huge dome in 1997. Supported by a grant from CSMF, the University of Michigan-Flint erected a new building to house classrooms. Today the University covers a large part of the downtown area.

Provide Entertainment and Events

Most of the visible redevelopments of downtown Flint have been related to entertainment and events. Several restaurants have opened within the downtown area. Blackstone's—the biggest among them—was opened with money from CSMF. Two other restaurants are located within the Community Foundation building, which was remodeled with the help of CSMF. Downtown Flint has attracted and organized several events in 2010. Among others these included the Crim Festival of Races, Back to the Bricks and the Bikes on the Bricks Festival. During these weekend events Saginaw Street is crowded with visitors from many regions. In 2010 the conference facilities at the Hyatt Regency Hotel reopened and hosted conferences and a movie festival. Flint's strategies of downtown revitalization have always favored the supply side of the market over demand. While the first attempt provided potentials for the tourist industry, the second attempt focuses on residents and creates housing opportunities especially for students.

Brownfield Site Handling[9]

In the inner city and the Northern part of Flint, the former car factories left large spaces of unused, mostly contaminated land. The three biggest— "Buick City", "Chevy in the Hole", and the "Fisher Body Plant"—are concrete sealed areas located close to downtown (Fig. 2). The Green City Coordinator, in one of our interviews summarized the whole industrial land, which is unused in Flint, as follows:

"Throughout the city we have about 1,000 acres or what would be about four million square meters [4 km2] vacant industrial property. And it is primarily located in these areas. Now, we have also quite a bit of area that we currently don't consider to be industrial brownfield, which is a lot of our rail lines, which sit more or less vacant and unused at this point, but they still have rail, they still have capacity. So we are not considering them a sort of abandoned like a lot of our property would be, but they are significantly underutilized." (Kubiak 2011, 131)

A very important part of the Green City Coordinator's job is to administer the prospective use of the abandoned industrialized properties in Flint. He is coordinating the demolition of the industrials facilities and trying to find

9 This part of the paper is a strongly reduced, revised and updated version of Kubiak 2011.

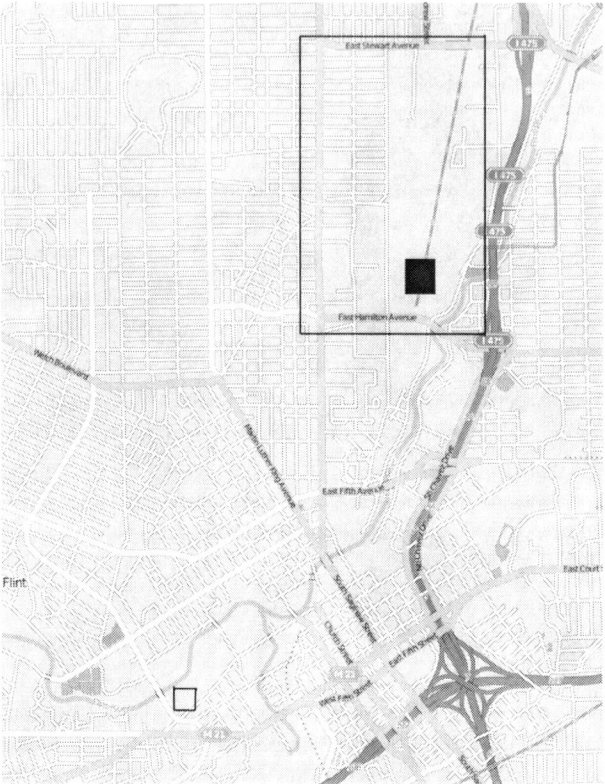

*Fig. 2: Location of Chevy in the Hole plant (small square),
Buick City plant (black square) and North Oak Park (big rectangle)
within the city of Flint*

*(Source: Ryan 2012, 18; own compilation © OpenStreetMap 2013.
04/25/2013, http://www.openstreetmap.org/)*

new enterprises, which could take over the unused space. This is planned mostly for Buick City and Delphi. In Chevy in the Hole the Green City Coordinator is mostly responsible for greening the property. For this he started a compost program.

The Green City Coordinator mostly wants to green the Chevy in the Hole property. Some parts of this property will be developed by the Kettering University (formerly General Motors University), but the larger part of this area will be developed as a park, which is located very close to downtown. Big trucks are driving through the city to collect all the organic waste, such as leaves and branches, which are then brought to the "park in the making"-site. The piles of compost are growing and growing. The idea of composting is not supported by all members of the community, because the wind often carries its foul, unpleasant smell over the city.

The latest ecological improvement to be presented is the Swedish Biogas Plant in Flint. Swedish Biogas is an enterprise located in Linköping, Sweden (in Swedish: Svenska Biogas). The enterprise invented a big net of biogas electricity plants as well as other uses of biogas. An example is a train operated with biogas driving 50 miles from Linköping to the Baltic Sea. CSMF sent the Mayor of Flint and the Green City Coordinator to Sweden in order to receive information about how biogas could be used. Together with the Governor of Michigan and Swedish Biogas International they returned with the idea of building a biogas electricity plant in Flint.

The Flint Neighborhood Improvement & Preservation Project[10]

The Flint Neighborhood Improvement & Preservation Project Inc. (Flint NIPP) is a community development corporation that aims at improving "the conditions that stabilize, revitalize, and provide affordable housing within Flint & Genesee County" (2010). Founded in 1976 by the then mayor, this nonprofit project has been providing housing and neighborhood services to over 30,000 families through two types of activities: the implementation of federal or state housing programs as well as building and revitalizing communities in the neighborhoods (Flint NIPP 2010).

The former area of activities is composed of a variety of programs that include the purchase, refurbishment, and resale of houses, repair assistance, ownership counseling, foreclosure counseling, etc. These activities are intended to provide citizens in need with the skills, financial and/or material aid to maintain or acquire houses. Most of the programs have been created by federal or state agencies—Flint NIPP received more than 40 million dollars over the last 33 years.

The second type of activities consists in supporting efforts that result in a vital community such as organizing block clubs (according to their own statement Flint NIPP founded more than 200 clubs since they started), as-

---

10 This part of the paper is a strongly reduced, revised and updated version of Schmidt-Roßleben 2011.

sisting neighborhood groups to become legally acknowledged, helping them raise funds for collective activities and much more.

Due to its dependence on federal subsidies, the organization is limited in defining its unique strategy. There are, however, two aspects that characterize its work. First of all, Flint NIPP understands its activities as complementing other actors' plans. This is why they decided to focus on the historic inner city—the Carriage Town district—that is close to Downtown Flint. Parts of the redevelopment efforts are currently taking place there. Flint NIPP has renovated and sold several historic houses. They are also a subcontractor of the Genesee County Land Bank receiving federal subsidies for their properties in Carriage Town[11].

Secondly, Flint NIPP has tried to be flexible and responsive to what the city and the residents need. For instance, as it became clear that many people waiting to buy a home were not able to meet the official mortgage criteria during the mortgage crisis, Flint NIPP decided to buy the mortgage and allow people to pay them rather than the bank. Moreover, after having been approached by community members, they managed to open a much needed grocery store—"Witherbee's Market"—in Carriage Town which remains the only grocery store in Downtown Flint.

Both the Mott Foundations and NIPP dominate Flint's nonprofit sector in the area of housing, community, and economic development. Together, they constitute a powerful alliance, which can be defined as a regime since they share essential goals and strategies, pool resources and expertise. By doing so, they have been able to independently design, finance, and implement measures aiming at revitalizing the community. Though their impacts are still small-scale, their holistic approach, which combines many activities and resources in specific target areas, has generated some successes regarding housing conditions, economic development, and community engagement. The case of Flint illustrates that the cooperation between and with local municipalities is important in terms of securing sustainable, long-term planning in a democratic manner.

Were one to analyze the whole history of city planning since the decline in Flint has started, one would have to consider the power of the Mott-Foundations. The Foundations, rather than the municipality, have been the

---

11 This project is part of the "Cities of Promise Initiative". The Michigan State Housing Development Authority (MSHDA) leads this initiative, which helps "to redevelop eight of Michigan's most distressed areas into thriving, vibrant cities that attract and retain jobs and people" (Keenon 2009, 1).

driving force. A spectacular example of this is the promotion of tourism in the 1980s. The decline of the auto industry prompted the city to attract mobile capital in manufacturing. Everybody knew that Flint's economy was too dependent on one industry. "However, try it as it might the community had never been able to attract other mobile capital. The high wage base provided by the oligopolized auto industry and the fact that the community is a very strong union town, with a long history of labor/management strife, made it unattractive to potential investors." (Lord and Price 1992, 158)

Left with no other choice the urban authority of Flint, as usual together with the Mott Foundation, made plans to turn Flint into a tourist city in the 1980s. In today's language this plan would be called "Theme Park City". Two main pillars were: building a Hyatt Hotel and second developing an "Auto World". "The concept of developing a luxury hotel in downtown Flint was a curious one since the Durant Hotel (an older luxury hotel) and a more modest Holiday Inn located within two blocks of the Hyatt site had already failed." (Lord and Price 1992, 159) "AutoWorld" should be a huge urban indoor theme park enthusiastically praising the virtues of the automobile. Both projects immediately ran into financial difficulties and were closed.

Conclusion: from General Motors to "General Mott"

The strategies of coping with the urban decline in Flint outlined above have one special 'motor'. All these activities have been initialized, financed and supported in several ways by two foundations, above of all by the Charles Stewart Mott Foundation (CSMF). This charitable foundation is located in Flint and was founded Charles Stewart Mott, an "automotive pioneer and original partner in the creation of the General Motors Corporation", in 1926 (CSMF 2013). Of the top 100 US foundations it ranks 26th, with total assets of more than two billion dollars (Foundation Center 2013). The foundation is inherently connected with the city's history since its assets are basically rooted in the industrial success and wealth of GM from the first half of the 20th century.

Charles Stewart Mott donated a considerable amount of time and money to the city and its community: He brought the University of Michigan-Flint to the city and was the founding father of the Charles Stewart Mott Children's Hospital at the university. He was a crucial supporter of the community school model in Flint and was elected mayor of the city twice. Being one of the largest philanthropists whose legacy is omnipresent even today, he was also called "Mr. Flint" (Dandaneau 1996, 194). Over the years the foundation has expanded its activities in five different areas worldwide. A total of 89 million dollars were donated in 2011, approximately 26 percent or almost 24 million dollars were allocated to the Flint area program with its three branches "community revitalization and economic development", "arts, culture and education" as well as "special initiatives" (CSMF 2012, 46–49). The foundation does not operate any programs itself but—according to its publications —funds and supports a broad range of activities in the city.

The 'second' Mott is the Ruth Mott Foundation (RMF)—also a charitable foundation located in Flint. Its donor, Ruth Mott, was the third wife of Charles Stewart Mott and equally committed to philanthropy (RMF 2013). Her scope of activities was to some extent different as she focused more on arts, health promotion, and beautification. These principles were adopted by the foundation and constitute three of the four areas for which grants can be obtained (the fourth area is called "special initiatives"). Since the foundation was created in 2001, it has been steadily growing in both numbers of staff and grants—today almost 7 million dollars per year are being donated through its grants program to projects in Flint and the surrounding county. Besides giving grants the foundation is also responsible for maintaining and operating "Applewood", the historic Mott family estate where public events now take place (RMF 2008; 2011). These two foundations are currently the main action groups involved in city development in Flint. While the RMF is playing a supporting act, the main actor is the CSMF. "For decades it had been acknowledged that Flint's economy was too dependent on one industry (automobile manufacturing), in fact on one corporation (GM)." (Lord and Price 1992, 158) Today this reliance on one single actor is still apparent, yet has turned into a dependency on the Mott-Foundations. In fact the city is about to live on the grants of one foundation, which receives its money from GM-revenues.

For without "General" Mott(s) there would be no Flint in Michigan anymore. In 1992, the US-American social scientist George F. Lord and Albert C. Price published an article "Growth Ideology in a Period of Decline: Deindustrialization and Restructuring, Flint-Style" in the top-tier peer-reviewed journal "*Social Problems*". They stated that "Flint presents a unique situation in which to examine the ideology of growth for two important reasons: 1) the extent of deindustrialization, and 2) the scope of the failed redevelopment efforts […]. Our analysis suggests that the ideology of growth obscures the problem. In contemporary urban settings, perhaps the ideology of local growth is—like a cage—a critical constraint." (Lord and Price 1992, 158, 167) Exactly 20 years later the analysis suggests the ideology of economic growth is history. It is also too euphemistic to speak about smart decline. Flint is muddling through with the necessary assistance of the Mott Foundations. After all, even the presentation of the Sloan-Museum is stating a vague outlook into the future after giving a very short but brilliant abstract of the city development:

"Flint of the 21st Century probably will be smaller, yet more racially and ethnically diverse. The people will need to be better educated and trained to fit the changing needs of a high tech, high skill workplace. Finally, the people will be less dependent on a single corporation for their welfare. Will the future be better than the past? For those who are waiting for the good old days to return, the future holds little hope. But for those who are able to prepare for change, and are willing to participate in forging a plan for the future, the years ahead may be bright indeed." (Sloan-Museum n.d.)

Therefore a necessary change of attitudes in the urban development ideology is slowly developing in Flint. "The American Assembly at Columbia University, which recently published a report on post-industrial cities, used the term 'legacy cities' as 'shrinking' and 'resizing' can have negative connotations." (Anon. 2011) Maybe that is the future. In any case this change of attitudes implies accepting the fact that Flint is a smaller, shrinking, downsizing city.

Works Cited

Anon. (2011). Smaller is more beautiful. *The Economist*, 10/22/2011. 02/18/2013, http://www.economist.com/node/21533417.

Bassett, E. M., J. Schweitzer, and S. Panken (2006). *Understanding Housing Abandonment and Owner Decision-Making in Flint, Michigan: An Exploratory Analysis.* 08/08/2010, http://www.geneseeinstitute.org/downloads/Bassett_Understanding_Owner_Decision.pdf.

Beauregard, R. A. (2009). Urban population loss in historical perspective: United States, 1820–2000. *Environment and Planning A*, 41, 514–528.

BMVBW (2000)—Bundesministerium für Verkehr-, Bau- und Wohnungswesen (2000). *Wohnungswirtschaftlicher Strukturwandel in den neuen Ländern. Bericht der Kommission.* Berlin: BMVBW.

Boardman, L. (2008). As residents leave, locals shrink smartly: Cities make plans as populations decline. *American City & County,* 123, 15–16.

CSMF (2012)—Charles Stewart Mott Foundation (2012). *Annual Report 2011.* 03/06/2013, http://www.mott.org/files/publications/AR2011.pdf.

CSMF (2013)—Charles Stewart Mott Foundation (2013). *Our Founder.* 03/06/2013, http://www.mott.org/about/OurOrganization/ourfounder.

Crow, C. (1945). *The City of Flint Grows up: The Success story of an American Community.* New York: Harper.

Dandaneau, S. P. (1996). *A Town Abandoned. Flint, Michigan, Confronts Deindustrialization.* Albany: State University of New York Press.

Flint NIPP (2010)—Flint Neighborhood Improvement & Preservation Project (2010). *Welcome to Flint NIPP.* 12/10/2010, http://wordpress.fnipp.org/.

Foundation Center (2013). *Top Funders. Top 100 U.S. Foundations by Asset Size.* 03/07/2013, http://foundationcenter.org/findfunders/topfunders/top100assets. html;jsessionid=ML2K11AGBGSWVLAQBQ4CGW15AAAACI2F.

Gillotti, T., and D. Kildee (2009). Land Banks as Revitalization Tools: The example of Genesee County and the City of Flint, Michigan. In K. Pallagst et al. (eds.). *The Future of Shrinking Cities: Problems, Patterns and Strategies of Urban Transformation in a Global Context,* 139–148. Berkeley: Institute of Urban and Regional Development.

Hannemann, C. (2003). Schrumpfende Städte in Ostdeutschland—Ursachen und Folgen einer Stadtentwicklung ohne Wirtschaftswachstum. *Aus Politik und Zeitgeschichte,* (28), 16–23.

Hannemann, C. (2004). *Marginalisierte Städte. Probleme, Differenzierungen und Chancen ostdeutscher Kleinstädte im Schrumpfungsprozess.* Berlin: Humboldt-Universität.

Hannemann, C. (2005a). Editorial. In N. Gestring et al. (eds.). *Jahrbuch StadtRegion 2004/05. Schwerpunkt: Schrumpfende Städte,* 9–16. Wiesbaden: Verlag für Sozialwissenschaften.

Hannemann, C. (ed.). (2005b). *Luckenwalde: Soziale Ressourcen im städtischen Wandel. Ein Lehrforschungsprojekt im Diplomstudiengang Sozialwissenschaften, Lehrgebiet für Stadt- und Regionalsoziologie.* Berlin: Humboldt-Universität.

Hannemann, C. (ed.). (2006). *Eberswalde: Identitätsbrüche auf dem Weg von einer Industrie- zur Dienstleistungsstadt. Ein Lehrforschungsprojekt im Diplomstudiengang Sozialwissenschaften, Lehrgebiet für Stadt- und Regionalsoziologie.* Berlin: Humboldt-Universität.

Hannemann, C. (ed.). (2007). *Saint-Etienne. Stadtpolitik in einer schrumpfenden Stadt. Ein Lehrforschungsprojekt im Masterstudiengang Sozialwissenschaften, Lehrgebiet Stadt- und Regionalsoziologie.* Berlin: Humboldt-Universität.

Hannemann, C. (2009). Saint-Etienne: Stadtpolitik in einer schrumpfenden Stadt. *Revue d'Allemagne et des pays de langue allemande*, 41 (3), 359–378.

Hannemann. C. (ed.). (2011). *Space Available Urban Policies in a Shrinking US-American City. Ein Lehrforschungsprojekt im Masterstudiengang Sozialwissenschaften, Lehrgebiet Stadt- und Regionalsoziologie.* Berlin: Humboldt-Universität.

Highsmith, A. R. (2009). *Demolition Means Progress: Race, Class, and the Deconstruction of the American Dream in Flint, Michigan.* PhD diss., University of Michigan.

Hollander, J. B. (2010). Moving Toward a Shrinking Cities Metric: Analyzing Land Use Changes Associated With Depopulation in Flint, Michigan. *Cityscape: A Journal of Policy Development and Research*, 12 (1), 133–152.

Keenon, M. L. (2009). *Cities of Promise initiative brings hope for the future to eight Michigan cities.* 03/13/2013, http://www.planningmi.org/downloads/cities_of_promise_article.pdf.

Kubiak, D. (2011). Facing the Problem. Many Ideas, no Money, no Staff, Ecological Strategies in Flint, Michigan. In C. Hannemann (ed.). *Space Available Urban Policies in a Shrinking US-American City. Ein Lehrforschungsprojekt im Masterstudiengang Sozialwissenschaften, Lehrgebiet Stadt- und Regionalsoziologie*, 125–145. Berlin: Humboldt-Universität.

Lord, G. F., and A. Price (1992). Growth Ideology in a Period of Decline: Deindustrialization and Restructuring, Flint Style. *Social Problems*, 39 (2), 155–169.

McIntyre, D. A. (2010). America's Ten Dead Cities: From Detroit to New Orleans. *24/7 Wall St.*, 8/23/2010. 03/09/2013, http://247wallst.com/2010/08/23/americas-ten-dead-cities-from-detroit-to-new-orleans/2/.

Moore, M. (2009). *Goodbye, GM ...by Michael Moore.* 03/06/2013, http://www.michaelmoore.com/words/mikes-letter/goodbye-gm-by-michael-moore.

Oswalt, P. (2005). Introduction. In P. Oswalt (ed.). *Shrinking cities, Vol. 1: International research*, 12–17. Ostfildern-Ruit: Hatje Cantz.

Pallagst K., et al. (eds.). (2009). *The Future of Shrinking Cities. Problems, Patterns and Strategies of Urban Transformation in a Global Context.* Berkeley: Institute of Urban and Regional Development.

Popper, D., and F. Popper (2002). Small Can Be Beautiful: Coming to Terms with Decline. *Planning*, 68 (7), 20–23.

Richards, A. (2006). Genesee County Land Bank. Putting property back into productive use. *Mott Mosaic*, 5 (1), 2–10.

RMF (2008)—Ruth Mott Foundation (2008). *Community Report 2008. Grants by Program Area.* 01/15/2011, http://www.ruthmottreport.org/Financial.html.

RMF (2011)—Ruth Mott Foundation (2011). *About RMF/Programs/Grants.* 01/15/2011, http://www.ruthmottfoundation.org/Default.aspx.

RMF (2013)—Ruth Mott Foundation (2013). Our Founder: Ruth Rawlings Mott 1901–1999. 03/07/2013, http://www.ruthmottfoundation.org/history.

Roberts, L. (1999). *General Motors closes Buick City complex in Flint, Michigan.* 06/16/2010, www.wsws.org/articels/1999/jul1999/auto-j02.shtml.

Rogge, J.-C. (2011). The Genesee County Land Bank. Dealing with Tax-Foreclosed Properties and Urban Planning in the Face of Urban Decline. In C. Hannemann (ed.). *Space Available Urban Policies in a Shrinking US-American City. Ein Lehrforschungsprojekt im Masterstudiengang Sozialwissenschaften, Lehrgebiet Stadt- und Regionalsoziologie*, 71–95. Berlin: Humboldt-Universität.

Ryan, B. D. (2012). *Shrinking-City Urban Form as a Determinant of Urban Policy: the case of Flint, Michigan, USA.* Paper, presented at 48th ISOCARP Congress 2012. 09/20/2012, http://www.isocarp.net/Data/case_studies/2253.pdf.

Schmidt-Roßleben, L. (2011). Planting Seeds: A Case Study on Non-Profit Organizations and their Effect on Revitalization Efforts in the Shrinking City Flint, Michigan. In C. Hannemann (ed.). *Space Available Urban Policies in a Shrinking US-American City. Ein Lehrforschungsprojekt im Masterstudiengang Sozialwissenschaften Lehrgebiet Stadt- und Regionalsoziologie*, 146–181. Berlin: Humboldt-Universität.

Sloan-Museum (2013)—Alfred P. Sloan-Museum Flint, MI (2013). *Permanent Exhibits at Sloan Museum.* 03/05/2013, http://www.sloanlongway.org/sloan-museum/exhibits-and-galleries/permanent-exhibits.

Sloan-Museum (n. d.)—Alfred P. Sloan-Museum Flint, MI (n.d.). *Permanent Exhibition in the 20th Century Gallery—Flint and The American Dream.*

Sloan-Museum Auto Fair (2013). *Past Fairs.* 03/05/2013, http://www.sloanautofair.com.

SOCDS (2013)—State of the Cities Data Systems (2013). *SOCDS Census Data: Output for Flint city, MI.* 03/06/2013, http://socds.huduser.org/Census/-Census_java.html.

Streitfeld, D. (2009). *An Effort to Save Flint, Mich., by Shrinking it.* 02/21/2013, http://www.nytimes.com/2009/04/22/business/22flint.html.

Tesch, J. (2011). Dough for the Doughnut Hole. The Second Attempt of Downtown Revitalization in Flint. In C. Hannemann (ed.). *Space Available Urban Policies in a Shrinking US-American City. Ein Lehrforschungsprojekt im Masterstudiengang Sozialwissenschaften, Lehrgebiet Stadt- und Regionalsoziologie*, 96–124. Berlin: Humboldt-Universität.

Touché, J., et al. (2005). Bau an! *Archplus*, 173, 44–47.

UAW (2012)—The International Union, United Automobile, Aerospace and Agricultural Implement Workers of America (2012). *Who we are and Quick Facts.* 09/20/2012, http://uaw.org/page/who-we-are.

Crisis in Automotive Cities: The Ambivalent Role of the Car Industry in the "Autostadt"[1] Wolfsburg and "Motor Town" Detroit

Martina Heßler

Industrial cities have always been dependent on their industry. Their histories are intimately connected with their industries. While times of economic growth are times of expanding and booming industrial cities, processes of de-industrialization and industrial decline are likewise times of urban crisis. Cities have then been confronted with tremendous challenges, which have sometimes led to structural changes, sometimes to urban decline or even urban bankruptcy as recently in the city of Detroit.

The emergence and growth of industrial cities in the 19th century is a well-researched topic in urban history. However, research has often focused on the social and environmental problems of early industrial cities and has drawn a rather negative picture of these cities (Reif 2012). Shrinking industrial cities have also attracted much interest among academics. Urban history thus tends to convey the impression that the history of industrial cities is one of "rise and fall". Yet, this is only part of the story. Not only does the narration of rise and fall misconceive the global dimension of the history of industrial cities by focusing on Western cities only, the concept also results from centering on the history of old-industrial cities, while other types of industrial cities have not drawn enough scholarly attention.

This article thus focuses on automotive cities, claiming that they are a particular type of industrial cities. Firstly, it considers its specificity and questions which consequences may be drawn from it. Researching industrial cities from the angle of their industry carries a promising potential. In order to unveil this potential, urban history has to open the black box of industry, since the predominant industry has also shaped the spatial structure of any given city, an observation that applies equally to their social structure, their mode of governance, and their economic base. Secondly, the article will focus on the specific role of automotive companies in the history of automobile cities. While times of economic boom and growth will be less of interest,

---

1 This term was coined by Horst Mönnich (1951).

the article rather concentrates on their crises. It seems to be a trivial observation that the automotive industry has always played a decisive role in urban crises in automotive cities. This article therefore sheds light on its ambivalent role: automobile companies are considered both a cause of crises as well as an actor in strategies to overcome *urban* crises.

Especially within the context of urban crisis and shrinking cities, research has focused on new modes of urban governance. Urban sociology and political science have emphasized that processes of de-industrialization and the erosion of the economic base of cities have led to changes in the mode of urban governance. A major focus within these debates is the relationship between local authority and business. David Harvey, for instance, has written about an „entrepreneurial mode of urban governance" and thus described how local authorities have begun to boost the economy, to encourage investment, stimulate growth and create jobs (Harvey 1989). Efforts to revitalize downtown as well as the establishment of public-private partnerships are quintessential components of the entrepreneurial mode of urban governance. Well-known and often cited examples are Baltimore (Levine 1987; Stocker 1987), Birmingham or Manchester, (Bailey and Chapain 2011; Beer and Evans 2010; Bodenschatz 2008), but also automotive cities such as Torino (Power et al. 2010) or Wolfsburg and Detroit, which will be scrutinized in this article. Most scholars have pointed out that the influence of private developers and investors on cities has seen a tremendous increase.

In what follows the focus will be on the influence of the automotive industry within automotive cities in times of crisis. As Jürgen Friedrichs has stated, the role and attitude of the industry is decisive in the process of urban decline. The less diversified a city's economic base, unsurprisingly the more vulnerable it becomes. Furthermore, the stronger the local corporate actors, the better their odds are to "control the labour market and prevent smaller companies from locating in the city due to the high wages paid by the dominant company or industry" (Friedrich 1993, 909). This means that the difficulty of any diversification of the economic base will tend to rise parallel to the degree of one company's or industry's dominance within a given city. However, the industry does not only play a role in the economic decline of cities, but, and that will be of special interest here, corporate actors also have a stake in responding to urban crisis. Friedrich has underlined that in some cities coalitions have formed against structural change. In such cases, the prevalent local industry has tried to recover and did not show any interest in the city's activities to attract new business (Friedrich 1993, 912).

The automobile city of Wolfsburg, where the Volkswagen Corporation has allegedly prevented the location of additional factories in the city by paying high wages and absorbing the potential workforce of the city has been named as an example (Harth et. al. 2010, 32). Considering Detroit, Clavel and Kleniewski have argued that in the beginning of the 1980s, "a recovery programme 'Rational Reindustrialization: An Economic Development Agenda for Detroit' was proposed by two economic analysts, who suggested a strategic retreat from automobiles into related manufactures" (cited after: Clavel and Klenieweksi 1990, 213). According to them however, "(n)either industry leaders, the United Auto Workers union, nor city officials were willing to shift away from an auto-related industrial strategy" (Clavel and Klenieweksi 1990, 213).

By focusing on Wolfsburg and Detroit, this article would like to put forward the argument that things are more complicated than that, and that the role of the automobile industry within its hometown deserves to become a topic of further research in the near future. Before considering the role of the auto industry, the article starts with reflections on the term "automotive cities" (Heßler 2014).

Automotive Cities—a special type of industrial cities

Automotive cities do, of course, host the car industry. Most of these cities, although not all of them, are mono-industrial cities. Their social and economic structure has been heavily influenced by the car industry. Their history is closely linked to the company's history and the economic ups and downs of the car industry. As already mentioned, the lower the industrial diversity, the more vulnerable the economic base of cities. Moreover, corporate actors have a strong influence on such mono-industrial cities (Friedrich 1993, 913). This is doubtlessly a central issue in times of crisis, when strategies of revitalization or economic recovery are discussed in cities.

Secondly, automotive cities are strongly perceived as such. Wolfsburg was already called an automotive city in the early 1950s; German author Horst Mönnich entitled his 1951 novel on Wolfsburg „Autostadt" (Mönnich 1951). Rüsselsheim is called the "Opel-Stadt", "Toyota-City" even got its official name from a car brand. Everybody associates cars when someone refers to

Detroit, while Fiat is inseparably affiliated with Torino. The Chinese automotive city of Changchung even refers to itself as "Detroit of the East".

Thirdly, automotive cities are distinct in a sense that their inhabitants are strongly attached to the cars produced there. Cars are of great significance for the modern lifestyle. They are a consumer good, objects of daily experience, of pride and prestige, and they carry a high societal relevance (Volti 2004). Workers are proud to assemble cars and proud to live in an automotive city. This strong involvement of inhabitants with their city and industry might be one aspect of a path dependency, which has often barred structural changes from coming to people's minds. The strong "car identity" might make any re-orientation of these cities less expectable. More research into this question is still needed, though.

Fourthly, in contrast to other Western industrial cities, automotive cities are cities of the 20th, but also of the 21st century. Western automobile cities have emerged since the beginning of the 20th century. Their boom periods were the 1920s and 1930s in the United States, and the 1950s and 1960s in Western Europe. In Eastern Europe, automotive cities came into being since the 1970s, with examples such as Togliatti or Nishni Novgorod (Siegelbaum 2008). In Japan, Toyota-City was built in 1959 by transforming a small village into an automotive city that nowadays hosts about twelve Toyota plants and hundreds of suppliers (Schmidtpott 2012). In China, automotive cities have emerged more recently in Anting and Changchun (Stein 2012).

Their topography has become a global one and their economic condition is heavily influenced by the global economy (Heßler 2011). The car industry in Detroit for instance experienced a heavy crisis in the context of global competition (Hill 1986, 113–116).

The car industry remains a key industry to this day in the Western World. Many jobs and a whole set of branches are still dependent on the car industry. It is a consumer goods industry, and as such differs from heavy industry. Up to now, urban history has mainly focussed on industrial cities with heavy industry. However, the particular logic of different industries and their consequences for their hometowns should be taken into closer consideration. The car industry is characterised by great dynamic and has lived through more than one instance of cycles and restructuring. It comprises specific supply chains, specific spatial structures, and so on. All these features determine the history of automotive cities. The economic fluidity in particular, as well as the repeated restructuring of the global market, makes the history of automotive cities a complicated business. Cities like Wolfsburg have not yet been challenged by an economic decline that would have threatened the existence of the city, which turned out to be the case for Detroit, but the uncertainty of their future economic base remains a latent question, making urban governance more complicated.

Fifthly, the histories of automotive cities are therefore manifold. We can distinguish different developments of automotive cities since the 1970s. Almost all automotive cities have experienced crises, particularly since the 1970s, which does not mean that they all had to adopt a process of fundamental restructuring. Some had to deal with cyclical crises and uncertainty, but still rely heavily on the car industry. Others have experienced—very much like cities of heavy industry—fundamental crises and plant closures. There is no doubt that cities of this kind had to manage a fundamental process of restructuring, such as Birmingham (Beer and Evans 2010; Bodenschatz 2008), Cowley, Oxford (Hayter and Harvey 1993), or Torino (Power et al. 2010).

Another issue that differentiates automotive cities from cities with heavy industry is the massive change in the composition of the workforce in the car industry. The relative number of workers has declined, while the share of managers, administration, engineers, designers and employees in research and development has increased. The city of Wolfsburg again serves as an example. In 1982 Herlyn stated that the share of employees had tripled between 1960 and 1980 (Herlyn 1982, 89–91). The table shows the increase of employees and the decrease of workers in the Volkswagen Company from the 1970s to today. Here, the tertiarization of the economy takes place within the car industry.

The social structure of the cities changed, while the industry itself remained the same. Some automotive cities have started to transform themselves into event and/or tourism cities by basically celebrating the car in theme parks. Wolfsburg, Rüsselsheim, Stuttgart, and Flint/Michigan have made strong efforts to establish theme parks or museums that stage and acclaim the car as a consumer good. The Volkswagen Corporation even claims to have a patent on the term "Autostadt" that is serving as brand for the theme park. Rüsselsheim and Flint have made similar efforts but failed.[2] Hence, some prove successful, while others do not. But all in all, we can describe them as a new type of city, namely a hybrid: an industrial city where cars are still being manufactured and simultaneously become a post-industri-

---

2 See Zimmermann (2014) and the contribution of Christine Hannemann in this volume.

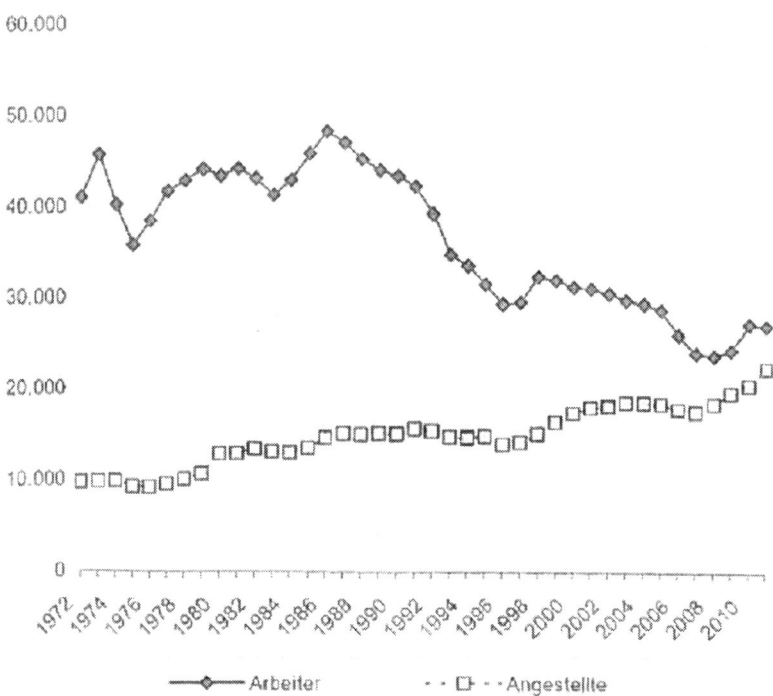

Fig. 1: Workers (Arbeiter) and employees (Angestellte) at Volkswagen
(Source: Herlyn et al. 2012, 82)

al city, where cars are now part of an event, of a theme park. Wolfsburg is an outstanding example here, but it is not the only one. If we look at Changchun, we can see that the newly built automotive city has been planned from scratch as such a hybrid of theme park, center of research and development, and site of car production. Such cities remain automotive (industrial) cities, but they are not simply industrial cities any longer.

Reflecting on the concept of the industrial city in this way might raise interesting questions for urban history. It implies that we have to stop talking primarily about the rise and fall of industrial cities. Instead we will have to focus on transforming industries and the changing formats and faces of their cities, and opening the "black box of industry".

The following considers the role of the automotive industry within this process of transformation. Detroit and Wolfsburg will serve as case studies.

The ambivalent role of the automobile industry

In their home countries both Detroit and Wolfsburg are strongly perceived as the most important automobile cities. The early histories of both cities are impressive stories of success. They have symbolized economic growth, affordability and modernity. The automotive industries in Detroit and Wolfsburg have been characterized as their nation's engines of economic growth. Detroit has been the paradigm of American progress, Wolfsburg has symbolized the "economic miracle" of the early Federal Republic of Germany. However, while the city of Wolfsburg managed to deal with several crises and is still a successful automobile city, the city of Detroit has recently declined even beyond bankruptcy.

The aim of this article is not to explain the differences in the history of these two automobile cities, which is a very complex matter. Instead it focuses on the car industry's relationship to the two cities and on its consequences for any process of transformation. In certain aspects, automobile cities are not different from other Western industrial cities, which were challenged by crises since the 1970s at the latest. The economic cycles of the industry have determined the economic condition of cities. Sales crisis, lay-offs, or the relocation of the production have strongly influenced the economic situation of cities. But in Wolfsburg and Detroit, more than just that, the automobile industry has not only been a cause of crisis, but simultaneously taken the role of an initiator of urban revitalization to overcome the crisis. An analysis of the role of the car industry as a cause of crisis as well as a player in overcoming the urban crisis is important, since the corporate actors of the car industry represent a strong local elite within these cities, as emphasized above. These cities are economically dependent on their industry. The trouble in times of crisis is, not surprisingly, that the city administration has almost no options to act as an entrepreneur, but to encourage investment or stimulate growth. Accordingly, the option of a public-private partnership is of great interest to urban governments in order to regain their capacity to act. The automobile industry in crisis does not seem to be a natural born partner to come in. However, one example from each city, Detroit and Wolfsburg, suggests exactly this to be the case. The article cannot offer more than a glimpse of the long history of the relationship between corporate actors and local authorities in both cities. It is nevertheless promising to take a look at the role of the automobile companies in times of crisis and the strategies for revitalization in the course of history. Particularly in Detroit, many different actors and various coalitions have over time developed different strategies to overcome the urban crisis. It is up to further research to analyze the efforts for urban recovery in Detroit in a historical perspective in order to specifically ask about the role of the automotive industry. In the following sections, one of the initiatives in Detroit, namely the building of the Renaissance Center in the 1970s, will be compared with a similar initiative in Wolfsburg around the turn of the century.

Detroit: the deserted city

The U.S. automobile industry came to Detroit right at the beginning of the 20th century: Ford Motor Company in 1903, General Motors in 1908 and the Chrysler Corporation in 1924 (Oswalt 2004a, 228). Since then, Detroit has evolved as the most important location of the automobile industry in the

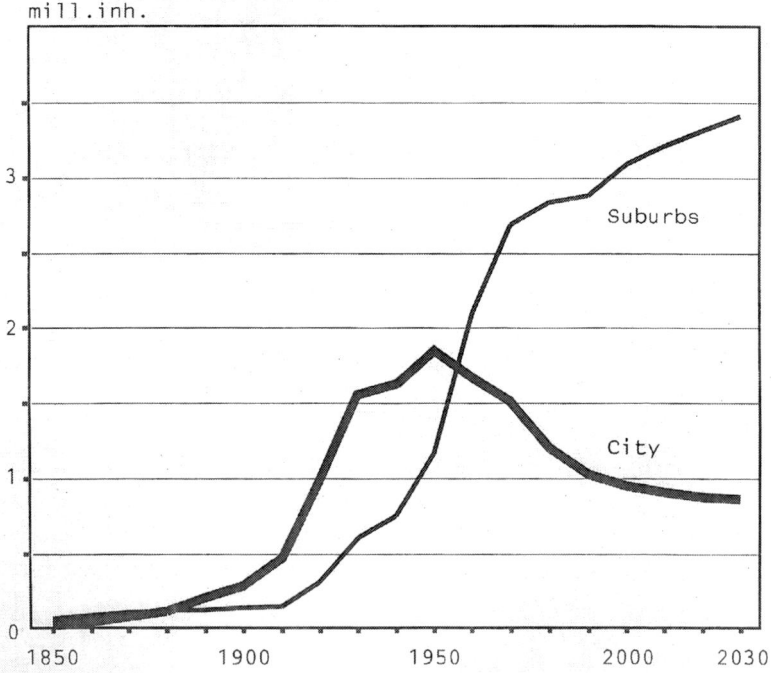

Fig. 2: Population development in the city of Detroit and suburbs, 1850–2030

(Source: Hagemann and Möller 2004, 7)

United States. From the beginning the city was a mainly mono-industrial city. Until the 1950s the city had been growing constantly. From 1900 to 1953 the number of inhabitants increased from 250,000 to 1.85 million (Hill 1986, 83). Detroit was called the "powerhouse" of the United States (Mende and Oswalt 2004, 3). It was a symbol of modernity and an engine of growth for Detroit and the US as a whole (Hill 1986).

The earliest signs of Detroit's urban crisis can be traced back to the 1950s (Hill 1986, 88). Detroit is an extraordinary example of a shrinking city due to its massive suburbanization. The city of Detroit lost over one million inhabitants over the last five decades, effectively more than half of its population. Simultaneously the suburbs gained inhabitants, companies, and jobs (Oswalt 2004b, 14; Fishmann 2004). Today, some 700,000 residents live in a 139-square-mile city that once had been the home of almost two million people. As one regional planning group has forecast, the number of inhabitants might decrease even further to 600,000 by 2030 (Davey and Walsh 2013).

Especially since the riots of 1967, more and more white residents had left the city. In 1990, the city of Detroit was 76 percent black (Orr and Stoker 1994, 52), with today's figures standing at around 82 percent, while the suburbs are mostly white.

This was accompanied by a tremendous cutback in jobs. From 1947 to 1963, Detroit saw a loss of about 137,000 jobs in the industry (Sugrue 2004, 233). During the 1970s, Detroit lost another 208,000 industrial jobs (Mende and Oswalt 2004, 3), while figures for the suburbs have simultaneously been on the rise. The reduction of jobs has continued since then.

Thomas Sugrue has thoroughly described the development and the beginning of urban crisis in an outstanding work (Sugrue 1995). Decentralization and suburbanization of factories and inhabitants reinforced racial segregation. A further factor was the process of automation in the car industry, called „Detroit Automation". The automation process affected in particular poorly qualified black people. But even if they had been better qualified, the automobile companies favored white workers. Moreover, between 1947 and 1959, the Big Three (the three big companies Ford, General Motors, and Chrysler) "built twenty-five new plants in the metropolitan Detroit area, all of them in suburban communities, most more than fifteen miles from the center city" (Sugrue 2005, 128; Darden et. al. 1987, 15–16). The companies fled the city, with great consequences for the place they left, particularly regarding racial problems.

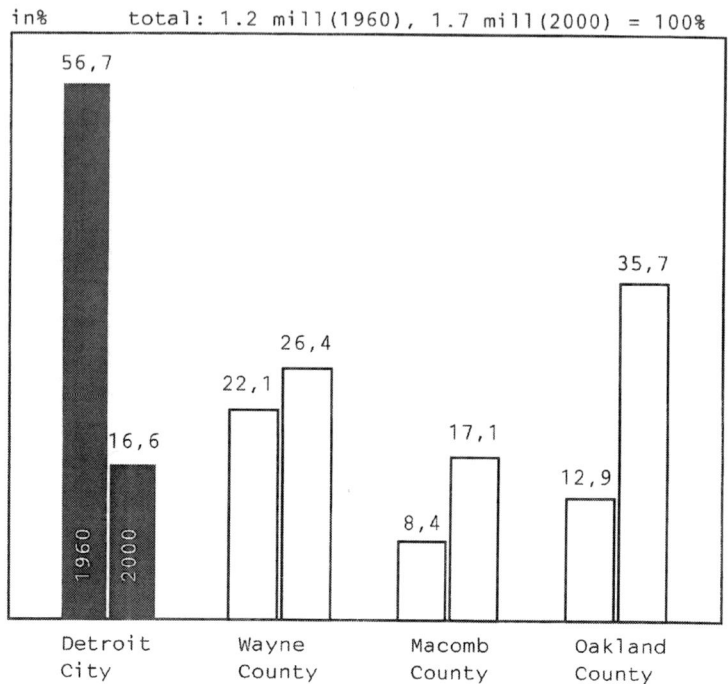

in%   total: 1.2 mill(1960), 1.7 mill(2000) = 100%

Fig. 3: Distribution of jobs in city and suburbs, 1960 and 2000

(Source: Hagemann and Möller 2004, 8)

In the 1960s, the Ford Company located its world headquarter in the suburb of Dearborn. In the late 1960s Ford employed no workers within Detroit's city limits. Moreover, the company had developed Fairlane Town Center, a mall and hotel complex near its suburban headquarters. In 1974, William Clay Ford even moved the Detroit Lions football team from the city to the new, suburban Pontiac Metropolitan Stadium (Desiderio 2009, 86).

Ford was acting in line with the other automobile companies. Today, General Motors employs only 2000 people within the city limits of Detroit, but still a total of 50,000 in the state of Michigan.

Although the city administration made attempts to relocate the automotive companies to the city of Detroit, these efforts were to no avail and drew heavy criticism. The General Motors Corporation announced plans for a new assembly plant called Poletown, effectively promising to build a factory within the city of Detroit—the first one since 1928—(Poremba 2001, 40). However, the proposed site included the northern third of the Poletown

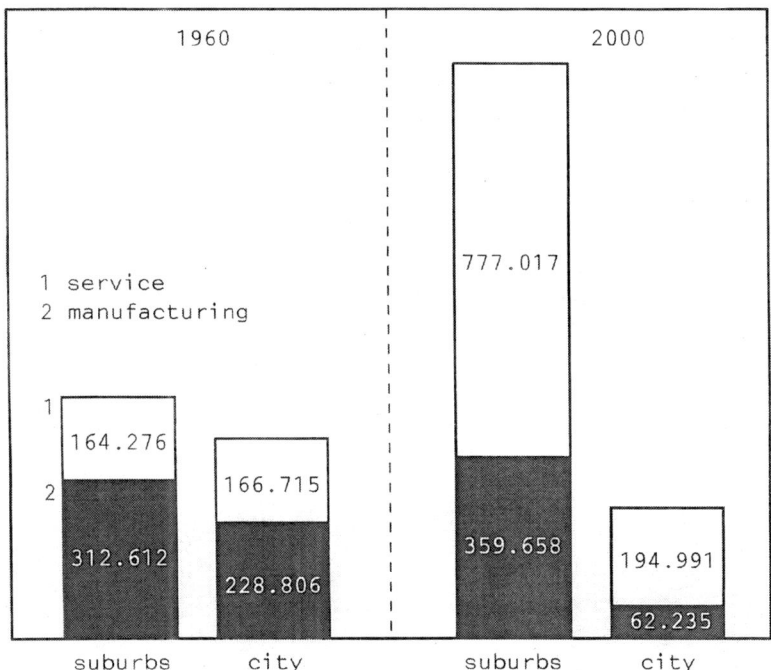

Fig. 4: People employed in manufacturing and service-based jobs, 1960 and 2000
(Source: Hagemann and Möller 2004, 8)

neighbourhood, an area of about 1.25 square kilometres. It was criticised on the grounds as presenting a destruction of Poletown (Hall and Hall 1993, 28; Sugrue 2004, 236). At the end of the 1980s, the same applied to a Chrysler factory. However, both companies did not employ more than a few thousand workers (Sugrue 2004, 236–237). Moreover, the Poletown plant cost the city 200 million Dollar in public subsidies (DiGeatano 1999, 561).

Since the 1950s, the city of Detroit has experienced a loss of population, workplaces and white inhabitants. The automobile industry had a big share in this process. Decentralization of factories as well as automation and job reduction contributed to a process that saw Detroit developing into a deeply divided city, both in terms of a city-suburb-divide as well as racial polarization. The riots from 1967 had reinforced this trend towards suburbanization. Detroit's image started to deteriorate. Subsequently, various actors and co-alitions emerged within the city of Detroit in order to develop strategies in response to the urban crisis, on of which was the construction of the aptly named "Renaissance Center".

Detroit Renaissance: corporate actors and the efforts to revitalize downton Detroit

The Renaissance Center, containing a hotel, restaurants, shops, entertainment facilities and offices, was built in the 1970s in downtown Detroit at a cost of about 340 million Dollars. It was designed by architect John Portman. Renewal projects in Pittsburgh and Atlanta served as models (Desiderio 2009, 87).

The project was initiated by a private non-profit leadership organization that closely cooperated with the city administration and called "Detroit Renaissance". It was founded in 1970 in order to address the urban crisis after the riots (Hall and Hall 1993, 23–25). Detroit businessmen such as Henry Ford II, financier and developer Max Fisher, and Robert Surdam, president of the National Bank of Detroit, alongside then Mayor Roman Gribbs and Michigan's governor George Romney, established Detroit Renaissance, Inc. to attract new business and to revitalize Downtown Detroit (Darden et al. 1987, 46–48).

This coalition comprised auto industry leaders, private developers, and members of the city administration, featuring the influential black mayor Coleman Young as a very strong actor among them since 1974. One of the big players was Henry Ford II, who showed great personal commitment. In 1971, he presented a development plan to Mayor Roman Gribbs and Detroit city Council, featuring hotels, offices, shops, and residential areas at the riverfront. The City Council approved the plan one year later (Detroit News 2001). Ford Motor Company took the lead on the project, but was not willing to be the only contributor to the bill. Accordingly, Ford coordinated a fund-raising and forged what was at the time the "largest private investment group ever assembled in the U.S. for an urban real estate project" (Darden et al. 1987, 48). He aimed at convincing all automotive companies to get involved. He was able to persuade General Motors, and soon the other corporations followed. They obviously felt obliged to Motor Town as a symbol of the American automobile industry and Ford had after all been blamed by locals for abandoning the city of Detroit before (Desiderio 2009, 87).

The aim of the project was the revitalization of downtown. The project still saw opposition, since many people did not believe that it was an adequate solution for Detroit's problems, particularly the racial tensions. Ford however advertised the Renaissance Center as a "catalyst for downtown development" (cited in: Desiderio 2009, 83), since Detroit's central business district had seen massive decline. Stores, business, and offices had left the area throughout the 1960s and 1970s (Desiderio 2009, 85), and new business and jobs—although in many cases low paid jobs—were to be brought into the city by means of the Renaissance Center. People such as architect Portman, Henry Ford, and parts of the local authorities believed in the success of the project. Mayor Roman Gribbs saw the "beginning of a vast revitalization of our riverfront which will stretch from bridge to bridge" (cited in: Desiderio 2009, 96).

In the beginning, the idea did in fact seem to be a success. People flocked into downtown to get their own impression of the Renaissance Center. As Desiderio puts it, the Center, "if only briefly, became a popular destination for locals and tourists alike" (Desiderio 2009, 83). However, the curiosity of tourists soon faded away. Before long, office spaces became vacant. Therefore, the Ford Corporation moved 1,700 employees from Dearborn to downtown Detroit, which made Ford—paradoxically—the Center's largest tenant. However, Ford employees resisted to work in Detroit. They were worried about security and long commutes (Darden et al. 1987, 51–52). Moreover, costs overran and the high rate of vacancy led to bankruptcy (Hall and Hall 1993, 23). Desiderio concluded: "The Renaissance Center did not become the 'catalyst' for the city that Henry Ford II had envisioned. The initial warm reception it received from business interests and some politicians was not enough to ensure its success; the structure failed to appeal to workers, shoppers and Detroiters" (Desiderio 2009, 106).

The Renaissance Center was criticized for being a city within the city. The architecture was often called "fortresslike" (Darden et al. 1987, 50). Access to the building was not easy, particularly for pedestrians. The Renaissance Center was separated from the city, not integrated into Downtown's structure. The shops attracted middle- und upper class people. The jobs did not fit the needs of former automobile workers. One critic talked of a "capitalist plot against the city" (Desiderio 2009, 102). Desiderio characterized the Renaissance center as a suburb in the city. It was safe and convenient, but did not revitalize the city (Desiderio 2009, 101).

In the long run, the flagship project did not contribute to bring new businesses, jobs and the revitalization to Downtown Detroit. The focus on flagship projects and the stimulation of tourism, shopping and new business in the inner city seems to serve as a typical example for the city as a "growth machine" (Logan and Molotch 1987), which means that a private growth coalition and the city government worked together first and above all to promote growth and employment. DiGaetano and Klemanski spoke of a "progrowth strategy" in Detroit (DiGaetano and Klemanski 1993, 381). But as Orr and Stoker have pointed out: "Key downtown interests and other standard elements of a growth machine have been conspicuously absent in Detroit." While Ford junior and some other investors as well as mayor Coleman aimed at revitalizing downtown, hotels, office buildings, and retail centers left the city at the same time the Renaissance Center opened (Orr and Stoker 1994, 57) and so foiled all efforts to revitalize the inner city.

By 1971, the Kresge Company had moved its headquarters to the suburbs. In 1972, Motown Records moved to Hollywood (Poremaba 2001, 137). The trend continued, as American Motors Corporation (AMC) moved its headquarters to Southfield. In 1974, even the football team left the city (Poremba 2001, 138). In 1983, when Hudson's closed its doors for good, the central city was no longer home to even a single major regional shopping area or complex (Darden et al. 1987, 26).

Thus, the project did not bring the flight from the city to a halt. The process of suburbanization continued. Orr and Stoker have come to the conclusion that an effective public-private partnership did not emerge. While a few strong actors, such as Mayor Coleman and Henry Ford, Junior, worked hard for the project, the efforts to revitalize the inner city did not draw sufficient support from the key elites of local business. Moreover, the automotive industry experienced a deep crisis during the 1970s, and was strongly hit by recession. General Motors laid off 38,000 workers and put another 48,000 on short-term leave (Poremba 2001, 137; Hill 1986, 113–115).

The „Detroit Renaissance" coalition and the „Renaissance Center" project are just one example of how various actors respond to crisis. What is of special interest here is the role of the automotive corporations, which added to the causes of urban crisis by way of their politics of decentralization and automation. To make things worse, they were hit by the recession of the 1970s and challenged heavily by global competition and the Japanese car industry. Simultaneously, the automobile companies, particularly Henry Ford, initiated a typical flagship project in order to revitalize downtown and to bring new business into the city. While the car industry left the city, it nevertheless became part of a growth coalition, aiming at the revitalization of Downtown and the diversification of the city's economic base. However, the initiative proved unable to stop the process of suburbanization and urban decline.

The City of Wolfsburg—Transformation processes in an automobile city

Like Detroit, Wolfsburg was an icon of modernity and a symbol of wealth and success. Founded during the Third Reich as production site for a cheap car for the masses, the Volkswagen, it has never been anything else than an automotive city. In the 1950s Wolfsburg became a symbol of the German economic miracle. For a long time, Wolfsburg was one of the most affluent cities in Germany. To this day, the city is heavily dependent on the car industry.

There are some important differences to Detroit, though. Wolfsburg has never experienced a suburbanization process or the flight of its inhabitants from the city as was the case in Detroit. Today's figures of inhabitants have been more or less stable for decades of 120,000 (Harth 2010, 26). Although Wolfsburg integrated foreign workers from Italy, who initially were socially and spatially segregated from the German inhabitants, the city had never experienced any serious trouble in this respect (Uliczka 1993; Grieger 2009). Besides, the city is much smaller. Finally, there is only one big corporate player in the city, namely the Volkswagen corporation, rather than the "Big Three" in Detroit. However, like in Detroit, the automobile industry is a very strong local actor that has influenced the development of the city in many respects—and was also both a cause of crisis and simultaneously part of a coalition to address the crisis.

From the early beginnings of the city's history, the company has played an enormous role within its development. Earlier research has described the patriarchal Nordhoff system, a term that reflects the influence of the company's first director Heinrich Nordhoff on the city's development, which back then seemed to be an unquestioned matter of course.

Even if the company ceased to have such comparably complete and unquestioned influence on the city's decisions after Nordhoff, the bonds between the city government and the company have nevertheless always been very tight. Sociological research and political science in particular have discussed the relationship between the company and local authorities since the 1950s (Schwonke and Herlyn 1967; Hilterscheid 1970; Herlyn et al. 1982; Harth et al. 2000; 2010). However, it is not the purpose of this article to give an overview of the changing relationship of the business elite and the local authorities in Wolfsburg in the course of the city's history. Instead it will focus on the role of the car industry in times of crisis.

Crisis

Wolfsburg did not experience a serious crisis before 1966/67 and the 1970s. But as a mono-industrial city it was heavily dependent on the car industry. As long as the company's sales boomed, this dependency was not perceived as a problem. After the crisis in the 1960s, Volkswagen reduced its workforce for the very first time in the history of the city. Between 1965 and 1967, the number of workers and employees declined from 48,600 to 45,600; between 1970 and 1972 from 59,200 to 51,800. And things got even worse. In 1974 and 1975, the workforce was cut back again. This time, lay-offs reached figures of around 10,000 people. (Harth et al. 2000, 14; Grieger 2008). The city experienced a slight decline of inhabitants and of tax revenues, and for the first time in its history ran into financial debt.

However, due to the quick recovery of Volkswagen in the second half of the 1970s, the city administration did not undertake serious efforts to restructure or redevelop the city. The workforce grew again, and so did the tax revenues.

It was not before the crisis of 1992/93 that new concepts of city planning were being discussed. Harth et al. have talked of a "turning point in city's history" (Harth et al. 2000). During these years, Volkswagen went through a deep depression. In Wolfsburg, lay-offs cut back the workforce from 60,000 in 1986 to 45,000 in 1996. At this time, just as in the 1960s, about 60 percent of all jobs in Wolfsburg were with Volkswagen (Harth 2000, 45–46). As a consequence, the unemployment rate climbed from a mere 7.6 percent in 1991 to a 17.9 percent in 1996. And again, the city ran into financial debt.

Now concepts for Wolfsburg's redevelopment were being devised. Just like in Detroit, the automotive company was a central actor in getting a restructuring process for the city off the ground. Although the city administration itself had started to develop strategies to respond to the crisis (Harth

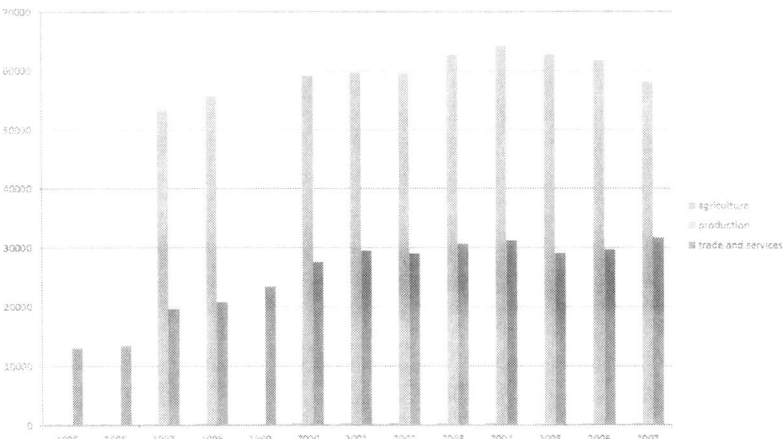

Fig. 5: Employees in Wolfsburg by sector 1995 to 2007
(Source: Statistische Jahrbücher Stadt Wolfsburg)

2010, 31–33), the role of the company was central for any further development. In 1998, the Volkswagen corporation presented to the city a concept for urban redevelopment called „AutoVision". Like in Detroit in the 1970s, it suggested flagship-projects. In 1999, a private-public-partnership was forged, the „Wolfsburg AG", „Wolfsburg Incorporated". Its board is being made up by city administrators and the Volkswagen Corporation. This public private partnership realized various flagship projects. Since the end of the 1990s, Wolfsburg has begun to transform into an event city. The company itself built a huge theme park called „Autostadt" (*auto city*). Moreover, a science center (by architect Zaha Hadid) was being established, alongside a new sports stadium, a water park, and a design outlet center. In addition, festivals are now being held in Wolfsburg, and an innovation campus has been built (Harth et al. 2010; Schrödel 2010). Flagship projects were seen as the silver bullet, very much like Detroit's "catalyst for urban development".[3] Both the corporate actor and the local authorities took great efforts to diversify the city's economic base. A typical growth coalition promoted growth and employment in the city. It was the VW corporation that initiated a public-private-partnership and became an important player. As one actor from Volkswagen stated, it was as important for the company as it was for

---

3 See the citation above of Desiderio (2009, 83).

the city to overcome the mono-industrial base of the city (Harth et al. 2010, 38). Thus, the company became a driving force for diversification in order to avoid the heavy burden of being solely responsible for the city's wellbeing. The share of jobs at the Volkswagen AG (compared to all jobs in Wolfsburg) actually decreased from 64 percent in 1998 to 44.4 percent in 2008 (Harth et al. 2010, 69). At the same time, the unemployment rate decreased from 14.2 percent to 6.0 percent. While in 1997 about 73 percent of Wolfsburg's total workforce had jobs in the second sector, this figure has fallen to a mere 57 percent in 2011. During the same period, the relative share in the service sector has been on the rise.

However, Wolfsburg's economy is still centered around the car. The innovation campus focuses on the car industry's needs, and the "Autostadt" theme park is one of the most important attractions in town. To this day, the Wolfsburg AG proved a successful coalition. Without doubt, the company was a core player within these strategies. It had an enormous influence on the process of the city's transformation. This is not to say, however, that the city administration was a weak actor. Contrary to Detroit, though, in Wolfsburg all players were fully committed to the agenda, even though conflicts and struggles were part of that cooperation.

Just as in Detroit, the cycles and crises of the automotive industry brought crises to Wolfsburg, which is not surprising considering its strong mono-industrial economic base. But contrary to Detroit, the Volkswagen Corporation did not question Wolfsburg as the site of their world headquarter and as a place for manufacturing cars, although it has since erected many new factories in the region, in Germany and all over the world. However, processes of automation as well as cycles still led to lay-offs. But Volkswagen introduced new models of work, like the "4-day-week" to prevent job cuts. The model of the "atmende Fabrik" (which translates to "breathing factory" and refers to a flexible workforce) was invented in order not to lay off workers in large quantities. Thus, without suburbanization of either factories or inhabitants, and without any tremendous cut backs of jobs and without Detroit's widespread segregation and racism the crisis was far from what it was in Detroit.

As in Detroit, when crisis hit the city, the corporate actors initiated a project in order to encourage investment and new business in Wolfsburg, with consumers and tourists being the target groups. Until now, this project is regarded as successful. Contrary to Detroit, it was not a single architectural project, but part of a city development plan, into which the projects were to be integrated. Without doubt, devising a strategy for redevelopment was less complicated in Wolfsburg, since it incorporates only one strong business actor, as the city is smaller, and because it was able to resort to a long standing relationship between corporate actors and the local authorities.

Conclusion

It does not come as a surprise that the automotive industry plays as decisive role for the history of automobile cities, both in terms of growth and boom as in times of crisis. That is particularly true for mono-industrial cities as Detroit and Wolfsburg. In both cities, crises originated from within the automobile industry. Nevertheless, there were fundamental differences. While the automotive industry gradually left the city of Detroit, the Volkswagen Corporation remained the main employer in Wolfsburg. While the city of Detroit lost almost all of its jobs in the car industry due to decentralization and automation, the number of jobs in Wolfsburg has been mainly dependent on the cycles of the car industry.

In terms of the role the car industry during times of crisis, the two case studies show very similar attitudes of the corporate actors. Both initiated a growth coalition, which aimed at flagship projects to bring new business, to attract tourists and to diversify the economic base of their respective city. The latter aspect needs to be stressed, since it was the automotive industry itself that aimed at a diversification of the industrial base of their city, instead of putting the brakes on attracting new businesses, something that can be observed among other corporate actors during urban decline. The city of Hamburg might serve as an example here. In time of crisis, "the traditional 'port and trade' elite has been losing part of its economic position to the new mass media elite, but actually tried to preserve it by promoting the traditions of the city and lobbying for subsidies for shipbuilding" (Friedrich 1993, 911–912). Contrary to that, the corporate actors in Wolfsburg and Detroit opted for diversification of the economic base, which was additionally motivated by the prospect to be released from their responsibility for the city's development. This responsibility was ascribed to the Volkswagen Corporation by local authorities and inhabitants because of the mono-industrial base and the intimate and long lasting connection of the city with the automotive industry. Regarding Detroit, as mentioned above, local elites and inhabitants blamed Henry Ford for abandoning the city.

While the growth coalition was not successful in 1970s Detroit, it is regarded as a success in Wolfsburg, at least until now. It was not the intention of this article to explain success and failure of these projects, let alone to explain the different histories of Wolfsburg and Detroit. This article proposed to open a window for further research on industrial cities, particularly on automobile cities and the role of the industry in economic and urban crisis. As it turned out, in both Detroit and Wolfsburg the automotive industry played an ambivalent role, proving to be both, a cause of crisis and simultaneously part of a growth coalition aiming at diversifying the mono-industrial base. This article can only offer a glimpse on a complicated subject of research. Further research, particularly long-time research in different cities, would be necessary. Take Oxford, UK as an example. Teresa Hayter and David Harvey blamed the Rover Company in Cowley, Oxford for closing the car plant and leaving the city behind. They criticized that the company first utilized on the city's resources, but then closed the factory while shifting the responsibility for the urban problems to the local authorities (Hayter and Harvey 1993). Contrary to that, Henry Ford claimed that he had started the initiative of 1970 because he felt committed to Detroit—which nevertheless did not stop the company from leaving the city. Volkswagen surely felt committed to Wolfsburg, but it also wanted to prevent Wolfsburg from becoming a symbol of urban decline or a "murder city", since it is home of its headquarters. Without doubt, both cities, Wolfsburg and Detroit, have had a long history as automobile cities with traditional and intimate connections to the car industry. And yet, the question of how the automobile industry reacts during economic crises, how deeply it feels committed to its location, and how it influences the development of the city during times of crisis still remains an open question for many automobile cities.

Works Cited

Anon. (2001). How the Renaissance Center changed the landscape of Detroit, The Detroit News, 9/29/2001, http://apps.detnews.com/apps/history/index.php?id=122.

Bailey, D., and C. Chapain (2011). The Recession and Beyond: Local and Regional Responses to the Downturn. In D. Bailey and C. Chapain (eds.), *The Recession and Beyond: The Role of Local Authorities in dealing with the Downturn*, 1–24, London: Taylor and Francis.

Beer, A., and H. Evans (2010). *The Impacts of Automotive Plant Closure. A Tale of Two Cities.* London and New York: Routledge.

Bodenschatz, H. (2008). Urban Renaissance in Birmingham und Manchester. In H. Bodenschatz and U. Laible (eds.). *Großstädte von morgen. Internationale Strategien des Stadtumbaus.* Berlin: Verlagshaus Braun.

Clavel, P., and C. Kleniewksi (1990). Space for progressive local policy: Examples from the United States and the United Kingdom. In J.R. Logan and T. Swanson (eds.). *Beyond the City Limits: Urban Policy and Economic Restructuring in Comparative Perspective,* 199-234 Philadelphia: Temple University Press.

Darden, J., et al. (1987). *Detroit: Race and uneven development. Philadelphia,* PA: Temple Press.

Davey, M., and M. Williams Walsh (2013). For Detroit, a Crisis Born of Bad Decisions and Crossed Fingers. *New Work Times,* 3/11/2013.

Desiderio, F. (2009). "A Catalyst for Downtown": Detroit's Renaissance Center. *Michigan Historical Review,* 35, 83–112.

DiGaetano, A., and J. S. Klemanski (1993). Urban Regime Capacity: A Comparison of Birmingham, England, and Detroit, Michigan. *Journal of Urban Affairs,* 15, 367-384.

DiGaetona, A. (1999). Urban Governance and Industrial Decline: Governing Structures and Policy Agendas in Birmingham and Sheffield, England, and Detroit, Michigan, 1980-1997. *Urban Affairs Review,* 34, 546-577.

Fishman, R. (2004). Suburbanisierung: USA. In P. Oswalt (ed). *Schrumpfende Städte, Vol. 1. Internationale Untersuchung.* 64-73. Bonn: Hatje Canz.

Friedrich, J. (1993). A Theory of Urban Decline: Economy, Demography and Political Elites. *Urban Studies,* 30, 901-917.

Gerrit, S. (2010). *Erlebnisgesellschaft in Wolfsburg. Freizeitkulturen und Stadtentwicklungspolitik seit 1990.* Braunschweig: Appelhans Verlag.

Grieger, M. (2008). Der neue Geist im Volkswagenwerk. Produktinnovation, Kapazitätsabbau und Mitbestimmungsmodernisierung, 1968–1976. In M. Reitmayer and R. Rosenberger (eds.). *Unternehmen am Ende des „goldenen Zeitalters". Die 1970er Jahre in unternehmens- und wirtschaftshistorischer Perspektive,* 31-66. Essen: Klartext.

Grieger, M. (2009). Zuwanderung und junge Industriestadt. Wolfsburg und die Migranten seit 1938. *Niedersächsisches Jahrbuch für Landesgeschichte,* 81, 177-210.

Hagemann, A., and N. Möller (2004). Statistical Data: Detroit. In P. Oswalt (ed). *Schrumpfende Städte, Vol. 1. Internationale Untersuchung.* 6-10. Bonn: Hatje Canz.

Hall, L. M, and M. F. Hall (1993). Detroit's Urban Regime: Composition and Consequence. *Mid-American Review of Sociology,* 17, 19–37.

Harth, A., et al. (2000). *Wolfsburg: Stadt am Wendepunkt. Eine dritte soziologische Untersuchung.* Opladen: Leske und Budrich.

Harth, A., et al. (2010). *Stadt als Erlebnis: Wolfsburg. Zur stadtkulturellen Bedeutung von Großprojekten.* Wiesbaden: Verlag für Sozialwissenschaften.

Harvey, D. (1989). From Managerialism to entrepreneurialism: The Transformation in urban governance in late capitalism. *Geografiska Annaler*, 71 B, 3–17.

Hayter, T., and D. Harvey (1993). *The Factory and the City. The Story of Cowley Automobile Workers in Oxford*. London and New York: Thomson Learning.

Herlyn, U., et al. (1982). *Stadt im Wandel. Eine Wiederholungsuntersuchung der Stadt Wolfsburg nach 20 Jahren*. Frankfurt am Main: Campus.

Herlyn, U., et al. (2012). Faszination Wolfsburg 1938–2012. Wiesbaden: Springer.

Heßler, M. (2011). Geschichte von Autostädten in globaler Perspektive: Plädoyer für eine global orientierte Zeitgeschichtsschreibung. *Informationen zur modernen Stadtgeschichte*, (1), 91–100.

Heßler, M. (2014). Autostädte und ihre Geshcichten. In M. Heßler und G. Riederer (eds.). *Autostädte. Wachstums- und Schrumpfprozesse in globaler Perspektive*. Stuttgart: Steiner (forthcoming, probable title).

Hill, R. C. (1986). Crisis in the Motor City. In N. Fainstein and S. Fainstein (eds.). *Restructuring the Ciy: the political economy of urban redevelopment*, 81–125. New York: Longman.

Hilterscheid, H. (1970). *Industrie und Gemeinde. Die Beziehung zwischen der Stadt Wolfsburg und dem Volkswagenwerk und ihre Auswirkungen auf die kommunale Selbstverwaltung*. Berlin: Berlin Verlag.

Levine, M. (1987). Downtown development as an urban growth: A critical appraisal of Baltimore Renaissance. *Journal of Urban Affairs*, 9, 103–123.

Logan, J., and H. Mototch (1987). *Urban fortunes: The political economy of place*. Berkeley: University of California Press.

Mende, D., and P. Oswalt (2004). Summary. In P. Oswalt (ed). *Working Papers, Detroit III*, 3–4. http://www.shrinkingcities.com/fileadmin/shrink/downloads/pdfs/WP-Band_III_Detroit.pdf.

Mönnich, H. (1951). *Die Autostadt*. München and Wien: Wilhelm Andermann Verlag.

Orr, M. E., and G. Stoker (1994). Urban Regimes and Leadership in Detroit. *Urban affairs review*, 30, 43–73.

Oswalt, P. (ed.). (2004a). *Schrumpfende Städte, Vol. 1. Internationale Untersuchung*. Bonn: Hatje Canz.

Oswalt, P. (2004b). Einleitung. In P. Oswalt (ed). *Schrumpfende Städte, Vol. 1. Internationale Untersuchung*, 12–17. Bonn: Hatje Canz.

Poremba, D. L. (2001). *Detroit. A Motor City History*. Chicago: Arcadia Publishing.

Power, A., J. Plöger, and A. Winkler (2010). Phoenix *Cities. The fall and rise of great industrial cities*. Bristol: Policy Press.

Reif, H. (2012). Städte und Städteagglomerationen der Montanindustrie in Deutschland, 1850–1914. *Informationen zur modernen Stadtgeschichte*, (1), 15–28.

Schmidtpott, K. (2012). Neue Perspektiven der historischen Industriestadtforschung in Japan. *Informationen zur modernen Stadtgeschichte*, (1), 87–103.

Schwonke, M., and U. Herlyn (1967). Wolfsburg. Soziologische Analyse einer jungen Industriestadt. Göttinger Abhandlungen zur Soziologie und ihrer Grenzgebiete. Stuttgart: Enke.

Siegelbaum, L. H. (2008). *Cars for Comrades. The Life of the Soviet Automobile*. Ithaca and London: Cornell University Press.

Stein, S. (2012). „Ein Wald rauchender Fabrikschornsteine". Rückblicke auf die chinesische „Produktionsstadt" der 1950er Jahre. *Informationen zur modernen Stadtgeschichte*, (1), 69–86.

Stoker, R. (1987). Baltimore: The self-evaluating city? In C. Stone and H. Sanders (eds.). *The politics of urban development*, 269–90. Lawrence: University Press of Kansas.

Sugrue, T. J. (1995). *The Origins of the Urban Crisis*. Princeton: Princeton University Press.

Sugrue, T. J. (2004). Niedergang durch Rassismus. In P. Oswalt (ed.). *Schrumpfende Städte, Vol. 1. Internationale Untersuchung*, 231–241, Bonn: Hatje Canz.

Uliczka, M. (1993). *Berufsbiographie und Flüchtlingsschicksal: VW-Arbeiter in der Nachkriegszeit*. Hannover: Hahnsche Buchhandlung.

Volti, R. (2004). *Cars and Culture. The Life of a Technology*, Baltimore: Johns Hopkins.

Zimmermann, C. (2014). Autostadt Rüsselsheim: Räume, Akteure und Selbstbilder zwischen Lokalität und Globalität. In M. Heßler (ed.). *Autostädte. Wachstums- und Schrumpfungsprozesse in globaler Perspektive*. Stuttgart: Steiner (forthcoming).

Comeback Cities? Urban Recovery Approaches in European Industrial Cities

Jörg Plöger

Weak Market Cities and recovery

The decline of cities in the industrialized world is usually a direct consequence of the process of economic restructuring. The collapse of the industrial base in these cities has been the main cause for many of the subsequent urban problems such as rising unemployment and welfare-dependency, population decline and out-migration or physical decay of the urban environment. This contribution will examine the impact of deindustrialization on older industrial cities throughout Europe and then highlight some of the approaches and strategies that have been used to overcome the problems associated with urban decline and 'shrinkage'. The main research questions are: Can we identify a common trajectory of growth, crisis, decline and—possibly—recovery for industrial cities? In case of signs for recovery, what were the contributing factors? Is the resurgence strong enough notwithstanding further urban challenges such as the most recent recession? The assumption is that, although the urban development process is largely driven by exogenous factors—outside of their immediate sphere of influence, the actions taken by cities themselves do have a local impact. A city that is responding to an urban crisis with dedicated, well-prepared and innovative approaches is thus likely to outperform its peers with similar problems. The evidence provided here is drawn from research about so-called 'Weak Market Cities'. These are older industrial cities in a transitory phase. On the one hand they have experienced and are still experiencing decline due to economic restructuring (covered in the second section). Despite the persistence of structural weaknesses, these cities are also showing—more or less pronounced—signs of urban recovery on the other hand (Power et al. 2010, 271–289). A detailed account of this process is provided in the third section.

The selection of case studies therefore includes cities in an intermediate phase of recovery that have neither reached advanced stages of recovery such as some larger old-industrial cities (e.g. Barcelona, Milan or Manchester) nor are they still in full decline as are several smaller, often mono-industrial cities located in Europe's 'rust belts' (e.g. in the Ruhr Area in Germany or Northern England). The sample thus includes cities in Western Europe that are showing fragile signs of recovery, yet are still struggling with considerable problems.[1] The following cities were chosen: Sheffield (England) and Belfast (Northern Ireland) in the United Kingdom, Leipzig (East) and Bremen (West) in Germany, Bilbao in Spain, Torino in Italy and Saint Etienne in France. All of these were important industrial cities within their respective countries. With the exception of Saint Etienne, they are also centers of regional importance within their national contexts.

Cities on the edge—severe urban decline

The emergence of industrial cities

Industrialization had a profound impact on rapidly transforming societies across Europe and fueled urbanization. However, regional differences can be distinguished; among them the timing of industrialization. The Industrial Revolution started almost simultaneously in English cities such as Manchester and Birmingham in the second half of the 18th century. Following Britain, the 'wave' of industrialization spread to the European continent and North America.

Frequently industrialization occurred disconnected from previous urban development, hence by-passing historic city roles such as being a convenient market-place, a safe bastion or a religious or political center (Hohenberg and Lees 1985). It involved cities with important functions such as London, Cologne or Amsterdam as well as places that previously were merely villages or small towns. The latter case involves some of the cities that emerged in the Ruhr Area in Western Germany, where the location of mines and industrial

---

1 Western Europe as applied here refers to countries with market-economies and democratic political systems as opposed to the former Eastern Bloc countries which had socialist regimes and state-controlled economies. It comprises countries in Southern European such as Spain and Italy. The only exception is Leipzig in East Germany, which became part of Western Europe with the collapse of the GDR and integration into West Germany after reunification.

plants since the 19th century transformed a mostly rural hinterland into a major industrial agglomeration.

In contrast to later urban development in the US (Roberts and Steadman 1999), the selected European cities were founded in medieval times and had already acquired specific functions—especially trade and administration—before being transformed by industrialization. Bremen had evolved as a major port associated with the prosperous Hanseatic League. Relative political autonomy grounded on its role as transport and trading hub, which today is reflected in its status as a city-state. Further south, Bilbao fulfilled similar functions as a port and trading center. Belfast, also a port city, became the administrative center for the British colonization of the Ulster region in Ireland from the 17th century onwards. Aided by its location, Torino developed into a gateway city on important transportation routes. In the 16th century it also became capital of the Duchy of Savoy and in the 19th century the first Italian national capital after the unification of Italy. Likewise, Leipzig benefited from its location on transportation routes in Central Europe and emerged as a crucial trading center in the Late Middle Ages. In Saint Etienne proto-industrial activities pre-dated its emergence as a major industrial city in the 19th century.

The rise of industrial cities was linked to their locations. The first industries emerged in close proximity to natural resources such as coal or iron ore. Favorable transportation infrastructure subsequently facilitated the movement of raw materials and processed products, which gave rise to urban growth adjacent to important waterways, roads and—particularly—railway lines. In some of the studied cities, proto-industrial activities had already emerged in the 18th century, including coal mining and steel production in Sheffield, textile manufacturing in Belfast or ship-building in Bremen. In the 19th century these cities quickly evolved into industrial giants, building on their strategic and productive advantages (Power et al. 2010, 9–11). Their enormous urban growth was fueled by a constant inflow of workers from other regions. As shown in Figure 1, the sharpest rise in population usually occurred in the period between the final quarter of the 19th century and the outbreak of World War I in 1914. Industrialization saw the emergence of large industrial companies as Harland & Wolff in Belfast, at one point the world's largest shipbuilding company, steel producers in Sheffield and arms manufacturers in Saint Etienne. Moreover, further technological progress spurred the rise of newer industries. Examples include aircraft production in Bremen, chemical industries in Leipzig, engineering in Belfast or automobile production in Torino.

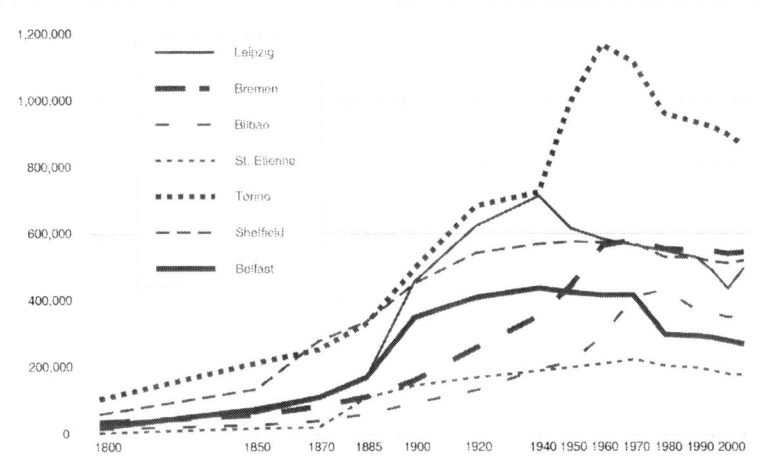

Fig. 1: Population development, 1800–2005

(Source: Adapted from Power et al. (2010, 13); official data from national, regional and city statistics offices[2])

Economic restructuring and urban decline

The collapse of key industries in these cities cannot be viewed in isolation from global processes of economic restructuring. Although some industries such as mining and steel production were already facing problems, economic growth of the post-war period and the rise of other—more elaborate—industries did initially not provide reasons for concern. A shift occurred in the early 1970s when the industrialized countries entered economic recession, symbolized by the oil crisis in 1973.

The global economy was undergoing a profound transformation. The Fordist mode of mass production was gradually being replaced by the Post-Fordist mode of flexible production (Clark et al. 2000). In an increasingly connected world, companies were constantly forced to adapt to shifts in the

---

2 If not otherwise mentioned, the many sources of statistical data used to produce the graphs and tables are not specified throughout the text for simplification (see Power et al. 2010 for detailed information). Furthermore, comparing statistical data across European countries is problematic due to variations in measurement and data availability.

City	Year	No.	Year	No.	Loss No.	Loss %
Bremen	1970	122,730	2003	67,966	55,000	45
Leipzig	1989	101,095	2004	13,648	87,447	87
Belfast	1973	*67,000*	2001	15,828	51,172	76
Sheffield	1971	117,100	2004	30,810	86,290	74
Bilbao	1970	124,539	2001	68,066	56,473	45
Torino	1971	492,791	2005	*322,000*	170,791	35
St. Etienne	1977	69,727	2001	41,104	28,623	41

Fig. 2: Loss of manufacturing jobs, 1970–2005

(Sources: Official data from national, regional and city statistics offices)

Note: data either for city level (Bremen, Leipzig, Belfast, Sheffield) or metropolitan/provincial level (Bilbao, Torino, Saint Etienne); in italics: rounded.

global marketplace. Decreasing transportation costs and the rise of new communication technologies furthered the development of new globally linked production systems and commodity chains.

These factors contributed to an increasing global division of labor (Amin 1994). To reduce production costs and to react to growing international competition, companies started out-sourcing production to countries with lower production and workforce costs. Initially, this included mainly low-skilled, low-tech parts of the production process, but later—with the development of a skills base in industrializing countries—more complex elements followed. This process often resulted in the collapse of certain industrial sectors and a dramatic workforce reduction in manufacturing in older industrial cities. In most such cities, moves toward a service economy have not yet compensated for those job losses (e.g. Daniels 1993).

The impact of economic restructuring on older industrial cities was substantial, although it varied from city to city. Cities dependent on heavy industries such as mining (e.g. Sheffield, Saint Etienne, Leipzig), steel (e.g. Bilbao, Sheffield) or ship-building (e.g. Bremen, Bilbao, Belfast) generally suffered the most. The degree of modernization and the level of diversification of the industrial structure were equally important factors. Mono-industrial or "one-company" cities lost their economic rationale when their major

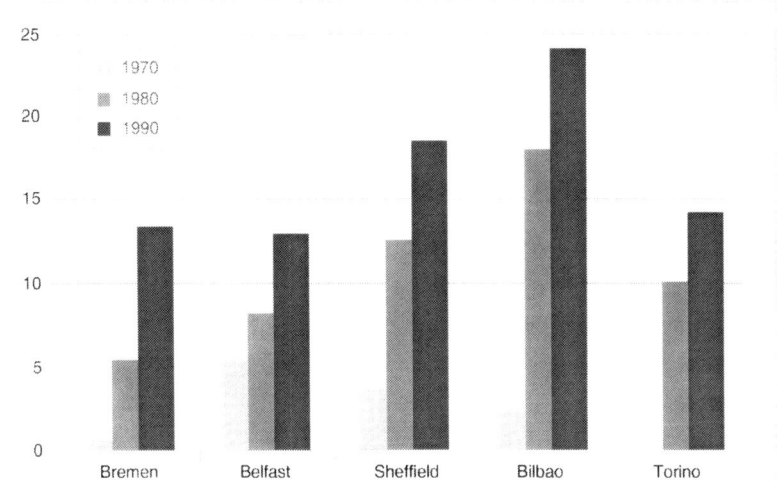

Fig. 3: Unemployment rates for selected cities, 1970–1990 (in %)

(Sources: Official data from national, regional and city statistics offices)

Note: Leipzig and Saint Etienne not included due to lack of data before 1990

employer collapsed. Cities that were once driving forces of economic growth to their respective countries became liabilities heavily dependent on transfer funds (Power et al. 2010, 24).

Economic restructuring is clearly illustrated by the massive loss of industrial employment between 1970 and 2005 (Fig. 2). From the early 1970s to the early 2000s these cities lost between 35 percent (Torino) and 76 percent (Belfast) of all industrial jobs. Leipzig experienced an even more dramatic decline (87 percent) in a very short period of time after the transition from a socialist to a market economy in 1990.

These job losses resulted in serious social problems such as unemployment and welfare dependency but also fierce labor struggles. Sheffield, for example, played a prominent role during the national miners' strike in the UK in the early 1980s just as dockers and other workers went on lengthy strikes in Bilbao and Bremen. In Belfast the loss of industrial employment exacerbated already hostile relationships between the Protestant and Catholic communities (e.g. Murtagh 2002). In most of these cities unemployment peaked in the mid to late 1980s. Figure 3 shows the steep increase in unemployment rates between 1970 and 1990 for the studied cities. Industrial decline particularly affected the low-skilled workforce, which were generally the first to lose their jobs when companies started reducing their workforce or moving parts of their production to lower-cost locations. They have also encountered the biggest difficulties in reentering the labor market, making them vulnerable for long-term unemployment and de facto exclusion from secure employment. These social grievances translated into increasing sociospatial inequalities. Traditional working-class neighborhoods, which also received the main influx of labor immigrants, were hit hardest by job losses and showed increasing indices of deprivation as disadvantaged groups concentrated there.

With the economic boom of the post-war period and the rise of white-collar employment, industries were in demand of workers, which set in motion manifold migratory processes from less developed regions and countries. Yet, with ongoing deindustrialization, industrial cities experienced a population decline (Fig. 4). Similar to developments in the US, UK cities such as Sheffield and Belfast already started losing their population in the 1950s, mostly due to suburbanization. The remaining cities experienced this decline from the 1970s onwards (Turok and Mykhnenko 2007, 169–170). Unlike the unemployment rates which usually peaked during the 1980s, most cities reached their lowest population in the late 1990s or later—or have continued to decline like Belfast.

Population decline was caused by a negative natural population balance due to ageing populations and by increasing out-migration; the latter being related to two main processes. While younger, more mobile and higher qualified persons moved towards

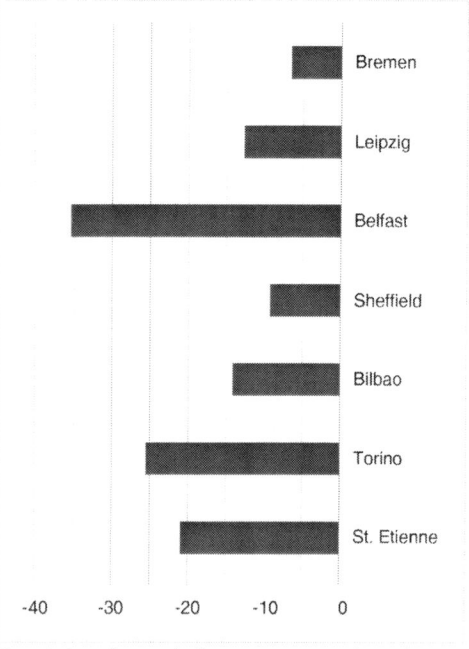

Fig. 4: Population decline, 1970–2005 (in %)

(Sources: Official data from national, regional and city statistics offices)

employment opportunities in more economically dynamic regions, middle-class families fleeing urban decay, social problems and low quality of life relocated to suburban locations. Suburbanization has increased in all studied cities since around 1970 and is causing increasing problems around issues such as taxation, unsustainable sprawl, car-dependency, rising social inequalities or costly infrastructures. In East Germany, cities had practically no suburbs until 1990 due to strict regulations on settlement patterns. Following reunification, the mostly rural municipalities surrounding Leipzig were transformed by new residential and commercial developments in a rapid process of "Wild East suburbanization" (Nuissl and Rink 2005, 127).

At the same time, these cities were confronted with further challenges associated with urban decline and shrinkage. The physical decay of the city with an increasing number of derelict buildings and vacant brownfields due to abandonment and lack of investment created a negative image and provoked a housing market crisis. In Leipzig, more than 60,000 units, 20 percent of the entire stock, had fallen vacant by the year 2000 (e.g. Herfert and Röhl 2001; City of Leipzig 2006, 13). Simultaneously, it became increasingly difficult to attract and retain professionals since modern amenities such as specific housing types or cultural and leisure facilities or quality of life in general was lacking. Low quality of life was in parts due to environmental problems. For example Leipzig's air, water and soil were heavily polluted through chemical plants, coal-fired power plants and open-cast lignite mining. Increasingly, budgetary crises restrict the ability of cities to shape future developments owing to insufficient funding, the inability to maintain infrastructures and services for a declining population, decreasing tax-bases and rising public debt (e.g. Plöger and Kohlhaas-Weber 2013).

Modes of recovery

The cities applied a wide range of strategies and measures in their search for a way out of their crisis. This section analyzes the approaches confronting the many challenges. It will present findings by focusing on the topics strategy development, new agencies, neighborhood renewal, and skills development. Before doing so, the following section provides information about individual recovery trajectories.

Trajectories

In order to understand the sequence of events and actions, we considered the period from the early 1970s until the mid 2000s. The following questions are addressed: How was recovery initiated? Was there an identifiable turning point? Who were the main actors involved? Did leadership play a role? Which focus for future development was identified? In order to analyze recovery trajectories we investigated whether a turnaround point or phase could be identified for each of the cities. A turnaround indicates that the low point of decline has been reached and that signs of urban recovery can be observed (Paddison 2001, 152). Turning points do not suggest, however, that all problems associated with the urban crisis are resolved or that all measurable indicators report a positive trend. Rather they constitute symbolic moments that may reflect real or perceived recovery. Different factors may indicate a turnaround, such as new landmark buildings representing physical renewal, a shift towards optimism for the future, new political leadership or a more dynamic labor market (Power et al. 2010, 27–57).

Turning points or in some cases turning phases could be identified for most cities with the possible exceptions of Saint Etienne and Belfast, which still showed significant problems. The timing of the turning points varied. In Bilbao and Torino, local decision-makers and urban experts placed them in the first half of the 1990s. In Sheffield, Leipzig and Bremen they were identified for the second half of the 1990s, sometimes extending into the early

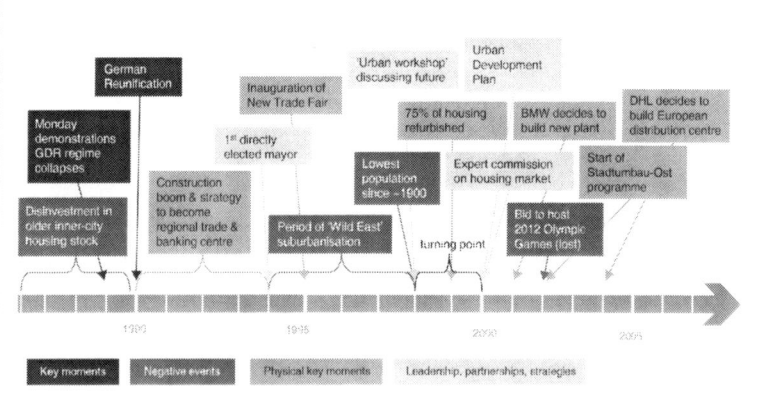

Fig. 5: Timeline of important events, Leipzig

(Source: Adapted from Power et al. (2010, 129))

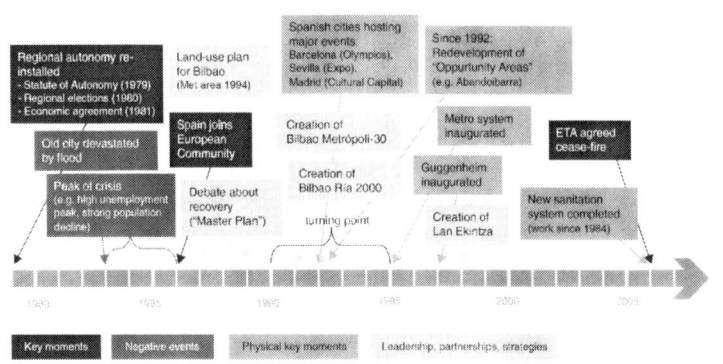

Fig. 6: Timeline of important events, Bilbao

(Source: Adapted from Power et al. (2010, 216))

2000s. As the timelines for Bilbao and Leipzig demonstrate (Fig. 5 and 6), individual recovery trajectories can be framed as constellations of specific events, political shifts, involvement by particular actors, and physical landmarks, among other factors. All trajectories shared common characteristics, yet varied in other aspects.

We can distinguish between endogenous and exogenous factors throughout the process. A starting point was the eventual recognition from within the city leadership that economic restructuring was unavoidable and that responding to the crisis was urgent. In order to be successful, new approaches had to be supported by a coalition of actors. This involved a difficult process of negotiation, consensus-building and multi-sectoral collaboration.

Strong leadership was important throughout the process. In cases like Leipzig a new leadership had emerged with the political transformation after the German Reunification. They were joined by an urban civil society, which was suppressed but had reemerged with demonstrations against the GDR regime. In combination with the optimism of the post-unification period this created momentum for change. In Sheffield a partnership-based approach to urban policy-making with a new Chief Executive replaced former 'old industrial' power constellations (Booth 2005). Support for interventions came from new funding streams to core cities by the newly elected Labour government. In Torino, a decisive change came with the first directly elected mayor in 1993 and the increasing involvement of local bank foundations in regeneration projects (Pinson 2002).

Employing regeneration discourse, city leaders attempted to convince the urban public of the need for readjustment. The change of mindset from the former industrial self-conception towards a new post-industrial identity was a difficult task. In order to succeed city leaders had to propose a new vision for the future. Every city emphasized different objectives. In the case of Bremen for instance, city leaders started shaping the transition from 'port city'—based on harbor-related activities and shipbuilding—to 'city of science'—based on high-tech sectors and research and development (Warsewa 2006, 24).

Apart from framing local conditions, these approaches need to be seen in combination with further exogenous factors. Major political events in the 1990s like the German Reunification's impact (Leipzig) and the peace process in Northern Ireland (Belfast) allowed for change. Several of the case study cities benefited from the devolution of power to regional and local governments throughout the last decades. After Spain returned to democracy in the 1970s, its regions were reinstated as important levels of government. The Basque Country was particularly successful in negotiating a substantial degree of autonomy from the central government. In combination with a reemerging strong Basque leadership, autonomy was instrumental to the recovery process of Bilbao, the region's largest city. Elsewhere, local political leadership was strengthened in the 1990s by the implementation of the direct election of mayors in Torino, Saint Etienne and Leipzig.

Throughout Europe recovery actions were supported by the availability of funding programs from different tiers of government that were designed to help cities and regions experiencing structural change. EU structural funds for regional cohesion granted substantial resources to less competitive, including old-industrial, regions. Since 1994, the *Urban* program of the EU addressed the issue of urban polarization and supported measures in disadvantaged urban neighborhoods. On the national level programs like *Soziale Stadt (Socially-Integrative City)*, implemented by the federal and state governments in Germany in 1999, offered funding for integrative renewal approaches in deprived neighborhoods. In many cases, city governments also designed their own programs in order to confront specific problems when external funding was regarded insufficient.

Strategic approaches

All of the cities in the sample developed urban strategies in order to over-come their crises, which varied in their actual implementation. While cities like Leipzig used them to inform local planning and policy-making, cities like Belfast considered them advisory documents not necessarily connected with actual implementation. The overall strategy was sometimes shaped by a forward-looking vision about how a city tried to reinvent itself in order to be 'equipped for the future' (e.g. Bremen). In Leipzig, it was more closely related to the actual problems and focused on ways to deal with them. The following part illustrates these different approaches.

In the late 1980s all tiers of government in Bilbao started working to-wards a Strategic Plan. The main objectives were to reverse the image of a declining, polluted city with concentrated social problems and to become an attractive location for investors and tourists alike. A project-oriented ap-proach was chosen to deal with urban decline and a new agency set up (see below).

For Leipzig we can identify two main strands of action: After the collapse of most of its economic base, the first strategy focused on economic develop-ment. An investor-friendly strategy was designed with the aim of attracting new companies and becoming more competitive (e.g. interview L06). It suc-ceeded in attracting two car manufacturing plants by BMW and Porsche. With large-scale investments in the airport and in highways, the city also attracted several logistics companies including online retailer Amazon and freight company DHL.

The second strand of action was designed to deal with what can be la-beled as 'shrinking city[3] problems' such as population decline, weak hous-ing markets with high vacancy rates, physical decay of many buildings and costly, oversized infrastructure (e.g. interviews L02, L13). A major objec-tive was to increase the appeal of the city as a residential location in order to attract and retain inhabitants. Due to the magnitude of these problems, Leipzig was forced to engage in new areas of policy development, hosting several roundtables and workshops in the late 1990s to discuss approaches for the future. The strategic focus on urban renewal was supported by many different, often innovative, approaches and instruments, some of which are discussed below. In 2001, Leipzig's experiences formed the basis of a major

---

3 See the chapters of Christine Hannemann and Martina Heßler in this book.

federal urban renewal program confronting the problems of shrinking cities, known as *Stadtumbau*.

The thematic focus of these cities' strategies was informed by a) other approaches that were tried elsewhere, b) local innovative ideas and c) building on functions perceived as strengths. Bilbao and Bremen illustrate how some of the local ideas were influenced from developments elsewhere. In Bilbao, decision-makers learnt from key regeneration programs in other Spanish cities since the late 1980s (González 2006, 842), particularly those associated with three major events during the 'Spanish year' of 1992, when Barcelona hosted the Summer Olympics, Seville the World Expo and Madrid became the European Capital of Culture. In other respects, local planners and decision-makers gathered ideas about how to regenerate the riverfront by visiting early waterfront redevelopments in Baltimore and Glasgow.

In Bremen, the recognition of the need for ongoing economic restructuring during the 1980s was combined with the belief that future economic success depended on high technology and knowledge-based innovation sectors. The growth of Silicon Valley and its link to higher education institutions gave rise to ideas for strengthening the technology and natural sciences profile of the University of Bremen and linking it with new high-tech sectors.[4] The creation of a technology-based business park on land surrounding the university physically reflects this approach (Fig. 7). The *Economic Policy Action Program* initiated in the mid 1980s and the *Special Investment Program* throughout the 1990s provided significant support for these objectives. The latter was made possible through substantial financial aid (2.6 billion Euros) from the federal government to avoid its bankruptcy (Prognos 2002, 23). The political decision-makers managed to convince the supervising bodies to invest a portion of these resources to support economic restructuring and urban regeneration rather than using it entirely for debt repayment.

Leaders in several cities used the work of scholars on urban or regional development to inform their policy approaches. In Leipzig, economic development policy focused on the identification of viable clusters with the work of economist Michael Porter being a main source of inspiration. Richard Florida's ideas about the importance of the so-called "creative class" and the three T's (talent, technology, tolerance) for attracting them was picked up eagerly in many cities (Florida 2002). Saint Etienne for example supports a

---

4 In Germany, educational policy is determined at the state-level. Being a city-state, Bremen is thus able to design its own higher education strategy.

local gay pride parade and focuses on its fashion design sectors. Manuel Castell's idea of "nodes" and "networks" in a globalized world informed the strategic vision of Bilbao to become a major regional hub (Del Cerro 2007). In Belfast, renowned academics and policy-advisors like Michael Parkinson have repeatedly been involved in producing strategy papers outlining future urban development (see Belfast City Council 2004).

Fig. 7: Technology Park Bremen, adjacent to university

(Source: Photo: J. Plöger)

New governance constellations

Since the 1990s, the urban public sector underwent a process of restructuring in many countries. This can be understood as a direct consequence of trying to be more competitive in a context of globalization and the need to adapt to rapid change. Neo-liberal policy approaches introducing market principles to formerly state-controlled sectors and the downsizing of state functions were widely applied (Heinz 2008, 45). In Germany, older industrial cities are chronically under-financed and have amassed huge debts (Holtkamp 2011, 16). Forced to balance their budgets and to reduce debts they responded by privatizing city services (e.g. utility companies) or even leasing them to foreign corporations, selling city-owned land, buildings and infrastructure and reducing the number of public employees.

Partnerships between the public and the private sectors became more common, with an early example being urban development corporations in Sheffield and Belfast. A further step was the formation of publicly owned agencies operating as private companies to carry out defined tasks such as economic or project development. Although they are essentially public sector bodies, they operate at arm's length from the core government.

An interesting example representing this new project-based approach in urban regeneration is Bilbao Ría 2000. This not-for-profit public-public partnership was set up in 1992 by the local, provincial, regional and national government to act as a project developer for major redevelopment sites formerly in harbor, railway or industrial use in the Bilbao area. Decision-making in Bilbao is located at different administrative levels; e.g. urban planning by the local government, fiscal power by provincial government and ownership of the land often by central government authorities. For political reasons, the Basque and national government entities each hold half of the shares. The public landowners contributed land to the company's portfolio; in return they were compensated with development permissions or modernized infrastructures elsewhere. After taking control of the land, Bilbao Ría 2000 carried out redevelopment activities in designated 'opportunity zones', the best known of these being Abandoibarra on the riverfront, now famous for the landmark Guggenheim Museum (e.g. Plaza 2007). Bilbao Ria 2000 plans the sites and changes the designated land-uses with the intention of increasing the land value before the land is sold to developers, with profits re-invested in further urban regeneration. This self-financing mechanism is considered highly significant for its success. The agency has de facto become the major planning and regeneration body in Bilbao, which has been criticized due to its semi-public and non-participative set-up (Rodríguez et al. 2001).

Neighborhood renewal

In European cities, two main types of disadvantaged neighborhoods can be distinguished. Firstly, traditional working-class neighborhoods in inner-city locations which were most affected by the consequences of industrial decline. They are often characterized by a low share of people in secure employment, lack of amenities, physical decay, housing vacancies, concentrated deprivation, a bad image, out-migration of remaining middle-class house-

Fig. 8: Patchwork of refurbished and derelict housing stock in Leipzig
(Source: Photo: J. Plöger)

holds, and lastly fragile community relations between long-term residents and—mostly migrant—newcomers. Examples include Gröpelingen in Bremen, East Leipzig, North Belfast or the left-bank urban communities in the Bilbao metropolitan area.

The second type comprises large mass-housing estates built between the late 1960s and early 1980s. Tenever in Bremen, Grünau in Leipzig or Otxarkoaga in Bilbao fall into this category. The socio-economic structure of these estates has shifted towards a concentration of disadvantaged groups. Their often unfavorable locations on the urban periphery may result in inadequate connections to the public transport system. As a response to various problems and increasing vacancies, their size has often been reduced through partial demolition.

In Europe, cities have been heavily reliant on public funding streams. Different layers of government (i.e. EU, national, regional and local) offered funding for neighborhood renewal approaches, enabling a long-term commitment to certain areas and preventing further neighborhood decay.

Several of the studied cities (e.g. Bilbao, Bremen, Leipzig) have implemented monitoring systems on social, economic, demographic, and housing data. Monitoring has become an important tool to measure local development, plan resource allocation and design specific area-based approaches.

In Bremen the main rationale behind supporting disadvantaged neighborhoods is social cohesion. Bremen's approach for neighborhood renewal entailed the identification of the most deprived areas and the allocation of available resources including through the federal and regional government program *Soziale Stadt* as well as its very own program *Wohnen in Nachbarschaften*. Apart from investments in physical infrastructure and the built environment this program also supports events, courses and neighborhood management.

Due to a particularly great population decline in the 1990s, the main objective in Leipzig was to attract and retain residents and to stabilize the housing market. Interventions focused on the renewal of the existing housing stock and the creation of new housing options. Considering the lack of examples to draw from, the city designed several innovative instruments and projects, including the promotion of inner-city town-houses to offer attractive housing options for middle-class families; a refurbishment incentive providing tenants with financial assistance for semi-derelict buildings in order to stop the decline of the housing stock; a self-user program advising owner groups to consolidate the older housing stock; vacant 'guardian houses' as symbolic interventions offered rent-free to creative groups such as artists and students in order to stabilize neighborhoods or the interim use of vacant sites (after demolition of derelict buildings) as public space in order to temporarily increase the quality of life in certain areas (Power et al. 2010, 119).

Confronting the skills mismatch

In some cities the industries that declined have not completely disappeared. Many companies—sometimes with public-sector support—managed to adapt older skills to more advanced types of manufacturing. In Saint Etienne a specialist optic lenses cluster has emerged on the site of the former arms factory. It is built on the earlier experience in arms manufacturing, particularly the precision engineering used for the production of gun lenses. In Sheffield, health-related engineering (e.g. laser technologies) uses former expertise in stainless steel, knife making and metal processing technologies. In Bremen the offshore wind energy sector uses former shipyards.

Ultimately, new jobs in the service economy or the advanced manufacturing sector require a skill-set different from that required in previous manufacturing jobs. The inability of some of the unemployed to gain access to new jobs is attributed to this skills mismatch. In most of these cities this was considered a major problem (Plöger and Weck 2013). On the one hand, city leaders became worried about working-class populations increasingly losing access to the labor market. Improving skills was thus regarded as a way of strengthening the most affected communities (Power et al. 2010, 99–102). On the other hand, these cities needed a qualified workforce as a key asset in order to attract potential investors. As a result they implemented several skills initiatives and programs, often supported by different tiers of government. The individual design, objectives and target groups of these programs varied between the cities. Their tasks include training, information about job opportunities, recruitment or supporting self-employment.

Resurgent cities

Most of the cities studied here show signs of recovery. Their recovery, although still relatively fragile and sometimes modest, nevertheless marks a trend reversal. Even so we can identify varying levels of resurgence.

This recovery is reflected in the most common statistical indicators such as population growth or unemployment rates (Fig. 9 and 10). Apart from Saint Etienne and Belfast, which continued to lose population, the other cities showed at least modest population growth since 2000. Unemployment rates dropped from their high 1990 levels in most cities. Torino, Bilbao and the two UK cities even saw their unemployment rates cut by more than half. In Bremen and Saint Etienne unemployment remained relatively stable and only Leipzig experienced an extreme increase, which is explained by the rapid transformation after German Reunification. Most of these cities—once characterized by severe social problems—now even show unemployment rates below their respective national average.

An in-depth analysis of both quantitative and qualitative data indicates that these cities have reached different stages of recovery (Power et al. 2010, 287–288) as illustrated by assessing a set of 14 quantitative indicators including

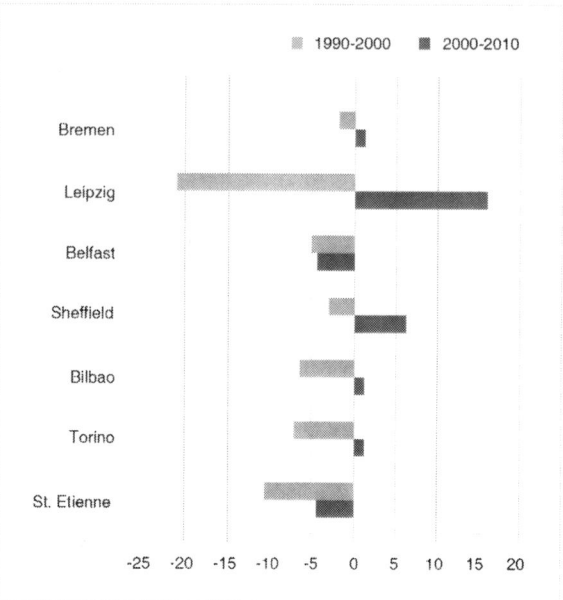

Fig. 9: Population change, 1990–2010 (in %)

(Sources: Official data from national, regional and city statistics offices)

population change, unemployment, qualification levels of residents, employment, GDP, and sprawl for the period between 1990 and 2008. According to this analysis, Bilbao shows the greatest progress, while Bremen, Sheffield and Torino also performed relatively well. Yet Leipzig, Belfast and Saint Etienne have not been able to recover to the same extent and still confront major challenges (ibid., 280).

As statistical information may disguise specific development patterns and comparisons between countries are problematic due to data inconsistencies, this analysis was supported with qualitative information on several themes (ibid., 282–286), including the evaluation of projects, approaches and other interventions whose outcomes may be difficult to measure in quantitative terms. This information is based on personal observations during fieldwork, the analysis of policy-documents, a literature review and interviews with key experts and policy-makers. Strikingly, this analysis results in a slightly different ranking. Bremen scores highest, followed by Leipzig and Torino; Sheffield, Belfast and Bilbao follow albeit with some distance, while Saint Etienne trails behind (ibid., 285).

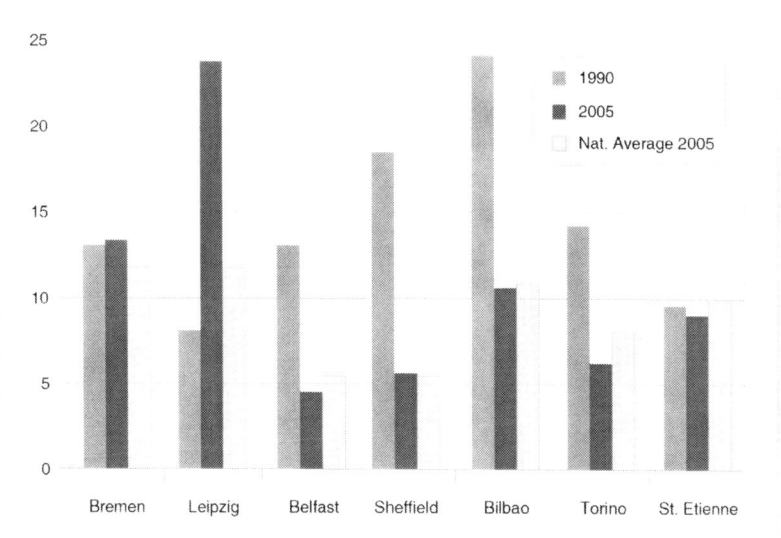

Fig. 10: Unemployment rates, 1990–2005 (in %)

(Sources: Official data from national, regional and city statistics offices)

Conclusion—At a crossroads: Further recovery or ongoing struggle?

Industrial cities have been reliant on external funding (e.g. regional, national, EU) during their transformation process. Notably, all cities produced urban strategies during their recovery path, which then served as guidelines for future actions. The main policy objectives however varied between cities, which is reflected in their focus on specific issues. This may include prioritizing the attraction of companies and inward investment, focusing on retaining and attracting high-skilled groups, reacting to shrinkage and its associated problems, or improving community and social cohesion.

Economic restructuring is an ongoing process in all cities, affecting industrial and other sectors failing to remain competitive. Economic development policies have however focused on creating a more resilient economic base built around innovative and knowledge-intensive sectors. As the German example shows, the industrial sector can continue to be an important economic driver when constantly adapted to new requirements. Some successful examples indicate that former functions can inform future options by building on traditional strengths.

Shaping individual recovery actions, these cities generally follow a rationale of urban competition, increasingly focusing not only on investors and companies but also on the highly skilled. Throughout the most recent financial crisis, those cities continue to address social inequalities and disadvantaged neighborhoods, often using innovative approaches. The overall effect of prestigious urban regeneration projects is less evident however. Only a few apparent examples stand out, while others may eventually not justify their high development and maintenance costs.

In terms of regional and local governance several shifts can be observed. Regional cooperation is increasing so as to create a more sustainable allocation of resources. Political leadership and the formation of new actor constellations can also play a role in shaping policy reorientations. Lastly, more democratic and accountable forms of decision-making along with a stronger involvement of civic society have gained importance.

Whilst the situation in these cities has improved considerably, many structural problems such as less competitive economic sectors or a prevalence of vulnerable social groups remain. In addition, new challenges have arisen that are potentially detrimental to the progress achieved so far (Kunzmann 2010, 603). One example is the deteriorating budgetary crisis of many municipal governments in Germany, with struggling, older-industrial cities being particularly affected by high debt levels and austerity measures—thus further restricting their ability to actively confront urban decline (Holtkamp 2010, 18). These industrial cities have however gained substantial experience in dealing with decline, providing them with valuable knowledge regarding crisis-intervention and at least some level of resilience.

Works Cited

Amin, A. (1994). Post-Fordism: models, fantasies and phantoms of transition. In: A. Amin (ed.). *Post-Fordism. A reader*. Cambridge, Mass.: Blackwell.

Belfast City Council (2004). *Belfast: State of the City. Conference Report*. Belfast City Council.

Booth, P. (2005). Partnerships and networks: the governance of urban regeneration in Britain. *Journal of Housing and the Built Environment*, 20 (3), 257–269.

City of Leipzig, Dept. of Urban Development (ed.). (2006). *Monitoringbericht 2006—kleinräumiges Monitoring des Stadtumbaus in Leipzig*. Stadt Leipzig.

Clark, G., M. Feldman, and M. Gertler (2000). *The Oxford Handbook of Economic Geography*. Oxford: Oxford Univ. Press.

Del Cerro Santamaría, G. (2007). *Bilbao: Basque Pathways to Globalisation*. Oxford: Elsevier.

Daniels, P. (1993). *Service Industries in the World Economy*. Cambridge, Mass.: Blackwell.

Florida, R. (2002). *The Rise of the Creative Class: And how it's transforming work, leisure, community & everyday life*. New York: Basic Books.

González, S. (2005). Scalar Narratives in Bilbao: A Cultural Politics of Scales Approach to the Study of Urban Policy. *International Journal of Urban and Regional Research*, 30 (4), 836–857.

Heinz, W. (2008). *Der große Umbruch—Deutsche Städte und Globalisierung*. Berlin: Difu.

Herfert, G., and D. Röhl (2001). Leipzig—Region zwischen Boom und Leerstand. In: K. Brake, J. Dangschat and G. Herfert (eds.). *Suburbanisierung in Deutschland—aktuelle Tendenzen*, Opladen: Leske & Budrich.

Hohenberg, P., and L. Hollen Lees (1985). *The Making of Urban Europe, 1000–1950*. Cambridge, Mass.: Harvard Univ. Press.

Holtkamp, L. (2010). Kommunale Haushaltspolitik bei leeren Kassen. *Aus Politik und Zeitgeschichte*, 7/8, 13–19.

Jungfer, K. (2005). *Die Stadt in der Krise—Ein Manifest für starke Kommunen*. Bonn: Bundeszentrale für politische Bildung.

Kunzmann, K. (2010). After the global economic crisis: policy implications for the future of the European territory. *Informationen zur Raumentwicklung*, 8, 601–612.

Murtagh, B. (2002). *The politics of territory—policy and segregation in Northern Ireland*. Houndsmill: Palgrave.

Nuissl, H., and D. Rink (2005). The 'production' of urban sprawl in Eastern Germany as a phenomenon of post-socialist transformation. *Cities*, 22 (2), 123–124.

Oswalt, P. (ed.). (2005). *Shrinking cities, Vol. 1, International research*, Ostfildern-Ruit: Hatje Crantz.

Paddison, R. (ed.). (2001). *Handbook of Urban Studies*. London: Sage.

Pinson, G. (2002). Political government and governance: strategic planning and the reshaping of political capacity in Turin. *International Journal of Urban and Regional Research*, 26 (3), 477–493.

Plaza, B. (2007). The return on investment of the Guggenheim Museum in Bilbao. *International Journal of Urban and Regional Research*, 30 (2), 452–467.

Plöger, J., and S. Weck (2013). Confronting Out-Migration and the Skills Gap in Declining German Cities. *European Planning Studies* (forthcoming).

Plöger, J., and I. Kohlhaas-Weber (2013). Shock-proof cities? The impact of and responses to the recent financial and economic crisis in older industrial cities. *Journal of Urban Regeneration & Renewal* (forthcoming).

Power, A., J. Plöger, and A. Winkler (2008). *Transforming cities across Europe—an interim report on problems and progress.* CASE Report 49. London: LSE.

Power, A., J. Plöger, and A. Winkler (2010). *Phoenix Cities—the fall and rise of great industrial cities.* Bristol: Policy Press.

Prognos (2002). *Wirkungsanalyse des Investitionssonderprogramms (ISP) des Landes Bremen.* Evaluierungsgutachten, Bremen.

Roberts, G., and P. Steadman (1999). *American Cities & Technology—Wilderness to wired city.* London: Routledge.

Rodríguez, A., E. Martínez, and G. Guenaga (2001). Uneven Redevelopment—New Urban Policies and Socio-Spatial Fragmentation in Metropolitan Bilbao. *European Urban and Regional Studies*, 8 (2), 161–178.

Turok, I., and V. Mykhnenko (2007). The trajectories of European cities, 1960–2005. *Cities*, 24 (3), 165–182.

Warsewa, G. (2006). *The transformation of European Port Cities—Final report on the new EPOC Port City Audit.* IAW Research Report, 11.

Part III
Cultural and Sociological Concepts

Fordist Elements of the Industrial City in Germany and the United States

Adelheid von Saldern

To be sure, a Fordist industrial city has always been a social construction, an imaginary picture and a utopian vision rather than a fixed reality. Apart from some elements that were realized in a linear way, no linearly planned industrial city has (ever) been realized, neither in Germany nor in the US. A Fordist industrial city was a model built after the model of assembly lines by referring in particular to Henry Ford's well-known automobile factories in and around Detroit that had introduced assembly lines in 1913. As known, assembly lines signified the division of labor in piece-meal activities determined by the conveyor belt's speed in order to achieve high efficiency in time, space and with respect to human labor, a maximum of output n production and profit due to mass production and relative high wages in order to generate mass consumption.

American city planners and architects did not use the term *Fordist (industrial) city*. Instead, they preferred the more general term *functionalism* (Hård and Misa 2008).[1] To be sure, these terms as well as the term Taylorism[2] were not synonyms for Fordism, but they expressed the same goal: to achieve an optimum of efficiency. In the following paper, I firstly describe the plans of industrial city that ironically contrasted Henry Ford's own ideas regarding the spatial order of industry. Furthermore, I consider the question which elements of functionalism and of Fordist industrial city plans were implemented in the US and in Germany and how workers' private lives were affected from these transformations. The last part of the paper addresses the international retrospective views on "Fordist cities" in the decades after 1945.

---

1 In combination with the term *European modernism*, the term *functionalism* dominates the American secondary literature.

2 Taylorism addressed a maximum of efficiency of labor independent of machines. As an overview on industrial cities: Heßler and Zimmermann (2011).

The European Model of a Fordist Industrial City

Two models in particular influenced city planning during the 20th century, the garden city and the functionalist city. The two concepts shared some overlapping features, especially in the way they rejected the existing cities. The latter were perceived as disarranged, wasteful, and damaged by allegedly dangerous masses. Nevertheless, the two concepts were widely interpreted as two disparate alternatives.[3] The British garden city-model by Ebenezer Howard (Howard 1898, 1902) focused on a nature-bound and co-operative urban culture and zoned communities. The zones were conceptualized as concentric circles around a civic center. The model also integrated some smaller scale industry in separated zones at the edges of the city, but did not address large industrial estates.

The second model was the functionalist city that was more committed to achieving a maximum of efficiency, functionality and rationalization, but the special type of a Fordist industrial city was more: it was characterized by an overall plan of spatial order in the fashion of a linear city (*Bandstadt*), as developed in Europe in the late 1920s. The Fordist linear industrial city radicalized the general principles of a functionalist city insofar as it created an entire new spatial order that abolished concentric city models (*Auflösung der Städte*) in favor of lines running in parallel similar to the assembly lines on the factory floor.

One of the greatest European promoters of a Fordist linear industrial city was Le Corbusier.[4] In 1929, when he travelled to Moscow he was influenced by the Russian anti-urbanists and by N.A. Miljutin who had conceptualized the linear city Sozgorod by 1930 (Fehl and Rodriguez-Lores 1997, 156). In 1930, the Bauhaus-founder Walter Gropius wanted to build a city exactly like a modern plant, a city without a social and cultural center (*Stadtkrone*), with separated lines (*getrennte Spuren*) and cul-de-sacs (*Stichstraßen*) analogous to the linkages between the assembly lines in factories (*Förderbänder*)

---

3 To be sure, there were also some other models of an industrial city. The best known stems from Tony Garnier. However, this model was not committed to functionalism and Fordism, and instead was conceptualized as a "Mediterranean socialist arcadia" with a Greek agora (Frampton 1986, 10). Another early example was Madrid. When this city expanded in 1882, city planner Arturo Soria y Mata materialized the principle of linearity to some extent.

4 Le Corbusier was a Swiss architect who lived in France. His widespread influence in Europe pushed national boundaries. This is the reason why I take him into account in this article.

(Fehl 1990, 64.) The highly valued Berlin city-planner Martin Wagner also had the vision of „creating new towns corresponding to a perfect machine" (quoted after Fehl 1990, 65; Scarpa 1986, 10–11).

As already mentioned, the essence of the various Fordist concepts of an industrial city was linearity.[5] Apart from linearity, this model had other features that corresponded with the general type of functionalist cities: Firstly, Fordist industrial cities were to be located in a decentralized spatial order of the region. The difference between town and hinterland was to be eliminated. Secondly this city type was to have a decentralized structure without any civic and cultural center (*Stadtkrone*). Thirdly, corresponding with the assembly lines in factories (*Förderbänder*), industrial plants and residential areas were to be located along parallel running lines (*getrennte Spuren*) cut by a greenbelt. Le Corbusier correspondingly created the slogans "green factory" and "vertical garden city". Cul-de-sacs (*Stichstraßen*) ensured that the distances between the lines, i.e. between home and workplace, were short. Fourthly, resembling the special function of each assembly line on the factory floor the linear industrial city featured lines exclusively serving traffic, partly railways, partly motorways. Fifthly, the plans also integrated recreational areas, opportunities for compensating the intensified labor and precondition for the maintenance of the workers' health. As the concept of a linear industrial city foresaw similar living conditions for all people, the distances from homes to recreational space and countryside were to be equalized.

The American Model of a Decentralized Industrial City

The American model of industrial cities, however, did not correspond with the European Fordist model of a linear industrial city, although the "general disorder and vileness" of many factory districts and the "desolateness of the common American industrial town" (Mumford 1922, 12) were vehemently criticized on both sides of the Atlantic and transatlantic circles of experts equally propagated decentralization. However, American city planners, such as the social philosopher and regional planner Lewis Mumford, held the gar-

---

5 There were more than a hundred variations of Fordist linear industrial cities. The architect Ludwig Hilberseimer developed a special kind of the linear city in 1927. He subdivided the linearity into settlement units of 4,000–10,000 inhabitants in the way that the linear development looked like a pearl necklace (Fehl and Rodriguez-Lores 1997, 38).

den city-founder Ebenezer Howard as well as the Scottish city and regional planner Patrick Geddes in much higher esteem than the Fordist city planners and architects. In this cultural context, he together with other American regional and urban reformers, including Henry Wright and Clarence Stein, founded the *Regional Planning Association of America* in 1923 that became the leading think tank in this field.

According to these Americans, decentralization stood for the creation of new regional communities in the hinterland with complete infrastructure, each one designed for 10,000 to 50,000 people divided by zoning and surrounded by open agricultural land. This idea was interpreted as the nucleus of a new polycentric structured country based on "natural conditions" that was thought to overcome the allegedly mechanized cosmopolitanism of big cities with their bulk of seemingly dangerous masses (Boyer 1983, 191, 193; Grandin 2009, 66–67). Instead, a new type of family was to develop with an income based on both, subsistence farming and wage labor.

Subsistence farming, also favored by architect Frank Lloyd Wright, however, did not meet with Le Corbusier's approval, because he preferred farmers and industrial workers to live side by side (Fehl and Rodriguez-Lores 1997, 162–163, 173, 175). The dissonances with Le Corbusier were even greater with regard to the principle of linearity, which did not become an element of the American city planners' concepts.

The greatest difference between the camps on both sides of the Atlantic concerned the idea of how people's homes were to be designed. In contrast to Le Corbusier and Gropius, the well-known architect Frank Lloyd Wright rejected the radical, machine-oriented formalism and functionalism of European Fordists. Instead, he favored well-grounded projects (*Bodenhaftung*) and took into account *natural* resources. Fearing the urban "mob", Wright increasingly followed the traces of a *romantic modernism* (Gartman 2009, 174–175). Thus he wanted to build "mass-produced homes" that would not resemble the "look of factory standardization" (ibid., 177). Wright's opinion was not an isolated one. In general, American architects considered the functions of a home to be completely different from those of a machine or a steam-ship. Radical functionalism seemingly did not match American individualism. Frank Lloyd Wright called his concept both an "organic modernity" and a genuine "American modernity" in the age of the machine (Tichi 1967, 17–18). The so-called Prairie-Style, fostered by him and some other architects and marked "by flowing lines, open space, and a functionalist absence of fussiness" (Green 2010, 56), was interpreted as "organic modern style" consciously developed as counterpart to European radical functional-ism. The director of the new *Museum of Modern Art*, Alfred H. Barr Jr., a great admirer of the Bauhaus, stated as early as 1932, that in general Ameri-can architects only slowly began to accept radical functionalism and its char-acteristic features of "restraint and discipline". He explained this reluctance on the part of American architects and planners by arguing that they did not want an infiltration through European architects any longer. „American nationalists will also oppose the [functionalist] Style as another European invasion" (Hitchcock and Johnson 1966 [1932], 13–15).

When Wright created the American "organic modern style" he inte-grated some elements of a linear city in his low-density model *Broadacre City* (1932)[6] designated for 2,300 people. As a critic of condensed urbanity, Wright here followed his self-obligation to the principles of decentralization, urban-rural fusion, section-building, spacious grid system, separated high-speed traffic lines, and subsistence farming on a patch of one acre per person. He also integrated some features of a linear city profile by foreseeing not only single-family houses but also superblocks in a line of one to two kilometer length. (Fehl and Rodriguez-Lores 1997, 39). Wright's vague Broadacre con-cept that mixed garden city-elements with functionalist features expressed more the architect's passion for pragmatist-experimental planning in general terms and perspectives than an explicit plan of an industrial city of his day.

In sum, although Henry Ford's assembly lines symbolized the Fordist idea per se, in the areas of architecture and planning the American top 'ex-perts' were less inspired by functionalism and much less by Fordism than the European vanguard. Thus, Fordist ideas in architecture and city planning were predominantly a European concern.

Divergence between Concepts and Realities in the United States

Zoning was the most widespread impact of functionalism on actual US-city planning during the 1920s. Zoning created not only new structures within suburbanization combined with class and racial segregation, but also the

---

6 Wright developed this model as a result of his book *The Disappearing City* in 1932, repub-lished under the title *The Living City* in 1958.

separation of factories from the residential districts similar to the European understanding of zoning. Although zoning corresponded with the idea of functionalism, it did not generate a Fordist linear industrial city.[7] To be sure, the older settlements of the mid 19th century constructed along the new US-railroad system had been built in just this way, but later on they were no longer models for the development of new industrial agglomerations. Not surprisingly, many industrial cities, such as Detroit, suffered from uncontrolled growth, as the 1920/21 edition of the Detroit city directory shows:

"There are no well-defined factory districts, such as are found in most cities. Instead the plants are to be found in every section. The rapid increase in population since 1910 has caused the city to spread out, so the many large plants, which only a few years ago were located far outside the city limits now are found in the center of some otherwise pleasant residence district or even far downtown in the neighborhood of office buildings, shops and theatres" (Zunz 1982, 308).

Thus, Henry Ford's Detroit became a "metropolitan community" with multiple industrial nuclei across the city. Henry Ford rejected this mixture of industrial and residential areas in 'his' city. Refusing urban life for ordinary people and fearing allegedly dangerous urban masses, Ford favored the idea of decentralization as did Lewis Mumford and other regional planners of the time. As a consequence, Ford developed a village industry concept. Thus, an impressive suburbanization process of Fords' plants took place, especially in the twenties, and Ford's workers also suburbanized from Detroit to Highland Park, Hamtrack, Greenfield Village (near Ford's River Rouge plant) and Dearborn to live closer to, but separated from the factories. Moreover, Ford radicalized his concept of decentralization by outsourcing parts of his car production. As a result, there were nineteen "villages" erected solely within the vicinity of his River Rouge complex (Grandin 2009, 58, 65, 74–75).

Decentralization and zoning were also the main characteristic of other company towns.[8] The totally planned and fully equipped Pullman town, already built in the 1880s near Chicago, had an attractive community center with Victorian architecture, moreover a wide boulevard that separated the factory from the community, long rows of two story brick homes in quiet

---

7 In Prussia zoning was already introduced in the 1880s.
8 At their peak about 2.500 company towns were counted. By 1930 more than two million people lived in such towns. The settlements were often characterized by detrimental living conditions for the new European immigrants (Handlin 1951, 168–169).

streets and barrack tenements at the edge of the town.[9] After the City of Chicago had incorporated Pullman in 1889, Pullman, however, developed as an "ordinary industrial community" in the following years. In 1910, the original residents "were almost completely replaced by newcomers seeking the cheaper rents of Pullman" (Buder 1967, 215 and 222). Therefore Pullman lost its profile as a company town in its own right.

As Pullman town displayed scarce signatures of functionalism-Fordism, the Company town Gary, founded in 1906 by the United Steel Corporation, had more resemblance with functionalist-Fordist ideas, especially in the 1920s when the company modernized and enhanced Gary's infrastructure. It even became the blue print for the linear industrial city Magnitogorsk in the Soviet Union (Hård and Misa 2008, 17). In Gary, functionalist-Fordist elements were the zoned separation of industrial from residential areas, the standardized and uniformed mass production of homes for the white (skilled) workers and the grid-pattern of the city plan, although the grid system was, as known, much older than functionalism/Fordism (Green 2010). Similar to Gary, the "Motor-City" Flint in Michigan, founded in 1908 by General Motors, also had settlements that resembled functionalist-Fordist ideas, but the core idea of a Fordist industrial city, namely linearity, was abandoned. Even the separation of plants from settlements was not satisfying, because the settlements, occupied by many black migrants from the South, were originally very close to the factories. It was only after WWII that General Motors relocated their factories to the environs of the city (Volkmann and Walther 2012, 30–31, 34).

Looking at the South, the "standard layout of the vernacular textile mill village" comes to mind. This kind of settlement was characterized by evidently older and patriarchal features than functionalist-Fordist. The plants were often located in the center of the settlements, the overseers' house was strategically placed in order to control the workers' residential areas; the church and the school as well as the company drugstore surrounded the mill; houses for the blacks were set aside (Crawford 1995, 187).

In sum, although company towns had some functionalist-Fordist elements, conceptual linkages to functionalism and Fordist urban planning were not expressed. Instead, these components were embedded within older traditions and regulations such as the grid pattern and the patriarchal order,

---

9 African Americans were housed in segregated slum areas, and Mexicans did not live in much better circumstances.

the latter especially in the Southern textile mill villages. In other cases, these elements were already part of common trends, above all the decentralization of industries and the separation of factories from residential areas through zoning and green belts. Or they were embedded due to market processes such as the pre-fabrication of the workers' houses.[10] In sum, "functionalist urban planning in the 1920s and 1930s did not resonate in the United States" (Hård and Misa 2008, 16). Correspondingly, Le Corbusier labeled the USA as "the land of the timid" when he visited the country in 1935 (Hård and Misa 2008, 17).

The rejection of European functionalism and Fordism by American regional planners also characterized the activities of American industrial architects, such as those of the well-known Albert Kahn. To be sure, Kahn strongly supported modern construction of plants, e.g. when he drafted Ford's plant River Rouge. However, he often tended to hide it behind traditional decorations and historical styles. Although designated as *romantic modernism,* this kind of American aesthetic "retained the mechanical connotations of speed and efficiency" (Gartmann 2008, 123). Unified "by antiurban references and an obsession with reuniting people with nature", vernacular architectures corresponded with different regional traditions (ibid.). *Romantic modernism* of the 1920s as well as the streamlined designs of the New Deal period conveyed the "wishful dominion of humanity over the mass-produced machine by covering over inhuman fragmentation with the soft, organic look of the human body" (ibid., 163). In company towns, especially in Henry Ford's factory districts, this American mainstream architecture characterized the workers' settlements. Here, the endless rows of pre-fabricated and widely standardized bungalows for blue-collar homeowners did not always look simple, but partly featured a "picturesque artistic design" (Crawford 1995, 206). Henry Ford evidently supported the widespread American belief that visible functionalism and Fordism in architecture destroyed the inhabitants' need of cozy, romantic, and decorative homes.[11]

---

10 The model city Radburn built in the 1920s was not an industrial city, nevertheless its profile followed the idea of functional separated zones, one for foot-traffic, the other for wheeled traffic. Free from through roads the residential areas were conceptualized as self-sufficient neighborhood-units corresponding to the idea of Clarence Arthur Perry who had developed the *Regional Plan for New York and Environs* (1929) (Mumford 1938, 490).

11 There were, however some exceptions. In the workers' neighborhood Ambridge Mann in Gary, the architecture consisted of many houses not only in Prairie Style but also in Art Deco. In Downtown Gary, developed in the early 20th century, even Frank Lloyd Wright designed some buildings.

Divergences between Concepts and Realities in Germany

In Germany, during the 19th century factories were usually integrated into the already existing cities. When big companies such as Siemens in Berlin wanted to expand, they often moved to the fringe of the city. In the case of Siemens, new settlements were built close to the factory, but separated from it. The company's architect Hans C. Hertlein built two settlements for the employees (Siemensstadt, 1928–1935 and Siedlung Heimat, 1930–1935), both in a traditional architectural style, called German style (*Deutscher Baustil*). In contrast to these two settlements, the housing settlement Großsiedlung Siemensstadt (1929–1931) was carried out by a non-profit company in cooperation with the municipal administration and some modern architects, such as Walter Gropius, Hugo Häring, Fred Forbat, Hans B. Scharoun and Otto Bartning. Siemensstadt corresponded with the principles of zoning as green belts were inserted between the rows of houses (*Zeilenbau*). Although the concept departed from the model of a Fordist linear industrial city, the settlement—providing three- or four-storied houses for more than 1,300 households—featured a modern structure and design with flat roofs in contrast to most of the settlement houses in American company towns. In some ways, the Siemensstadt was, however, an exception, because at that time, the well-known modern settlements usually were located at the fringes of already existing cities, e.g. in Frankfurt/Main, rather than close to industrial plants. Although these reform settlements corresponded more or less with the principles of functionalism, they had nothing in common with a Fordist linear industrial city.

The industrial city foundations of Salzgitter and Wolfsburg during the NS-period were laid partly in the green countryside, partly as an amalgamation of already existing villages. The war-oriented foundation of the "city of the Hermann-Göring-Werke" Salzgitter with its coalmine and steel plants was committed to the new concept of a scattered and green city (Durth 1997, 39; Benz 1992). As far as parts of the city were newly planned, an East-West axis dominated with a monumental NS-building on one end and the administration buildings of the city and the Hermann-Göring-Werke on the other. The plan respected the division of functions (*Funktionstrennung*), and the housing settlements, subdivided in easily controlled neighborhoods, were built in the conservative *Heimatstil* and took up diverse elements of the garden city-model (Fritzsche 1992, 238–242). In contrast to the principles of a Fordist linear industrial city, the Nazis followed the idea of building a city with an inner center that corresponded with the specific NS-idea of socially controlled urbanity and expansive party representation.

To be sure, at first glance, Wolfsburg really looked like a Fordist linear industrial city because the plant featured a conspicuously long linear front similar to Ford's half-a-mile long factory River Rouge in Dearborn. Moreover, the VW-plant ran parallel to the Mittelland-Canal and to the railroad tracks and it was located apart from the city-agglomeration and separated from the various residential areas. However, it differed from the model of a Fordist linear industrial city insofar as the housing settlements were not located in lines parallel to the factory building, the Canal and the railroad tracks. Instead, the diverse plans followed more or less the idea of erecting a scattered city with polycentric housing settlements and an administrative and cultural center as well as a broad boulevard and a NS-temple hall. However, neither the boulevard nor the temple hall project have actually been built. Instead, city planning halted during World War II except for the erection of barracks for forced labor and KZ-prisoners.

Only the Soviet Union created more or less Fordist linear industrial cities. This was a result of the singular combination of a dictatorship and its total will of industrialization based on heavy industry as well as on motorization (Siegelbaum 2011) and limitless disposal of land that provided the opportunities for new Fordist city foundations, although gaps between plans and realities could not be avoided, especially in the era of infrastructure and air pollution. Ironically, only the communist countries adopted the principles of capitalist Fordism in city planning. City planners such as Ernst May were given an opportunity only in the Soviet Union and not in Germany to carry out the erection of some linear industrial cities such as Magnitogorsk, Volgograd and Sotsgorad. Ernst May was not the only one of Western experts in the Soviet Union. At the end of the first Five-Year-Plan (1928–1933), around 35,000 engineers, architects and city planners from the West lived temporarily in the Soviet Union to shape the new industrialization of this huge country (Jaješniak-Quast 2008, 201), However, as early as in 1932, one year before the second Five Year Plan, party leaders damned modern functionalism and interpreted it as Western cosmopolitanism (Altrock et al. 2003). Consequently, by the mid 1930s, the Soviet Union changed their principles of Fordist city planning and promoted "socialist realism" with architectural replicas from the past.

Recreation and *Social Engineering*: Fordist Models of Family Life and Housing

The scientific insight into the intimate dependence between good labor, good recreation and good housing influenced industrial welfare programs, especially in American company towns. The companies believed that a rationalized way of workers' life at home was one of the preconditions for worker's best recreation. Accordingly Ford proclaimed "[…] a man who is living right will do his work right" (quoted after Gartman 2009, 50). To be sure, this was all but new insofar as it was also an integral element of older paternalism, carried out not only in Pullman town,[12] but also in other company towns as well as in the vernacular textile mill villages across the American South. The German company settlements, above all those in the Ruhr district that produced coal and steel, were also characterized by a strict paternalistic order that determined the spatial pattern as well as social life. Although such a configuration had some effects that were similar to Fordism, e.g. disciplined workers' behavior, they belonged to a pre-Fordist understanding of "human capital". Thus, at the turn of the 20th century paternalism was seen as un-American. Although the Fordist *social engineering* concepts (Etzemüller 2009) kept some paternalist elements, as e.g. surveillance, a sample of new features led to an alteration. While paternalism 'only' promoted a decent life for workers, *social engineering* also integrated aspects of modernity into their uplifting program that was conveyed less by direct methods of disciplining than by media messages, e.g. through magazines, advertisement and movie stories as well as by professional advice from scientific 'experts'. The reformers wanted to transfer a growing mass society to an overall system of order that placed everybody along the line of his or her functions for society. While industrial workers had to adapt to the factory order during their workdays, they were free citizens after they left the factory gates in the evening. This was seemingly regarded as a potential danger for public order as well as for the necessary recreation of industrial workers. Because the entrepreneurs knew that the permanently increasing intensification of labor required intensified recreation, they often supported the rise of modern sports and the installment of useful sport and leisure facilities.

Henry Ford, the very personification of Fordism, was an example of demonstrating such a mixed type of paternalism and modernism. He employed

---

12 Pullman's idea of order and morals excluded any alcohol consumption in the town.

many new immigrants from South and Eastern Europe (Sugrue 1996, 25), who were seemingly educable and willing to assimilate. In his view, good wages were a precondition for achieving the demanded family and gender order. He did not want his workers' wives to seek any outside-employments, except if temporarily in times of absolute need. Wives were considered responsible for best practices at home in favor to their husbands' recreation. Ford lent his (skilled) workers money for home ownership and in reverse expected the full acceptance of the modern norms of cleanliness, hygiene, good housekeeping, health protection, nutrition, and morals, that were checked by his Factory Inspectors (Ford 1924, 148–150; Ford 1926; Fehl 1995, 20).[13] As the Factory Inspectors' work was based on the investigations of the *Sociological Department* within the company, Ford mixed traditional practices of rigid surveillance and coercion (especially in the 1920s: Grandin 2009, 92–95) with modern scientific knowledge of workers' habitual mentalities. Presumably, such a mixture of old and new was characteristic of many American company towns if the entrepreneurs financed or credited workers' houses and so received a better opportunity to surveil and elevate workers' life-styles as 'experts', not least via the media.

Although concepts of creating a well-ordered new society with "new men" circulated among all urban social reformers in the US and in Europe, European functionalists and Fordists were more radical and deeply convinced that the renewal of societies did not begin merely with family order but with workers' dwellings. After 1925, when the Bauhaus' messages favored the „analogy [of a house] to a plant (*Analogie zur Fabrik*) (Bodenschatz 1995, 43), Fordist ideas were integrated into the architectural concepts of prefabricated houses.[14] Le Corbusier promoted the construction of houses as "living machines" (quoted after Hilpert 1978, 14). Bauhaus founder Walter Gropius who correspondingly saw himself as "housing-Ford" (*Wohn-Ford*) promoted standardized small dwelling-cells (*Wohnzellen*) for families.[15] Such cells were not only interpreted as a consequence of a lack of money for larger dwellings,

---

13 Such a linkage between efficiency in production and life-styles at home also characterized the concepts of big European companies, e.g. Siemens (Sachse 1990, 27–28).

14 Highly influenced by Fordism, the newly founded *Congrès Internationaux d'Architecture Moderne* (CIAM) propagated the erection of large housing estates in 1928/29, whereby the three or four-storied houses were to be erected in parallel rows (*Zeilenbauweise*). And in 1929, facing the huge housing misery the concept of "dwelling for the existence minimum" (*Wohnung für das Existenzminimum*) was created with usually around 40 square meters for a family with two children.

15 Gropius wanted cells with a lot of light, air and sun (Fehl 1990, 64).

but also as cultural progress[16] in order to achieve a rationalized and disciplined life-style for the inhabitants not at least by way of space and architecture (Hilpert 1978, 40; Moos 1983, 78; Saldern 1991, 168). In the European functionalists' view, Fordist house constructions also demanded certain materials, especially glass, steel and concrete, as well as certain forms, in particular non-ornamented ones, which expressed modernity, rationalization, and mass production. According to functional principles, the ground plans, transferring the city zoning system onto dwellings, allocated special functions exclusively to specific rooms, e.g. the very small kitchen only served for cooking and not for eating.

The individual was regarded as an „abstract dwelling being" (*abstraktes Wohnwesen*) (Adolf Behne, quoted after Fehl 1995, 32); people were compared with bees and their small dwellings with honey combs not only by Le Corbusier but also by Walter Gropius and the well-known city planner of Frankfurt/Main, Ernst May (Hilpert 1978, 92). Similar to labor at assembly lines, the homes were thought of as spaces where individuals could be educated in a mute way. Martin Wagner wanted to create dwellings in which „the life of the dwellers are adjusted to endurance runs (*Dauerlauf*), to ganging (*Gleichlauf*) and to the fast and cheap run (*Lauf*) of the machines" (quoted after Fehl 1990, 65; Scarpa 1986, 10–11; Thöner 2006, 158). In sum, the rules of Fordist labor at assembly lines were transferred to the private sphere (Hilpert 1978, 14).

Fordist views on technological progress and the intricate dependence between an optimal family order and optimal labor achievements also led to the Taylorization and Fordization of housekeeping. Many efforts were directed at the mechanization, rationalization and professionalization of housework. Such efforts addressed the general model of modern kitchens (and not especially the kitchens in industrial cities), reducing their size and abolishing the traditional workers' kitchen-cum-living room in Europe and in the US. Le Corbusier also wanted to place the kitchen equipment analog to the results of the motion studies, hoping that this would reduce the women's efforts of chores. He and other functionalists in Germany as well as the *home economists* in the US usually still promoted conventional gender roles, but on a technologically modernized and rationalized basis.

---

16 The executive director of CIAM, Siegfried Giedion, interpreted *New Living* also as an opportunity of distancing from bourgeois conventions (Sturm 2006).

In transatlantic comparison, most of the architects and *home economists* were more market-oriented in the US than their colleagues in Europe (Saldern 1997). The reason for this difference was firstly the greater importance of consumerism in American society and culture. Secondly, in contrast to Germany, the US did not have a remarkable subsidized housing program in the 1920s. In the 1930s, the New Deal housing program "only" relieved the housing misery of the very poor in poorly designed inner urban areas (Gartman 2009, 157). Looking at Germany, the huge subsidized housing construction program of the 1920s, addressed at the lower middle and the upper working classes, was as model for a new societal order including the "new men".

Thirdly, while American reformers were committed to the neighbor-unit plan with community centers, as successfully developed by the sociologist Clarence Arthur Perry by 1920 for general urban planning, the European modernists primarily focused on housing and the renewal of the single family-nucleus, therefore neglecting the erection of community centers within the settlements (Domhardt 2012, 114–121).[17] There certainly was an extensive fluctuation of ideas across the Atlantic (Rodgers 1998), but this does not mean that transatlantic differences were being eliminated (Hård and Stippak 2008, 123) as their preconditions, constellations, and feasibilities varied substantially.

Although *social engineering* characterized a great part of all family reforms in the private sphere, a "colonization of life-styles" from above had not be achieved either in the United States or in Europe. To be sure, they did have impacts on the customs and attitudes over a long time, especially in the areas of hygiene and homemaking. Families and individuals, however, had a number of opportunities to subvert the given norms and rules or to adapt them in their own ways, giving them their own meaning. Thus, the variety of the interiors in standardized fabricated houses of company towns demonstrated the capability of being arbitrarily appropriated by the inhabitants (Wright 1981, 189–190). Furthermore, since the 1920s, the auto-mobilization of many American workers made it possible to escape the repressive side of living in company towns. "The new mobility encouraged individual mores instead of the community ethos that formed the social basis of the company town" (Crawford 1995, 201).

---

17 In 1938, after Gropius had migrated to the US, he eventually took over the idea of planning neighborhood-units, although more theoretically than in his concrete drafts (Domhardt 2012, 117).

Functionalist-Fordist residential concepts were combined with the hope that these models of settlement houses would gradually determine how society as a whole would live in the future. Indeed, functionalist-Fordist living ideas had been conceptualized beyond Fordist industrial city models and partly even materialized in settlements remote from industries. The protagonists, however, considered functionalist-Fordist living as a precondition for perfect social order of their visions of society, including (linear) industrial cities of the future.

The "Fordist City" and its Decline in the Second Half of the 20th Century

In a retrospective view of Social Scientists, Fordism characterized the whole society between the 1950s and the 1970s,[18] characterized by mass production and mass consumption as well as institutional and interactional regulations of various aspects of society. A Fordist economy combined with so-called Fordist regimes brought about the most dynamic forces in society during this period. These basic assumptions pervaded city planning and architecture and therefore led to the establishment of the term "Fordist city" as the dominant city model in this period. The term did, however, not refer to the concept of a Fordist linear industrial city as such, although Le Corbusier already promoted it then (Le Corbusier 1945, 72–73). In Germany, a model that had already emerged during the Nazi-period (H. B. Reichow)—the so-called urban landscape (*Stadtlandschaft*) and the "structured (zoned) and scattered city" (*gegliederte and aufgelockerte Stadt*)—combined functionalist and organic features as was common in Britain and France in that period.[19]

With regards to the GDR, a special type of industrial city was developed in Eisenhüttenstadt (1953–1961: Stalinstadt) with its huge factory for iron and steel production. Here, the principles of separated functions by means of zoning were accepted and balanced with spatial vicinity of factory, settlement houses, and countryside. In contrast to the model of a Fordist linear in-

---

18 The so-called Regulationists, i.e. the *école de la regulation* in France (Michel Aglietta et al.) supplied political-economic analyses on the Fordist organization of society.

19 Committed to the NS-state, H.B. Reichow developed a linear extension of Stettin and the creation of a town-landscape (*Stadtlandschaft*) in 1940 (Fehl and Rodriguez-Lores 1997, 16).

dustrial city, the Eisenhüttenstadt-plan, drafted by architect Kurt W. Leucht, did not accept the Fordist idea of a city without any center (*Auflösung der Städte*). Thus, Leucht also rejected former plans that had propagated merely a functionalist conglomeration of the industrial plant and the settlement houses. Instead, Leucht conceptualized subdivided workers' settlements (*Wohnkomplexe*), each equipped with an infrastructure for basic needs and a separated system of footpaths. Furthermore, Eisenhüttenstadt received the profile of a "compact city" with a big square as its center, where the city hall and the "house of culture" (*Kulturhaus*) were located. Corresponding with the dominant principles of the early 1950 the representative buildings displayed a style called "national architecture" with colonnades and decorations on the facades. As typical for socialist city planning, the broad boulevard (*Magistrale*) that was used for parades, connected the city center with the factory and its huge administration building. Although there was a moderate distance between the plant and the city, the overall spatial figuration of this "city of a new type" (*Stadt neuen Typs*) symbolized the central importance of the factory for the city and its inhabitants (May 1999, 141–167). Some years later, new large residential units with pre-fabricated super-blocs were developed in order to decrease the cost of house production and to rationalize the use of infrastructural facilities. As a result, Fordist elements of mass production of construction more and more characterized the silhouette of the city including the large settlements with their high degree of standardization and uniformity. This pattern, however, was less a peculiarity of an industrial city but a characteristic of all newly built neighborhoods in socialist cities—and more or less in western cities as well.

In general, functionalism gained more and more influence in European and American city building processes. Thus, the principles of zoning were elaborated, construction of city-highways for the increasing number of mass-produced cars extended, and suburban growth of pre-fabricated single-family homes in rows expanded, especially in the US, where Levittown of the early postwar-era was considered a model. Finally, since the late 1950s, huge multi-storied super dwelling-blocks were built especially at the fringes of both industrial and non-industrial cities, if more often in Europe than in the US.[20]

---

20 These satellites consisted of mass-produced steel and concrete constructions and an architecture that represented, however, mainly just a degeneration and vulgarization of what younger European architects (such as the British architects Alison and Peter Smithson) originally wanted to express under the label of "new brutalism" (or "brutal humanism" as

When mass production became less profitable in the 1970s economy, the companies' strategy shifted towards more flexibility and diversity of their production. This corresponded with the demands of the global economy as well as with people's changing tastes who favored more individualistic and pluralistic life-styles. Consequently, cities with Fordist mass production such as the automobile city Detroit and several other American company towns, rapidly deteriorated. Although Fordist plants with monotonous labor at assembly lines continued to exist (up to now), all the visions inherent in the Fordist model of society and in the "experts'" wisdom and their planning capacity rapidly faded away.

Due to the decline of Fordism in the production era, the basic ideas of the Fordist linear industrial cities collapsed as well. The professional "experts" increasingly had to cope with critical civic movements that demanded more participation and rejected the dominance of functionalism and Fordism. The massive countertrends included a new acceptance of urban complexity, ambiguity, and a spatial logic beyond linearity (Hilpert 1995, 144). Post-Fordism blurred the spatial barriers between various functions of the urban zones (Hilpert 1995, 144–147; Gartman 2009, 313) and propagated flexible and open structures to promote urbanity. While post-functionalist architectural "whateverism" swept over many cities, so-called deconstructive architecture with its focus on displaying societal fragmentation characterized the post-Fordist era.

In this post-Fordist era, electronics and High Tech companies simultaneously developed a new kind of industrial settlement represented in Silicon Valley that actually consisted of several already existing agglomerations and small towns. This region with its many dispersed company buildings became a symbol of both, the 'old' suburban space figuration typical for American sprawl and the new network society. The lack of available homes, the monotonous widespread suburbs and the employees' dependence on automobiles are, however, all but models of environmental sustainability in post-Fordist industrial cities. Although some Fordist elements can be still found here, such as the trend of a 'dissolution of cities' in favor of a network system as

---

Le Corbusier called his *Unité d'Habitation* in Marseille). The ambivalent aesthetic of the "new brutalism" was based on the dominance of concrete as a material to demonstrate the obligation to honesty. Thus, it "exposed the crude, primitive side of machine civilization and set the stage for the explosion of aesthetic and political protests of the 1960s" (Gartman 2009, 193), simultaneously symbolizing the end of Fordism as a model for society and cities.

well as the companies' embeddedness in the landscape, Silicon Valley nevertheless demonstrates that the formerly comprehensive concepts of a Fordist linear industrial city have completely worn out and that the great societal visions of Fordism and Fordist planning as a comprehensive concept for shaping society have definitely ended.

Conclusion

The subject *Fordism and industrial cities* presents itself as an extremely tricky one for two reasons. Above all, leading city planners and architects in the US and in Germany show different levels of respect for functionalism and Fordism. The distancing from functionalism in the US was not least due to American nationalism in the early 20th century that was characterized by the will to differ from Europe and to develop a genuine American culture. The dense transatlantic network of architects and city planners and the displayed interest in the concepts of the "other side" did not eliminate the search for American originality and difference, among others, expressed by the term *organic modernity*. This led to a rejection of European's *functionalism* (and Fordism) as an overall concept in city planning and architecture. To be sure, many elements in American city planning and architecture were based on the idea of functionalism, above all zoning and the prefabrication of houses, but these practices were embedded in other contexts, i.e. market processes, and not seriously theorized. Functionalism in architecture did not even succeed in industrial cities in a country where replica and ornaments were popular. Functionalist elements of settlement houses in industrial agglomerations were therefore often hidden behind vernacular styles, and this was justified with traces of people's individuality and romanticism outside the (assembly lined) factories.

On both sides of the Atlantic, planners of industrial agglomerations rejected the existing cities because of the "dangerous masses", in Germany on the additional grounds of the allegedly restricted functionality of their 'classic' concentric profiles. The solutions on both sides, however differed considerably. The American planners, primarily committed to regional planning, were, above all, anxious to decentralize industrial agglomerations across a region and were less interested in developing a special model for the inner structure of such an industrial agglomeration (except zoning and green belts). The German Fordists equally wanted to develop decentralized industrial agglomerations, but in addition a strict linear inner structure of the agglomeration that corresponded with the configuration of assembly lines on huge factory floors. As this ambitious concept of such a Fordist linear industrial city could not be materialized in Germany (only more or less in the Soviet Union), functionalist architects focused on settlement houses. They influenced several relative powerful municipalities to align the newly built settlement houses at the fringes of the already existing cities with the principles of Fordism as far as possible. Yet representative centers were not relinquished in the new industrial cities, Salzgitter and Wolfsburg in the NS-period and Eisenhüttenstadt in the GDR, built under two different dictatorships. As an overall principle, linearity thus was not a component of the plans. The long and linear boulevards (in the GDR: *Magistrale*), connecting the factory with the city center, demonstrated the importance of the factory for the whole city. Rather than representing the Fordist principle however, they primarily served the purposes of party representation.

The other reason the subject *Fordism and industrial cities* is tricky is that functionalist elements penetrated the general 'zeitgeist'. For example, zoning and green belts (as medium of segregating the zones from each other) were components of many highly different city plans during the first half of the 20th century, including the garden city-model. The same can be said for the attempts to shape people's behavior that were not at all restricted to industrial workers in industrial agglomerations. Instead, *social engineering* was an ingredient of many different discourses in the US as well as in Germany, e.g. in the area of health, hygiene and home economics.

Readers may be concerned about the Fordists' view of people as bees and machines and of their hubris of trying to shape them after the best tools for industrial labor. In their self concept, Fordist city planners and architects were committed to reform society and adapt it to the necessities and opportunities of industrial modernity. As Fordism was polyvalent and compatible with every political system, they aspired to Fordism in the hope to create a new societal order with new human beings. In thinking so, they lost their grip on reality. In this respect, the American colleagues were more down-to-earth and moderate. They left the assembly line on the factory floor and looked for market-conform compensation outside.

After 1945, the wide generalization of functionalism and Fordism among Social Scientists and urban planners consequently led to the term "Fordist city" (after 1970: "post-Fordist city") as characteristic of the "Fordist society" without differentiating between industrial cities and non-industrial cities. This is a chance for historians to take a closer look at the special type of existing industrial cities in a transnational perspective and at investigations that consider the impacts new industrial branches and new modes of production by High Tech have on urban spaces.

Works Cited

Altrock, U., et al. (2003). *Die internationale Suche nach der sozialistischen Stadt in der Sowjetunion 1929–1935*. Berlin: Braun.

Benz, W. (ed.) (1992). *Salzgitter. Geschichte und Gegenwart einer deutschen Stadt 1942–1992*. München: C.H. Beck.

Bodenschatz, H. (1995). Analogismus von Fabrikarbeit und Alltag außerhalb der Fabrik: Ein Essential des Fordismus? In Stiftung Bauhaus Dessau and RWTH Aachen (eds.). *Zukunft aus Amerika. Fordismus in der Zwischenkriegszeit*, 39–43. Dessau: Stiftung Bauhaus.

Boyer, M. C. (1983). *Dreaming the Rational City. The Myth of American City Planning*. Cambridge, Mass. and London: MIT.

Buder, S. (1967). *Pullman. An Experiment in Industrial Order and Community Planning 1880–1930*. New York and Oxford: Oxford University Press.

Crawford, M. (1995). *Building the Workingsman's Paradise. The Design of American Company Towns*. London and New York: Verso.

Domhardt, K. S. (2012). Individuum und Stadtgemeinschaft: Die Nachbarschaftsidee in den amerikanischen Stadtentwürfen von Walter Gropius. *Informationen zur modernen Stadtgeschichte* (1), 108–127.

Durth, W. (1997). Städtebau und Weltanschauung. In R. Beier (ed.). *Aufbau west aufbau ost. Die Planstädte Wolfsburg und Eisenhüttenstadt in der Nachkriegszeit*. 35–50. Ostfildern-Ruit: Gert Hatje Verlag.

Etzemüller, T. (2009). *Die Ordnung der Moderne. Social Engineering im 20. Jahrhundert*. Bielefeld: Transcript.

Fehl, G. (1990). Fordismus und Städtebau um 1930. *Wissenschaftliche Zeitschrift*, 36 (1/2), 61–66.

Fehl, G. (1995). Welcher Fordismus eigentlich? In Stiftung Bauhaus Dessau and RWTH Aachen (eds.). *Zukunft aus Amerika. Fordismus in der Zwischenkriegszeit*, 18–37. Dessau: Stiftung Bauhaus.

Fehl, G., and J. Rodriguez-Lores (eds.). (1997). *„Die Stadt wird in der Landschaft sein und die Landschaft in der Stadt". Bandstadt und Bandstruktur als Leitbilder des modernen Städtebaus*. Basel: Birkhäuser.

Ford, H. (1924). *Mein Leben und Werk*. Leipzig: List.

Ford, H. (1926). *Das große Heute, das große Morgen*. Leipzig: List.

Framton, K. (1986). *Modern architecture, a critical history.* London: Thames and Hudson.

Fritzsche, S. (1992). Stadtgründungen im 20. Jahrhundert—Salzgitter im internationalen Vergleich. In W. Benz (ed.). *Salzgitter. Geschichte und Gegenwart einer deutschen Stadt 1942–1992,* 233–280. München: C.H. Beck.

Gartman, D. (2009). *From Autos to Architecture. Fordism and Architectural Aesthetics in the Twentieth Century.* New York: Princeton Architectural Press.

Grandin, G. (2009). *Fordlandia. The Rise and Fall of Henry Ford's Forgotten Jungle City.* New York: Metropolitan Books, Henry Holt and Company.

Green, H. (2010). *The Company Town. The Industrial Edens and Satanic Mills That Shaped the American Economy.* New York: Basic Books.

Handlin, O. (1951). *The Uprooted. The Epic Story of the Great Migrations That Made the American People.* New York: Grosset & Dunlap.

Hård, M., and M. Stippak (2008). The new German city in Britain and the United States. In M. Hård and T. J. Misa (eds.). *Urban Machinery. Inside Modern European Cities,* 121–140. Cambridge, Mass. and London: MIT Press.

Hård, M., and T. J. Misa (2008). Modernizing European Cities: Typically Uniformity and Cultural Distinction. In M. Hård and T. J. Misa (eds.). *Urban Machinery. Inside Modern Európean Cities,* 1–20. Cambridge, Mass. and London: MIT Press.

Heßler, M., and C. Zimmermann (2011). Perspektiven historischer Industriestadtforschung. Neubetrachtungen eines etablierten Forschungsfelds. *Archiv für Sozialgeschichte,* 51, 661–694.

Hilpert, T. (1978). *Die funktionelle Stadt. Le Corbusiers Stadtvision—Bedingungen, Motive, Hintergründe.* Braunschweig: Vieweg.

Hilpert, T. (1995). Die postfordistische Stadt. Suche nach einer Gestaltkultur der offenen Form. In Stiftung Bauhaus Dessau and RWTH Aachen (eds.). *Zukunft aus Amerika. Fordismus in der Zwischenkriegszeit,* 135–147, Dessau: Stiftung Bauhaus Dessau.

Hitchcock, H.-R, and P. Johnson (1966 [1932]). *The International Style.* New York and London: Norton.

Howard, E. (1898). *Tomorrow. A Peaceful Path to Real Reform.* London: Swann Sonnenschein.

Jajeśniak-Quast, D. (2008). Steel towns in Postwar Eastern Europe. In M. Hård and T. J. Misa (eds.). *Urban Machinery. Inside Modern European Cities,* 187–210. Cambridge, Mass. and London: MIT Press.

Le Corbusier (1945). *Grundfragen des Städtebaus.* Stuttgart: Hatje.

May, R. (1999). *Planstadt Stalinstadt. Ein Grundriß der frühen DDR—aufgesucht in Eisenhüttenstadt,* Dortmund: Institut für Raumplanung, Universität Dortmund (IRPUD).

Moos, S. von (1983). Le Corbusier und Gabriel Voisin. In S. von Moos and C. Smeenk (eds.). *Avant Garde und Industrie,* 77–102. Delft: University Press.

Mumford, L. (1922). The City. In H. E. Stearns (ed.). *Civilization of the United States. An Inquiry by Thirty Americans,* 3–20. New York: Harcourt, Brace.

Mumford, L. (1938). *The Culture of Cities*. New York: Harcourt, Brace.

Rodgers, D. T. (1998). *Atlantic Crossings. Social Politics in a Progressive Age*. Cambridge, Mass: Belknap Press of Harvard University Press.

Sachse, C. (1990). *Siemens, der Nationalsozialismus und die moderne Familie. Eine Untersuchung zur sozialen Rationalisierung in Deutschland im 20. Jahrhundert*. Hamburg: Rasch and Röhring.

Saldern, A. von (1991). „Statt Kathedralen die Wohnmaschine". Paradoxien der Rationalisierung im Kontext der Moderne. In F. Bajohr, W. Johe and U. Lohalm (eds.). *Zivilisation und Barbarei. Gedenkschrift für Detlev J.K. Peukert*, 168–192. Hamburg: Christians.

Saldern, A. von (1997). Social Rationalization of Living and Housework in Germany and United States in the 1920s. *The History of the Family: An International Quarterly*, 2 (1), 73–97.

Scarpa, L. (1986). Martin Wagner oder die Rationalisierung des Glücks. In *Martin Wagner 1885–1957. Wohnungsbau und Weltstadtplanung. Die Rationalisierung des Glücks*, 8–23. Berlin: Akademie der Künste.

Siegelbaum, L. A. (2011). *The Socialist Car. Automobility in the Eastern Bloc*. Ithaca: Cornell University Press.

Sturm, H. (2006). Die zweite Entdeckung Amerikas. Amerikanische Mechanisierung und europäische Kunst. In F. Kelleter and W. Knöbl (eds.). *Amerika und Deutschland. Ambivalente Begegnungen*, 133–154. Göttingen: Wallstein.

Sugrue, T. J. (1996). *The Origins of the Urban Crisis. Race and Inequality in Postwar Detroit*. Princeton: Princeton University Press.

Thöner, W. (2006). Deutschland, USA und das Bauhaus. In F. Kelleter and W. Knöbl (eds.). *Amerika und Deutschland. Ambivalente Begegnungen*. 155–170. Göttingen: Wallstein.

Tichi, C. (1987). *Shifting Gears. Technology, Literature, Culture in Modernist America*. Chapel Hill and London: North Carolina Press.

Volkmann, A., and U.-J. Walther (2012). Aufstieg und Fall der Stadt Flint, Michigan … end of story? *Informationen zur modernen Stadtgeschichte*, (1), 29–44.

Wright, F. L. (1995). *The Phoenix Papers. Vol. 1: Broadacre City*. Tuscon: University of Arizona Press.

Wright, G. (1981). *Building the Dream. A Social History of Housing in America*. Cambridge, Mass.: MIT Press.

Zunz, O. (1982). *The Changing Face of Inequality. Urbanization, Industrial Development, and Immigrants in Detroit, 1880–1920*. Chicago and London: University of Chicago Press.

The Utopian Industrial City: The Case of the Baťa City of Zlín (Republic of Czechoslovakia)[1]

Martin Jemelka and Ondřej Ševeček

Introduction

During the interwar years, the footwear industry was confronted with simi-larly revolutionary changes and processes to those in the automobile indus-try that are often associated with the name of Henry Ford. The originally very modest enterprise of the Baťa siblings turned into the equivalent of Ford's vehicle as over the first half of the 20th century, it grew into a gigantic concern with global reach. From today's perspective, the Baťa concern can be considered a textbook example of a modern enterprise oriented toward mass production of consumer goods which was constituted based on Ford-ian principles. In the first three decades of the 20th century, a progressive model of enterprise took shape there, the substantive components of which included not only production, technological, and managerial elements, but also social rationalization supported by a vision of a new industrial culture which seemed to be inseparably linked to the new concept of organizing hu-man life and labor.[2]

An integral part of the concern's program became the establishment of company towns. These were built starting in the 1930s not only in Czecho-slovakia, but also in other countries in Europe, the Americas, and Asia. They were comprehensive projects, and in their time truly represented the pin-nacle of private capitalist urban planning. The reference model for their de-velopment became the concern's headquarters in Zlín, Czechoslovakia, today the Czech Republic. It was precisely in the space of this originally inconse-quential rural town that the concern began to realize its urban vision, and

---

1 This paper was produced within the scope of grant project no. P410/10/1995 "Company Towns of the Baťa Concern" supported by the Czech Science Foundation.
2 The basic literature on the history of the Baťa concern consists (and has consisted for five decades) of two works by Bohumil Lehár (1960; 1963). A useful research aid for orienting oneself in the large number of publications on the topic is the expanding bibliography accessible through the website www.tomasbata.com.

Fig. 1: The Zlín garden quarters of Zálešná, Podvesná, and Díly with standardized development of family houses. View from the northeast, 1942

(Source: Moravian Provincial Archives in Brno, State District Archives in Zlín—Photographic Archives)

over time created a specific model of industrial organization, which—like its other products—it gradually exported to a range of countries around the world (Ševeček 2013, 33–36). The activities of the Baťa concern received significant attention in relatively short terms. The so-called "Baťa system" became the subject of a range of discussions and polemical debates even in the international context. From the beginning, however, these discussions were markedly polarized. On the one hand, in the eyes of certain contemporaries of the concern (primarily among entrepreneurs and the technical intelligentsia), it manifested period views of the ideal of modern industrial organization; on the other hand, for many of its critics (especially among the union movement, the left-wing intelligentsia, and probably also Baťa's competitors) it represented an embodiment of modern capitalist tyranny. Furthermore, the global method of expansion, involving not merely the sale of Czechoslovak products on foreign markets but increasingly the relocation of production abroad, provoked in many places tempestuous reactions and was often the target of mass campaigns of various types and aims. It is significative that this interest in Baťa was far from being merely a matter for a narrow group of experts from the footwear industry or of entrepreneurs and managers; soon, it became a focus of attention for a certain segment of architects, urbanists, politicians, and reform-minded intellectuals ruminating over new trends in the development of cities and the urban way of life, or over the role of the new industrial means in society and politics. In time, the concern's practices were thus pulled into the referential framework (as a relatively well-known example) of debates on the shape of modern industrial society (Fig. 1).

Towards a model company town of the Fordist era

The company town as a specific type of industrial settlement

The fact that the case of Zlín and other Baťa towns can be classified as a type of industrial settlement built and administered by a single enterprise—known since the initial phases of industrialization—becomes significant in an historical perspective. For this specific type of industrial settlement, the term "company town"[3] is used in the literature, and this can be considered to be undoubtedly one of the characteristic residential types of the industrial era. Moreover, research currently underway has drawn attention not only to the growing relevance of their study and the significance of these localities for historical science, but also to the fact that they were more widespread than has been assumed hitherto.[4] After the onset of industrialization, the number of company towns grew in particular in countries that had adopted capital-

---

3 This is a modern term. According to J. S. Garner, it first appeared in America at the end of the 19th century and was used to designate mining and smelting colonies in parts of Appalachia and the Monongahela River Valley. In the beginning, it had a pejorative meaning, and the negative connotations (reflecting the poor living conditions in these types of colonies) remained with it for a long time. Only gradually did this designation begin to be used for other settlements dependent on a single company operating in other segments. Initially, this concerned mainly settlements established around textile mills (*mill towns*) as well as various industrial villages. Subsequently, the term also encompassed model company towns established by reform- or paternalistically-minded entrepreneurs (Garner 1992, 3–14).

4 An example is ongoing research as part of the the project "Company Towns in the World. Origins, Evolution and Rehabilitation (16th–20th centuries)", coordinated in the History Department of Padua University. More information about this interdisciplinary project, which also involves the creation of an extensive database and atlas of company towns, can be found at http://www.companytown.net.

ism and free-market principles. They often belonged to entrepreneurs whose companies contributed to the industrial revolution's takeoff. They were often localized in sparsely populated and 'backward' areas. In the early phases of industrialization, the availability of raw materials was frequently the determinative factor for their establishment. Through their generally poor living conditions, these places often symbolized the unresolved relationship between the emerging industrial civilization and the environment. Concepts like "production," "exploitation," and "profit" serve well to describe the main purpose of their establishment (Garner 1992, 3).

Relatively early, however, entrepreneurs began to appear (such as Robert Owen, George Pullman, William Hesketh Lever, George and Richard Cadbury, etc.) who were willing to accept a greater level of responsibility for the environment, which surrounded their factories, as well as for their employees' living conditions. Some of the housing experiments they initiated became well known, and influenced future developments in the urban and social area. It is difficult to overstate the significance of these "model company towns," as they tend to be called, because they introduced into the conceptual thinking of the time a compelling moral stimulus which drew attention to maintaining a certain order in the social and urban sphere, thus contributing significantly to the establishment of social policy and industrial urbanism (Kiess 1991).

The motivations with which industrialists approached this type of local engagement were quite varied, however (ranging from the purely pragmatic to the sacrosanct endeavoring for example to elevate and cultivate the labor force). Most of them opted for an extensive paternalistic policy, especially in an attempt to recruit and stabilize a qualified workforce, to valorize their investment in buildings and land, to prevent speculation on the housing market, or to better direct and administer the management of resources. If there was another alternative, however, entrepreneurs usually preferred not to construct apartments and residential infrastructure at their own expense, but especially enterprises developing in isolated and unpopulated areas often had little choice. On the other hand, it is clear that certain industrialists took a real interest in the prosperity of their employees, even though their engagement in local matters was in many cases perceived ambivalently or even criticized as authoritarian. It was precisely the model company towns that were intended to become the embodiment of their views and ideas about the new organization of industrial society. This was not just about innovations in architecture and urban planning, however (these towns were often designed by prominent architects of their time). In conjunction with their industrial activities, investors' attention was also concentrated on extensive social programs that even encompassed workers' families. From this point of view, it is thus impossible to interpret the phenomenon of company towns merely as sites of experimentation with new architectural and urban planning solutions. Many of them became true laboratories of the dawning industrial age—places in which through everyday encounters with practical issues of production and societal relations, in dialogues and conflicts between employers and employees, industrial civilization emerged and took shape (Garner 1992; Kiess 1991; Teuteberg 1985).

Baťa towns: main features and characteristics[5]

It is thus also possible to view the case of Baťa towns as an extraordinarily interesting articulation of the old repertoire of problems, which entrepreneurs had faced since the early phases of industrialization. In this context, the concern's program can be interpreted as an attempt at a modernist reinvention of the concept of the model company town. It is obvious that many substantive aspects of the case in point fundamentally correspond with the typological classification (model company town). Also, practically everything in Baťa towns was closely linked to the company. It owned a significant portion of the property and real estate. These settlements were relatively small geographically, and the number of residents was directly proportional to the size of the factory (normally around one thousands residents). These towns usually reached a larger size (sometimes even on the order of tens of thousands of residents) if they developed in conjunction with some original settlement, or if they were able to integrate new productive functions into their structure. The localization of Baťa towns was based on the famous thesis (hearkening back in certain respects to a conception prevalent in reform circles since the 19th century) that industry which was established in large cities did not measure up with new and rationalistic aims of planned development. It seems, however, that the concern's management used this premise rather to place emphasis on its own vision of society than to accentuate the issue of residents' living conditions in its own right.[6] The main principles of local-

5 We base this section in particular on Ševeček (2013).

6 According to the Baťa concern's management, the societal form necessary for industrial development does not emerge in the environment of large cities. On the contrary, the

izing Baťa towns were also based in certain important respects on the logic that underpinned many previous projects. This mainly concerns their establishment in economically less-developed, rural regions (at a sufficient distance from large cities) with the required labor force. At the same time, these should also be localities with inexpensive and available land of a suitable size and quality, not only supplied with appropriate transportation links (a navigable river and a railway), but also sufficient raw materials and resources (in particular construction materials, as well as potable and service water). These were the basic parameters which—in the concern's experience—determined whether a new company town could successfully develop and prosper.

In terms of planning, the concern—like many of its predecessors—produced an elaborate and comprehensive design of each company town according to which it was established. The actual urban design was influenced on the one hand by the garden city movement and the concept of the functional city (in particular regarding its approach to the relationship between housing, work, and recreation), and on the other hand to a significant degree by the effects of Fordism. The following main principles influenced the character of the urban environment of Baťa designs throughout the interwar period: open development on a greenfield site, zoning with functionally defined areas, an economy of movement from the point of view of pedestrian traffic, standardization and economization of construction, and family accommodation in houses.

Social relations in company towns always had specific features, and in certain substantive respects the Baťa projects did not depart from these. Firstly, this involved the specific industrial life style which existed in them. Their crystalized core was the industrial enterprise, which was not only a vehicle of social order (rules were implemented here mostly in a top-down manner), but also a guarantor of social reconciliation. The enterprise's control of the town was legitimized by the ideal of softening social tensions and to rise industrial productivity. This was often reflected in the company town's political leadership. The Baťa concern always endeavored either to establish an independent administrative status for its company towns, or—after the Zlín model—to exercise fundamental influence on (or control over) the existing municipal administration to which the given company town was subordinated. Local politics were thus directly integrated into the enterprise,

---

placement of industry in a large city was seen to lead to social dysfunction and the creation of crowds of individuals who do not (and cannot) possess the necessary level of appreciation for industrial cooperation (Baťa 1939, 1–3).

and the municipal administration was basically considered to be one of the enterprise's departments (here, it was assumed that the factory and town shared common interests and goals, according to the motto: "What is good for the plant is good for the town and vice versa."). The political sphere thus marginalized a central dimension of modern urban life—public space no longer represented the political ideal of a heterogeneous public but instead reified community ideals. Organizations of workers deemed undesirable by the management (a typical example being labor unions), for instance, were not tolerated in Bat'a towns.

Before focusing on a more detailed analysis and characterization of the Zlín situation, we wish to foreshadow an answer to an important question: In what respect can Bata towns be considered to represent qualitatively new and particular cases? First of all, one must take into account the fact that the concern's program was developed under new structural conditions of the interwar period—that is, at a time when entrepreneurs from around the world were embarking on "pilgrimages" to Henry Ford's American plants, which had become the generally respected ideal of a large production enterprise, and when concepts such as rationalization, standardization, and scientific management were a ubiquitous incantation. The enterprise's founder, Tomáš Bat'a (1876–1932), set out in this direction as well, and became a passionate protagonist of the new industrial means. He understood them not merely as a prerequisite for economic growth; rather, he viewed them as a powerful, positive, and autonomous force which—when released—could provide an ever-increasing level of material security and comfort for the whole world while at the same time contributing to the new, rational organization of industrial society (Bat'a 1932). If we were to look for the keystone of the concern's program of the 1920s and 1930s, the technological scheme (or, perhaps more precisely, the method of thinking strongly bound to technical and technological premises), which stood at the enterprise's foundations, cannot be overlooked. Not only did it result in a revolutionary transformation of factory production, it is also reflected in ideas about the arrangement, role, and functions of urban space, as well as in its societal and cultural characteristics.

At its core, the Bat'a program was founded on the utopian idea that this technological scheme that fundamentally changed the method of production could be transferred relatively easily (using scientific methods) to other areas of life in society. This idea hence formed the basis of the concept of the industrial town that the concern developed in the 1920s and 1930s: a town that in quite substantive respects was seen as mere extension of modern large scale industry. It was primarily considered a place established by mass production, and secondarily one of mass consumption. At the same time, the town itself was an industrial product, and as such it was not only produced and consumed, but also presented. It became a living showcase of the "new world" and the new lifestyle produced by large industrial organizations (Ševeček 2013, 28).

As already hinted at above, in attempting to distinguish Baťa projects qualitatively from the aims of other entrepreneurs known from the past, it seems difficult to dispense with the concepts of Fordism (Saldern et al. 2009) and the Fordist Industrial City.[7] Baťa towns can basically be understood as a model case of an urban environment in which a private capitalist enterprise of the Fordist type was able to realize its vision without a significant counterweight. In so doing, they embodied the ambition to embrace and transform the town in its totality—materially, socially, and culturally. Baťa projects were characterized by a concerted effort to permeate architecture and society. Architecture and social interaction served to create a homogeneous world—a world whose spatial arrangement would immediately reflect the new way of life. Architecture and urbanism played an extremely important role in this conception. They were built with the intention to embody the new rational order introduced by the Fordist factory and to establish its very dominance.

Societal relations in Baťa towns were influenced by intensive interventions into the structure of the labor force, which immediately reflected the new division of industrial labor in rationalized production operations. There was the result of many years of experiments, during which new scientific techniques found broad application (e.g. studies of time and movement, psychotechnical, psychological, and health tests, etc.). In conjunction with these processes, the concern particularly concentrated on the realm of social and personnel policy. In addition to social programs and other motivational stimuli, another integral component of its management practice involved sophisticated methods of supervising and disciplining employees. Importantly, the enterprise's personnel department systematically monitored employees—not only in the workplace, but also in their private lives. It is precisely these surveillance and control measures that constituted important elements of the firm's program and a focus of its critics (Fig. 2).

---

7 See the article of Adelheid von Saldern in this volume.

Fig. 2: A sewing workshop in rationalized footwear production, 1939

(Source: Moravian Provincial Archives in Brno, State District Archives in Zlín—Photographic Archives)

It was already noticed in period commentaries that what they called the "Baťa system" went much further in the social and urban spheres than the famous American enterprises did. It seems that in these contexts it is important to direct our attention toward the actual production program which the Baťa towns constituted. Baťa towns emerged in the circumstances of an industrial organization, which required a relatively high degree of human intervention in the manufacturing process and was equally characterized by a relatively high degree of flexibility in production. The quality of the main footwear outputs was not primarily a result of the level of the technologies— these were more of a prerequisite in order to increase efficiency throughout the organization—but a result of the quality and productivity of human labor. Under these conditions and circumstances, the way in which the relationship between the enterprise and its employees was regulated was of key importance in many respects. It is for this reason that the model of the "social person"—sensitive to the work climate and the environment—was met with greater acceptance. The concern's practice was based on the assumption that through a certain arrangement of conditions in the workplace and in employees' home environments it was possible to achieve the necessary commitment and loyalty (or, rather, identification on the part of employees with the goals defined by the organization). New rules in the area of work were condensed into a formula, which the company sought to integrate into the workers' social and cultural lives. Through gradual sedimentation, this led to the emergence of a highly comprehensive system that embodied the ambition to legitimize even certain negative costs accompanying the world of mass production (Ševeček 2009, 71–72).

Baťa's Zlín[8]

Zlín is not an example of a new city built on a greenfield site, although some studies of the Zlín case suggest this. From the beginning, its modern development was closely linked to the original provincial settlement core whose urban tradition stretches back to the Middle Ages. It is important to mention this not only because this constellation influenced the character of the Baťa urban program to a certain extent. More importantly, it characterized the environment (especially with respect to its culture and values) from which Tomáš Baťa as many of his closest collaborators emerged. At the time the Baťa enterprise was established (1894), Zlín was a backward, provincial town with approximately three thousand residents. Most of them made their living in the crafts, small trading, or agriculture. Very soon, however, the growth of local industry radically transformed conditions in the municipality. By the end of the 1930s, Zlín had become a major industrial center with forty thousand residents (Fig. 3) (Pokluda 2006).

Since the First World War, industrial development was closely tied to one expanding private capitalist entity—the Baťa company. In the 1923 communal elections, after a candidate list of Baťa employees obtained an absolute majority of mandates in the municipal council, the indirect influence exerted on Zlín by the industrial enterprise until that point became a conscious effort on the part of the enterprise to direct and regulate the town's development. In the following years, Zlín acquired its distinctive character, which from an architectural and urbanist point of view has significantly determined its form to the present day. This was an equally determining moment for

---

8 Unless stated otherwise, this section is based on research conducted between 2002 and 2005 by Ondřej Ševeček. His results are summarized in Ševeček (2009).

Fig. 3: A factory building of the company T. & A, built in 1906. Photo taken between 1910–1915

(*Source: Moravian Provincial Archives in Brno, State District Archives in Zlín—Photographic Archives*)

the Baťa enterprise; at approximately the same time, it initiated an extensive reorganization and reconstruction of the plant, which transformed the Zlín factory into one of the most progressive operations of its time (Lehár 1960).

It is possible to enumerate many reasons and motivations for why the Baťa company embarked upon such a pronounced and fundamental engagement in the urban space—ranging from those pertaining to the still unsustainable situation in the town (sanitation and health risks, the housing shortage, social instability, insufficient water supplies, etc.), to those immediately connected to the enterprise's economic interests (the needs of production, the conservation of real estate investments, the stabilization of core employees, etc.), to those reasons which in certain respects refer to the ideological roots and principles upon which the new model of enterprise was built. At this point, we will emphasize at least one motivating factor that seems to have been especially significant for the development in Zlín, as it reveals one of the constitutive elements of the Baťa business model and relates to the form and methods of its expansion.

If we were to examine the character of the Baťa factories' economic growth and the attendant transformation of their structure in greater detail, we would see that in addition to a range of situational factors the practice of certain successful large enterprises (particularly American ones) evidently served as a model. These enterprises were able to exploit advantages resulting from their size—advantages which Alfred Chandler (1962; 1990) called the advantages of "SST-economies" (Scale, Scope, Transaction-cost). One of the substantive principles upon which enterprises of this type were built was vertical integration. This was to ensure the fastest value chain flow—from deliveries of raw materials, to production, to sales. Based on this model, the Baťa company gradually internalized activities connected to procuring a range of basic raw materials, built an extensive complex of auxiliary production facilities, and developed an extensive distribution organization with its own retail chain at its core (Lehár 1960; 1963). The enterprise's development was characterized by an effort to be self-sufficient in all substantive areas of its activity. It seems that, among other things, the path of vertical integration on which the Baťa enterprise embarked and which transformed it into a textbook example of a modern business enterprise, also was a significant factor in the genesis of the specific "company town" model—or, rather, that a certain (and, it seems, not insignificant) analogy can be traced in these processes. This propensity toward internalizing a range of activities essential for the enterprise's operations was one of the important motivating factors that gradually led the dynamically expanding Baťa enterprise (in the locally specific circumstances of Zlín) to a certain form of internalization of the town itself. In this respect social and personnel policies also played a substantive role—in addition to the need to quickly remedy the dismal housing conditions in Zlín—, which in this labor-intensive sector were intended to ensure smooth operations and high efficiency in production (Ševeček 2013, 26–32).

Urban space

In the existing literature, the urbanised organization of Zlín is usually placed into context with the concepts of functional city[9] or garden city. While there is no doubt that many elements characteristic of Zlín's development relate well to these concepts, it seems that this tremendously overestimates their role in the processes of shaping the town's spatial organization (Ševeček and Zahrádková 1995). The development of the town's new spatial organization started with the residential unit as housing was the most pressing issue that led the concern to embark on a more significant intervention into urban

---

9 Zlín's urbanistic organization is most often conceived as a contribution to the concept of the Functional City. According to certain urbanists, Zlín's separated zones anticipated the principles of the Athens Charter announced by the CIAM conference in 1933.

Fig. 4: View of Fordian architecture in the company quarter of Nad Ovčírnou, 1935
(Source: Moravian Provincial Archives in Brno, State District Archives in Zlín—Photographic Archives)

planning in Zlín. Hence, the first land-use plans that emerged in Zlín in rapid succession starting in 1915 are focused on this area. In the factory housing sector, which unequivocally dominated the town (in the 1930s, it housed approximately 60–70 percent of the town's residents and approximately 70 percent of the enterprise's employees), two main types of residential structure existed alongside one another: the family house and the dormitory. It was precisely the accentuation of these two construction types that significantly determined the character and spatial relationships within the town (Fig. 4).

It is no accident that a family house in the garden quarter became the promoted symbol of the new Zlín, even though a larger portion of the enterprise's employees (more than 40 percent of the workers) lived in factory dormitories. The family house was unequivocally the most common construction type in the town (approximately two thousand company houses had been built in Zlín's garden quarters by 1938, in which 36 percent of the town's population lived), as well as a reification of the new lifestyle that the enterprise supported universally. The family house with a small garden was not only one of the key elements of Zlín's urbanism, but also a reflection of the family-policy ideal advocated by the enterprise. This ideal was established to emphasize family life. After the wedding, the wife was to stay at home and take care of running the household (in this model, the recognition of women's work in the household was reflected in the man's wage as the family's breadwinner).

The model's role in the society of the company town was aimed on the one hand at worker activity in the workplace (the ideal of family life brings a new identity to the man/worker and a new ethos to men's work, which in this model fostered great achievements in the workplace), and on the other at worker behavior outside the workplace (in the best case, the family was to replace workers' clubs, professional associations and even unions). In this regard, it is important to note that all factory apartments were rented to employees based on a supplement to the wage contract—the use of the (in reform circles often-criticized) wage-rent ratio. This model did not enable employees to buy the houses provided by the company, which ensured the enterprise's relative power to influence employees even in the political sphere.

During the construction of the garden quarters, Fordist principles found wide application—in particular the use of rationalized production methods, standardization, and large-scale production. These principles were reflected by the architectural and urban shape of the residential quarters, which fascinated many architects at the time. The economic model assumption was that expenditures on rent should not exceed a certain percentage (set at 5–7 percent) of employees' wages, since these expenditures affected the calculations for production itself: The more an employee had to pay for housing, the greater his wage had to be, which thus increased production costs and the price of products (Ševeček 2013, 43). In a similar vein, the semi-detached house became a characteristic building arrangement in Zlín. It offered all the advantages of an individual structure (the company ideal of a family house in a garden quarter) while at the same time taking up less land, public roads, and municipal installations than the "idealized" detached house.

The launch of rationalized housing development in the 1920s was accompanied by an important changes in the spatial organization of social life. It was no accident that the former spatial separation of housing for clerks and workers disappeared from the family quarters. Pursuing a Fordist vision, the Baťa company attempted to build in Zlín a stable and optimized cooperating "workers' Community" the composition of which better matched the social mix (workers and higher-level employees were to continue to live together in the same family quarter). Potential differences in family housing standards (quarter-detached, semi-detached or detached) were concealed behind a standardized architectural form. This does not mean, of course, that there were no social differences between the residents of factory districts—these were clearly present due to the different positions held by employees in the company's functional hierarchy. Of much greater importance of this vision was the question of a shared lifestyle shaped by the factory, the new industrial culture, and its products—one of which was of course the company family house.

Considerations about urban space, its structure, and architecture in Zlín were closely linked to technological bases. This can be demonstrated vividly by one of the substantive principles of the construction of Zlín—namely, that all buildings and municipal structures were understood as principally temporary. Already at construction stage, it was reckoned that due to technological progress all buildings would be obsolete roughly forty years later (only thirty years in the case of certain structures more closely linked to the development of technology and science—e.g. hospitals), and would need to be demolished and rebuilt according to future needs. Urban development was thus calculated in such a way that investments in construction would be amortized before the buildings would be surpassed by technical and technological progress (Fig. 5).

Fig. 5: Labor Square in front of the entrance to the Baťa factory in May 1935

(Source: Moravian Provincial Archives in Brno, State District Archives in Zlín—Photographic Archives)

Zlín's spatial composition was based on the principle of free development with airy open spaces and extensive greenery. Development in closed blocks was to be preserved only in its historical center. The new center of urban life, Labor Square (located in front of the factory's entrance) and featuring a cinema, hotel, and department stores, was designed—like the extensive factory grounds, the boarding-house district, the school quarter, the Baťa hospital, and other groups of public buildings—as a set of autonomous, open developments. The land-use plans reserved large areas of the town for the establishment of orchards, parks, and recreational zones. Zlín thus gradually acquired a garden character featuring wide boulevards and large open spaces scaled for the mass movement of people during times of peak use (the character of the urban space was significantly influenced by the time schedule set by the Baťa factory; during brief periods of time—the start of work, the lunch break, the end of work—the town and its infrastructure had to handle the onslaught of thousands of factory employees). In addition to expanding the strip of greenery in the town's center, the regulation plan also reckoned with the establishment of forested parks in areas adjacent to the town. Emphasis on the town's "green character" and its programmatic integration with the surrounding landscape were important components of Zlín's urbanism. Its development was informed by the idea that modern industry and the natural environment embody a state of equilibrium (or rather the idea of nature as a counterweight to rationalized and stereotyped production), which was venerated by both of modern Zlín's main creators—the industrialist Tomáš Baťa and his architect František Lydie Gahura.

Urban society

In attempting to characterize Zlín's development in the interwar years, one must mention first and foremost the societal vision of the concern's founder, Tomáš Baťa, and his ideas about the social order that modern factories were to produce. This is how Baťa the industrialist later recalled the societal ideas of his twenties:

"I was a collectivist and something like a communist, but decidedly a socialist. […] I dreamed of Tolstoy's simple life. After I'd paid off my debts […] I'd buy a small country manor and sow only what I needed for myself and my family. Towns existed only

Fig. 6: View of the crystallizing core of Baťa's Zlín, mid-1930s

(*Source: Moravian Provincial Archives in Brno, State District Archives in Zlín—Photographic Archives*)

to enslave farmers, and factories to enslave workers; merchants to live like parasites from the work of others."[10]

Tomáš Baťa soon turned away from his initial agrarian-socialist ideals, however—or, rather, he transformed them. After visiting major industrial areas in Europe and America, the factory came to be increasingly central to his thinking—not merely as the essential element of a new economic system, however, but also as an entity establishing a certain new form of sociality. In the years following the First World War, Tomáš Baťa, already unequivocally oscillated in his ideas between industrial paternalism and Fordism. After his death in 1932, the concern under its new chief, Jan Antonín Baťa (1898–1965), increasingly accentuated Fordism, scientific management, and the role of technocratic power, which—in the ideal case—was intended to create through gradual reforms the political conditions under which the enterprise's societal vision could be realized. In the area of urban planning, this was mainly a vision of the ideal industrial town as a settlement on a smaller scale, with one enterprise and one main industrial product (Fig. 6) (Baťa 1939, 1–3).

---

10 Quoted from Tomáš Baťa (1932, 25).

In conjunction with these ideas, Zlín became an experimental space which endeavored—using scientific methods and a combination of disciplinary mechanisms and social benefits—to realize the vision of a society of work characterized by exemplary cooperation. It was to be an environment where the worker would meet his foreman or supervisor after work and they would share a range of important events in their lives. It soon became clear, however, that this idealized way of life was developing significant cracks. It was unanticipated, and came from those very employees who had been expected to be the most loyal—from the ambitious and increasingly significant echelon of professional managers. They were the first to begin to leave the factory family quarter (shared lifestyle). By the second half of the 1930s, the emergence of their own individual housing can be observed in Zlín—a sign of the urban society's budding emancipation from the factory and of the gradual erosion of the collectivist socialist vision from which this arrangement arose.

The enterprise's growing influence on the town was also intensively reflected in the composition of Zlín's population. Its main features began to distinctly reflect the requirements of rationalized production as early as during the 1920s. An important role in the recruitment of employees in Zlín was played by scientifically based personnel management, as well as the concern's strategy of preferentially employing very young people from poor backgrounds and without previous work experience. It was precisely these people who were best able to adapt to the enterprise's requirements and the specific conditions of living and working in Baťa's Zlín. Thus, in the interwar years, the town's population evidenced a range of sociologically and demographically peripheral features: almost two thirds of the town's residents were aged 15 to 30 years, 67 percent were unmarried, 68 percent were economically active, and 99 percent were literate (data from 1930). With respect to age and gender, the town's population in 1930 was dominated by men aged 15 to 29 (30 percent of Zlín's population) and women aged 15 to 24 (27 percent of Zlín's population). These women found employment in Zlín mainly as production workers, and their work activity was limited to the period of life preceding marriage; married women worked in the Baťa factory only exceptionally. It is evident that even this constellation, reflecting primarily an effort to achieve the thorough rationalization of production (minimization of costs and maximal efficiency of all enterprise activities), had in many respects a determinative role for the "new town" project, and significantly facilitated the societal underpinning of the Baťa urban vision.

The gradual absorption of Zlín by the concern played out on a range of levels. It has already been mentioned that political control of the municipality passed into the hands of the concern following elections in 1923. Relatively soon thereafter, the concern took over control over almost everything concerning distribution (water, electricity, gas, food, medication, etc.). Such an intensive and extensive incorporation of the town enabled the concern, among other things, to plan and direct the municipal economy in a very comprehensive manner. The plans from the 1930s for the economic development of the new Baťa towns clearly demonstrate how far this model had progressed. It included a calculation of the expenditures of individual households of which it was assumed that most would return in large part to the concern through its various facilities, services, or stores (from the power plant to the cinema).[11]

The Baťa concern expanded into other areas of urban life and culture in Zlín in a similar manner. In particular education, healthcare and sports became priorities for the Baťa management. Thus, among other things, several notable ensembles of modern buildings emerged in interwar Zlín, of which at least the school quarter (five modern school buildings, an auditorium, gymnasium, playground, and outdoor swimming pool) and the Baťa Hospital complex (situated in a tranquil zone in the town's eastern periphery and constructed with a system of free-standing, single-story pavilions surrounded by greenery) must be mentioned. Yet this was not merely an architectural design; the very method of organizing the Zlín Experimental School (as it was called at the time) and healthcare also became widely known in expert circles. Moreover, the concern made very skillful use of these areas—which it considered to be important pillars of its program—to promote its own brands and its ideas about modern society. The area of company training and education in particular was to play a key role in this conception by spreading the new values and the new way of life (Vrána 1939).

---

11 To illustrate this, the 1939 book *Průmyslové město* gives the following calculation of expenses for employee wages: housing 7%, lighting 1%, heating 2%, food 40%, clothing, shoes, linens 20%, entertainment 4%, training 3%, travel 3%, sick leave 5%, insurance 2%, savings 10%, other expenses 3% (*Průmyslové město* 1939, 573).

In the 1920s and 1930s, new media and methods of communication entered the urban space in a dramatic manner. The company press in particular was of special significance, alongside radio and film. The beginnings of Zlín's corporate press stretch back to the First World War. At the close of the interwar period, the company produced these publications (important for Zlín and its surroundings): *Zlín, Magazine of Baťa Workers* published every Friday, *Zlín, Big Edition* published on Wednesdays, and *Zlín, Monday Paper for the Zlín Region*. The Friday *Zlín*—which soon reached a print run of 38,000 copies—was focused first and foremost on informing employees about goings-on at the company. Wednesday's big edition covered mainly important world news in brief, and reached a print run of 100,000 copies. The Monday edition focused on society and important events in Zlín and its surroundings (promotion of the purposive development of the district of Zlín), and also included a sports column and a brief overview of world news. From the beginning, the company press was closely tied to the Baťa concern's ideology and political interests (Cekota 1931).

A new radio culture quickly took root in Zlín as well. The use of radio at the enterprise level reached a qualitatively new dimension when it launched its own radio broadcasts. From the start of broadcasting, there was no doubt that its content profile would be completely dependent on the strong societal vision of the concern's management and in this sense would launch and fill out another dimension of the development of media in the model company town.[12] On the other hand, due to the easy availability of other competing programs, radio also brought quite a different dimension into the urban environment, which completely surpassed local conditions and influences. It was significant for the town's development that this medium—despite its

---

12 The regular program of Baťa radio was divided into two main parts. The first, which actually started the working day, lasted fifteen minutes and was broadcast at a time (from 6:30 to 6:45 a.m.) when concern employees were coming to the factory. With respect to content, it consisted of rhythmic marches played from phonograph records. The second, central part of the broadcast, which ran during the main morning break (at 9:00 a.m.) for 10 minutes, usually began with a brief musical extract, followed by news focused mainly on events in the factory and in the town; edifying slogans were often read out as well. The transmission usually concluded with a lecture on organizational, ethical, safety, and other issues of factory work. It was also common for information to be provided about the offerings of factory cinemas. The factory radio station, which by the end of the 1930s broadcast regularly every day, did not cover merely the factory grounds in Zlín, but was also transmitted to various company facilities (Szczepanik 2005, 37–38, 51).

focus on the individual and the family—created in the urban space a distinct public sphere, which was not directly subject to the concern's influence.

In a workers' town like Zlín, film played a far greater role than any other new media, and became the most widespread form of entertainment generally. The growing demand for film entertainment was satisfied with the construction of the grandiose Grand Cinema (1932), in which an audience of up to 2,500 could view a screening, and which thus became by far the largest cinema in Czechoslovakia. The Zlín environment was not merely a place for enjoying film and entertainment, however. Very soon, the Baťa management came to understand the significance of the latest media technologies for an industrial society, and the possibilities that their exploitation would offer for modern business activities. Zlín thus took its place among the immensely lively focal points of film creation. From the end of the 1920s until the mid-1940s, the Baťa company produced or commissioned approximately 170 films (Szczepanik 2005, 43). The significance the enterprise ascribed to film production is evidenced by the conditions created for this thriving segment of activity, especially in the second half of the 1930s. A decision by the concern's management led to the start of construction on the Zlín Film Studios in 1935.

In the shadow of the Baťa factory, the youngest town in Czechoslovakia emerged as a project of the rising postwar generation—a town developing at a frantic pace, blazing with optimism and faith in the future of the industrial society which, it seemed, could be planned and produced. Baťa's Zlín captivated many visitors with its special charm. It seemed to be the realization of an old dream of harmony and unity—a reification of an urban utopia that became achievable due to modern technology and a strictly scientific approach. The concern contributed to the development of this utopian imagination in no small way. This did not involve only propaganda, however; the town in tow of the factory became a construction site on which a whole new worldview was built with ambitions to gain control of the totality of lived reality. The new Zlín was not only engineered according to the "factory," but also measured and interpreted through its logic. In its space, new cultural and expressive forms found broad application. A key role was played in particular by Fordist architecture, industrial design, and film, all of which significantly influenced the newly constituting society (Fig. 7).

The town became a venue for spectacular mass celebrations and events, where thousands of young uniformed employees marched side by side. Their bodies were an integral component of mass rituals repeating on various occa-

Fig. 7: May Day 1937, view of some of the participants in the Labor Day celebration

(Source: Moravian Provincial Archives in Brno, State District Archives in Zlín—Photographic Archives)

sions (Labor Day, commemorative celebrations, funerals of leading concern personalities, etc.). Ultimately they referenced the collective character of industrial work, reinforced the enterprise's authority and employees' sense of belonging, and manifested a perfect concert of residents. Most often, it was sporting events that pulled the town and its residents out of their everyday routine. Sports were broadly supported by the concern, not only due to the ideal of physical prowess and stamina, but also in order to cultivate a spirit of competition and to build character—traits and values which were of such importance for the new industrial man. It was this way of life that accompanied Zlín to the brink of the Second World War.

Postscript and Conclusion: From Zlín to Gottwaldov and back

In November 1948, a birthday celebration was held in Zlín's Grand Cinema for Czechoslovakia's first Communist president, Klement Gottwald. On this occasion, a proposal to change the town's name to Gottwaldov was adopted.

This was implemented officially on the day on which the first five-year plan was launched—on January 1, 1949. At the same time, the enterprise was renamed as well—the Baťa national enterprise[13] became the Svit national enterprise (Kraus 1984, 21). The two new names were the symbolic culmination of the reversal which took place in Zlín during the initial postwar years. The private capitalist company town became socialist Gottwaldov. Despite the radical Communist rhetoric after taking power in February 1948—dealing in various ways with so-called Batism, which was designated one of the most sophisticated forms of capitalist exploitation, and distancing itself from the Baťa past identified with the Nazi regime—it soon became obvious that both the town and the factory would return (in many important respects) to a well-worn path. After the intensive anti-Baťa campaign had subsided and the political situation had calmed down, an appreciable line of continuity emerged between the old regime and the new.

It seems that the Zlín environment (as a strictly hierarchical society directed in an authoritarian manner) adapted relatively quickly after 1948 to the new political requirements, and soon accepted even the new ideological tools of the ascendant Communist regime. These processes also eased the forced departure of the Baťa top management and numerous changes in important positions in the leadership of the enterprise and of the town, as did, more generally, the fact that there was a natural inclination at the enterprise to pursue primarily goals in the economic and production areas, with everything else traditionally subordinated to these objectives. "Old" tools and methods, which formerly had a strong influence on employees and urban society (from personnel policies to a network of media) found application in socialist practice as well. If a range of original structures and elements of the Baťa system were accepted—whether acknowledged as such or not—in designing now the model socialist town (technologies, production processes, and procedures, methods of organization and management, planning and development, healthcare, education, etc.), there were of course also areas where application of the original model ran up against relatively fundamental problems and obstacles. This concerned the areas of personnel and social policy, for example, in which the state as well as the Communist Party and its associated organizations interfered with increasing forcefulness. In accordance with the new position of women in socialist society, for example, the

---

13 Already in May 1945, the company Baťa, a. s. came under so-called national administration. Its nationalization took place on the basis of a presidential decree in October 1945 (Karkošková et al. 2000, 103–107).

Baťa family policy ideal and model of the woman as homemaker employed only prior to marriage was completely abandoned. Thus, the proportion of women working at the enterprise rose quickly and stabilized in the second half of the 1980s at approximately 58 percent (*Statistická ročenka* 1961, 4; *Statistická ročenka* 1991, 84).

In view of further development, it was important that during the period following the Second World War (essentially until the end of the 1990s), the town's development continued to be planned and directed in close connection with the needs and requirements of local industry. Under socialist conditions (i.e. under the conditions of a directed economy and socialist land-use planning), the town and the enterprise continued to develop dynamically. At the beginning of the 1950s, the nationalized enterprise reached its prewar production level (in 1939, total footwear production was 33,408,000 pairs, in 1945 just 7,743,000 pairs, and in 1950 33,396,000 pairs).[14] After a reorganization in 1958 involving the abolishment of the main administrations of several footwear companies, the renamed Gottwaldov became the main headquarters of the Svit national enterprise as an "economic production unit" associating the formerly independent enterprises of Svit (Gottwaldov), Botana (Skuteč), Sázavan (Zruč nad Sázavou), and Závody Gustava Klimenta (Třebíč). A significant portion of the Czechoslovak footwear industry's production capacity was thus once again directed from there (i.e. similarly to the period when the Baťa concern structure was in operation). The associated economic production units reached their production peak in the 1960s and 1970s. The Gottwaldov enterprise itself produced the most footwear in 1969 (54,053,000 pairs; *Statistická ročenka* 1991, 74–77). Starting in the mid-1970s, a slight declining tendency in footwear production could be discerned, which accelerated in the mid-1980s. In 1989, when the Communist regime was abolished, total production at the Svit enterprise was 63,584,000 pairs of shoes. In this context, it must be underscored that, in addition to the main area of footwear production, other industrial sectors—the establishment of which was also connected with the activities of the Baťa concern—developed in the town as well, involving mainly the engineering and construction industries. Thus, in 1988 four industrial enterprises were the largest employers in Gottwaldov (Svit with 14,926 employees, Závody přesného strojírenství with 5,351 employees, Průmyslové stavby with

---

14 In this context, it must be mentioned that the Zlín factory was damaged extensively in an aerial bombardment in 1944, which also had repercussions for the procedure for resuming production (*Statistická ročenka* 1991, 76).

2,981 employees, and Pozemní stavby with 2,980 employees) employing a total of 26,238 workers (*Vybrané údaje* 1990, 5).

Industrial production can also be correlated with the growth of the town's population, which peaked in the second half of the 1940s, and again in the 1960s and 1970s; growth slowed perceptibly from the 1980s on.[15] Starting in 1994, Zlín's population began to decline slowly but persistently due to a natural population decline (i.e. more deaths than births) as a result of negative migration (i.e. more emigrants than immigrants). As a consequence of this trend, Zlín's population declined by more than 5,000 between 1991 and 2011.[16]

These trends in population development are directly linked to the start of extensive housing construction initiatives, which were considered a task of utmost importance in the postwar period. Between 1945 and 1969, a total of 8,393 new apartments were built in the town (*Gottwaldov* 1970, 6). The nature of development however changed completely; the model of family houses in garden quarters was abandoned, and a new form of housing development was sought which accentuaed housing in multi-story residential buildings. In this connection, it must be emphasized that Zlín/Gottwaldov became one of the important centers of socialist urban planning in the years following the Second World War. It is not surprising during the genesis of the new model of massive postwar development oriented toward prefabrication, standardization, and typification that a pioneering role was given to architects with links to the former Baťa design office. In 1953, the first all-panel building in Czechoslovakia was built in Gottwaldov (the so-called type G-40, i.e. a five-story panel building with 40 apartments, intended for Gottwaldov). Significant advances in panel construction were achieved in particular thanks to experiments in panel development undertaken at the Baťa concern as early as during the Second World War (Zarecor 2011).

---

15 The postwar development of the population of *Greater Zlín* (i.e. the town including its incorporated municipalities) is captured by the following statistical data: 1945—49,800; 1950—61,021; 1961—63,038; 1970—70,252; 1980—79,519; 1991—83,126; 2001—80,854 (*Statistický lexikon* 2005, 21).

16 This figure does not reflect the decline in population due to territorial changes connected with the partition of certain parts of the municipality (this decline was 3,625 persons between 1991 and 2011). Databáze demografických údajů za obce ČR (Database of demographic information for municipalities in the Czech Republic), publicly accessible from the website of the Czech Statistical Office on http://www.zlin.czso.cz/cz/obce_d/index. htm.

The events of 1989—combined with a radical change in the political situation, the breakup of the Soviet bloc, and the fall of Communist regimes in Eastern Europe—brought about a fundamental turning point for the town's further development, and it entered 1990 again with its historical name—Zlín. The start of the 1990s is of course also connected with the beginning of an extensive economic transformation, which was accompanied in Zlín by rapid deindustrialization. During the very brief period of one decade, the town's traditional industrial structure—which had determined its character throughout the previous century—broke down and disappeared. Despite the range of problems these processes brought about, their anticipated social impact was largely muted by rapid creation of new jobs in the service sector (ca. 55 percent of the town's economically active population in 2001), the development of Small and Medium-sized Enterprises (SMEs), and the possibility of commuting to work outside the town (this was the case for 17 percent of the economically active population in 2001) (*Statistický lexikon* 2005, 1072–1073). The course of the transformation process was also influenced by the administrative reform occurring in the Czech Republic in 2000, as a result of which Zlín became the regional capital of the Zlín Region (i.e. one of the 14 administrative regions into which the territory of the Czech Republic was divided). Thanks to this reform, the deindustrialized town managed to integrate new functions into its structure, compensating for the decline in the traditional footwear and engineering industries. The basic character of the town's transformation during the last two decades reflects current data from the register of economic entities, which show that the largest employers headquartered in Zlín today are the Tomáš Baťa Regional Hospital (440 employees), the public Tomáš Baťa University (410 employees), and the restored company Baťa, 410 employees, although these worked across the Czech Republic) which does not produce any footwear in Zlín anymore, however.[17] Zlín thus avoided the major decline many other industrial towns experienced and are experiencing in Europe and North America (and of course elsewhere as well). The question remains, however, what will become of the regional capital and its slowing economy in the future.

---

17 Data for the purposes of this paper were provided by the Register of Economic Subjects of the Czech Statistical Office's regional branch in Zlín. The data reflect the state of affairs as of January 31, 2013.

Works Cited

Baťa, J. A. (1939). *Ideální průmyslové město*. In *Průmyslové město*, 1–3. Zlín.

Baťa, T. (1932). *Úvahy a projevy*. Zlín.

Cekota, A. (1931). *Zásady pro zpravodaje časopisu „Zlín"*. Zlín.

Chandler, A. D. (1962). *Strategy and Structure: Chapters in the History of the Industrial Enterprise*. Garden City and New York: Anchor Books.

Chandler, A. D. (1990). *Scale and Scope: The Dynamics of Industrial Capitalism*. Cambridge, Mass.: Belknap Press of Harvard University Press.

Garner, J. (ed.). (1992). *The Company Town. Architecture and Society in the Early Industrial Age*. New York and Oxford: Oxford University Press.

Gottwaldov (1970). *Gottwaldov 1945–1970. 25 let budování města a socialistické společnosti*. Gottwaldov.

Karkošková, A., Z. Pokluda, and V. Štroblík. (2000). Znárodnění průmyslu ve Zlíně 1945–1948. *Zlínsko od minulosti k současnosti*, 17, 103–107.

Kiess, W. (1991). *Urbanismus im Industriezeitalter. Von der klassizistischen Stadt zur Garden City*. Berlin: Ernst & Sohn.

Kraus, L. (ed.). (1984). *Od verpánku k světovosti. Druhá část třídílné publikace o historii VHJ Svit, oborový podnik Gottwaldov, retrospektiva let 1945–80*. Gottwaldov: Svit.

Lehár, B. (1960). *Dějiny Baťova koncernu (1894–1945)*. Praha: Státní nakladatelství politické literatury.

Lehár, B. (1963). The Economic Expansion of the Baťa Concern in Czechoslovakia and Abroad, 1929–1938. *Historica*, 5, 147–188.

Pokluda, Z. (2006). *Sedm století zlínských dějin*. Zlín.

Průmyslové město (1939). Zlín.

Saldern, A. von, R. Hachtmann, and J. H. Kirsch (eds.). (2009). Fordismus. *Zeithistorische Forschungen*, Online-Ausgabe, 6, H. 2. 02.02.2012 http://www.zeithistorische-forschungen.de/16126041-Inhalt-2-2009.

Ševeček, L., and M. Zahrádková (eds.) (1995). *Kulturní fenomén funkcionalismu. Sborník příspěvků konference*. Zlín: Státní galerie ve Zlíně.

Ševeček, O. (2009). *Zrození Baťovy průmyslové metropole. Továrna, městský prostor a společnost ve Zlíně v letech 1900–1938*. České Budějovice and Ostrava: Veduta and Ostravská univerzita v Ostravě.

Ševeček, O. (2013). The Case of Company Towns of the Baťa Concern. In O. Ševeček and M. Jemelka (eds.). *Company Towns of the Baťa Concern: History—Cases—Architecture*, 15–47. Stuttgart: Franz Steiner Verlag.

Statistická ročenka 1960. VHJ Svit. (1961). Gottwaldov: Svit.

Statistická ročenka 90. (1991). Zlín: Svit akciová společnost.

Statistický lexikon obcí České republiky. (2005). Praha: Ottovo nakladatelství.

Szczepanik, P. (2005). Mediální výstavba Ideálního průmyslového města. Síť médií v Baťově Zlíně 30. let. In P. Skopal (ed.). *Kinematografie a město. Studie z dějin lokální filmové kultury*, 23–55. Brno: Masarykova universita.

Teuteberg, H. J. (ed.). (1985). *Homo Habitans. Zur Sozialgeschichte des ländlichen und städtischen Wohnens in der Neuzeit.* Münster: Coppenrath.

Vrána, S. (1939). *Deset let pokusné práce na měšťanských školách ve Zlíně 1929–1939.* Zlín.

Vybrané údaje o obcích v okrese Zlín. (1990). Zlín: Okresní oddělení Českého statistického úřadu ve Zlíně.

Zarecor, K. (2011). *Manufacturing a Socialist Modernity. Housing in Czechoslovakia, 1945–1960.* Pittsburgh: University of Pittsburgh Press.

Social Engineering, the Factory and Urban Environment: Cadbury/Bournville and Opel/Rüsselsheim (1878–1960)

Timo Luks

This article is concerned with Cadbury and Opel; and with Bournville and Rüsselsheim. A comparative analysis of these two case studies aims to shed light on one distinctive way in which industrial factories are integrated into their urban environments. Both companies are of continued interest for historical research because Cadbury and Opel pioneered advanced methods of (mass) production and welfare policies. Apart from that, their extraordinary public reputation can be seen to also rest on the fact that both companies deliver two very iconic products of modern societies for now more than a century: cars and chocolate bars.

Cadbury/Bournville and Opel/Rüsselsheim share some striking features that distinguish them from other cases. Neither Bournville nor Rüsselsheim fit into the categories of large industrial cities like Manchester or highly agglomerated industrial regions like the Ruhr area. Whereas Manchester, the Ruhr area and many other examples symbolized all the alleged evils of unchecked industrialization and urbanization and evoked a somewhat utopian counter-image of a bucolic idyll (Zimmermann and Reulecke 1999), Cadbury/Bournville and Opel/Rüsselsheim seemed to embody a successful compromise of rural and industrial ways of living. In both cases, *one single company* was willing, able and expected to take responsibility for maintaining wellbeing, social order and stability within its immediate hinterland.

The following article does not give a detailed analysis of company housing nor is it a case study in architecture and urban planning. Instead, I will concentrate on the production of meaning and the politics of representation that were essential for the integration of the industrial factory into its urban environment. In order to be considered an 'industrial city' it was necessary, but not sufficient, to attract a considerable industry within its reaches. Further minimal criteria for defining industrial cities are a large percentage of workers and an economic performance that depended on industrial companies. But the point is, that being an industrial city meant nothing less than developing an imagery that not only transcended traditional skepticism that was wielded against large factories, but rather promoted factories as a harmoniously integrated part of urban 'landscapes'. This shift was accompanied and fostered by the rise of new protagonists in public debates: social reformers and "experts" (e.g. early "sociologists") as opposed to the formerly dominant bourgeois writers and cultural critics. Therefore, a study on industrial cities must bear in mind the complex overlapping of social, economic and cultural history. The following article is mainly concerned with one aspect in this field of study: the "boundary-work" (Gieryn 1983, 781–795) carried out by journalists, industrial reformers and sociologists in order to relate and integrate factories and their environment. The ways in which this work was carried out was heavily determined by one particular mode of problematizing modern industry and its effects on society—social engineering. Hence, the opening paragraphs of my article are concerned with the concept of social engineering. The subsequent paragraphs will analyze the two case studies of Cadbury's and Opel's, followed by an attempt to situate the case studies within a broader context.

The Concept of Social Engineering

From the 1880s onwards, rapid urbanization and industrialization led to profound changes in the social order. Contemporary observers interpreted these developments in terms of 'crisis' (Föllmer and Graf 2005; Graf 2008; Hardtwig 2007). The crisis trope generated the new practice of social engineering, providing sociologists, architects, welfare workers and engineers with scientific tools to tackle social problems in a 'rational' manner. Social engineering can be defined as a mode of rethinking and reworking modernity in order to overthrow what seemed to be a seriously threatening process of social disintegration and fragmentation. Social engineers tried to restore social order by focusing on middle-range social formations, e.g. industrial work and the factory, traffic and transportation, urban planning and architecture, population and social policy (Etzemüller 2009; 2010; Kuchenbuch 2012; Luks 2010; Schlimm 2011; Jackson 1990; Jordan 1994; McClymer 1980).

The concept of social engineering has been introduced by Zygmunt Bauman to highlight specific features of modernity within which the holocaust could be situated (Luks 2012). "I suggest", Bauman (1989, 18) argues, "that the bureaucratic culture which prompts us to view society as an object of administration, as a collection of so many 'problems' to be solved, as 'nature' to be 'controlled', 'mastered' and 'improved' or 'remade', as a legitimate target for 'social engineering', and in general a garden to be designed and kept in the planned shape by force (the gardening posture divides vegetation into 'cultured plants' to be taken care of, and weeds to be exterminated), was the very atmosphere in which the idea of the Holocaust could be conceived, slowly yet consistently developed, and brought to its conclusion." The Holocaust, in Bauman's view, did not suspend main features of modernity, but rather drew its most "radical" conclusion by using scientific methods (e.g. statistics, biology, demography) to identify sections of the population to be 'exterminated'. Extermination, many Nazis officials argued within this context, should be implemented by 'rational planning'—translating racism and anti-Semitism into terms of 'problem solving'. This meant: isolating different 'problems' from each other and suspending moral reflection in favor of technical solution—which, in Nazi terminology, included extermination. None of this was unique to Nazi Germany, but rather, as Bauman indicates, to the central tenets of modernity itself. 'Problem solving' depended on scientific expertise, empirical research and social analysis. Hence, applied (social) sciences became one of the most important instruments to design social order. This process paved the way for a permanent presence of experts within administrations, parliaments, political parties, pressure groups, industrial factories and so on (Raphael 1996; Szöllösi-Janze 2004; Edgerton 2005; Brückweh 2012). From the 1880s onwards, one can witness the rise of a professional society. As Harold Perkin (1989, 123) put it:

"In all its manifestations, liberal, conservative or socialist, the professional social ideal consistently applied the tests of justification by service to society and, in one form or another, of the greatest happiness of the greatest number, to the analysis and criticism of contemporary society. Down to about 1880, however, such criticisms were a disconnected series of individual correctives to the excessive materialism of capitalist system while in no way threatening its continued existence. From the 1880s by contrast, concomitantly with the accelerated growth of professional occupations of all kinds, it began to take shape in a form that appeared to many landowners and business men to be an organized threat to the rights if not indeed to the security of private property and so the foundations of capitalist society."

Professional society and social engineering—on the one hand a discursive formation, on the other hand a practice shared by many (industrial) sociologists, reformers and production engineers—did not necessarily threaten private property and "the foundations of capitalist society", as Perkin argues. It rather marked a profound change within industrial and capitalist society. On the one hand, industrial production became central to society as a whole. The term 'industrialism' increasingly replaced 'capitalism' within discourses on professionalism and social reform that were aimed, in the first place, at the urban environment and, then, at the channeling of industrialization. Social reform in this sense soon became a forerunner of social engineering. On the other hand, 'rational planning' and 'efficiency' became the hallmarks of social order. Industrial experts had a fair share in these developments.

Among other aspects, social engineering was concerned with the development of industrial landscapes and industrial cities. It was an important motor not only for planning and designing (industrial) model towns and villages or company housing but also for far reaching discourses on the need and the opportunity to integrate living space and workplace likewise. Social engineering supported ideas of an ever increasing responsibility of industrial companies for their workmen and, most important, workmen's *environment*. Social engineering in this respect was an attempt to assure the stability and morality of socio-spatial milieus. In contrast to earlier rejections of industrial factories and across-the-board damnation of its effects on social order, these new attempts tried to prove that modern industry was not necessarily incommensurate with social coherence and harmony (Heald 1970; Kasson 1976). Referring to the United States, Morrell Heald (1970, 27) argues that from the beginning of the 20th century businessmen, social workers and political reformers shared a new awareness for the mutual dependency of industry and urban communities. "From this new awareness would grow new forms of community organization, which, in time, would bind business closely into the web of urban welfare institutions." The "quality of urban life" became something of utmost importance (ibid., 34). From the turn of the century, these efforts gained momentum. They re-vitalized and, in many ways, reinvented traditional paternalist attitudes in business. Patrick Joyce (1980, 90–133) analyzes in detail the rise of powerful discourses and social practices in Britain that stressed the necessity of employers to exert "social hegemony" over "their" municipalities. Joyce highlights the consolidation of factory towns, urban-industrial neighborhoods and an accompanying "sense of community" since the second half of the 19th century. In Britain and elsewhere, a "culture of the factory" emerged that fostered corporate 'investment' in its surrounding (urban) milieu. Patrick Joyce addresses these developments as "new paternalism" that even pervaded the symbolic representation of many companies.

"The ritual of the factory extended the symbolic boundary from the factory to the neighbourhood, celebrating the connection of the employer and the community. The basic constituent of this ritual was undoubtedly the mythology of the employer family. The history and destiny of the factory was made one with the saga of family life, so enforcing the fiction of community." (ibid., 181)

Arguably, the paternalist tradition from the beginning of the 20th century became less and less important. In order to highlight the decrease of paternalism and the increase of more 'scientific' approaches I use the term social engineering to describe one particular mode of designing social and industrial order. The discourse on social engineering slowly faded away in the late 1950s and early 1960s. The erosion of social engineering can be related to the rise of *flexible* mass production, new forms of individualization within the workplace and so on (Luks 2010, 272–279). These changes echoed new developments in urban history, mainly a massive politics of modernization and the rise of automotive cities (Gunn 2011; Heßler and Zimmermann 2011).

The Factory in the Garden: Cadbury and Bournville

The history of the Cadbury Cocoa Works has been mainly discussed with regard to its company culture (Dellheim 1987) and welfare policy (Robertson et al. 2007), the underlying Quaker ethics (Bradley 1987; Child 1964) and, of course, different aspects of business history and production organization in general (Fitzgerald 2005; Jones 1984; Rowlinson 1988). Beyond these topics, special attention has been paid to Cadbury's efforts in urban planning and housing, especially after the relocation of the works from Birmingham to Bournville in 1878/79 that led to the engineering of a model village and its subsequent transformation into a garden suburb (Chance 2007; Harrison 1999).

Cadbury's efforts in industrial reform, welfare work, urban planning and housing policy have been largely influenced by the religious ethics of the Quaker community. John Child (1964, 294) identifies four main precepts of Quaker ethics in relation to modern business: "(i) a dislike of the exploitation and profit of one man at the expense of another, (ii) a traditionally puritan view of the 'stewardship of talents', stressing the value of hard work, lack of waste, the careful organization of resources, and a personal renunciation, all for the service of others, (iii) a tradition of egalitarianism and democratic relationships, and (iv) an abhorrence of conflict between men." These ethics' 'bounded individualism' became the hallmark of a preoccupation with the social problems of modern industrial society. Cadbury and other Quaker companies, therefore, were engaged in an enduring struggle to reconcile their religious ethics with the requirements of modern industry and to unfold a business culture that would be able to 'cure' the 'social ills' of industrial societies. "Quakers have not failed to apply their ethical criteria to the conditions of modern industry. Not surprisingly, their chief concerns have been the quality of social relationships within the factory, the conditions of work in this environment, and the division of the rewards of this toil" (ibid.). The Quaker ideal in industrial relations was a state of mutual understanding, goodwill and the absence of conflict. A sense for the development of workmen's 'personality' led Cadbury and others to questions of designing factory premises, housing estates and so on.

For many decades, the Cadbury company was located in Birmingham, one of Britain's most important industrial cities throughout the 19th century. In 1831, when John Cadbury opened his factory and started a manufacturing business in Crooked Lane, "a winding back street" (Iolo A. Williams), Birmingham's industry was dominated by a plethora of small-scale workshops. The heyday of large industrial factories was still to come. Things changed in the last third of the 19th century. Birmingham now housed a couple of large factories; the city witnessed an altered spatial structure and a dwelling situation that became worse and worse. This triggered a vivid discussion about the future of social order. Critics of industrial and urban life strongly fostered the idea of a pastoral way of living, a "village and cottage ideal", time and again. Aesthetical objections against fast growing industrial cities and workers' dwelling quarters in the name of a new romanticism, an idealization of nature and so on resonated with ideas of social harmony and powered different approaches of social and industrial reform (Harrison 1999, 1–16).

In the late 1870s, Cadbury decided to leave the urban-industrial moloch and to relocate its factory in the countryside. Initially, Cadbury's move was motivated by a typical mixture of business and philanthropic motives. The Birmingham production site had become too small and thus a hindrance for further expansion. Instead of moving to a slightly larger site in Birmingham, which would have forced a lot of compromises and cut backs upon the

company, its directors—the Cadbury family—opted for a new beginning
(Williams 1931, 54–76). Relocating its main factory to the countryside was
driven by the aim to offer the workers a better livelihood. It was a conscious
attempt to escape from the 'social ills' associated with an expanding industrial city. The company started to buy landed property beyond the newly
built factory and facilitated housing and infrastructure. Yet, in contrast to
many other firms, Cadbury did not restrict its use to its own employees.
Bournville was neither planned nor executed as a "company town" in a narrow and traditional sense.[1] To ensure formal, legal and—in theory—financial
independence from the company, Cadbury endowed the landed property
and the buildings to the newly found Bournville Village Trust. The idea was
to strengthen local self-government rather than exercising power in a 'feudal'
manner (Dellheim 1987, 20).

When moving to the countryside, Cadbury was anxious about the effects
that a large factory would possibly have on the Bournville area. The "factory
in the garden" should preserve a sustainably pastoral way of living—and
not duplicate or transfer the problems of large industrial settlements. The
planners and architects—Alfred Pickard Walker, William Alexander Harvey,
and Henry Bedford Tyler—approached the task by designing and building
low priced but high quality dwellings that preserved aesthetic and social visions of pastoral life. Their attention was not limited by the shape of the
buildings or the layout of the flats and also included an ambitious program
of landscaping and the design of the surrounding environment. Especially
Harvey was keen to combine efforts in housing reform with ideas of the Arts
and Crafts Movement and, therefore, soon became a leading figure in discussing (and solving) the so-called cheap cottage-problem (Harrison 1999,
33–94; Lees 1985). From the beginning, Harvey „expressed his disgust at
overcrowded slums and his distaste for the 'desolate row upon row' of ugly
and cramped villas which threatened to engulf Britain's cities. […] Harvey
soon began to deliberately produce more varied streetscapes in the village.
He sought to emulate the picturesque patterns he admiringly noted in pre-
industrial villages" (Harrison 2004, 2–3).

From the start, the provision of open-air recreation facilities was a main
feature of Bournville. To those in charge the Bournville factory garden
seemed to be as important as the village itself. The factory garden, estab-

---

1 The concept of company towns is of American origin (Buder 1967) and, in Britain, was
  frequently discussed not as a model fit for adoption but rather an erroneous way of inte-
  grating urban and industrial developments that should not be repeated.

lished in 1893 and just like the housing managed independently from the company, and the "Arcadian allegory" (Helena Chance) were meant to be a model recreation development and to distinguish Bournville from other attempts in urban and industrial reform. Although landscaping and recreation were part of a larger reform discourse, Cadbury used these topics to highlight his own industrial and pastoral impetus. Reformers "harnessed landscape in this period as a form of social engineering designed to attract and maintain a quality workforce for maximum profit" (Chance 2007, 199). Helena Chance argues that Cadbury's introduction of the garden(ing) ideal into the realm of industrial organization, beyond its already mentioned functions, reaffirmed a highly gendered approach to the workforce. While the men's open-air recreation ground was nothing else but a sports field, the so-called Girls Ground, opened in 1896, was mainly a garden. Gardening was considered to be a mainly "female" activity and an effective way to give "the (working) girls" a sense of (feminine) respectability. Cadbury integrated images of the "Cadbury's Angels", as the working girls were referred to in official publications, into the firm's public relations-strategy. "Symbolic ideas of gardens are represented using metaphor and allegory to project Arcadian images of factory life. The Cadbury's Angels are portrayed as ideal women, according to Christian morality, and the photographs provide mirror images for the girls, reflecting their status as angels in the garden. [...] In all the photographs that were kept, the women look modest and the setting, the garden, reinforces this message" (ibid., 209). While displaying the working girls within a garden setting was in the firm's view the best way to illustrate what Cadbury and Bournville were all about, Bournville as a whole became

"the living symbol of the Cadbury's vision of industry. It was captured in a brilliant metaphor, 'the factory in a garden', evoking the union of industry and nature. [...] For George Cadbury, the benefits of country life were immeasurable. 'If the Works had been in Birmingham,' he told a visiting journalist, 'instead of lying at their ease there in the fresh air, with the grass beneath them and the blue sky above them, they would have had nowhere to pass their rest hours except the dingy streets, or perhaps some narrow, evil-smelling court, and they might even have been tempted to spend it in the cheerier surroundings of a drink shop—and who can blame them?' Rural pleasures, then, served moral purposes, enabling workers to lead the good life or, at least, the good life according to George Cadbury." (Dellheim 1987, 31)

The prominence of Bournville and its model character owed much not only, as mentioned, to the continuous public relation-strategy of the firm itself, but also to the fact that members of the Cadbury family and the board of management—notably Edward Cadbury—published a number of successful books on different topics in industrial relations. This approach led to the inscription of an otherwise somewhat arbitrary example into the much broader framework of industrial sociology and industrial reform. Edward Cadbury (1873–1948), author and co-author of several influential books (Cadbury and Shann 1907; Cadbury, Matheson and Shann 1907; Cadbury 1912), entered the Cadbury family business in 1893, when his father and uncle were in charge. In 1899 Edward Cadbury became Managing Director and took charge of the company's export business and women workers. From 1937 until his death in 1943 he was chairman of the board of management. His most important book *Experiments in Industrial Organisation* was published in 1912. The book was not so much a theoretical study of the possibilities, limits and perspectives of modern management and industrial organization as it was a guidebook, a collection of examples and a portrait of the Cadbury firm. His book, he wrote, was meant to give a description of one particular large factory, the Bournville Works, and the continuous efforts of the Cadbury Management. Referring to the different measures and facilities, Cadbury (1912, XVII) pointed out that "the varied schemes involved have not come into being in any haphazard or accidental way", but were the result of ongoing reflection and experimentation.

Although the company planned, designed and maintained a whole village, Edward Cadbury did not consider the approach of attempting to enrich workers' whole lives as being paternalistic. Rather, taking responsibility for much more than factory life in a narrow sense was presented first as a necessity of business efficiency and second as an essential service required due to an otherwise absent urban and civic infrastructure. Not in each and every case, Edward Cadbury wrote, is it desirable to turn the factory into the center of workers' lives. In case the factory was located in a larger town, this would not even be possible.

"But in the case of a factory that is in a village, or on the outskirts of a large town, the circumstances seem to be somewhat different. In such places, as a rule, there is very little opportunity for social recreation, and since a considerable part, if not the majority, of the community are dependent for their livelihood directly or indirectly on the large Works situated in their midst, it seems natural that their social life should focus round this centre." (ibid., 259)

Considering Cadbury's relocation of its own factory, it becomes clear that the company created the exact situation Edward Cadbury identified as requirement and legitimation to expand a company's responsibility. What is striking about the Cadbury case is the move to reconfigure paternalism by situating it within a more 'scientific' framework. This tendency was accompanied by a pro-industrial attitude and the firm belief that it was possible to reconcile nature and industry.

Industrial Village: Opel and Rüsselsheim

The history of Opel is well known to historians of modern industry, although an overall synthesis is still lacking. A broad panorama in terms of social and business history is given by Bernd Heyl and Andrea Neugebauer (1997) who focus on Opel during the Weimar and Nazi period, while Henry A. Turner's (2005) study is concerned with "the struggle for control of Opel" between General Motors and Nazi Germany. Main developments in labor history and production organization have been analyzed by Anita Kugler (1985), Andrea Neugebauer (1999) and Peter Schirmbeck (1988). We therefore know a lot about trade unionism, everyday working lives, and the composition of the workforce in terms of age, gender, social and regional background, vocational training and qualification. Opel, of course, is frequently discussed by scholars who are interested in the history of the automobile industry or assembly line production in general due to Opel's pioneering role in introducing elements of the so called American system of mass production, including the early introduction of conveyor belts (Bönig 1993; Flik 2001; Laux 1992; Stahlmann 1993).

During the heyday of social engineering Opel and Rüsselsheim have frequently been discussed whenever someone felt the need to 'prove' that modern industry does not necessary lead to chaotic urbanization. Decade after decade, Opel and Rüsselsheim seemed to reconfirm the hopes that pastoral life and industrial production could be reconciled and coexist in perfect harmony. It was not accidental that well-known journalists like Heinrich Hauser (1901–1955) were fascinated by Opel and Rüsselsheim. Hauser was highly popular and successful during Weimar and early Nazi Germany. As a journalist he was influenced by the so-called *Neue Sachlichkeit*. With other representatives of this cultural trend he shared an extensive interest in machines, industry, and workers as embodiment of modernity. But in terms of style his books and reportages differed significant from the mainstream of *Neue Sach-*

lichkeit. When writing about Opel, his favorite topic of choice[2], Hauser usually preferred a highly metaphorical language, applying romanticist images of nature and natural harmony to industrial production. He usually did not only focus on efficiency and functionality, but highlighted in particular the 'beauty' of machines and industrial production. Repeatedly Hauser depicted the 'journey' of raw materials, beginning with their entrance into the 'sphere of production' until the finished car left the factory building. Metaphors of nature were used within this context to interpret the many single processes of production as being part of an 'organic whole' (Neugebauer 1987, 59–67; Graebner 2001). Apart from his interest in what happened behind factory gates, Hauser had a keen interest in the ways modern industry was embedded into the surrounding environment. His book *Am laufenden Band (At the Assembly Line)*, published in 1936, stressed this point time and again: "The factory and the workers' housing settlements strongly determine the face of the small town [Rüsselsheim], but, still, its rural character proved indestructible. One has to walk just a few steps to leave these walls behind and to enter the woods, the vineyards or the large River Main meadows" (Hauser 1936a, 10). Heinrich Hauser illustrated his description with some photographs, stressing what he called a successful integration of industry and nature.

Fig. 1: The Opel Tower Midst Natural Beauty

(Source: Hauser 1936a, 9)

2 Hauser wrote several books on Opel whose immediate success and enduring popularity seems to be a result not so much of Hauser's somewhat mannered writing but the iconic photographs, particularly by Paul Wolff: *Am laufenden Band* (1936); *Opel, ein deutsches Tor zur Welt* (1937); *Im Kraftfeld von Rüsselsheim. Mit 80 Farbphotos von Paul Wolff* (1940); *Bevor dies Stahlherz schlägt* (1951); *Dein Haus hat Räder* (1952).

Fig. 2: The Factory as Horizon

(Source: Hauser, 1936a, 12)

These pictures visualized Hauser's firm belief in the possibility of embedding industry into nature 'harmoniously' and 'organically'. According to this view, factory premises and factory buildings do not disturb the pastoral and bucolic sight or the agricultural activities in any way. On the contrary, Hauser (1936a, 13) wrote, "the factory rises from the undulating sheaves just like an island". Hauser's pictures do not accuse factory buildings of disrupting nature's order and beauty or of being erratic. The Opel Tower (Fig. 1) rises up in the middle of blooming trees and seems to be a part of this harmonious landscape. The factory premises are the natural horizon, not so much limiting as a point of rest. The factory premises could equally be an alpine panorama, at least in visual terms (Fig. 2). If one is resting from a hard day's work, the picture appears to be saying, take a glance and enjoy the calming aesthetic of the factory premises. Hauser's respective Wolff's pictures invert the classic and traditional view insofar as the usual postcard image directs the gaze into the opposite direction: from the industrial and urban vantage point towards the landscape. Hauser not only includes a praise of Opel[3], but also tries to establish one particular aesthetic measure to judge the ways in which factories and natural landscapes are integrated. Opel and Rüsselsheim, in this regard, turn into a model of harmonious and 'organic' integration.

Hauser's suggestive pattern became common sense. Of course, one anonymous visitor stated in the journal of the metal workers' union (Anon. 1950, 4), there was a significant contrast between the "rural peace" around the river Main on the one hand and the "aura of industrial agility within the Opel factory premises" on the other hand, but this *contrast* in the case of Opel never turned into a *conflict*. Rather, Opel and Rüsselsheim seemed to signify a state of utopian potential and perfection that irritated contemporaries just because such a harmony between industry, nature and settlement was so rarely seen elsewhere. Opel and Rüsselsheim, therefore, turned into a model for a future integration of large-scale industrial production with its huge factories into the surrounding environment. German sociologist Karl Weigand wrote in 1956—following the pattern of stressing Russelsheim's uniqueness—that this small town exercised a very strong influence "on the design of the cultural landscape in the Rhine-Main-Area" (Weigand 1956, 10). Opel determines, he wrote, "the image of its business community (*Betriebsgemeinde*), which owes its latter-day size and urban character to the company" (ibid.). In contrast to other industrial cities, Weigand argued, Rüsselsheim never became an unmanageable urban-industrial moloch. Rüsselsheim was hailed for being and remaining a "workmen's village" (*Arbeiterdorf*) that

"was different from its neighbor villages due to the fact that a distinct 'factory town' existed right beside the residential buildings on an ample factory estate, which had been grown in the first place without its own factory borough, but rather attracted its workers from other places. [...] The village character changed when larger settlements were built. Just like the 'Opel colony' these settlements occupied an ample space outside the traditional residential belt. [...] But a decisive inner change did not occur before the end of World War II. Only now a distinct business community was established that even in the expansion during the thirties was still lacking." (ibid., 42–43)

Cultural representation, for example in terms of journalistic popularization (Hauser) or scientific discovery (Weigand), was just one way to put forward statements about the inseparability of Opel and Rüsselsheim and, fur-

---

3 It was the company itself that ordered the richly illustrated book and published some chapters in the company's official journal *Opel-Kamerad* (Hauser 1936b).

thermore, nature, quasi-urban settlements and industry. Another way were the manifold efforts in planning and building factory housing, guaranteeing a continuous 'material' presence of the factory within a city or village. Opel took part in attempts to build company housing. In 1935 the company newspaper proudly announced the topping out ceremony of a new Opel colony (Anon. 1935, 4). The official Opel press constantly covered the *Opel-Wohnungsbaugesellschaft's* progress (Otto 1939). In 1939 the journal *Opel-Kamerad* reported on the state of the art in the new settlement and gave an illuminating impression of a walkabout:

"At the colony cottage's area", our anonymous author wrote, "I always feel overwhelmed by some kind of sanctification. A bright earnestness is dominating [this place]. No one is living for the day, but continuously working with well-considered purpose until evening or even nightfalls. [...] Pediments are glancing over the small gardens at the beautiful wooded environment in dignified humility." (Anon. 1939, 77)

The anonymous author of this little piece of writing stressed the "factual beauty" and the "flawless appearance" of the settlement. He watched the settlers handing over "fresh products of gardening" through the windows and witnessed "healthy children" that made his or her heart sing out of joy because of "this modest, but self-achieved and therefore precious prosperity" (ibid., 78).[4] All these admired characteristics, the author continued, were echoed inside the cottages whose furniture was "appropriate and without any disrupting decoration". The interior was as "rational and reasonable" as the residents themselves. No one indulged any "false illusiveness" (ibid.). The Opel settlement is presented and discussed as a perfect embodiment of a stable social 'order' beyond what was referred to as liberal and individualistic chaos, fragmentation, egoism, and alienation. This very effective idea(l) of order became evident in highly suggestive photographs (Fig. 3).

Images such as this stressed the similarity and well-ordered composition of the detached houses and their place within the settlement as a whole. Even houses and dwellings should avoid, one could argue, standing alone in a 'fragmented' and 'isolated' way associated with 'liberalism' and 'individual-

---

4 "Health" was an important topic within discourses of industrial settlements and workmen's dwellings but cannot be discussed here in detail. In 1940 the journal *Opel-Kamerad* enthusiastically reported on "healthy children with chubby cheeks". Every settler, the article claimed, confirmed a significant change in terms of health and nutrition after moving in. "The families' health is ensured by the healthy dwelling in the colony in an excellent way; and by living in comfortable, healthy and bright rooms" (Anon. 1940, 234).

Fig. 3: Opel Settlement—Infrastructure of Social Order

(Anon. 1939, 77)

ism'. The picture stressed affinity, connectivity and so on yet the writing simultaneously denied that these characteristics led to uniformity. On the one hand, the houses and gardens looked strung up like pearls on a chain. The street and the fence highlighted the straightforwardness of this order. On the other hand, different vantage points and framings pointed towards the distinctive and distinguishing elements. *Within* the pictured and built *serial* order, within 'reasonable limits', variation was possible. Where variation on a pictorial level was invisible, it had to be posited. "The latitude (*Spielraum*) for a particular taste that still exists despite the [settlement's] unity is used—in favor of the overall picture of the colony, too—very beneficial. [...] The more or less visible order that here determines everything does not allow any unchecked capriciousness. But the effect is never burdensome or constricted" (Anon. 1939, 78).

Debates about Opel and Rüsselsheim usually stressed the preexistence of a beautiful landscape and village and the fact that its inhabitants were 'rooted in the soil'. The story told about Opel and Rüsselsheim was one of a factory welcomed by its pastoral environment. It was a story about a factory that acknowledged the values of rural life—a story about the ways in which both were beneficial to each other.

Conclusion

The analyzed cases in one way or another imply the possibility and even necessity to design urban and rural environments by designing factory premises and factory buildings. Because industrial sociologists, welfare workers and others acknowledged the manifold interrelations between factories and their environment, the factories had to be held responsible for social order as a whole. This belief was a main element of the particular mode of problematizing industrial work in the first half of the 20th century I have been referring to as 'social engineering'. Social engineering in many respects turned earlier paternalist practices and utopian visions into something new. Employers' paternalist dreams turned into a highly 'rational' task for industrial sociologists and welfare workers to design a 'rational' factory order and to situate the factory within its environment. Efforts in designing industrial settlements and dwellings were frequently echoed by contemporary sociological reflection and analysis in Britain and Germany. Employers, industrial sociologist Ludwig Heinrich Adolph Geck wrote in 1931, had always tried to "design the factory's social order along the lines of fundamental principles and to influence social order outside the factory" (Geck 1931, 313). Certain firms, British industrial sociologist J. Henry Richardson wrote two years later,

"appear to aim at the creation of a model community in which the workpeople shall find full scope for their physical, mental and moral development. Not only are the best possible arrangements made for the comfort of the workpeople inside the factory, and the work organized so as to involve the least possible strain, but all such matters are being considered in consultation with the representatives of the employees. Outside the factory facilities are provided for a wide variety of social, educational and recreational activities." (Richardson 1933, 179)

Between the 1920s and 1950s, as these quotations indicate, questions of boundary work became prevalent. Many companies, sociologists, industrial reformers and even production engineers felt the need to answer the question where to draw the line between a factory and its environment. Historical studies in industrial cities and landscapes should integrate the dynamics and practices of "boundary-work" into its realm. By doing so, one can analyze the *making of* industrial cities and landscapes from the vantage point of cultural history.

Works Cited

Anon. (1935). Die Opelstadt wächst. Richtfest der neuen Opel-Siedlung (1935). *Opel-Werksgemeinschaft*, 12/6/1935, 4.

Anon. (1939). Schönes und Frohes aus der Opel-Siedlung (1939). *Opel-Kamerad*, 4/10/1939, 77–79.

Anon. (1940). Vorbildliche Leistungen in der Opel-Siedlung Rüsselsheim (1940). *Opel-Kamerad*, 9/11/1940, 233–235.

Anon. (1950). Ein Besuch bei Opel Rüsselsheim am Main (1950). *Metall*, 5/2/1950, 4.

Bauman, Z. (1989). *Modernity and the Holocaust*. Cambridge: Polity Press.

Bönig, J. (1993). *Die Einführung von Fließbandarbeit in Deutschland bis 1933. Zur Geschichte einer Sozialinnovation*. Münster and Hamburg: LIT.

Bradley, I. C. (1987): *Enlightened Entrepreneurs. Business Ethics in Victorian Britain*, London: Lion Books.

Brückweh, K. (ed.). (2012). *Engineering Society. The Role of the Human and Social Sciences in Modern Societies, 1880–1980*. Basingstoke: Palgrave.

Buder, S. (1967). *Pullman. An Experiment in Industrial Order and Community Planning 1880–1930*. New York: Oxford University Press.

Cadbury, E. (1912). *Experiments in Industrial Organisation*. London et al: Longmans.

Cadbury, E., and G. Shann (1907). *Sweating*. London: T. Fisher Unwin.

Cadbury, E., M. C. Matheson, and G. Shann (1907). *Women's Work and Wages. A Phase Of Life In An Industrial City*. London: T. Fisher Unwin.

Chance, H. (2007). The Angel on the Garden Suburb. Arcadian Allegory in the "Girls Ground" at the Cadbury Factory, Bournville, England, 1880–1930. *Studies in the History of Gardens & Designed Landscapes*, 3/27/2007, 197–217.

Child, J. (1964). Quaker Employers and Industrial Relations. *Sociological Review*, 12, 293–315.

Dellheim, C. (1987). The Creation of a Company Culture. Cadburys, 1861–1931. *American Historical Rreview*, 92, 13–44.

Edgerton, D. (2005). Science and the Nation. Towards New Histories of Twentieth-Century Britain. *Historical Research*, 78, 96–112.

Etzemüller, T. (ed.). (2009). *Die Ordnung der Moderne. Social Engineering im 20. Jahrhundert*. Bielefeld: transcript.

Etzemüller, T. (2010). *Die Romantik der Rationalität. Alva & Gunnar Myrdal—Social Engineering in Schweden*. Bielefeld: transcript.

Fitzgerald, R. (2005). Products, Firms and Consumption. Cadbury and the Development of Marketing, 1900–1939. *Business History*, 47, 511–531.

Flik, R. (2001). *Von Ford lernen? Automobilbau und Motorisierung in Deutschland bis 1933*. Köln, Weimar and Wien: Böhlau.

Föllmer, M., and R. Graf (eds.). (2005). *Die Krise der Weimarer Republik. Zur Kritik eines Deutungsmusters*. Frankfurt am Main and New York: Campus.

Geck, L. H. A. (1931). „Autonom-betriebliche Sozialpolitik". In Görres-Gesellschaft (ed.). *Die soziale Frage und der Katholizismus. Festschrift zum 40jährigen Jubiläum der Enzyklika Rerum novarum*, 312–333. Paderborn: Schöningh.

Gieryn, T. F. (1983). „Boundary-Work" and the Demarcation on Science from Non-Science. Strains and Interests in Professional Ideologies of Scientists. *American Sociological Rewiew*, 48, 781–795.

Graebner, G. (2001). *"Dem Leben unter die Haut kriechen…". Heinrich Hauser. Leben und Werk. Eine kritisch-biographische Werk-Bibliographie*. Aachen: shaker.

Graf, R. (2008). *Die Zukunft der Weimarer Republik. Krisen und Zukunftsaneignungen in Deutschland 1918–1933*. München: Oldenbourg.

Gunn, S. (2011). The Buchanan Report, Environment and the Problem of Traffic in 1960s Britain, in: *Twentieth Century British History*, 22 (4), 521–542.

Hardtwig, W. (ed.). (2007). *Ordnungen in der Krise. Zur politischen Kulturgeschichte Deutschlands 1900–1933*. München: Oldenbourg.

Harrison, M. (1999). *Bournville. Model Village to Garden Suburb*. Chichester: The History Press.

Harrison, M. (2004). *William Alexander Harvey (1874–1951)—Bournville and after*. http://www-etsav.upc.es/personals/iphs2004/pdf/082_p.pdf.

Hauser, H. (1936a). *Am laufenden Band*. Frankfurt/Main: Hauserpresse.

Hauser, H. (1936b). Ein Auto wie aus einem Stück gebaut. *Opel-Kamerad*, 2/7/1936, 34–39.

Heald, M. (1988). *The Social Responsibilities of Business. Company and Community, 1900–1960*. New Brunswick, New Jersey and Oxford: Transaction Publishers.

Heßler, M., and C. Zimmermann (2011). Perspektiven historischer Industriestadtforschung: Neubetrachtungen eines etablierten Forschungsfeldes. *Archiv für Sozialgeschichte*, 51, 661–694.

Heyl, B., and A. Neugebauer (eds.). (1997). *"… ohne Rücksicht auf die Verhältnisse". Opel zwischen Weltwirtschaftskrise und Wiederaufbau*. Frankfurt am Main: Brandes & Aspel.

Jackson, D. W. A. (1990). *Gunnar Myrdal and America's Conscience. Social Engineering and Radical Liberalism, 1938–1987*. Chapel Hill, North Carolina: University of North Carolina Press.

Jones, G. (1984). Multinational Chocolate. Cadbury Overseas, 1918–1939. *Business History*, 26, 59–75.

Jordan, J. M. (1994). *Machine-Age Ideology. Social Engineering and American Liberalism 1911–1939*. Chapel Hill, North Carolina: University of North Carolina Press.

Joyce, P. (1980): *Work, Society and Politics. The Culture of the Factory in Later Victorian England*, Chapel Hill, North Carolina: Rutgers University Press.

Kasson, J. F. (1999). *Civilizing the Machine. Technology and Republican Values in America, 1776–1900*. New York: Hill and Wang.

Kuchenbuch, D. (2010). *Geordnete Gemeinschaft. Architekten als Sozialingenieure—Deutschland und Schweden im 20. Jahrhundert*. Bielefeld: transcript.

Kugler, A. (1985). *Arbeitsorganisation und Produktionstechnologie der Adam Opel Werke von 1900–1929.* Berlin: WZB.

Laux, J. M. (1992). *The European Automobile Industry.* New York: Twayne.

Lees, A. (1985). *Cities Perceived. Urban Society in European and American Thought 1820–1940.* Manchester: Manchester University Press.

Luks, T. (2010). *Der Betrieb als Ort der Moderne. Zur Geschichte von Industriearbeit, Ordnungsdenken und Social Engineering im 20. Jahrhundert.* Bielefeld: transcript.

Luks, T. (2012). Eine Moderne im Normalzustand. Ordnungsdenken und Social Engineering in der ersten Hälfte des 20. Jahrhunderts. *Österreichische Zeitschrift für Geschichtswissenschaften,* 2/23/2012, 15–38.

McClymer, J. F. (1980). *War and Welfare. Social Engineering in America 1890–1925.* Westport and London: Greenwood.

Neugebauer, A. (1987). *"Die Macht sachlicher Informationen". Zur Funktion einer Werkzeitschrift—die Opel-Post.* Unpublished MA Thesis, University of Frankfurt am Main.

Neugebauer, A. (1999). "Frauen, welche ein Hauswesen zu versorgen haben, werden nicht angenommen". Frauenarbeit in den Opelwerken 1880 bis 1945. *Zeitschrift für Unternehmensgeschichte,* 44, 172–195.

Otto, R. (1939). Gemeinnützige Opel-Wohnbaugesellschaft. *Opel-Kamerad,* 1/10/1939, 12–13.

Perkin, H. (1989): *The Rise of Professional Society. England since 1880.* London and New York: Routledge.

Raphael, L. (1996). Die Verwissenschaftlichung des Sozialen als methodische und konzeptionelle Herausforderung für eine Sozialgeschichte des 20. Jahrhunderts. *Geschichte und Gesellschaft,* 22, 165–193.

Richardson, J. H. (1933). *Industrial Relations in Great Britain.* London: P.S. King.

Robertson, E., M. Korczynski, and M. Pickering (2007). Harmonious Relations? Music at Work in the Rowntree und Cadbury Factories. *Business History,* 49, 211–234.

Rowlinson, M. (1988). The Early Application of Scientific Management by Cadbury. *Business History,* 30, 377–395.

Schirmbeck, P., and A. Dresler (eds.). (1988): *"Morgen kommst du nach Amerika". Erinnerungen an die Arbeit bei Opel 1917–1987,* Bonn and Berlin: Dietz.

Schlimm, A. (2011). *Ordnungen des Verkehrs. Arbeit an der Moderne—deutsche und britische Verkehrsexpertise im 20. Jahrhundert.* Bielefeld: transcript.

Stahlmann, Michael (1993). *Die erste Revolution in der Autoindustrie. Management und Arbeitspolitik von 1900–1940.* Frankfurt am Main and New York: Campus.

Szöllösi-Janze, M. (2004). Wissensgesellschaft in Deutschland: Überlegungen zur Neubestimmung der deutschen Zeitgeschichte über Verwissenschaftlichungsprozesse. *Geschichte und Gesellschaft,* 30, 277–313.

Turner, H. A. (2005). *General Motors and the Nazis: The Struggle for Control of Opel, Europe's Biggest Carmaker.* New Haven and London: Yale University Press.

Weigand, K. (1956). *Rüsselsheim und die Funktion der Stadt im Rhein-Main-Gebiet (mit besonderer Berücksichtigung der Pendelwanderung)*. Frankfurt am Main: Kramer.

Williams, I. A. (1931). *The Firm of Cadbury, 1831–1931*. London: Constable.

Zimmermann, C., and J. Reulecke (eds.). (1999). *Die Stadt als Moloch? Das Land als Kraftquell? Wahrnehmungen und Wirkungen der Großstädte um 1900*. Basel, Boston and Berlin: Birkhäuser.

A Town Without Memory?
Inferring the Industrial Past:
Clydebank Re-built, 1941–2013

Rebecca Madgin

"We lost everything [...] it was raining incendiary bombs [...] I counted seven which had burnt out in my small back garden. They were all over the roads and gardens [...] losing everything like that [...] it gave us a deep sense of value [...] we really appreciated what we had from then on." The Blitz of the 13 and 14 March 1941 is etched into the collective memory of Clydebank. Far from being erased through the passing of time and the creation of new urban spaces, the physical and psychological trauma caused by wartime destruction was compounded by the urban renewal initiatives of the post World War II period. "Years later [...] I cried when they pulled down Singer's Clock [...] you could see it from anywhere in Clydebank [...] I thought [...] Oh, God! It was the only thing left [...] it came through the Blitz untouched [...] it was a symbol of survival and meant so much to the people of Clydebank. I hate them for that" (McKendrick 1986, 11). An increased awareness of what was valuable in the urban landscape ensured that the loss of the Clock left an indelible scar on both the physical and mental urban landscape. Furthermore, the testimonies illustrated that the "continued existence of familiar surroundings may satisfy a psychological need, which even if irrational, is very real. Nothing gives more tangible assurance of stability than bricks and mortar" (Hubbard 1993, 363).

The chapter will consider this connection between the mental and physical urban landscape as Clydebank tried to regenerate its industrial landscape between 1941 and 2013. In doing so the chapter will engage with a neglected area of research, namely the role of collective memory and emotional value in the transition from an industrial to post-industrial town.

The cumulative loss of the built environment during both wartime destruction and post-war reconstruction reshaped the look and the feel of Clydebank. The Blitz of 1941, so eloquently remembered in the oral testimony, left only seven houses out of 12,000 intact (Hood 1988, 168). This destruction did not spare the schools, hospitals, churches, factories and shipyards as the tapestry of urban development unravelled thread-by-thread. Post-war reconstruction continued to erase the town's physical markers as the mindset of demolish and rebuild continued with pace into the 1960s.

The repeated loss of industrial landmarks such as the Singer Clock in 1963, the factory in 1981 as well as the closure of the shipyards in 2001 left Clydebank suffering from the amnesia of architectural memory loss. Allied to this were several urban renewal initiatives during the 1960s and 1970s, each of which favoured comprehensive redevelopment. Clydebank, with its dual industrial structure of shipbuilding and manufacturing sewing machines, was in a constant state of flux as both industries suffered from rationalisation and increasing foreign competition. The urban environment was also continually modified and redeveloped to meet the needs of post-war society. Clydebank is thus characterised by a curious mix of permanence and impermanence. For over one hundred years Clydebank maintained this dual industrial structure. However, within this façade of stability were severe fluctuations in both employment levels and environmental cohesion as successive urban policies re-shaped the town. What remains today are vivid memories of a proud industrial past located in a landscape stripped of its physical industrial legacy. In the absence of a critical mass of former industrial buildings, Clydebank could not adaptively re-use the physical legacy. Instead, the creation of the Urban Regeneration Company in 2002 wove the collective memories of the town into a renewed urban fabric. The ways in which this collective memory was mobilised as part of urban redevelopment moves the debate about the future of industrial cities away from one that focuses solely of property-led regeneration. The chapter, in the absence of the built industrial legacy in Clydebank, centres on the adaptive re-use of the mental landscape.

Between the Physical and the Mental Landscape

The relationship between collective memory and physical places is complex and despite the attention of scholars in disparate disciplines is not yet fully understood. Without physical places, Poulet, states humans would be "mere abstractions" (Malpas 1999, 176). Ruskin believed that although "we may live without her (architecture) [...] we cannot remember without her" (Ruskin 1880, 178). In his view the physical structure triggered memory and allowed future generations to connect with the "passing waves of humanity" (ibid.). Morris demonstrated the emotional connection to existing structures through his powerful plea to prevent the "grievous loss we incur by their destruction" (SPAB 1878). These early moves to retain the familiar environment illustrated the connection between mental space and physical place. Debates surrounding the emotional value of physical structures reached their clearest expression during the second half of the 20th century. Using the notion of *Heimat*, Arnold examined how a sense of belonging to a physical place was conveyed in a teenager's diary following Allied bombings:

"I only mention these single buildings by name because they used to be familiar landmarks, but don't believe that they are the only sites of destruction, no, everything! [...] I pass through the Untere Konigsstrasse, and my blood runs cold: death and destruction! More and more I reach the conclusion: Kassel is no more! In a single dreadful night, Kassel has been razed to the ground!" (Arnold 2011, 40)

Grenville, applied the notion of ontological security to post-war Worcester: "I read [...] with horror of the proposed pulling down of Worcester brick by brick [...] Worcester is an old and faithful city and its charm lies in its ancient streets and buildings and lack of modern structures [...] The idea is nothing short of a scandal" (Grenville 2007, 455). These examples echo the oral testimonies of Clydebank to demonstrate that the dialectic between the mental and physical landscape plays a powerful role in the sense of place.

This literature on the reconstruction of bomb-damaged cities is well advanced but an under-researched area is how the transition from industrial to post-industrial is shaped by the emotional value of a lost environment.[1] The demands of a post-war planning framework to improve urban environments ensured that decisions concerning the value of the existing environment had to strike a fine line between sentiment and pragmatism. Abercrombie's desire to radically modernise post-war Edinburgh was tempered by his recognition that "nothing is so likely to arouse controversy and opposition as change or destruction of any of the ancient human landmarks of this city. This cherishing of the heritage of the past is laudable but it makes the work of the planner more perilous" (Abercrombie 1949, 53).

Urban renewal initiatives in the latter decades of the 20th century further disrupted the familiar environment. The predilection for comprehensive redevelopment left physical scars on both the physical and mental landscape. The "demolition of a building is a traumatic experience for the residents of a district whose daily life is framed by a built environment to which they are

---

1 Tim Edensor's work (2005) on industrial ruins is an exception but this focuses more on the re-appropriation of physical space rather than mobilising the memories attached to lost buildings to secure an urban renaissance.

unconsciously attached" (Council of Europe 1987, 44). Hubbard extended this point to note that "the demolition of prominent social or public buildings can have a deep-seated effect on a community, as it effectively wipes out a significant chapter in the history of a place and erases memories of its heritage for the majority of its present and future inhabitants"(Hubbard 1993, 366). These emotions were drawn upon by Porteous who described the sense of loss of historic buildings as "topocide" (ibid.), following on from Tuan's definition of the love of place as topophilia (1974). In the context of rationalisation, deindustrialisation and urban renewal redundant industrial sites were often planned for demolition.[2]

Pierre Nora's seminal work illustrated the multiplicity of ways in which memories were enshrined in place. For Nora these sites could be material or immaterial, or put another way tangible or intangible but common throughout was their capacity to "become a symbolic element of the memorial heritage of any community" (Nora 1996, xvii). Memory was therefore not static and rooted in one site at one time. Rather it is a fluid, pluralistic concept dependent on time, place and practice. Undeniably the physical environment acts as a trigger for recollection but in the context of redevelopment it is not desirable to create a single layered urban centre in which the city cannot "escape the tyranny of a single present, and the monotony of a future that consists in repeating only a single beat heard in the past" (Mumford 1938, 4). Within this process industrial buildings were demolished; all that remains in Clydebank is a former crane. Lowenthal's belief that "memory and history both derive and gain emphasis from physical remains" (1985, xxiii) should have ensured that Clydebank was a town without memory. The fetishsisation of re-using industrial buildings displayed in numerous conservation-led regeneration initiatives in the 1980s should have ensured that Clydebank was also a town without a future. However, neither was the case, as the memory of the lost heritage remained embedded in the mental landscape and eventually woven in to the new physical landscape.

If the existing built environment was a repository of emotional value, by the 1980s, it also signalled economic value. The fall of industry and the consequent rise of property-led urban regeneration led to the adaptive re-use of physical structures. These schemes developed in many countries with

---

2 Examples include the Coal Exchange and Euston Arch in London. The retention of industrial structures was often either through planning blight as attention turned to other sites or conservation as, from the late 1960s, industrial structures started to be given statutory protection through the listing system.

notable early examples in the United States with Lowell National Heritage Park (1978), in France with the rehabilitation of the Le Blan complex in Lille by Reichen & Roberts (1980) and in Britain with Dean Clough in Halifax (1983). Each of these buildings were restored and re-used for housing, offices and leisure as well as exploiting the tourist industry. From the end of the 1970s there was an increasing realisation in the Western world of the economic potential of the existing industrial environment to regenerate urban areas.

The *Urban Development Corporations* (UDC) during the 1980s[3] used the industrial successes of the 19th century to fuel the transition to a service-sector led post-industrial city. Along with re-use, the UDC's also branded and marketed the city along clear lines:

"Manchester was at the forefront of the industrial revolution in the 18th and 19th centuries. It was the first Industrial City. It was a city rich in ideas and with the people possessing the initiative, drive and determination to turn those ideas into reality. The legacy of the invention, prosperity and confidence of this period of bold growth remains: canals, railways, mills, warehouses and offices." (Central Manchester Development Corporation 1988, point 1.1)

If the body and the city could not be untangled in this vision then neither could the mental and physical legacy of the past. This legacy was selected and managed by a combination of the public and private sector. Following on from Ruskinian notions of architecture and memory, the visual symbols of the industrial city were woven into the future mindscape of the city (Madgin 2009). Put another way, both the economic and emotional value of the industrial past were harnessed to re-imagine a post-industrial future. Allied to this was a plethora of funding mechanisms designed to unlock the economic value of former industrial sites. The *European Regional Development Fund* (established in 1975) added an international source to British initiatives such as the Urban Grant, the *Architectural Heritage Fund*, the *Townscape Heritage Initiative* and the tax-breaks designed to encourage the private sector to re-use buildings and be "handsomely rewarded by profit" (Binney 1990, 13). The physical legacy in mind and money reigned supreme.

The *Urban Regeneration Companies* (URC)[4] that succeeded the UDCs post-1997 maintained this emphasis on property-led urban regeneration.

---

3 The Urban Development Corporations (UDC) were a quasi-qutonomous national government organisation established under the local government planning and land act 1980.

4 The Urban Regeneration Companies (URC) were established in 1999. The aim is to unite public and private sector partners to deliver sustainable regeneration and stimulate invest-

However, reflecting the neo-liberal Third Way of New Labour the early 21st century also saw a renewed focus on social regeneration. However, as New East Manchester URC demonstrated, the historic environment in Ancoats largely catered for incoming residents as existing residents were moved out of the self-styled 'urban village'. The capacity of the former industrial environment to meet urban agendas, such as the need for sustainable Brownfield development, the desire to support the cultural and creative industries, and the creation of an urban lifestyle retained the emphasis on re-use (Madgin 2008). Indeed, New East Manchester was convinced that the industrial legacy could be "rehabilitated to create an environment for living and working that has proved highly successful elsewhere" (NEM 2001, 7). The re-use of industrial heritage was a mechanism to unlock latent economic value in deprived urban areas.

The cumulative loss of industrial heritage in Clydebank ensured the town was therefore at a distinct disadvantage when considered against the critical mass of buildings found in Ancoats and Castlefield, Manchester or the Kulturbrauerei, Berlin or the iconic structures of Motte-Bossut, Roubaix or the Cable Factory in Helsinki. Compared to over twenty listed buildings[5] in Castlefield[6], Clydebank had only twelve. Only the Grade A listed Titan Crane was explicitly connected to the town's industrial development. The others such as the Grade B Town Hall, the library and the Co-operative retail buildings and numerous churches were the consequences rather than the cause of industrial Clydebank. However, the area, unlike Castlefield did retain a critical mass of people with memories and meanings embedded in the urban landscape.

The Rhetoric and Reality of Post-War Urban Renewal

"I was surprised at how passionate and loyal people are to Clydebank and how at times they shun the developments, but this is just with the fear that Clydebank will lose its history. Once they were assured that everything was being done to preserve

ment in towns and cities. They are independent companies established by the relevant local authority and regional development agency (RDA).

5 English Heritage list the buildings in England and Historic Scotland in Scotland.

6 http://www.manchester.gov.uk/downloads/file/12609/castlefield_conservation_area_map

the history of Clydebank, they opened up and began to embrace the developments."
(Clydebank rebuilt 2007, n.p.)

Clydebank can be characterized by the continual and comprehensive reinvention of its built form. Essentially, Clydebank was a Victorian new town
formed from the relocation of two firms: the shipbuilders, J. & G. Thomson in 1871 (later John Brown), and the Singer Sewing Machine Company in 1881. Consequently, the town grew exponentially from a population
of 3,000 in 1881 to over 43,000 in 1913 as people sought work in one of
the two industries (Hood 1988, 1). The population of Clydebank increased
to just over 50,000 in 1982 and remained at approximately 45,000 for the
Clydebank region into the 21st century.[7] This dense working-class community were housed sequentially in sandstone tenements, prefabricated houses,
and high-rise blocks. The residential environment was supplemented by the
construction (and reconstruction) of social infrastructure such as a Town
Hall, library, shops, public baths and several public houses and churches.
Clydebank fostered a 'tradition of independent community organization'
(Collins 2008, 15). This was aided by the Trade Union and the Socialist Party
and took many forms. The spirit of the important 'Red Clydeside' movement[8] in 1911 and again 1917 was evident in the creation of the Unemployed
Action Group in the 1970s and is still evident in the 21st century (ibid.). Suc-
cessive urban agencies noted this 'deep pride in the community' (Clydebank
Task Force 1980, n.p.)[9], along with the 'indefatigable 'Clydebank spirit'
(Clydebank rebuilt 2004b, point 1.1) This largely resulted from industrial
successes as the Urban Task force (1980) recognized that 'Clyde Built' has become a "world wide synonym for quality" whereas the Urban Regeneration
Company (2002) focused on the history "which gives Clydebank people
their heart and pride" (ibid.). This focus on 'Clyde Built' gave the town an
embedded sense of place identity. Despite this the demands of a post-war
planning framework ensured that the external identity of Clydebank was
consistently shaped by official urban policies.

---

7 This also includes the expansion of the burgh to include Radnor (1906), Parkhall and
   Mountblow (1925), Whitecrook (1937), Faifley (1949) and finally Duntocher and Old
   Kilpatrick Faifley, Hardgate and Duntocher (1975).

8 See Russell, I. (1988). The Clydebank Rent Strike. In J. Hood (ed.). *The History of Clydebank*. Lancashire: Parthenon Publishing Ltd, Cornforth.

9 The 'Urban Task Force' was set up in 1980 by the Scottish Development Agency (SDA).
   The SDA was itself created in 1975 to further the development of Scotland's economy and
   improve its environment.

What followed was a confused period in which the redevelopment of the area oscillated between architectural amnesia and the rhetoric of remembrance. Successive urban renewal initiatives adopted a pragmatic approach to improve the living and working conditions of Clydebank's residents. As such the post-war priority to improve the condition of housing saw parts of Clydebank designated as a Central Redevelopment Area in 1948, and as Comprehensive Redevelopment Areas from 1963 onwards (Hood 1988, 170, 177). The rebuilding of the Singer Sewing factory in 1964, as well as several other urban improvement schemes, including Clydebank's classification as an Area for Priority Treatment in 1976, were further examples of this holistic approach to urban renewal. The closure of the Singer factory in 1980 marked the next wave of redevelopment. The site, once the world's largest factory, became the key component of Scotland's first Enterprise Zone in 1981. The Urban Task Force (UTF) set up to administer change recognised that the 'rapid redevelopment of the Singer site will give a new identity to the centre of Clydebank' (Clydebank Task Force, 1980, n.p.). Each of these policy initiatives left a lasting mark on the physical and social infrastructure of Clydebank, as the physical repositories of the town's industrial memories were continually erased in favour of a renewed and reinvented urban landscape.

Year	Urban Initiatives
1940 and 1950s	– Scottish Special Housing Association Limited – Central Redevelopment Area
1960s	– Comprehensive Redevelopment Areas (Kilbowie, Eastern and Dalmuir)
1970s	– Areas for Priority Treatment
1980s	– Urban Task Force: 'Clydebank Task Force' – Enterprise Zone
1990s	– Smaller Urban Regeneration Initiative – Priority Partnership Area – Social Inclusion Partnership
2000s	– Urban Regeneration Company: 'Clydebank rebuilt' – Community Planning Partnership

Tab. 1: Selected Urban Policies in Clydebank, 1940–present day

(Souce: Adapted from Hood (1988) and Collins (2008))

The reality of comprehensive redevelopment was massaged by the rhetoric of respecting Clydebank's industrial past. This was witnessed with the rebuilding of two housing estates completely destroyed during the Blitz. The identity of place was "conferred by the new street names" (Hood 1988, 173) as the streets in the area in the middle of the Clydebank, Singer and Drumry railway stations were named after the shipbuilding heritage. Hood, Vanguard, Queen Mary, York and Alsatian were all built in the Clyde shipyards and all played a role in securing an Allied victory. The second development, which was south of the railway line that connected Drumry and Singer stations, chose to respect the working-class past by weaving the names of the post-war Labour ministers, whose government had provided the subsidies to allow Clydebank to rebuild, into their urban fabric. Atlee Street and Bevan Street were just two of these iconic names. The new street names were the physical expression of the renewed 'sense of value' and emotional connection to the past as exemplified in the oral testimonies.[10]

This rhetoric of remembrance was again seen during the 1980s as the Urban Task Force chose to re-present the identity of the town. This was achieved through building on the 'proud tradition' in Clydebank and the fact that: "Enterprise isn't new to Clydebank. The town is perhaps best known for sewing machines and great ships—all of the 'Queens' were built here at John Brown's Yard. Part of the former Beardmore Yard at Dalmuir is now the site of the Agency's Clydebank Industrial Estate" (Clydebank Task Force 1980).[11] The similarity to the textual representation of Castlefield by the *Central Manchester Development Corporation* (CMDC) outlined earlier is clear. However, whilst CMDC incorporated the former industrial buildings, the UTF replaced them with light industrial units centred on a new business park. Furthermore, Clydebank's 19th-century motto "Labore et Scientia" (by hard work and by knowledge) was diluted by a new marketing motto, "Excellence and Enterprise" in 1986 (Hood 1986), The significant loss of architectural memory during the post-war period left post-1945 architecture juxtaposed with gap sites and the remnants of the industrial legacy.

In reality this rhetoric of respect neither extended to the physical or mental legacy of the town. The views of the established working-class community on how to regenerate their town were glossed over in favour of enterprise-led regeneration. Indeed, the long-established community group, by 1980 called

---

10 *Clydebank Burgh Council* and also the *Scottish Special Housing Association* reconfigured this symbolic built environment.
11 The Queen Mary, Elizabeth and Elizabeth 2 were all made in the John Brown shipyard.

the Clydebank Unemployed Workers' Centre, was advised by its landlord that its ongoing use of Clydebank Business Park premises "was not compatible with the image of a business park" (Collins 2008, 36). This, coincidentally, was the business park built on the site of the former Singer factory. The partnership agenda, seen in the names of urban initiatives in table 1, was little more than an externally imposed agenda by central and local government on local communities supported by the private sector. Communities were supposedly part of the process of urban change but whilst they were consulted they were rarely heard.

Clydebank rebuilt

"People were saying Clydebank was going to be left a ghost town—they were wondering what was going to happen to the Singer building and what was going to happen to Clydebank [...] Of course we survived—although maybe not as well as some would have liked." (Anon. 2010)

Just as the Blitz was etched into the collective memory of Clydebank so was the loss of the industrial past. The socio-economic consequences of deindustrialisation with the demolition of Singer's in 1981 followed by, the final nail in the industrial coffin, the closure of the shipyards in 2001 ensured that the narrative of loss continued into the 21st century: "Never again will the former John Brown Shipyard echo to the rattle of riveting hammers or the crackle of welding torches as thousands of men crafted ships and, for the past 30 years, platforms and rigs for the North Sea oil and gas industry" (The Scotsman 2001, 5). The terminal decline of the dual industrial structure ensured that both the urban sensescape and an embedded way of living and working were disrupted. This triggered a further urban renewal initiative. Just as the closure of Singer's in the 1980s led to the Enterprise Zone, the closure of the shipyards led to the creation of the *Urban Regeneration Company* (URC): 'Clydebank re-built', which was established in 2002. The remit of Scotland's URC was to 'reposition Clydebank as a creative, distinctive and successful regional centre within the Glasgow metropolitan area" (Clydebank rebuilt 2004b, point 3.1.1). In order to achieve this the URC combined public-sector money and partnership working to attract human and capital investment. Their strategy was based on four key areas: 1. Connected Clydebank, 2. Inclusive Clydebank, 3. Quality Clydebank and 4.

Competitive Clydebank. These were designed to lift the physical and psychological barriers to redevelopment and to secure the transition from an industrial to post-industrial town.

Clydebank rebuilt marked a break from previous urban policies; from the outset they recognized the importance of incorporating the collective memory of the town into its urban renaissance. In 2003 the URC announced that their community consultation had "demonstrated a strong pride in past achievements, and a more positive view of life in Clydebank today than many prophets of doom would have us believe. Recognising past achievements, and the current strengths of Clydebank, will be the solid building blocks of future development" (Clydebank rebuilt 2003, 2).

This rhetoric was similar to the emphasis on enterprise and tradition espoused by the Urban Task Force. However, this time the sentiment was matched by the reality of urban development. This was largely as a result of the formal involvement of residents in the regeneration of their town. From the outset, in line with both the New Labour and devolved Scottish governments' emphasis on community development, regular design forums, seminars, workshops, field-trips and exhibitions ran alongside the circulation of newsletters, an active presence in the local newspapers: the *Clydebank Post* and the *Glasgow Evening Times* as well as an online presence through the Clydebank rebuilt website. An average of 100 people attended seven design forums with a total of almost 4000 people recorded as attending at least one of the consultation events.[12]

The Design Forums were workshops at which residents, businesses, workers, and community group representatives worked with the URC, landowners and architects to shape the regeneration of the area. By the fourth Design Forum the role of collective memory in the regeneration of Clydebank was evident. A sense of historical looting and the loss of the physical legacy of the past revealed the impact of urban change on the mental landscape. A focus in the fourth Design Forum on the loss of iconic symbols such as the Clock and the Coat of Arms was matched by the belief that residents wanted to "hold on to the past and reclaim anything that has been lost" (Clydebank rebuilt 2004a, 6). The community favoured a representation of the Clock either through a "scale model, a replica, a clock face laid out in paving or parts of the clock featuring in other design works". Furthermore, the emotional

---

12 These figures do not include those design forums where the numbers were not reported as well as the informal engagement through newspaper campaigns.

impact of the loss of the shipbuilding industry was reflected in the desire to identify the Queens Quay as the "birth place of luxury liners" and that the waterfront area should be used to both "feature and document the shipping industry". Suggestions were made for "superimposed pictures of ships, ships numbers" and/or "names". Finally, despite the horrors of the wartime devastation it was suggested at the forum that the "Blitz should feature in any design proposals" (ibid.). This 'revitalized sensitivity to place' (Casey 1997, xiii) was directly as a result of the widespread upheaval and change wrought by wartime destruction and post-war reconstruction. The lingering sense of loss was still evident in 2012, as the demolition of the Clock continued to pervade the collective memory of the town "I still think the worst thing that happened was taking down the clock because you could check the time

Fig. 1: Road sign with motto

(Source: Photo: R. Madgin)

wherever you were in the town. No one really had watches because they were expensive." (Anon. 2012).

The scarcity of the physical environment, with no physical remnant of Singer's and only the Titan Crane from the shipbuilding industry, ensured that the almost "pathological attachment" to the remaining historic built environment (Lynch 1960, 42) could also be applied to the memory of the lost historic environment.

Turning Rhetoric into Reality

The rhetoric of lost heritage demonstrated at the Design Forums was incorporated into architects' design briefs and ensured that the industrial footprint was evident in the revitalized urban landscape. This took many forms, both subtle and explicit, in new buildings and in new urban spaces but each was united in its desire to embed Clydebank's re-development in the collective memory of the town. The motto was changed and strategically placed on entry points into the town. In this view Clydebank's 'proud past' would lead to its 'dynamic future' (see fig. 1).

The preoccupation with identity seen in the 1980s remained in the 2000s. Instead of creating a new identity through re-using the Singer site, the URC partnership felt Clydebank needed to regain its identity. This was to be achieved by having a 'strong focus on what Singer did for the town' (Clydebank rebuilt 2004a, 9). This was no longer possible following the demolition of the factory but was instead implemented in the designs for new buildings and public realm works. The first of these references to the past was the design for the John Knox workshops. Community involvement in the designs for the workshops (see fig. 2) was evident with the Fourth Design Forum on 13th September 2004 suggesting a 'representation of types of stitching from Singer factory in concrete slabbing' (ibid., 6). The URC issued the tender for the workshops on 17th September 2004 and work started on site on 29th November 2004. The final product showed the imprint of the Castle stitch on the exterior of the workshop.

This ethos of community involvement was further evident in the phase 4 design brief for the workshops in 2010 which stated that the architect-led scheme should "obtain community involvement in shaping proposals and outcomes through Clydebank re-built organised community consultation

Fig. 2: John Knox workshops and the stitch pattern
(Source: Photo: R. Madgin)

forums. This will assist in generating a sense of ownership of the project" (Clydebank rebuilt 2010b, point 4.17).

The John Knox workshops were successful in two different and connected ways. Firstly, the high levels of community ownership of the design resulted in "negligible vandalism in the last 5 years and to date, there has been no reported break-ins" (ibid.). Secondly, the workshops achieved 100 per cent occupancy rates for extended periods. The John Knox workshops thus illustrated how the collective memory of the past, fuelled by the emotional reaction to a lost heritage, was mobilized to drive forward the physical regeneration of the area.

This ethos of weaving the memory of the industrial past into the new urban fabric continued in a variety of guises. The Queen's Quay situated on the former John Brown's shipyard was a key site. This time new buildings were built to reflect the shipbuilding heritage. The Fifth Design Forum in January 2005 revealed that the community consultations indicated that:

"Designs should reflect the history of the area, particularly the heritage of the ship-building industry and era. As such, much of the development would depict/interpret the shipbuilding theme, with various art works along the promenade, and in the design of the buildings. The first of these to be built would be the new Enterprise Centre, the major design feature of which would incorporate an elevation at the front like the brow of a ship." (Clydebank rebuilt 2005a, 4)

The strength of pride in Clydebank's past and the vivid collective memory again drove the new urban design. However, caution was struck in the Queen's Quay area with a clear steer to both "incorporate modern design" and to ensure that the designs were of high quality (ibid.). 'Clydebank built' was a source of pride but equally the URC were keen to ensure that Clydebank rebuilt would also leave a lasting legacy. As such it was hoped that the design of the building would "create an architectural benchmark that people and other developers will take notice of'" (ibid.). The internationally renowned architectural firm Page/Park was commissioned to build the enterprise centre. The firm "designed the building to reflect the ship building legacy of the site in both form and materials". This was evident with both the "flaring cantilevered steps in the slabs at each level evoke a form reminiscent of a ships hull" and the "roofline which rises above along the length of the elevation into a prow at the eastern end of the building."[13]

Clydebank rebuilt also broke with tradition in retaining and re-using the former industrial environment. Following the first Design Forum in 2003 the URC announced that the Grade A listed "Titan crane is a potentially critical asset. It is a defining feature of Clydebank that provides a reminder of a proud past" (Clydebank rebuilt 2003, 6). The subsequent re-use of the crane as a visitor attraction ensured that Titan was "no longer just a crane, but a sculpture on the skyline, and a memorial to the proud tradition of the town" (Clydebank rebuilt 2006, n.p.). In a further illustration of the connection between people and place it was proposed in 2001 that the Titan became a community-owned asset (Clydebank rebuilt 2011, n.p.). The URC also listened to the suggestion that the Grade B listed Town Hall "should be reinvigorated as an icon building" (Clydebank rebuilt 2003, 6). The new Civic Quarter comprising of the refurbished Town Hall and the Central Library opposite the new Solidarity Plaza juxtaposed new urban design with pre-First World War buildings. The re-used buildings won a number of design awards such as a Civic Trust Award and the prestigious Chicago Athenaeum

---

13 For more information see: http://pagepark.co.uk/projects/titan-enterprise-centre.

Fig. 3: The re-used landscape: Titan Crane and the Town Hall

(Source: Photo: R. Madgin)

award. Award-winning and sustainable urban design was a central tenet of the URC's strategy. Creating the "kind of 'place' that ensures competitive advantage over rival areas" was tied to the quality of the environment and the image of the town (Clydebank rebuilt 2004b, point 1.5). Indeed in eleven years of operating, Clydebank rebuilt has received over twenty national and international awards and accolades.

The commitment of Clydebank rebuilt to respect the collective memory of the town was also witnessed in the design of new urban spaces either through public art or public realm works. Again these took a variety of different forms and were mainly located on the canal side. The installation of a "memory line [...] inscribed with stories, facts and figures about the Canal and Clydebank" was complemented by the "Bankie Benches" (Clydebank rebuilt 2009b, n.p.). These benches were inscribed with stories about the Singer clock and factory that were produced by local school children (ibid.). Further landscaping works represented the railway lines feeding into the Singer factory sidings and the incorporation of slipways into the design for walkways on the former John Brown's shipyard. In an echo of the immediate post-war period the new street names on the former shipyard were also

Fig. 4: "Bankie benches" and railway sidings

(Source: Photos: R. Madgin)

named after ships built in Clydebank. This was not a top-down process but rather decided after a newspaper advert placed by the URC.

The continued respect for the collective memory of the town through the design of new buildings, new spaces and the refurbishment of existing buildings marked a break from the rhetoric of remembrance favoured by the previous urban policies. Clydebank showed itself to be a town with both memory and through the Urban Regeneration Company it is now also a town with physical mnemonics.

Conclusion

Reversing the architectural amnesia of the industrial past added further layers to both the physical and mental palimpsest of Clydebank. As such the case study engages with an under-researched area of academic debate. There is a "sad lack of theory that would connect people's emotional bonds with the physical side of places" (Lewicka 2011, 218). Indeed the sense of loss demonstrated by the residents of Clydebank indicates that, contrary to the view of Altman and Low, physical spaces are more than mere "repositories and contexts within which interpersonal, community, and cultural relationships occur" (1992, 7). Rather the former industrial environment, whether retained or demolished, played a key role in guiding the future of Clydebank.

Despite the scarcity of physical mnemonics the collective memory of the area remained and was formally unlocked during the latest phase of urban regeneration.

The experience of Clydebank moves the debate surrounding the future of former industrial cities in to a different domain and one that privileges the mental landscape as much as the built environment. Indeed, there is a symbiotic relationship between the mental and the physical. Not only do physical changes alter the mental landscape but, as shown with the incorporation of collective memory in new urban spaces and buildings, the mental landscape can inform further urban development. This is an underplayed element of the transition from industrial to post-industrial as the instrumental values of re-using buildings took precedence in successive waves of urban policies from the 1970s onwards. The ancillary effects of converting former industrial sites into spaces of consumption ensured that economic values were privileged. The value of the former industrial city, in this context, rested with its capacity to reinvent its socio-economic base and to attract human and capital investment. However, Clydebank re-opens a debate concerning the ways in which collective memory and community involvement can enhance place attachment. Paradoxically, the sense of loss evident in Clydebank served to reinforce a sense of place. Rather than focusing on reclaiming place identity, like the Urban Task Force and the Urban Regeneration Company, reclaiming ownership of urban space drove the desire to respect the industrial past. The relatively low levels of vandalism across the new urban spaces, allied to the active involvement of a spectrum of Clydebank residents in the Design Forums, reflects this renewed sense of ownership.

Clydebank rebuilt's community focus ran contrary to the experience of property-led regeneration in Manchester where Central Manchester Development Corporation's boundaries were drawn to exclude "a string of impoverished areas [...] in a conscious effort to ensure that the Urban Development Corporation remained focused and single-minded in its efforts to secure property-led redevelopment and, at the same time, avoiding the supposed distractions of dealing directly with the residents of impoverished communities" (Imrie et al. 1999, 208–209, cited after Madgin 2009). This was further supported by the Urban Regeneration Company in Ancoats whose compulsory purchase order was considered to stand for "Communities Put Out" (Interview, 2005, Ancoats Resident). Rising house prices and the flow of new wealth into a deprived area exposed the polarities of the unskilled, unemployed council house tenants and the skilled workers living in luxury apartments (Madgin 2008). Labadi in her European-wide evaluation of the socio-economic impacts of heritage-led regeneration also lamented the 'erroneous assumption that rehabilitating historic urban areas with the aid of cultural or heritage projects always leads to an improvement for the local community' (2011, 112).

In this sense Clydebank's inclusive strategy of weaving collective memory should allow the 'proud past' to drive the 'dynamic future'. However, despite the involvement of residents, there was still a recognition that "all community members are still not aware, and there seems to be difficulty in getting the information and message to 'fan out' more widely" (Clydebank rebuilt 2007b, 9). Allied to this was the selectivity of the supposed collective memories. Dissenting voices at the Design Forums stressed the need to "need to look to the future—a lot of local people didn't like working in Singers and the shipping industry" (Clydebank rebuilt 2004a, 6). Furthermore, there was also the suggestion that the new designs should "feature people—it's not all ships and clocks" (ibid.). However, the majority of comments sought the inclusion of the lost industrial heritage in the new urban environment. This accords with Halbwachs' findings that collective memory' only "retains the elements which continue to live, or are capable of living in the consciousness of the group that keeps the memory alive" (Miller 2003, 16). Clydebank rebuilt provided the institutional space to ensure that these collective memories could inform the future development of the town.

Ultimately, though, the future of the area depends on more than the design of new buildings and spaces. Rather it is the function of these new spaces that will create jobs for the former industrial workers and their descendents. Without this, award-winning design that enshrines a single past will be unable to fuel the post-industrial future. This concern was exemplified a conference in 2006 entitled "For a People's Clydebank or Sold Doon the Watter? What does the 'regeneration' of our town mean for ordinary working class people?" (Collins 2008, 119).[14] This built on decades of dissatisfaction with urban policies that despite the rhetoric of partnership had seen them favour the public and private sectors.

Whether this policy to incorporate the industrial past is indicative of a 21st century version of Hewison's *Climate of Decline* (1984) is debatable. What is certain is that the role of collective memory can both be a benefit

---

14 Scots vernacular translated as 'sold down the water'. Going 'doon the watter' was a reference to the Glaswegians who sailed the River Clyde on paddle steamers en route to seaside towns during the Victorian era.

and burden to urban redevelopment. On the one hand the inclusive engagement practices of the URC allied to the realisation of memory in new spaces represents a move away from the top-down property-led urban regeneration schemes seen in the first post-industrial cities. On the other hand it enshrines a single narrative in physical place. The complexity of urban life is secured by the palimpsest of experience and function. Boyer connected this experience of place to memory and architecture believing that as 'spectators we travel through the city observing its architecture and constructed spaces, shifting contemporary scenes and reflections from the past until they thicken into a personalised image' (Boyer 1996, 32). These scenes and spaces need however to be multi-layered as urban areas consist of multiple and competing images. A "too well ordered" town, like the past, "loses its appeal" (Lowenthal 1985, 62). The URC tried to emphasise the role of the past, present and future (Clydebank rebuilt 2004c, point 5.1.2) in guiding the regeneration but what has resulted is an emphasis on the industrial past. As yet the post-industrial potential has not been fulfilled. Clydebank's "great and overwhelming past" is "at once a curse and a blessing" (Lowenthal 1985, 64). Clydebank rebuilt adds a further layer to the town's proud industrial past; securing a dynamic post-industrial future for both the mental and physical landscape will be eminently more challenging.

Works Cited

Primary Sources

Abercrombie, P. and D. Plumstead (1949). *A Civic Survey and Plan for the City and Royal Burgh of Edinburgh*, Edinburgh.
Anon. (2010). Nobody Thought Singer Would Close. *Clydebank Post*, 06/02/2010.
Anon. (2012). The Fabric of Society: The Singer's Story. *Clydebank Post*, 05/04/2012.
Central Manchester Development Corporation, (1988). *Strategy for Consultation*, Manchester: Central Manchester Development Corporation.
Clydebank rebuilt:
Architects Brief:
– JKS Phase 4: Site Preparation& Workshop Development, Design Team Services, Project Brief, September 2010b.

Design Forums:
– 1st Design Forum, April 2003

- 3rd Design Forum, May 2004
- 4th Design Forum, September 2004a
- 5th Design Forum, January 2005a
- 6th Design Forum, June 2005b
- 8th Design Forum, February 2006a
- 9th Design Forum, June 2006b
- 10th Design Forum, November 2006c
- 11th Design Forum, February 2007a
- 12th Design Forum, October 2007b
- 13th Design Forum, June 2008
- 15th Design Forum, September and October, 2010a
- 16th Design Forum, May 2011

Masterplan:
The Clydebank Plan, 2003-2010, 2004b.
Newsletter:
July 2009.
Public Art Strategy,
A Strategy for Art in Clydebank's Public Places, Consultation Draft, 2004-2010, 2004c.
Interview with Resident A, September 2005.
Interview with Clydebank rebuilt officer, September 2012.
New East Manchester (2001). *A New Town in the City, Regeneration Framework,* Manchester.
Society for the Protection of Ancient Buildings, *Annual Report of the SPAB* 1878
The Scotsman, Curtain goes down on the end of an era as Clydeside yard puts up for sale sign, 1 August 2001.

Secondary Sources

Arnold, J. (2011). *Allied Air War and Urban Memory, The Legacy of Strategic Bombing in Germany.* Cambridge: Cambridge University Press.
Binney, M. (1990). *Bright Future, The Re-use of Industrial Buildings.* London: SAVE Britain's Heritage.
Boyer, M. C. (1996). *The City of Collective Memory, Its Historical Imagery and Architectural Entertainments.* Cambridge, Mass.: MIT Press.
Casey, E. S. (1997). *The Fate of Place. A Philosophical History.* Berkeley: University of California Press.
Collins, C . (2008). *The Right to Exist: The Story of the Clydebank Independent Resource Centre.* Clydebank: Clydebank Independent Resource Centre.
Edensor, T. (2005). *Industrial Ruins: Space, Aesthetics, and Materiality.* New York: Berg.

Grenville, J. (2007). Conservation as Psychology: Ontological Security and the Built Environment. *International Journal of Heritage Studies*, 13 (6), 447–461.

Hewison, R. (1987). *The Heritage Industry: Britain in a Climate of Decline*. London: Methuen.

Hood, J. (ed.) (1986). *Clydebank: 100 Years*, Paisley: Clydebank District Council.

Hood, J. (ed.). (1988). *The History of Clydebank*. Lancashire: Parthenon Publishing Ltd, Cornforth.

Hubbard, P. (1993). The Value of Conservation: A Critical Review of Behavioural Research. *Town Planning Review*, 64 (4), 359–374.

Labadi, S. (2011). *Evaluating the Socio-Economic Impacts of Selected Regenerated Heritage Sites in Europe*. Amsterdam: European Cultural Foundation.

Lewicka, M. (2011). Place attachment: How far have we come in the last 40 years? *Journal of Environmental Psychology* 31, 207–230.

Lowenthal, D. (1985). *The Past is a Foreign Country*. Cambridge: Cambridge University Press.

Madgin, R. (2008). Making the Most of our Existing Urban Assets? New Labour's Focus on the Historic Urban Environment. In S. Nail and D. Fee (eds). *Vers une Renaissance Anglaise*. Paris: Presse de la Sorbonne Nouvelle.

Madgin R. (2009). *Heritage, Culture and Conservation: Managing the Urban Renaissance*. Saarbrücken: VDM Verlag.

Madgin R. (2010). Reconceptualising the Historic Urban Environment: Conservation and Regeneration in Castlefield, Manchester, 1960–2009. *Planning Perspectives*, 25 (1), 29–48.

Malpas, J. E. (1999). *Place and Experience, A Philosophical Topography*. Cambridge: Cambridge University Press.

McKendrick, T. (1986). *Clydebank Blitz*. Glasgow: McNaughtan & Sinclair.

Miller, M. J. (2003). *The Representation of Place, Urban Planning and Protest in France and Great Britain, 1950–1980*. Aldershot: Ashgate.

Mumford, L. (1938). *The Culture of Cities*. London: Secker & Warburg.

Nora, P. (1996). From Lieux de Mémoire to Realms of Memory. In P. Nora and L. Kritzman (eds.). *Realms of Memory: Rethinking the French Past*. New York: Columbia University Press.

Part IV
The Mediated Industrial City

Representing the Industrial City: Rotterdam, 1880–1970

Judith Thissen

This article examines the image of industrial Rotterdam in commercially—produced postcards and in avant-garde photography and film. In the late 19th century, picture postcards rapidly developed into a mass medium. Hundreds of different view cards of Rotterdam circulated during the "Golden Age" of the postcard, which lasted until the end of the 1910s. These cards promoted a particular vision of Rotterdam to tourists and people visiting for business, but also to the local population, thus shaping the city's self-image. At the other end of the cultural spectrum, avant-garde filmmakers and photographers visualized Rotterdam in radical new ways. Starting in the twenties, artists like Joris Ivens and Andor von Barsy redefined the aesthetic qualities of the urban landscape and disclosed the beauty of the industrial city to the general public. Their modernist perspectives on Rotterdam influenced the visual representation of the city well into the post-war period.

The visual materials I selected for my research are all photographic and there is a reason for this. From their invention, photography and the cinema were widely seen as part of the industrial age. Both media were also considered "objective" because photographic images are mechanically produced and reproduced. The industrial quality, combined with the ontological realism of the photographic image, made that photography and cinematography were frequently chosen to market the modern city and its industries (Schürmann 2008, 130–132). Obviously, the objectivity of photographic images should never be taken for granted. It is in fact highly ambiguous. Nonetheless, more than paintings, for instance, photographic images do bear a direct relationship with reality and this makes them particularly relevant for my own approach, which combines aesthetic analysis with social history. I am not interested in urban representation *per se* but in the historical relationship between the visualization of industrial Rotterdam and its "factual" development of as a port and industrial city. It is at the intersection of these phenomena, that we can understand the dynamics of medialisation in the context of large processes social and cultural change.

Postcards from a Family Album

When I moved to Rotterdam a few years ago, I was given a collection of 52 old postcards of my new hometown. They came from an album that once belonged to my great grandparents, who lived in a provincial town in the South-East of the Netherlands. They and their children received the postcards between 1902 and 1918. The majority of these cards belonged to a set. Selling packets of six, seven or eight different views of the same town was a common commercial practice in those days. The buyer would either send the individual cards to different addresses or, as in this case, to the same household. By receiving several cards of such a series or even the complete set within the time-span of a few days, my relatives shared in the traveler's metropolitan experience. My family did not visit Rotterdam until the 1920s. So I wondered what impression of the city did they get from these postcards.

Each set in the collection offers the spectator an overview of the city's touristic highlights: public buildings, bridges, historical statues, shopping streets and scenic views of the old town center (Fig. 1). However, what is conspicuously missing in the sets are images of Rotterdam as a modern industrial city. Only the old, 17th and 18th century pre-industrial harbors in the town center with their small sailing boats are represented on the cards. There are no pictures of the new docks on the South Bank, where the industrial port activities were concentrated. Neither do we find any pictures of warehouses or factories. Despite the fact that Rotterdam was widely perceived as an industrial city, its industrial character is exactly what these postcard series avoided to represent. In addition, the postcards favor a picturesque mode of representation, which in some series is enhanced by the use of a soft-tone coloring of the originally black-and-white photographs. Thus, the cards offer a romantic idealization of the present: an urban ideal image that focuses on the city's historical past. To be sure: there are some postcards in my collection that show the modern metropolitan qualities of Rotterdam: its elevated railway, the iron-work bridges and the White House skyscraper. Yet also for these emblems of modern life the same picturesque mode of representation prevails, domesticating urban modernity as it were.

Fig. 1: Postcard set Rotterdam, stamped 1903

(Source: Author's private collection, family album)

At this junction, I want to point that this collection may well be representative for a Dutch family album of the early 20th century, but it does not reflect the total offering on the market. In the 1900s, some local postcard publishers and the Verlag Dr. Trenkler, a Leipzig-based company that operated internationally, had views of the new docks on the South Bank in their assortment. Typically, these postcards featured the steam ships, grain elevators and cranes that epitomized the modern industrial port. (Fig. 2) We find several examples in the collections of German postcard dealers, but far less in Dutch archival collections. While this discrepancy requires further research, it suggests a difference in the city's perception between national and international publics. German visitors, many of whom might have been on business in Rotterdam, seem to have appreciated the industrial quality of the city well before the Dutch.

What can we learn from the case of my Rotterdam postcard collection? For one, in the opening decades of the 20th century, the production of commercial postcards was so large and their circulation so widespread in that it is difficult to give a comprehensive overview of the corpus. This is often the case with visual materials that were mechanically reproduced. Hence, one

Fig. 2: Postcard Rijnhaven, circa 1910

(Source: Author's private collection)

needs to carefully consider the limits and limitations of the corpus of images under consideration and situate the selection in the broader media landscape. Second, we have to be attentive to the fact that the industrial quality of an industrial city is not necessarily favored by mainstream visual media. Especially in metropolitan contexts, we will come across competing interpretations of modernity and urban life. In other words, there is not "one" industrial city and the absence of certain images may also be meaningful and needs to be explained. Thus a detour is necessary to understand why most Dutch postcard albums of the early 20th century do not contain images of industrial Rotterdam.

From Mercantile Town to Industrial City

Well into the 1830s, writers and visitors still praised Rotterdam for having kept the character of a Dutch mercantile town of the 17th and 18th century. As Paul van de Laar (1998) points out, the term mercantile town not only designated a city focused on trade but also implied an urban ideal image, which had its roots in the pre-industrial period and shaped for over two centuries the ways in which Rotterdam saw it self and represented itself to the larger world. In the mercantile town, the elite of merchant families set the political, social and cultural agenda, and the flourishing of commerce went hand in hand with a flowering of the arts stimulated by that same elite. The economy of Rotterdam, like that of other mercantile towns such as Amsterdam and Venice, was based upon the staple market system and entailed a particular model of spatial development characterized by a strong relationship between town and harbor, whereby the waterfront functioned as a showcase for the wealth of the city and its elite. (van Dijk and Avelar Pinheiro 2003, 91). In Rotterdam, it was on the *Boompjes* on the North Bank of the New Meuse that the most prosperous merchant families lived and did business.

The urban ideal of the mercantile town began to disintegrate in the second half of the 19th century under the pressures of reality. Due to innovations in transportation technology, investments in infrastructure and the rapid industrialization of the German hinterland, Rotterdam grew explosively and its port developed into one of the largest in continental Europe. Large-scale harbor expansion took place between 1880 and 1920, increasing the total port area from approximately 200 hectares to almost 1,800. The New Waterway canal improved the access route to the North Sea, especially for larger vessels. From the mid-1890s until the outbreak of the First World War, the port's annual growth in traffic was almost eight percent. In 1880, the port handled about 2.7 million tons, by 1913 the total volume of cargo had increased to 32 million tons. Nearly 75 percent of all goods were transit goods, coming from or going to Germany. The expansion in traffic went hand in hand with a fundamental shift in the port's economy. Rotterdam changed from a staple market system to a transit port. This meant that the core of economic activities no longer revolved around the trade in relatively high valued commodities shipped in small volumes, but on the throughput in bulk of raw materials, like iron ore, coal, grains, wood and, later also petroleum (van de Laar 2000, 2002; de Goey 2002).

Initially, the transformation of Rotterdam from a mercantile town into a *transitopolis* met with fierce resistance. During the first half of the 19th century, the Rotterdam merchant elite successfully used their political power to frustrate the reorientation of the port's function in order to protect their staple-market interests. According to Van de Laar, the city's business elite "was opposed against free trade, the abolition of Rhine tolls that would stimulate the port's transit function, and it did not like any modern railroad connections that could jeopardize the distributive function of the old merchant families" (2002, 64). By the 1870s, however, the resistance of the old merchant families was broken by a new breed of entrepreneurs and measures by the central government to liberalize the Dutch economy by putting an end to the nation's seaport monopolies, thus finally embracing the new international standards of free trade. From then on, Rotterdam could fully exploit the advantages of its geographic location and developed into a transit port. Between 1880 and 1914, the municipality invested almost eighty million guilders in the infrastructure of its harbors (van de Laar 2002, 66). The largest public investments went into a new harbor complex on the South Bank: the Rhine, Meuse and Waal docks. Specially built for the handling of bulk goods, these river docks allowed cargo-handling from ship to ship on stream via floating and shore-based grab cranes and elevators.

In this context of rapid economic and geographic expansion, the ideal of a town in which industry and trade harmoniously mixed with socio-cultural functions, gave way to a model of urban planning that separated the city from its industrial activities. From the 1900s onwards, we witness a growing spatial division between living and working and a process of decentralization, whereby the harbors moved to the western outskirts of Rotterdam towards the sea. This outward movement had its parallels in the realm of housing. Workers and their families continued to live near the harbors, docks and shipyards, but as early as the 1870s the wealthy upper class began to move out of the city. Rotterdam gained the reputation of being a *werkstad*—a workmen's city. Its largely working-class population continued to grow, from circa 100,000 inhabitants in 1850 to 470,000 in 1914 (van de Laar 1998, 24). After several decades of boomtown growth, Rotterdam was no longer a small, attractive mercantile town but a large, modern industrial city.

"Oh how ugly, ugly thou art. Industrial new Rotterdam", the Dutch poet E. J. Potgieter complained in 1879 (van de Laar 1998, 1). According to its critics, industrial Rotterdam and its business elite of *nouveau riche* cargo handlers and stevedores was solely focused on economic growth and material well-being. In the eyes of many contemporaries, the elevated railway that opened in 1877 exemplified par excellence the ugliness of the modern era and the barbarian character of the transit city, its lack of cultural sensibility and good taste in urban planning. There had been strong public resistance to the construction of the railway, not only on the part of the merchant elite but much broader sections of the population because the railway literally cut through the city's historic center (Fig. 1). With the railway, the new age had arrived. Its presence in the urban landscape was unavoidable for everybody who walked through the city. However, as my earlier analysis of the post cards revealed, decades after its actual demise, the inhabitants of Rotterdam and most Dutch visitors still clung to the ideal image of the mercantile city and its notions of urban beauty. Hence, they favored a picturesque mode of representation that softened the "ugliness" of the industrial city and soothed the anxiety associated with modern life.

The Beauty of the Industrial City

During the 1920s, the aesthetic esteem for the industrial city with its functionalist architecture changed radically. By the end of the decade, "modern, large, technological Rotterdam had become enormously popular both in artistic circles and among the city's inhabitants in general", art historian Patricia van Ulzen observes (2007, 55). Avant-garde movements like Russian Constructivism, German *Neue Sachlichkeit* and the Dutch movement *De*

Stijl provided new frameworks to appreciate the modern urbanity of Rotterdam. A city that had previously been branded as ugly, was suddenly considered beautiful (van Ulzen 2007, 49).

The beginnings of this shift in taste from a picturesque to a modern aesthetics can be situated with the emergence of a style that became known as the New Photography. This international movement advocated a documentary mode of representation that "objectively" reflected reality but from unusual angles and with strong contrasts in form and light to produce an effect of alienation and thus sensitize the spectator. Some of the leading exponents of the New Photography were based in Rotterdam, where they belonged to a creative milieu that included many prominent modernist architects, typographers, and industrial designers, including as J. A. Brinkman, J. J. P. Oud, W. H. Gispen, J. Kamman and P. Swart. They maintained extensive international contacts, especially with the Bauhaus, and exchanged ideas with other photographers and filmmakers through avant-garde platforms like *Internationale Revue i10* and *Filmliga* (Van Ulzen 2007, 55; Gierstberg 2011, 109; Paalman 2011, 67–111).

Embraced by the municipality, the local business community and the popular press, the New Photography became the aesthetic vehicle to promote the modernity of Rotterdam and its industrial port, especially the new docks on the South Bank. The ultimate symbol of the city's newly-discovered industrial beauty became *De Hef*—the high draw bridge over the New Meuse, which was inserted into the old elevated railway in 1927. In many respects, *De Hef*—the actual bridge and its visual representation on postcards, in the popular press and in avant-garde art—exemplified the shift towards a modernist aesthetic sensibility (Fig. 3). As we saw, the construction of the elevated railway had met with fierce resistance in the 1870s. Fifty years later, the public's response to the new bridge was decidedly more enthusiastic. Local newspapers reported with great excitement about the construction works and covered in detail the dismantling of the old bridge and the opening of the new one (Koot 2001). *De Hef* inspired the anonymous reporters of the popular, illustrated weekly *Groot*

Fig. 3: Postcard Rotterdam—Alles Staal (all Steel) with De Hef bridge, circa 1935

(Source: Author's private collection)

Rotterdam but also featured in the 1928 portfolio *Métal* by the prominent avant-garde photographer Germaine Krull.

Krull's photography had a strong influence on Joris Ivens, with whom she had a relationship when he shot *De Brug* (The Bridge), by far the most famous art work about *De Hef* and a film that was almost immediately recognized as a masterpiece of experimental cinema. Made in 1928, this short documentary (black & white, silent, 16 minutes) shows the movements of the lifting bridge, trains, and boats. By way of rhythmic editing and constructivist perspectives, alternating between different angles and with strong variations in shot size, Ivens creates a visual contrast between the different movements and forms. The film premiered in the art-cinema context of the *Filmliga* and then gained a much broader audience when its distribution was taken over by the Dutch branch of the UfA. In the national press, *De Brug* was highly praised and typically reviewed in terms of the "first Dutch art film", an "expression of modern times" and "modern beauty" (Koot 2001, 28).

The aesthetics of *De Brug* deserve a more detailed analysis, but I am primarily concerned here with questions of social history, in particular with the film's relationship to the actual industrial city. If we consider Ivens' cinematographic representation of the South Bank harbor from the perspective of social history, what strikes first and foremost is the almost total absence of people in the film. The filmmaker presents himself as the man behind the camera. The spectator sees the bridge through his eyes, but the other human beings in the film are merely abstract forms, instead of characters with inner emotions with whom the viewers can identify. In fact, in several shots, we only see an arm or hand that is operating a machine. In other words, the *werkstad* as a social space is absent. Rotterdam is emptied of its workers and its representation reduced to a visual spectacle of industrial architecture and transportation technologies.[1] This abstraction was a deliberate choice on the part of Ivens. While in the post-war era, the harbor became more and more disconnected from the city, this spatial division was not yet the case in the first half of the 20th century. Dockers and other laborers lived in working-classes neighborhoods on the South Bank because the combination of working and living was still the dominant urban pattern. Indeed, "the city" could

---

1 Obviously, this aesthetic strategy had its real-life counterpart in processes of mechanization in the harbor itself. For instance, a series of new techniques, especially the introduction of floating and shore-based grab cranes, had mechanized much of the handling of ore and coal, which had previously done manually by dock workers (van Driel 2002).

Fig. 4: Jan van Maanen, De Maas biedt velen arbeid/
The Maas provides work for many
(Source: Photo from Brusse and Oud (1938), 38)

not be entirely blocked out when shooting *De Brug*. In the far distance, framed by the bars of the bridge, the spectator gets a glimpse of street life on the quays. It is as if social reality breaks through the formal language of constructivism.

The dehumanization of the industrial city is not characteristic for Ivens' film alone. On the contrary. I would argue that it is emblematic for the New Photography. Take the work of Andor von Barsy, a Hungarian cameraman and photographer, who lived and worked in Rotterdam during the interwar period (Gierstberg 2011; Paalman 2011, 130–165). His series of photographs of the Rotterdam harbor—almost 300 in total—rarely represent workers and if they do, the rationale seems purely aesthetic. The same can be said for many of his films. For instance, Von Barsy's *Tusschen aankomst en ver-*

Fig. 5: Jan van Maanen, Het daverende lied van den arbeid/The booming song of labour

(Source: Photo from photo from Brusse and Oud (1938), 39)

trek (Between arrival and departure), a port promotion film, was described as "a voluminous symphony of cranes, crabs, tug-boats and ocean steamers" by a contemporary reviewer (quoted after Gierstberg 2011, 108). Another famous example is *De Schoonheid van Rotterdam* (the beauty of Rotterdam), a richly illustrated book that appeared in 1938 in a highly popular book series dedicated to beauty of the Netherlands (Brusse and Oud 1938). Most photographs in the Rotterdam volume are typical examples of the New Photography. They capture the city's industrial and modernist qualities "in black and white with strong contrasts that show the structure of the objects to better effect" (van Ulzen 2007, 49). Ships and industrial structures such as bridges, cranes and grabs dominate this visualization of Rotterdam. The absence of people is striking. Workers appear mostly in extreme long shots, which represent them as faceless, stylized figures in the industrial landscape (Fig. 4). Perhaps the most telling example in *De Schoonheid van Rotterdam* is the photograph "The booming song of labor" by Jan van Maanen (Fig. 5). In this shot of the harbor labor is understood as the fully mechanized labor of the cranes.

Until the outbreak of the Second World War, modernist representations of the South bank docks defined by and large the visual image of industrial Rotterdam. The older, more picturesque postcards of the industrial port, often with soft-tone coloring, disappeared from the market. The war years had their own iconography. In May 1940, the city's historic center, including the old Leuvehaven, was almost entirely destroyed by the German Air Force and the firestorm that followed the aerial bombardment. The new harbor complexes along the Meuse suffered very heavy damage in September 1944, when the German occupiers blew up the quays and warehouses on both the North and South banks and demolished the few remaining cranes and elevators. The majority of postcards of this period highlight the devastation in the city center, whereby visual contrasts are frequently used to enhance the picturesque quality and sense of drama inherent in wartime images.

Post-War Industrial Rotterdam: The Rush to the Coast

In the first two decades after the war, the modernist image of Rotterdam gained momentum. There was a strong continuity between the interwar-years and the period of post-war reconstruction in terms of architectural ideals. By the 1930s, Rotterdam was already highly praised for its modernist buildings. J. J. P. Oud acted as the Municipal Housing Architect for Rotterdam from 1918 until 1933. The utopian visions of city and society were embodied in the *Nieuwe Bouwen* projects of the Brinkman & Van der Vlugt firm, in particular in their Van Nelle factory (1931). During the reconstruction era, no other Dutch city accepted as thoroughly the modernist principles of architecture and urban planning defined by the CIAM (*Congrès International d'Architecture Moderne*). Thus, Rotterdam built the most modernist city center in the Netherlands and became a prime example for the international planning community (Rooijendijk 2005, 63). In "A Walk Through Rotterdam", for instance, Lewis Mumford discusses with unbridled enthusiasm the aesthetic and urban qualities of the *Lijnbaan*, the new open-air pedestrian shopping mall that formed the heart of the city's modernist center (Mumford 1953, 50–52). Not surprisingly, the favorite object of photographers and film makers became the new city center with its functionalist architecture (Andela and Wagenaar 1995; Blijstra 1965). On the other hand, the post-war interest in the city center and concomitant changes in the visual representation of modern Rotterdam should not be understood as a simple shift in subject matter. At stake was a major transformation in the relation between the city and its industrial port.

The so-called *Basisplan*, which was presented in 1946, defined the outlook for the future Rotterdam. As social geographer Cordula Rooijendijk
observes, the plan was "a turning point in history, since its aim was to realize a new utopian society on the basis of socioeconomic planning, marking
the end of laissez-faire and the beginning of the welfare state" (2005, 67). In
the new city, urban functions—dwelling, work, leisure and transportation—
were radically separated. Rotterdam was zoned into housing areas, recreational areas, and work areas. There was to be a central business district but
large industries and companies that had no need to be in the center, had to
be relocated to new industrial zones on the outskirts (Rooijendijk 2005, 74).
  The *Basisplan* had important consequences for the relation between city
and harbor. As a result of the decentralization policy, the port and related industries moved more and more westwards towards the coast during the post-
war era. This development was fostered by fundamental changes in transport technology and cargo handling, notably the introduction of containers
and the continuous increase of vessel size. Large-scale expansion of the port
surface further accelerated the ongoing separation between the city and its
harbor. With the Botlek Plan, the Europoort-Maasvlakte complex and the
opening of the Eemhaven, the total port area grew from 1,400 hectares in
1950 to some 7,600 hectares in 1975. These new harbors were much larger
than the ones that were developed before 1940. In particular, they accommo-
dated large petro-chemical plants and storage tanks. In the post-war period,
industrialization occupied a central place in port policies. Before the war,
Rotterdam's large scale industrialization remained limited to those sectors
that were directly connected to transshipment and shipping, that is ship
building and repair. After 1945, the city wanted to become less dependent
on the German hinterland and diversify its economy, especially by stimulat-
ing the oil business and related industries (van de Laar 2002; de Goey 2002).
  Because of the "rush to the coast", industrial Rotterdam moved literally
out of view. Whereas in the 1920s and 1930s, the segregation of city and
industry had been to a large extent a visual effect created by the New Photography, it became reality with the development of the Botlek, Europoort
and first Maasvlakte. To this day, the harbor remains a fundamental element
in the story of the city's identity and its economic success. However, the harbor figures primarily in written narratives. Since the 1960s, the port and its
industries can only be re-integrated into the visual representation of Rotterdam by way of montage. Let me illustrate this with two examples.

Representing Post-War Rotterdam

The first example concerns multi-picture postcards. After the war, this type of "greetings from" card, typically with four to eight photographs of a particular city in black-and-white or color, developed into one the most widely-spread commercial formats aimed at tourists. Clearly, the collage of different miniature views echoes the sets of the early 20th century. In the case of Rotterdam, the format was particular appropriate as it allowed to represent the city and the new, outlying harbors on a single card (Fig. 6). In fact, the dynamics of the industrial port could only be seized by offering a multi-picture overview (Fig. 7). Like the postcards and avant-garde photography of the Interwar period, the "greetings from Rotterdam" cards produced during the reconstruction era stress the modern and metropolitan quality of Rotterdam. However, unlike Van Ulzen, I would not conclude that there was a strong "continuity in the way the city's future was envisioned" (2007, 66). On the contrary, we can observe a radical break in perspective. The emphasis in the visual narrative about Rotterdam shifted in the postwar period from the harbor to the new city center, from industrial activity to consumption and entertainment. By the 1960s, the *Lijnbaan* shopping mall (van den Broek & Bakema, 1949–1953), department store *De Bijenkorf* (Breuer, 1953–1957)

Fig. 6: Postcard Greetings from Rotterdam, circa 1967

(Source: www.dekunstclub.nl)

Fig. 7: Postcard Greetings from Rotterdam, circa 1964

(Source: www.dekunstclub.nl)

and the Euromast (Maaskant, 1960), a space age observation tower for tourists, had become the city's new icons.

My second example is again taken from avant-garde cinematography. More than thirty years after the success of *De Brug* (1928), Joris Ivens was commissioned by the city council to make a promotional film about Rotterdam as the "gate of Europe". With a commentary written and narrated by the poet Gerrit Kouwenaar, *Rotterdam-Europoort* (1966, 20 minutes, color) can be best described as a cine-poem that combines fact and fiction. The film alternates between abstract images of the port and industrial activities, intimate documentary sequences portraying social life in the city, and staged scenes in which the fictional theme of the flying Dutchman is elaborated. The three story lines come together to tell a story of destruction and reconstruction: "this city I saw burning, this city I saw building" (commentary Kouwenaar).

In *Rotterdam-Europoort*, montage is essential to link the city and the harbor, to visualize the connection between "oil and grain and people [...] and oil and people" (Kouwenaar). Whereas in *De Brug*, social life and urban living could still break into the film's highly stylized representation of the industrial city, this was no longer an aesthetic choice when Ivens shot the Europoort film. Due to the rush to the coast, the geographic separation of city and port had become reality. The nearest harbors of the Botlek-Europort complex are situated at some twenty kilometers from the center of Rotterdam. Moreover, Ivens has to use extreme long shots and aerial photography to characterize the Europoort. The new harbor complex is not only situated far away from the city center and hence "out of view", but it also resists representation because of its scale and the nature of its industries. Only with an extreme distance between the camera and its object does the filmmaker manage to give the spectator an impression of the Europoort-Botlek complex. Such extreme long shots, by their very nature, render the human element invisible. In particular, the shots of the petro-chemical industry in *Rotterdam-Europoort* show an entirely desolate, dehumanized industrial landscape. It is almost as if we watch an apocalyptic scene in a science fiction film. The dehumanization of the industrial city that we observed in *De Brug* and other works of New Photography is brought to an extreme, but it is imposed by the landscape itself and not a matter of modernist aesthetics.

However, there is more at stake in *Rotterdam-Europoort* than just a new urban pattern that conditions and restructures the visual representation of the industrial city. Ivens deliberately reinforces the split between port and city, between working and living. Whereas the images of the *Europoort* evoke the formal aesthetics of the New Photography, most sequences in the city are shot in *cinema vérité* style, thus creating a strong aesthetic contrast between the port and the city center. Only when filming a new, modernist apartment block, an emblem of welfare state housing for the working classes, Ivens uses the same formalist language as when he films the harbor complex. But everyday life in the city center is captured in a far more direct and realist way. People are rendered as individuals, they literally have faces and their activities seem to unfold naturally before the camera. The inner city is primarily represented as a shopping and entertainment zone and the domain of the young. Many scenes shows acts of consumption and recreation: people are portrayed as smiling shoppers, cheerful cinemagoers, they are drinking coffee in a lunch room or enjoy themselves at night driving around on mopeds. The fourth urban function that Ivens isolates in the film is transportation: the bustle at the railway station, flows of people going by foot, bike or moped to work, home or into the shopping district. In sum, *Rotterdam-Europoort* endorses and visualizes the urban ideal image of the modernist city as defined in the *Basisplan* with its strict separation of urban society into industrial, housing and recreational zones that are connected by efficient transportation systems.

Conclusion

This article has examined how commercial postcards and some renowned works of avant-garde photography and cinematography represented Rotterdam as an industrial city. Given the centrality of the port for the city's identity and economy, my research focused on images of the harbors. For the period 1880–1970, we can distinguish three stages. During the first decades of industrialization (1880–1920), when Rotterdam rapidly developed into a major industrial port and big city, this urban and economic development was only marginally visible in the postcards of the period. In terms of subject matter, most view cards highlighted the city's historical center and the old Leuvehaven as if times had not changed and Rotterdam remained a mercantile town. Cards of the newly-built docks on the South Bank circulated on a limited scale, but they aimed primarily at foreign tourists. Aesthetically, the postcards of this period, even those of the new harbors, favored a picturesque mode of representation, often using soft-coloring to create a romantic effect.

Around 1920, as modernism came to the foreground in almost all realms of art, Rotterdam's industrial quality was reassessed and its functionalist beauty discovered by avant-garde photography and cinematography. This shift from a picturesque to a modernist aesthetic sensibility and the concomitant interest industrial Rotterdam was not restricted to the cultural elite. By the end of the twenties, modernism had gained a much wider audience thanks to illustrated magazines like *Groot Rotterdam*, the programming of avant-garde cinema in commercial movie theaters, modernist design and typography. During the next decade, the South Bank harbor complex figured prominently in the visual representation of Rotterdam. In the 1930s, postcard producers also adopted a more objective photographic style and they no longer applied the technique of soft-coloring. Finally, it is important to recall that despite their profound interest in the industrial port, avant-garde filmmakers and photographers largely ignored workers and working-class life in Rotterdam. There was a strong tendency to dehumanize the industrial landscape reducing it to functionalist architecture, bridges, cranes, machines, ships and trains.

During the post-war reconstruction era, modernism continued to be the dominant aesthetic regime. As Rotterdam and its new center became the mecca of modernist architects and urban planners, producers of visual images developed a strong interest in the inner city at the expense of the harbour. This visual marginalization of industrial Rotterdam went hand in hand with the physical movement of port activities towards the coast as a result modernist planning, which advocated a clear separation between different urban functions and relegated industrial activity to the outskirts of the city. In the second half of the 20th century, the physical and visual gap between the city and harbour grew to the point that both spaces could only be integrated into the same visual narrative by way of collage and montage. However, the mode of representation changed. The 1960s witnessed the beginning of a break away from modernism and a gradual humanization of the visualized urban landscape. This shift in aesthetics and subject matter was fostered by a shift towards a more personalized and intimate documentary style in film and photography. The inhabitants of Rotterdam first appeared as gratified consumers in the modernist décor of the new city center or tenants of comfortable welfare state apartments. Paradoxically, workers as real people with personal stories about Rotterdam as *werkstad* only came to the forefront of the city's visual representation at the beginning of the post-industrial era, that is during the seventies and eighties, when they went massively on strike to fight the growing redundancies in the port and related industries.

Works Cited

Andela, G., and C. Wagenaar (eds.). (1995). *Een stad voor het leven: Wederopbouw Rotterdam 1940–1965.* Rotterdam: Uitgeverij de Hef.

Blijstra, R. (1965). *Rotterdam: Stad in beweging.* Amsterdam: N.V. Arbeiderspers.

Brusse, M. J., and P. J. Oud (1938). *De schoonheid van ons land. Deel IV: Rotterdam.* Amsterdam: Uitgeverij Contact.

Dijk, H. van, and M. Avelar Pinheiro (2003). The changing face of European ports as a result of their evolving use since the nineteenth century. *Portuguese Journal of Social Science, 2,* 89–103.

Driel, H. van (2002). The first mechanization wave in coal and ore handling as an example of patterns of technological innovation in the port of Rotterdam. In R. Loyen, E. Buyst and G. Devos (eds.). *Struggling for leadership: Antwerp-Rotterdam port competition between 1870–2000,* 299–319. Heidelberg: Physica Verlag.

Gierstberg, F. (2011). The forgotten photography of Andor von Barsy. In F. Gierstberg and J. de Jong (eds.). *Andor von Barsy photographer.* Rotterdam: Gemeentearchief Rotterdam/Jap Sam Books.

Goey, F. de (2002). Port of Rotterdam: Land-use policy during the twentieth century. In R. Loyen, E. Buyst and G. Devos (eds.). *Struggling for leadership: Antwerp-*

Rotterdam port competition between 1870–2000, 221–234. Heidelberg: Physica Verlag.

Koot, R. (2001), De Hef en het imago van de modernste stad van Nederland. Een brug tussen haven en avant-garde. In M. Halbertsma and P. van Ulzen (eds.). *Interbellum Rotterdam. Kunst en cultuur 1918–1940*, 20–44. Rotterdam: NAi Uitgevers.

Laar, P. van de (1998). *Veranderingen in het geschiedbeeld van de koopstad Rotterdam.* Rotterdam: Erasmus University.

Laar, P. van de (2000). *Stad van formaat: Geschiedenis van Rotterdam in de negentiende en twintigste eeuw.* Zwolle: Waanders Uitgevers.

Laar, P. van de (2002). Port traffic in Rotterdam: The competitive edge of a Rhineport (1880–1914). In R. Loyen, E. Buyst and G. Devos (eds.). *Struggling for leadership: Antwerp-Rotterdam port competition between 1870–2000*, 63–85. Heidelberg: Physica Verlag.

Mumford, L. (1953). *The highway and the city.* London: Secker and Warburg.

Paalman, F. (2011), *Cinematic Rotterdam: The times and tides of a modern city.* Rotterdam: 010 Publishers.

Rooijendijk, C. (2005). *That city is mine! Urban ideal images in public debates and city plans, Amsterdam & Rotterdam 1945–1995.* Amsterdam: Amsterdam University Press.

Schürmann, S. (2008). Advertisers, Commercial Artists, and Photographers in Twentieth Century Hamburg. In M. Heßler and C. Zimmermann (eds.). *Creative urban milieus. Historical perspectives on culture, economy, and the city*, 119–136. Frankfurt am Main and New York: Campus Verlag.

Ulzen, P. van (2007). *Imagine a metropolis: Rotterdam's creative class, 1970–2000.* Rotterdam: 010 Publishers.

Representations of Industrial Cities in Photo Books and Promotional Films of the 1950s and 1960s

Rolf Sachsse

"Where there is order, wellness arises. Well divided into parts, even working class quarters win a high definition of architecture. All of this follows the plan" (Le Corbusier 2007, 54). This description by Le Corbusier provides a picture of the model of the *Cité industrielle* after the plans of Tony Garnier— and it describes an image, not a city map. It may even be understood as the scenery from a computer game: The virtual camera moves fast across wide streets without any obstacle, and the viewer registers a panoramic horizon with lines of factories. Le Corbusier wrote these words shortly after World War I and they were published around 1922 while Garnier's model of the industrial city originates in the years around 1912. Cinematographic and photographic representations hinder in nearly no other genre as thoroughly as in the display of industrial cities, be they medium or large sized but historically strictly bound to the 20th century.[1]

Both these forms of media have undergone serious changes within the last three decades, above all due to the technical developments commonly summarized as the digital revolution. Seen from the vantage point of media history, the processes of digitization have come to an end when differentiation replaces fundamental change. In the following, two short prehistories will serve to demonstrate the interdependencies of industrialization, media representation, and modern media in which these representations really took place. This argument will be followed by examples of the two media genres of the promotional film and the illustrated book in the form of short case studies. Although there are later samples of both films and books, this case study closes with the late 1970s.

---

1 The following is a corrected and extended version of an earlier draft (Sachsse 2012, 55–69). The author is especially grateful to Benjamin Heidersberger and Bernd Rodrian from the Heidersberger Institute, Wolfsburg, for additional information and copyright courtesy.

Industrialization and Medialisation until 1914

Hypothetically, industrial cities may be understood as affiliated with a history of the industrialization processes of the 19th or 20th century. These processes are mirrored in media and thus strictly bound to the economic stories of the cities or their surrounding countries. Visually, the industry of the first half of the 19th century manifested itself in steel etchings of industrial venues on calling cards and letterhead papers (Korzus 1980), in portraits like that of Isambard Kingdom Brunel taken by Robert Howlett in 1857 (Haworth-Booth 1984, 50, 61–65) or in big picture catalogues of industrial products as produced by Nicolas Henneman and others on behalf of Prince Albert after 1851 (Keeler 1982, 257–272). Larger amounts of photographic prints provided by manufacturing production allowed for various forms of media representation of industrial events, from luxuriously produced fair albums to large-sized cardboards handed over as presents to customers up to large issues of smaller picture copies for representatives and wholesalers (Kosok 1999).

Parallel to the development of the Autotype grid-printing practice of images, the genre of often very luxuriously produced company books in small editions emerged since the 1890s (Sachsse 2013). Especially cities with strong interests in the settlement of industrial companies adopted strategies similar to the public relation attempts of the industry. As early as 1863 the first illustrated book of the cities Elberfeld and Barmen in the Wupper Valley was published with a number of pasted photographs (Langewiesche 1863). Panoramas from a steeple or from the city hall tower, e.g. the one of the new city of Grand Island in Nebraska by J. R. Moeller from 1885, might have been placed on the desks of industrial estate agents at the time (Pare 1982, 256–257). As late as 1910 the architect Walter Gropius, as an employee in the AEG head quarters of Peter Behrens in Berlin gathered countless picture cards advertising the investment into US harbors and US grain silos in order to illustrate his talks on functional architecture with them (Brown 1993, 304–308).

Nearly at the same time, shortly before World War I, both forms of media that served to represent industrial cities were introduced to the German people: the documentary film and the photographically illustrated book. From 1908 on, Karl Robert Langewiesche edited his "Blaue Bücher" (blue books) claiming, due to the large numbers of printed issues, that he had brought the illustrated book into the houses of moderately earning citizens (Starl 1981, 73–81). At the same time, cinemas were moved from the fairground or the variety into their own buildings. The architecture of cinemas provided a space for a common ritual of reception of the presentation of features and documentaries (Brod 1992, 15–17). In 1910, Julius Pinschewer founded the first film-production company in Germany, concentrating on commissioned films. He became an early pioneer of the promotional city film in the 1920s and, among others, financed the works of Walter Ruttmann (Agde 1998, 20–23). However, it is important to that the introduction of these media processes was still fermenting at that time; neither a city film nor a photo book was issued on the subject of the industrial city before 1914—aside from a small book on the Hamburg harbor and some company publications (Jung 2000, 9–15; Meissner 1909).

Industrialized media and propaganda between the two World Wars

All functional forms of audio-visual media were established in the 1920s and 1930s; reviewing them from the vantage point of the 21st century, they can be considered analogue. For at least three to five generations in the Northern hemisphere, these media formats have strongly influenced the sensitive apparatus of social perception (Zielinsky 1989, 98–174). Similar observations have been made in an efficiency research into mass communication technically made possible through broadcasted and printed media that sought to manipulate whole nations or continents (Böckelmann 1975). The convergence of urban representations in photography and film is particularly important; however, descriptions of this convergence up to now can almost only be found in the context of picture-journalistic publications such as illustrated magazines and in rare city films (Bollerey 1995, 114–131).

In 1925, Walther Günther published a small polemic „City film. Remarks on an epidemic"; the work saw two editions and coined a genre of the same title (Günther 1925; 1928). At the time of the first edition, Adolf Trotz' first Berlin film had been shown in public (Goergen 2001a, 11–20). The second edition was printed in 1928, parallel to Walter Ruttmann's epochal opus "Berlin. Sinfonie einer Groszstadt" (Berlin. Symphony of a Metropolis), which almost over-represented the genre in later film history (Günther 2009, 235–244). Until then, numerous editions of projection slides (*Lichtbildreihen*) had been published by picture agencies such as Fritz Stoedtner's and had been presented in public spaces like the Urania halls. Increasing numbers of short city films were released and presented as a popular cultural addition to screenings or photo talks (Goergen 2001b, 34–38). With the establishment of the weekly Ufa newsreel in 1925, the short city films increasingly became a component of the journalistic news service. These films instigated the interest of many city governments. The highest priority was to attract public attention when providing editorial information, as was noted by Walter Lippmann and Edward Bernays in their well-known books (Lippmann 1922; Bernays 1928). Three styles of the genre "city film" were established until the beginning of World War II: feature length films were comparatively rare, short film sequences were often produced in a news context, and the real city film corresponded with the documentary with lengths of about 15 to 20 minutes (Zimmermann 2003, 59–73).

However, for the visual (self-)representation of industrial cities, this film wave had an equally minor impact as the starting boom in photographically illustrated books. Jeanpaul Goergen sums up the city film genre "cozy beauty", a concept equally applicable for the photographic slide shows of most cities (Goergen 1997, 4–6). When an otherwise very strict observer August Sander received the order of portraying the city of Viersen in 1939, he could hardly concentrate on anything but the idyll of the "romantic provincial city" before his camera, which had become an equally well-established title. There were a number of illustrated books depicting German cities between 1925 and 1940 comprising the industrial parts of these cities, e.g. Lübeck or Berlin. Yet these books were rather cultural than industrial self-representations. Of the volumes on Jena, photographed in 1925 by Paul Wolff, and on Lübeck, taken in 1928 by Albert Renger-Patzsch, as well as on Dresden, provided in 1929 by numerous Modernists of the craft, it is known that they were handed out as presents on behalf of the city to the participants of a teachers' association meeting there (Wolff 1925; Renger-Patzsch 1928; Dresdner Lehrerverein 1929). And like in the film of Walter Ruttmann, Sasha Stones' fascinating illustrated book defined Berlin itself also only partially as an industrial but in general an urban metropolis, including the industry as a foil, without symbolising the city as a whole (Behne and Stone 1929).

Only one illustrated book of 1937 on the city of Essen—partially illustrated with photographs of Albert Renger-Patzsch—shows this city as originally industrial although it is fashioned in the manner of the classical line of illustrated travel books introduced by Kurt Hielscher as a conservative form in the 1920s (Cremers 1937; Hielscher 1924). Even some volumes depicting the harbors of Bremen and Hamburg and published at various occasions between 1930 and 1939 concentrate on the technical quality of the harbor arrangements and much less on the idea of an industrial city (Verkehrsverein Bremen 1930; Kaufmann and von Seggern 1938; Hansa and Beutler 1939; Die deutschen Bücher 1939; Tietgens 1939). Thus, the inter-war decades had seen the introduction and, in some degree, the establishment of the genres displaying the (audio-)visual (self-)representation of industrial cities but not the public reception necessary for its constitution as a genre. And both media had to dismiss any possible convergences with each other due to NS media politics (Böhme 2004, 162–169). As the common representation of industrial cities in the period from the 1950s to the 1970s pursued different lines in both types of media, they need to be seen as distinct and will be introduced individually.

City films

As a genre, the city film on industrial cities as produced after 1945 in Europe and the US can be understood more in the vicinity of the industrial film than of the cultural and social documentary. After World War I, industrial films—e.g. "Vu Feier an Eisen (De fer et de feu)" by Gustave Labruyere in 1921—were produced in larger numbers, partially in full feature length like the Luxemburg example (CNA 1997). All these films follow—more than the later city films—a relatively schematic dramaturgy: Following a panoramic view looking over big industrial arrangements an introduction is given to the specific theme, now and then with the help of animated sequences, pointing out the big economic power and the uniqueness of what was shown. Then there are impressive pictures of the production process, mostly in close-up and American takes, before quieter sequences of the film are devoted to the social care of the enterprise ranging from the canteen supply over company sports to jubilee parties. In this setting, the industrial film has a similar plot to the book-shaped company publications or the archival constructions of most company photo archives; these only add portraits of the company founders, protagonists and associated of the enterprise (Langewiesche 1863; Zimmermann 2005; Thijssen 2002).

The genre "city film of industrial cities" is confronted with a number of difficulties in filmography; traditions of different types of media archives seem to depend on many random choices in terms of access that are directly connected to the production terms of the films: Numerous works were produced by small producers on local commission; usually camerawoman or cameraman were the same person, often a local journalist, now and then even a hairdresser's master craftswoman with amateurish ambitions (Jakob 2011). It is only with a certain degree of luck that these films can be traced through systematic archival care as it is the case with the media archive centre of Westphalia whose multimedia information centre allows to supplement historical-critical editions (Jakob 2009). Now and then industrial cities are also interested in publishing their former promotional films until today: The films produced yearly by the city of Gelsenkirchen between 1951 and 1996 can all be purchased online as DVD editions (Gelsenkirchen 2009). Here, even an alternative city film survived, the "Schmuddelecken" (*dirty corners*) from 1972—indeed classified by all protagonists as a „bad" film (Gelsenkirchen 2011).

Unfortunately, the sources for the Western Ruhr area within the Rhenish archives are equally bad for the North German and Saarland industrial cities. But the Westphalian examples, as that of the city of Gelsenkirchen, nevertheless precisely prove what the city film was about. The audio-visual account of one year brings to the fore the city's achievements in the best light, showing the industry as prosperity and bringing relief for the whole city, and concentrates upon the soft factors of urban development in culture, sport, consumption and health care. The dramaturgy of the films follows simple rules: The spectator approaches and enters the city by car, meets the modern traffic in the form of streetcars, coaches and well cleaned private cars until the camera touches the chimneys of industry works and finally reaches the interiors of the museums, theatres and swimming-pools. It was not allowed to film industrial companies themselves; industrial espionage was the big issue leading to the topological exclusion of all people apart from the employees. In the latter part of such city films shopping scenes from the high street depict nice happy citizens with an ice cream being slopped in bright sunlight before the viewer is cinematically engulfed by the evening coziness. Gelsenkirchen employed its own photojournalist as a city filmmaker; from 1965 onwards Werner Nickel produced not only the annual city film but also illustrated all books and advertising pamphlets of the city (Nickel 1965).

No city in Western Germany declined the opportunity to be represented in such films as particularly beautiful and desirable from the 1950s onward. A visual discussion on the heavy industry and its influence on the urban situation did not take place here. This is the exact opposite with Alfred Wagg's film "Germany: A Family of the Industrial Ruhr" of 1958, which is the reason of referring to it here (Wagg 1958). The film plot uses the help of a protagonist and his family for the depiction of the living situation in the Ruhr district: The family not only lives in the northern parts of Essen that are practically never shown in city films until these days; the strong side effects of industrialization in the form of dark clouds of smoke are as clearly displayed as the complicated procurement of food in everyday life (Führmann 2012). This film was not commissioned by a city government but an instructional film for US soldiers to be stationed in Western Germany and, besides this, it depended on the resemblances of northeastern American industrial locations to the German Federal ones: Essen is here compared to Pittsburgh in a similar way as the sensational report of W. Eugene Smith in Life magazine (Stevenson 2001).

In Eastern Germany, however, the economic achievements of socialism could only be communicated with considerable delay in comparison to the West, and thus the genre of the industrial city representation tended to be a challenge both for film and photography. Whilst company reports were produced, their public presentation was afflicted with all kinds of censorship problems (Mühlberg 2004, 147–167). In this respect, the impression that the city films of the GDR up to the building of the Berlin Wall concentrated extensively upon the damages of World War II is hardly refutable (Schenk 2000, 6–9).

During the 1960s, following the introduction of color television and in the context of new media uses, the genre of the city film started to erode (Günther 2009, 251–256; Ludes et al. 1994). The basically critical position of public media in Western Germany hardly admitted excessively positive representations of industrial city planning. In the 1970s, the first opposition stirred against the industrial city from an ecological perspective (Lehmbrock 1971). Throughout the 1980s, the industry faced closure in a number of German regions, and with this came the end of the self-image of the visual representation of industrial cities as reflected in photographic and cinematic productions (Eskildsen and Borsdorf 1987). Only the introduction of the Internet in the middle of the 1990s and through it forms of "viral marketing" in channels like YouTube since about 2007 provided for a renaissance of the representative city film, which also holds for Gelsenkirchen (Gelsenkirchen 2012).

First case study: The publishing house "Die schönen Bücher" (The beautiful books)

There are a lot more sources for documenting the self-representation of industrial cities in photographically illustrated books than for city films. A bibliography of photographic history from 1984, by no means complete, enumerates roughly fifty illustrated books of West German industrial cities from 1950–1968; some of them were issued in several editions with high numbers of printed copies (Heidtmann 1984, 575–583, Numbers 17543–17823). No less than fifteen of these illustrated books came from one photographer and publisher; these also experienced up to eight editions—although some were less popular with the public. Wolf Strache (1910–2001) had founded his own publishing company "Die schönen Bücher" (The beautiful books) in 1951 and published, besides countless scenery representations, nearly 40 monographs of German cities until 1979 when the company was closed (Heiting 1988, 70–71; Sachsse 2003a, 430–431). After the successful first edition on the city of Stuttgart where he had settled after World War II, he soon devoted himself to the city of Essen (1952), then Esslingen (1952), Hannover (1953), Recklinghausen (1953), Sindelfingen (1954), Leverkusen (1955), Oberhausen (1955), Braunschweig (1957), Düsseldorf (1959), Wolfsburg (1960), Neuss (1962), Moers (1965), Flensburg (1967), Mannheim (1968) and Lehrte (1971)—each of these cities can be apostrophized as industrial cities in one way or another.

The narrative of these books was always the same and based on a model that Strache had already tested successfully several times before World War II, although it was not concerned with the depiction of cities but with that of the "Autobahn" (*motor highway*) as an important propaganda subject of Germany's National Socialism: The trip is personalized by the look at one's own carriage or at a nice woman, and the viewers of the illustrated book are led as fellow-passengers through picturesque sceneries through the book itself (Strache 1939; Heiting and Wiegand 2011, 235). In the city books named above he used a similar narrative: Through blossoming sceneries one reaches the nice and clean city whose wealth exists either in a historical core—as in the volumes on Esslingen, Braunschweig and Düsseldorf—or is presented in the form of tidy places full of happy young people, like in the volumes on Hannover, Leverkusen, and Wolfsburg all of which saw several editions. The photographs were made with the least possible means: The photographer's archive in Baden-Württemberg's country media centre contains mostly small and medium sized negatives, the classical material of a photo-journalist operating alone and without aid (Kalisch 2009).

The distribution form was apparently always the same: The publishing house—Strache himself—offered the publication of an illustrated book to a given city government and negotiated a minimum delivery number for the first edition with which he could finance its production and printing. For the city it was interesting to be able to disseminate such an illustrated book as a public work seemingly independent and to see it discussed in technical periodicals as a photographic book and in the daily press under travel literature. On the average, the publishing house might have calculated the first edition to be sold out and/or given away after about one year—then the publisher began to really profit: New admissions and printing corrections were necessary for an updated new edition, and through these one could earn real money, for instance through the copyright shares. For six of the industrial cities mentioned above, up to eight editions were published over a period of about fifteen years—one of the safe business ideas of the German Federal economic miracle years.

Unsurprisingly Wolf Strache faced direct competition, for instance from the photographer Paul Swiridoff (1914–2002) (Teuber 2006). There were also cities that published such books under their own direction, particularly as public institutions still had decisive influence over the newspapers and magazine publishing houses throughout the 1950s and 1960s (Pohl 2010, 61–99). However, it remains remarkable that industry and cities hardly ever presented themselves together. The big industrial enterprises were proudly mentioned in the cityscape volumes, yet nearly no industrial photographer delivered more than one or two rather insignificant pictures to the volume. Vice versa, in the many company books published after 1950, there were hardly more than one or two pictures to be found of the city in which the respective enterprise was located. Various pictures of the photographer's family Angenendt are printed in Dortmund company books similar as in a city book and several of their works show the industrial scenery of Westphalia, but these never follow the same commissions, and there are no cross-references between these illustrations (Buberl 1996). The same is valid for the GDR where some books show urban representations, such as the book illustrated by Herbert Henschel on Jena published in 1959 (Deutscher Kulturbund 1959). Besides, there was a "Kleine Städtereihe" (*small city series*) from the Sachsenverlag Dresden between 1958 and 1962. These show images of the historical city—e.g. in the volumes on Dessau, Rostock and Freiberg—combined with a number of illustrations on smart new buildings, especially in new living quarters; the photographs mostly came from local sources (Usemann 1958; Fabian 1959; Brendel 1960). A publication on Stalinstadt/Eisenhüttenstadt is informative: Here the whole new building plan was displayed as a kind of a baroque city plan while the steel industry and the social institutions are shown as a pattern of future socialism (Hofmann and Oldenburg 1960). Only one city was comparable to this as work and city melted here with each other in the visual representation: Wolfsburg.

Second case study: The city of Wolfsburg

In 1960, the first illustrated book on Wolfsburg was published by Wolf Strache and his company "Die schönen Bücher", probably without much engagement on the part of the city. The "Wolfsburger Nachrichten" (Wolfsburg news) noted after its publication: „The arrangement of the booklet focused above all on nice architectural photographs one has, however, not always taken with enough care", the manager of the urban building society complained. After this criticism the city commissioned a second version of the book in 1962 which was evaluated by the "Wolfsburger Allgemeine Zeitung": "An illustrated book with good texts—images leave room for wishes—one may be curious how the illustrated book on Wolfsburg will look like that is put together by the city under its own supervision" (Rodrian 2008, 10–14, 11). However, Wolf Strache's book that was critiqued in this review was published again a year later (1961) in an unchanged second edition, in 1963, in 1965, and in 1966 again in the same versions, in 1969 in a changed, now the sixth edition, twice released again in 1973 and 1977—after all, the volume does not seem to have been received too badly. The second version mentioned contained images by two photographers: VW's industrial photographer Willi Luther (1909–1996) and by Heinrich Heidersberger (1906–2006) who had moved to Wolfsburg just in 1961 (Budde 1962; Junge-Gent 2001; Hoffmann 2007). If the volume of 1962 is only important because of the cooperation of a VW company photographer, then the volume on the city of Wolfsburg edited by Heinrich Heidersberger in 1963 presents a landmark of the German photographic book history (Fig. 1) (Heidersberger 1963; Heiting and Wiegand 2011, 396).

Fig. 1: Heinrich Heidersberger: The City of Wolfsburg

(Source: Heidersberger 1963, new edition Berlin 2007, Cover)

On the one hand, the volume contains pictures of a photographer who struggled for his lifetime to be recognized as an artist. On the other hand, no one but this photographer could afford to leave behind the principles of the illustrated tourist book. By the 1930s, with his book about the Heinkel works at Oranienburg, he had presented an absolutely unusual and hardly timely company publication (Mäckler 1940). What he had sketched in Wolfsburg—obviously in accordance with the modern management of the city under the administrative director Wolfgang Hesse, the son of the Lord Mayor of Dessau who had invited the Bauhaus in 1925—as a book was rather unusual in format, presentation, and dramaturgy. On many pages, the optical square format (h x w: 25.9 x 24.3 cm) is used for full page photographs, so that numerous pictures are printed in butt joints while double pages with white spaces made it possible to show wide angle panoramas that were absolutely unusual in photography at that time. One of these panorama images perfectly displays the role of industry in the self-representation of industrial cities (Fig. 2): The photograph shows the view of the city from a small hill

Fig. 2: Heinrich Heidersberger, View from the slide hill onto city, Wolfsburg 1961/63
(Source: Heidersberger 1963, n.p.)

in winter, the horizon being formed by the Volkswagen factory. Only at a second glance one can see that the chimneys and large halls are painted onto the photograph: When the original photograph was taken in 1961, the factory venues did not yet exist but when the book was published in 1963 these chimneys and the large hall had formed the city's horizon—so they had to be retouched (Rodrian 2008, 11–12). It is just this part of the factory of which Heinrich Heidersberger took a photograph in later years that was to become his most popular image (Dethier 1984, 391).

The book's narrative is divided into three parts: A prelude of the four seasons—closing with the mentioned winter panorama—is followed, as in Walter Ruttmann's Berlin film, by a daily routine of work and city more or less kept on parallel tracks The seasons are as mixed in it as the places of the city and the factory areas until dusk falls onto Schiller's pond; this panorama is the only one dominated by steeples rather than by the VW factory. The last parts of the book are fully dedicated to the urban culture and the thoroughfares to and from Wolfsburg, thus demonstrating the integration of the city into the Federal Republic—with its situation near the so-called "border area" of the GDR and its special cultural and economic support. The dust cover again depicts, cinematically in the form of a shot and a countershot, the factory and the canal. Tertium comparationis here is the wide streets for which the Volkswagen car is built in Wolfsburg.

When the book was published in 1963, Heinrich Heidersberger took a number of photographs for it, which did find their way into printed pages: In 1962, the first trains with Italian workers arrived, and there were barracks built as housing for them. Heidersberger took six photographs of these scenes as well of the workers being integrated into the work processes at the

Fig. 3: Heinrich Heidersberger, Migrant workers from Italy in front of their housings, Wolfsburg ca.1962/63

(Source: © Heinrich Heidersberger, Wolfsburg)

VW assembly lines but the city administration obviously did not dare to include these images into the book. Especially two of these photographs are remarkable and would have formed a good double page (Fig. 3 and 4): They show the same road with some of the men on the pavement and some of the barracks in the middle ground, the better quality housing for the German population forming the horizon. One photograph shows the men going to work, the second the same men returning from work with plastic bags in their hands—and with a VW beetle in the foreground. The narrative of the double page is easy to decipher: If they work as hard as their German co-workers these men will be able to both drive a VW beetle of their own and live with their families in the homes provided by the city. Even this optimistic reading did not find enough support in the group preparing the book and its contents, due to the ideology of the "the hard working German" it was difficult to deal with the idea that someone else could be achieving what they themselves had.

Until a second edition appeared in 2007, mainly for photo-historical reasons, the book had disappeared nearly completely from public perception. From his 75th birthday in 1981 onwards, Heinrich Heidersberger had the opportunity to show his photographs of the city every five years (in 1986, 1991 and later), and the catalogues available of these exhibitions compile additional motives of Wolfsburg over and over again. Another chapter of photographic history had been written for the city in its visual self-representation: In 1994, James Welling was invited to the opening of the local art

Fig. 4: Heinrich Heidersberger, Migrant workers from Italy in front of their housings, Wolfsburg ca. 1962/63

(Source: © Heinrich Heidersberger, Wolfsburg)

museum and to present his view of the city and the factory in yet another book. He devoted himself to the visual clichés of this city—the architecture of its early days in around 1939 and the company works with automated assembly lines (Heiting and Wiegand 2011, 413; Lockemann 2008, 33–42).

Changes of the media ensemble

Both the city film and the photographically illustrated book, lost ground around 1970 caused mainly by the emergence of moving image media and by a consistently more critical look at both the city and life in middle-class Germany. In addition to this, since the end of the 1960s the self-image of all industrial cities was threatened by global developments, which led to coal and steel crises as well as to sales decline of large-scale industrial products. Two books may be named here as symbolizing the end of an era. They show that the unique selling proposition of the visual representation in the photo book or in the city film disappears at the very moment at which the medium has gained respect in the art world and is no longer effective in society (Sickert 1983, 357–384; Sachsse 2003b, 7–11). The media society changes in the 1970s: The newsreel cinemas are closed, the edition figures of illustrated magazines decrease considerably, and the average edition numbers of photographically illustrated books declines (Jaeger 2005, 416–439). At the same time other forms of political representation assert themselves; presents to guests to a city no longer take the form of illustrated books—the event marketing begins.

One of the last volumes in the old fashion devoted to the industrial city already foreshadows that the time of uninhibited self-representation by the blessings of economy, modern architecture and social achievements came to an end: Helmut Kloth (Berlin 1937) took the photographs for an illustrated book published in 1966 with the dry title "Essen" and no subtitle (Bechthold 1966). All pictures are printed strictly in a square format, the light has broken, the skylight has turned from grey to medium grey, the sun seems only overcast. What especially becomes clear: the city has no centre anymore, i.e. the self-representation of this industrial city renounces a classical element of identity, it seems, as if it is recognized here tacitly that the city of Essen is, in fact, a mere agglomeration. More strictly than in former volumes the factories and industry as a whole are faded out almost completely. There are no shots of freight depots or harbors that had characterized former industrial city representations. Instead, the photographer pauses at a number of office houses that did not develop more interesting looks with help of a diagonal picture composition.

While the exhibition organizer Klaus Honnef already tries to catch the art of photography with the vocabulary of film theory, the commercial photographer Charles Wilp (1932–2005) makes the last attempt in rescuing the genre in 1979 with a stroke of genius in design and glamor: "Dazzledorf" (Dazzle village—a nickname for Düsseldorf) is actually a company publication of the armament group Rheinmetall. However, it is also presented as an homage to the city of Düsseldorf and to both the artists Joseph Beuys and Charles Wilp (Wilp 1979). Just like the last city films of the 1970s, this volume demonstrates that the genres are outdated. From the early 1980s, it took another two decades until new media offers of urban (self-)representation set up with homepages and offer Flickr and YouTube as forms of viral and/or event marketing; but looking back the signs of disintegration of an urban industrial self-image are already recognizable ever since the middle of the 1960s.

Works Cited

Agde, G. (1998). *Flimmernde Versprechen. Geschichte des deutschen Werbefilms im Kino seit 1897*. Berlin: Neuer Berliner Verlag.

Anon. (1939). *Hansestadt Hamburg*. Berlin: Die deutschen Bücher.

Bechthold, G. (1966). *Essen, Bild: Helmut Kloth*. Frankfurt am Main: Umschau. http://www.pixelprojekt-ruhrgebiet.de/serie.php?serien_id=6005237&id_language=1.

Behne, A., and S. Stone (1929). *Berlin in Bildern*. Wien: Dr. Hans Epstein.

Bernays, E. (1928). *Propaganda*. New York: Horace Liveright.

Böckelmann, F. (1975). *Theorie der Massenkommunikation. Das System hergestellter Öffentlichkeit, Wirkungsforschung und gesellschaftliche Kommunikationsverhältnisse*. Frankfurt am Main: Suhrkamp.

Böhme, G. (2004). Die Ästhetisierung der Politik. Kommunikationsdesign im Nationalsozialismus. In K. Buchholz and K. Wolbert (eds.). *Im Designerpark. Leben in künstlichen Welten*, 162–169. Darmstadt: Haeusser.media.

Bollerey, F. (1995). Die Großstadt—Mit den Augen von Künstlern, Literaten und Regisseuren. In W. Lippert (ed.). *Mit anderen Augen 1945 bis 1995. Düsseldorfer Architektur aus Photographensicht*, 114–131. Köln: Verlag der Buchhandlung Walther König.

Brendel, F. (1960). *Freiberg. Kleine Städtereihe 5*. Dresden: Sachsenverlag.

Brod, M. (1992). Kinematographentheater (1909). In J. Schweinitz (ed.). *Prolog vor dem Film, Nachdenken über ein neues Medium 1909–1914*, 15–17. Leipzig: Reclam.

Brown, W. J. (1993). Walter Gropius and Grain Elevators, Misreading Photographs. *History of Photography*, 17 (3), 304–308.

Buberl, B. (ed.). (1996). *Angenendt. Eine Fotografenfamilie. Erich Angenendt, Rudi Angenendt, Christian Angenendt*. Heidelberg: Braus.

Budde, R. (1962). *Wolfsburg. Texte und Bilder zur Geschichte und Gegenwart der Volkswagenstadt*. Braunschweig: Steinweg.

Cremers, P. J. (ed.). (1937). *Essen*. Berlin: Deutscher Kunstverlag.

Deutscher Kulturbund (ed.). (1959). *Jena, Stadt im Grünen. Bilder von Herbert Henschel*. Jena: Max Keßler.

Dresdner Lehrerverein (ed.). (1929). *Dresden. Ein Bilderbuch für die Teilnehmer an der Deutschen Lehrerversammlung*. Dresden: Meinhold & Söhne.

Eskildsen, U., and U. Borsdorf (eds.). (1987). *Endlich so wie überall? Bilder und Texte aus dem Ruhrgebiet*. Essen: Klartext.

Fabian, E. (1959). *Rostock. Kleine Städtereihe 3*. Dresden: Sachsenverlag.

Führmann, H. (2011). *Zu schön um wahr zu sein. Der neue Stadtfilm von Essen*. 01/02/2012, http://www.derwesten.de/staedte/essen/zu-schoen-um-wahr-zu-sein-id345947.html.

Gelsenkirchener Geschichten e. V. (ed.). *Gelsenkirchener Geschichten. Die interaktive Spurensammlung Gelsenkirchener Geschichte—Soziokulturelles von Gestern und*

Heute. Werner Nickel—Stadtfilmer & Photograf. 12/13/2011, http://www.gelsen-kirchener-geschichten.de/viewtopic.php?t=6095.

Goergen, J. (1997). Behagliche Schönheit. UfA-Städtefilme der 30er Jahre. *Filmblatt*, 2 (6), 4–6.

Goergen, J. (2001a). Die Angst vor dem Dokumentarischen. Die Stadt der Millionen. Ein Lebensbild Berlins. *Filmblatt*, 6 (16), 11–20.

Goergen, J. (2001b). Städtebilder und Lichtbildreihen. *Filmblatt*, 6 (16), 34–38.

Günther, L. P. (2009). *Die bildhafte Repräsentation deutscher Städte: Von den Chroniken der frühen Neuzeit zu den Web-Sites der Gegenwart.* Köln and Wien: Boehlau.

Günther, W. (1925). *Städtefilme. Bemerkungen zu einer Seuche.* n.p.: Bildwart-Publikation.

Günther, W. (1928). *Städtefilme.* Berlin: Bildwart-Publikationen.

Hammers, B. (2013). *Sasha Stone sieht noch mehr.* PhD diss., Aachen.

Haworth-Booth, M. (ed.). (1984). *The Golden Age of British Photography 1839–1900, Photographs from the Victoria and Albert Museum, London, with selections from the Philadelphia Museum of Art, Royal Archives, Windsor Castle, The Royal Photographic Society, Bath, Science Museum, London, Scottish National Portrait Gallery, Edinburgh.* Millerton, New York: Aperture.

Heidersberger, H. (1963). *Wolfsburg, Bilder einer jungen Stadt.* München: Bruckmann.

Heidtmann, F. (1984). *Bibliographie der Photographie. Deutschsprachige Publikationen der Jahre 1839–1984. Technik—Theorie—Bild.* München et al.: Saur.

Heiting, M. (ed.). (1988). *Zeitprofile. 30 Jahre Kulturpreis Deutsche Gesellschaft für Photographie 1959–1988.* Köln: photokina.

Heiting, M., and T. Wiegand (ed.). (2011). *Deutschland im Fotobuch. 287 Fotobücher zum Thema Deutschland aus der Zeit von 1915 bis 2009.* Göttingen: Steidl.

Hielscher, K. (1924). *Deutschland.* München: Albert Langen Verlag.

Hoffmann, T., and B. Rodrian (eds.). (2007). *Ästhetik der Moderne. Photographien von Heinrich Heidersberger.* Ingolstadt: Museum für Konkrete Kunst.

Hofmann, J., and E. Oldenburg (1960). *Stalinstadt. Kleine Städtereihe 6.* Dresden: Sachsenverlag.

Hoppè, E. O. (1929). *Romantik der Kleinstadt.* München: Bruckmann.

Jaeger, R. (2005). "Orbis Terrarum" und "Das Gesicht der Städte": Photobücher über Länder und Metropolen. In J. Holstein (ed.). *Blickfang. Bucheinbände und Schutzumschläge Berliner Verlage 1919–1933*, 416–439. Berlin: private print.

Jakob, V. (ed.). (2009). *Das Vest Recklighausen, Ein Kulturfilm von Karl-Heinz Kramer 1952.* Münster: LWL.

Jakob, V. (2011). *Egon, lass mal laufen! Die Filme der Elisabeth Wilms.* Münster: LWL.

Jung, U. (2000). Städtebilder und Lokalaufnahmen der Kaiserzeit. Ein auswertungsorientierter Zugang. *Filmblatt*, 5 (14), 9–15.

Junge-Gent, H. (ed.). (2001). *Willi Luther. Ausschnitte aus dem fotografischen Werk.* Gifhorn: Kunstverein Gifhorn.

Kalisch, C. (2009). *Vergänglichkeit oder gültige Aussage? Der Nachlass des Fotografen Wolf Strache im Fotoarchiv des LMZ.* 01/03/2012, http://www.lmz-bw.de/uploads/media/Vergaenglichkeit_oder_gueltige_Aussage.pdf.

Kaufmann, K. and H. Stiefelhäuser (eds.). (1938). *Hamburg. Das Tor zur Welt.* Hamburg: Hans Christians.

Keeler, N. B. (1982). Illustrating the 'Reports by the Juries' of the Great Exhibition of 1851. Talbot, Henneman, and Their Failed Commission. *History of Photography*, 6 (3), 257–272.

Korzus, B. (ed.). (1980). *Fabrik im Ornament, Ansichten auf Firmenbriefköpfen des 19. Jahrhunderts.* Münster: Landschaftsverband Westfalen-Lippe.

Kosok, L. (ed.). (1999). *Industrie und Fotografie. Sammlungen in Hamburger Unternehmensarchiven.* Hamburg: Museum der Arbeit.

Landesbildstelle Hansa (ed.) and W. Beutler (1939). *Der Hamburger Hafen.* Hamburg: Landesbildstelle.

Langewiesche, W. (ed.). (1863). *Elberfeld und Barmen. Beschreibung und Geschichte dieser Doppelstadt des Wupperthales, nebst besonderer Darstellung ihrer Industrie* [...], Barmen: Langewiesche.

Le Corbusier (2007). *Towards an Architecture.* Los Angeles: Getty Research Institute.

Lehmbrock, J. (ed.). (1971). *Profitopolis oder: Der Mensch braucht eine andere Stadt.* München: Die neue Sammlung.

Lippmann, W. (1922). *Public Opinion.* New York: The New Republic.

Lockemann, B. (2008). *Das Fremde sehen. Der europäische Blick auf Japan in der künstlerischen Dokumentarfotografie.* Bielefeld: transcript

Ludes, P., H. Schumacher, and P. Zimmermann (1994). *Geschichte des Fernsehens in der Bundesrepublik Deutschland. Bd. 3: Informations- und Dokumentarsendungen.* München: Wilhelm Fink.

Meissner, L. (ed.). (1909). *Hafen von Hamburg. Eine Rundfahrt durch die Hafenanlagen der Freien und Hansestadt Hamburg in 170 Heliogravüren nach photographischen Aufnahmen von Franz Schmidt und Otto Kufahl.* Hamburg: Meissner.

Mühlberg, D. (2004). Rekonstruktionsversuch einer ergebnislosen Betriebsreportage von 1956. In K. Hartewig and A. Lüdtke (eds.). *Die DDR im Bild. Zum Gebrauch der Fotografie im anderen deutschen Staat*, 147–167. Göttingen: Wallstein.

Pare, R. (ed.). (1982). *Photography and Architecture 1839–1939.* Montreal: CCA Callaway.

Pohl, N. (2010). Demokratisierung im inneren Widerspruch. Französische und saarländische Printmedienpolitik 1945–1955. In C. Zimmermann, R. Hudemann and M. Kuderna (eds.). *Medienlandschaft Saar von 1945 bis in die Gegenwart. Band 1: Medien zwischen Demokratisierung und Kontrolle (1945–1955)*, 61–99. München: Oldenbourg.

Renger-Patzsch, A. (1928). *Lübeck, 80 photographische Aufnahmen.* Berlin: Ernst Wasmuth.

Rodrian, B. (2008). Die fertige Stadt. In B. Heidersberger and B. Rodrian (eds.). *Wolfsburg. Bilder einer jungen Stadt. Beiträge zur Neuauflage*, 10–14. Berlin: Nicolaische Verlagsanstalt.

Sachsse, R. (1986). *August Sander in Viersen*. Viersen: Schriften der Stadt Viersen.

Sachsse, R. (2003). *Die Erziehung zum Wegsehen. Fotografie im NS-Staat*. n.p.: Philo Fine Arts.

Sachsse, R. (2003). *Fotografie. Vom technischen Bildmittel zur Krise der Repräsentation*. Köln: Deubner.

Sachsse, R. (2012). Kamerafahrt und Panoramablick. Repräsentation von Industriestädten in fotografischen Bildbänden und Werbefilmen der 1950er und 1960er Jahre. *Informationen zur modernen Stadtgeschichte*, (1), 55–69.

Sachsse, R. (2013). Firmenschriften. In M. Heiting and R. Jäger (eds.). *Autopsie. Deutschsprachige Fotobücher 1918–1945*. Göttingen: Steidl (forthcoming).

Schenk, R. (2000). Städtebilder aus der Trümmerzeit, DEFA—Dokumentarfilme von 1946. *Filmblatt*, 5 (13), 6–9.

Sickert, P. (1983). Film ist etwas Schnelllebiges. Gespräch mit […] über Werbung. In Alexander Kluge (ed.). *Bestandsaufnahme: Utopie Film*, 357–384. Frankfurt am Main: Zweitausendeins.

Starl, T. (1981). Die Bildbände der Reihe "Die Blauen Bücher". Zur Entstehungs- und Entwicklungsgeschichte einer Bildbandreihe. *Fotogeschichte. Beiträge zur Geschichte und Theorie der Fotografie*, 1 (1), 73–81.

Stephenson, S. (ed.). (2001). *Dream Street. W. Eugene Smith's Pittsburgh Project*. New York: Norton & Cie.

Strache, W. (1939). *Auf allen Autobahnen*. Darmstadt: Tatzelwurm.

Teuber, A. (2006). *Die Städtebilder von Paul Swiridoff*. PhD diss., Bonn.

The Internet Archive (ed.). *Germany: A Family of the Industrial Ruhr (1958)*. 01/02/2012, http://www.archive.org/details/GermanyA1958.

Thijsen, M. (2002). *Het Bedrijfsfotoboek 1945–1965. Professionalisering von fotografen in Nederland*. Rotterdam: 010 publishers.

Tietgens, R. (1939). *Der Hafen*. Hamburg: Hans Christians.

Usemann, W. (1958). *Dessau/Wörlitz. Kleine Städtereihe 2*. Dresden: Sachsenverlag.

Verkehrsverein Bremen (ed.). (1930). *Bremen. Die Stadt und der Hafen*. Leipzig: F.A.Brockhaus.

Wilp, C. (1979). *Dazzledorf, Düsseldorf "Vorort der Welt". 20 Jahre fotografiert*. Dreieich: Melzer.

Wolff, P. (1925). *Jena*. Rudolstadt: Müllersche Verlagsbuchhandlung.

Zielinski, S. (1989). *Audiovisionen. Kino und Fernsehen als Zwischenspiele in der Geschichte*. Reinbek: Rowohlt.

Zimmermann, C. (ed.). (2005). *Industriefotografie im Saarland*. Saarbrücken: Saarland University.

Zimmermann, P. (2003). Zwischen Sachlichkeit, Idylle und Propaganda. Der Kulturfilm im Dritten Reich. In P. Zimmermann and K. Hoffmann (eds.). *Triumph der Bilder. Kultur- und Dokumentarfilme vor 1945 im internationalen Vergleich*, 59–73. Konstanz: UVK.

Zitzewitz, D., et al. (ed.). *Gelsenkirchen Blog. Gedanken aus der lebendigen Metropole an der Emscher. Neuer Stadtfilm.* 01/02/2012, http://www.gelsenclan.de/index.php/neuer-stadtfilm/.

Tradition and Contrast: Industrial Cities and Industrial Work in the Documentaries of Michael Glawogger: From "Megacities" (1998) to "Working Man's Death" (2005)

Henry Keazor

"City of the Big Shoulders": Carl Sandburg's "Chicago"

"HOG Butcher for the World,
Tool Maker, Stacker of Wheat,
Player with Railroads and the Nation's Freight Handler;
Stormy, husky, brawling,
City of the Big Shoulders"

(Sandburg 1916/1992, 3)

With these words the American poet Carl Sandburg (1878–1967) opens his famous and often quoted poem "Chicago" from 1916 which stands at the beginning of his volume "Chicago Poems". If there is any doubt that Sandburg wants to sing in praise of the industrial city Chicago by opening with these lines, these doubts are dispersed in the further course of the poem and towards the end of the poem when the poet verbally even repeats the opening, but adds the words "proud to be" before the repetition of "Hog Butcher for the World,/Tool Maker, Stacker of Wheat" etc. Such pride is nevertheless something Sandburg develops and justifies throughout a process in which he responds to the reproaches of various critics against Chicago:[1] Yes, this industrial city has flaws such as prostitution, crime and social problems, but Sandburg turns the tables by demanding: "Come and show me another city with lifted head singing so proud to be alive and coarse and strong and cunning." Thus, Sandburg seems to imply that other cities have the same problems, and he calls those that do not "little soft cities." These are cities that cannot compete with Chicago, a place the poet characterizes through a series of metaphors which invoke animals such as dogs ("Fierce as a dog with

---

1 For this context see the introduction by John E. Hallwas (Sandburg 1916/1992, xx) who names William T. Stead and Upton Sinclair as examples for such critics.

*Fig. 1: Ricardo Galvez, poster commissioned by the Public Broad-casting Service (PBS) as promotion for the entry dedicated to Carl Sandburg in their biography TV-series „American Masters",
September 2012*

*(Source: PBS-website: http://www.pbs.org/wnet/americanmasters/episodes/
carl-sandburg/posters-how-carl-sandburg-saw-chicago/2215/)*

tongue lapping for action"), but especially the youth of humankind ("cun-ning as a savage pitted against the wilderness") as well as man ("here is a tall bold slugger set vivid against the little soft cities"/"Under the terrible burden of destiny laughing as a young man laughs"/"Laughing the stormy, husky, brawling laughter of Youth").

Power, strength, vitality, activism, optimism, and pride are hence set against the initial reproaches whose negative connotations now almost be-come necessary parts of the positive metaphor: This "savage", "slugger" and "young man" obviously also needs carnal pleasure, hence prostitution, and given the heated character of this vital being it does not surprise that there is also crime such as shootings among gunmen—finally, the invocation of the "savage" is in tune with the fight for survival of which "wanton hunger" is an expected part. In this way, Sandburg paints a picture of the industrial city of Chicago with its meat markets, its railroads, its exchanges and industries, which on the one hand portrays the "ideal-typical" Chicago-workman, while on the other hand witnesses a process of de- or super-individuation (Fig. 1). For Sandburg, the workman here functions as a representative monument for the industrial city in which he is active: it is not so much that Sandburg describes the city itself, he rather characterizes its features via its inhabitants by featuring their minor flaws and many virtues.

"City On the Move": Jim Coulthard's "Sheffield"

It might be a giant leap from Sandburg's poem from 1916 to the later documentary films on industrial cities, since we are not only skipping temporal gaps of more than fifty respectively eighty years as well as geographical borders, but also the various boundaries between the different media of text and film, a medium, however, closely linked to industry: the first film shown publicly and commercially on the 28th of December 1895 at the "Salon Indien du Grand Café à Paris" depicted "La Sortie de l'Usine Lumière à Lyon" and presented workers leaving the Lumìere-factory (Lanzoni 2002, 28; Pearson 1996, 14). However, it seems as if a certain tradition links a poem such as Sandburg's "Chicago" from 1916 to, for example, a film such as Jim Coulthard's (director and producer) and Wilfred Harrison's (text) Sheffield: "City on the Move?" from 1972. After its release, this promotional documentary garnered unexpected attention again in 1997 when parts of it were used for the opening of Peter Cattaneo's smash hit movie "The Full Monty": a wide part of its audience assumed that the shown footage was just a spoof,[2] but despite the fact that some of the voice-over commentary and the accompanying music were slightly altered, most of the borrowed footage was authentic.

In his film, Coulthard tries to show that the industrial city of Sheffield has lived through various watershed moments in history and that this booming place, destined for great things, is about to witness another one of these turning points. Of course, at that time the director could not have foreseen that this watershed would actually bring quite a cruel twist of fate only a few years after the completion of the film when Sheffield had to witness a declining and decimated steel industry and thousands of unemployed workers.

In order to bring his intended message home, Coulthard relies on two intertwined structures: in the first instance, Coulthard uses the classical sequence of the four elements (Fig. 2a–d). Hence a series of images and comments presents a city in which the four elements air, fire, water and earth are in perfect harmony. As a voiceover commentator explains, "thanks to a smokeless policy started in 1959," the air is smokeless and clean and Sheffield is "one of the cleanest industrial cities in Europe." This sentiment stands despite the fact that—and here we pass to the element fire—"steelmaking

---

2 On this, see the information provided on the back of the cover of the 2008 release of "Sheffield: City On The Move" in the context of the DVD "The Reel Monty" as well as the text on the website http://www.thereelmonty.com/ (last accessed 04/16/2013).

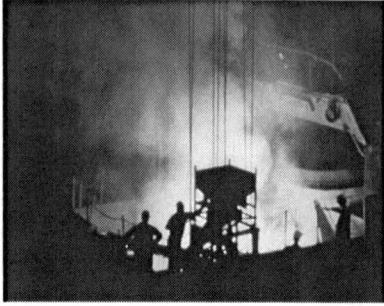

Fig. 2a–d: Screenshots from: Jim Coulthard/Wilfred Harrison, Sheffield: City on the Move, 1972

(Source: From the DVD "The Reel Monty", ACM retro, Sheffield)

is still at the heart of the city's heavy industry". The element water is introduced via reference to the reservoirs in the nearby hills, reportedly dubbed as "Sheffield's lake district", and the element of the earth is treated via the architecture of Sheffield, for example with reference to its famous "Hole in the Road", an award winning underground shopping precinct and concourse, sporting a "roof of sky".

These "eternal" elements are in some ways the fitting equivalent to the stable and enduring qualities of Sheffield, for the second structure of Coulthard's film relies on the opposition between tradition and innovation. Hence, Sheffield is on the one hand portrayed as a city that is deeply rooted in its history and its tradition (for example: the cutlers of the city still meet regularly with proper pomp and ceremony), while at the same time, the city is constantly evolving and aspiring to prosper. For example the University of Sheffield anticipated a student population of 10,000 during the 1980s and while Sheffield's nightlife before was not very sophisticated, it then featured the kind of nightlife expected of all modern cities of any substantial size, hence it was, with its "The Fiesta" nightclub, even home to the biggest nightclub in Europe. In this way, Coulthard makes his audience understand that Sheffield offers the best of all worlds: it is a city full of history, but also modern and characterized by striving; it is a place of hard work, but, thanks to the hard work of its people, also a place for leisure. Sheffield is a place of industry, but at the same time a very clean and green place.

The film constantly compares Sheffield to other cities in order to show that it is actually incomparable and unmatchable. For example, according to the film, no city north of London has more department stores than Sheffield; the Christmas illuminations are more extensive in this city than anywhere else in the country.

Like Sandburg, Coulthard never portrays any actual individuals, but rather their character, their collective efforts and endeavors as reflected in the history of the city. It is the appearance of Sheffield that serves, as in Sandburg's poem, as a kind of mirror of the "character" of the city of Sheffield. In the film as well as in the poem, the city and its inhabitants reflect each other. In both cases one could assume that this might be also due to the fact that both works, the poem as much as the film, were written and produced during a time when these respective industrial cities were "on the move", that is: aspiring, striving, ambitious and rising. Hence, each city easily serves as mirror images for a population that aimed at recognizing themselves in such emergent megacities.

But as the sarcastic and ironic use of Coulthard's "City on the move" in the context of Cattaneo's "The Full Monty" already demonstrates, things changed after the decline of the industry[3] and it is therefore interesting to see how documentaries are approaching the phenomenon of the declining industrial city in the following years.

Michael Glawogger and the change in documentary film

As an example I will focus on two films by Austrian director and filmmaker Michael Glawogger. Born in 1959 in Graz, Glawogger studied between 1981 and 1982 at the San Francisco Arts Institute before transferring to the film

---

3 See Taylor et al. (1996, 63–72): "The catastrophic decline of Sheffield's industrial district".

academy in Vienna where he studied from 1983 to 1989. In 1989, he presented his first film, "Krieg in Wien" ("War in Vienna"), which he had produced
together with his colleague Ulrich Seidl, another Austrian director, script-
writer and film producer.[4] "War in Vienna" portrays four days in the Austrian capital by combining news reports with interviews and observations. But
Glawogger is also a director of feature films, such as "Die Ameisenstraße"
from 1995 ("The Ant Trail"), and these two types of films—the scripted, fictional feature film on the one hand and the non-fictional documentary on
the other –, both equally practiced by Glawogger, already hint at the fact that
he is an advocate of a movement that denies a strict demarcation between
the scripted feature and the documentary film. In fact it can be argued that
a film such as Cattaneo's "The Full Monty" in a certain way also documents
something,[5] just as a documentary such as Coulthard's "City on the Move"
equally relies on scenes that are somewhat staged. In general the only seemingly entirely "objective" documentary actually already contains subjective
elements insofar as it depends on the filmmaker's decisions concerning the
material that is to be filmed, the angle and the point of view of the camera
and the latter's presence, something that influences the filmed surroundings
as well as its ensuing perception during the editing process.

It is hence debatable whether or not it makes sense to distinguish strictly
between the "fictional film" and the "non-fictional film", for instance when
concerned with an author such as Thorolf Lipp. In his book from 2012,
"Spielarten des Dokumentarischen" ("Varieties of the Documentary"), Lipp
explained his motive for disposing of the traditional notion "documentary"
by referring to the fact that in his view, entirely different forms such as a
three minute service for a cultural TV-program, a 20-minutes report, shot
and edited in three days, and a 90-minute film, produced over a period of
three long years, could not be properly called "documentaries" since their
"narrative form, artistic means, communicative aims and their temporal
extent would differ decisively" (Lipp 2012, 16). Lipp therefore prefers the

---

4 See for this the information on Glawogger's website http://www.glawogger.com/bio.php
(last access: 04/16/2013) as well as on http://de.wikipedia.org/wiki/Michael_Glawogger
(last access: 04/16/2013).

5 See for example Bill Nichols' position who considers feature films as a sort of a "documentary of wish-fulfillment" since according to his view, a movie documents the wishes of an
author, of the director or of the production company, or one could add: of the audience to
which the production company reacts. See for this Nichols (2001, 1). For further observations concerning the convergence of feature films and documentaries see for example the
foreword by W. C. Barg, K. Hoffmann and R. Kilborn in Hoffmann et al. (2012, 11).

term "non-fictional film" and distinguishes under this "umbrella term" further sub-categories or (as he calls them) "prototypes" such as the "plot-based documentary" (hence he does not eliminate the notion entirely as it sneaks back in at this stage), "non-verbal documentary", the simple "documentary", the "Direct Cinema" and the "Cinéma Vérité" (Lipp 2012, 12).

This is not the occasion to discuss the meaningfulness of such distinctions and labels (one could, for example, object that Lipp mingles formal criteria such as "plot-based" and "non-verbal" with historical phenomena such as the "Documentary" of the 1930s or the "Direct Cinema" of the 1960s), but Lipp's struggle shows that the "documentary" as a genre has entered a crisis which renders evident its claim to simply "document" something. As the Scottish documentary filmmaker John Grierson, who introduced the term "documentary" and who would ultimately become the revered 'father of British and Canadian documentary film', wrote in a 1926 review of Robert Flaherty's "Moana" (Grierson 1926):[6] "Documentary is a clumsy description, but let it stand" (Grierson 1932, 39).[7]

Glawogger seems to agree with Grierson because he frequently refers to term "documentary", but always based on the understanding that the documentary includes and adapts elements commonly found in fictional film. However, as Glawogger states, "film in the end is always composing. The way you chose your means, how you put up your camera, exactly how you are creating an image, how you edit it and how the sound is used, all this is composed in every respect" (quoted after Hoffmann 2012, 37). Yet Glawogger emphasizes at the same time: "But when working with film and especially with the documentary you can only truly compose in a good way with things that are there in reality anyway. […] I would never re-stage or enhance, single out or make clearer something that doesn't exist in reality anyway." (ibid.)

Indeed, Glawogger occasionally re-enacts prior experiences for the camera he has made without a camera with the help of his subjects, but in a way that the result looks like a spontaneously filmed, "real" event. Glawogger explains such a use of semi-documentary material by referring to the fact that the portrayed action would have never occurred in the presence of a camera

---

6 See Deacon (2005, 151).

7 For this discussion, see Hohenberger (1998, 24), who considers the fundamental problem of the theories on documentary to lie in the fact that the definition of the "fictional" is still too vague.

and that the re-enacted version of the previously experienced event looks much more authentic than had the real action been filmed.[8]

Glawogger's films on cities and labor

Two films show Glawogger's interest in the world of labor, its sites and cities: In 1998 he presented the documentary "Megacities", followed in 2005 by "Working Man's Death". The title of the latter is quite ambiguous insofar as it refers on the one hand to the brutal conditions under which humans have to work and how their labor reduces them to physical activities that might kill them sooner or later. On the other hand, the title poses the question of whether this type of hard work is about to become extinct in some countries or if it just becomes more and more invisible to us, that is: mainly the Western audience (and hence Glawogger aims to visually represent this type of work).

Both films function according to a similar principle: In a representative way a certain amount of phenomena is looked upon—thus, "Megacities" tells "12 stories about survival" ("12 Geschichten vom Überleben") in four cities (Mumbai, New York, Mexico and Moscow). In "Working Man's Death" "5 pictures " ("5 Bilder") are presented:

- Ukrainian colliers who illegally work in a deserted coal mine in the coal field of Donbass and earn their living under high risk and heavy physical strain,
- Indonesian workers extracting and transporting sulfur from a sulfur mine at the volcano Kawa Ijen,
- Nigerian workers in a slaughtering yard (or a field, rather) in Port Harcourt where animals such as goats and steers are killed, sold and processed in large masses,
- Pakistani workers in the wrecking wharfs at Gadani where scrapped deep-sea vessels from all over the world are being dismantled, and finally

---

8 In Lipp's terms Glawogger would have to be seen as a director of "simple documentaries" since Lipp (2012, 30) demands of this genre that "there a topic is dealt with in an especially reflected, perhaps even unique handwriting of the author, that is with artistic means which match as precisely as possible with the chosen topic."

– Chinese workers in the steel mill of Liáoníng, a province in the Northeast of China, traditionally an area of heavy industry.
– An epilogue, shot in Duisburg, presents scenes from a former steel mill that has been transformed into a leisure park. In this estheticized place adolescents are enjoying themselves and thus the film closes with reference to the increasing disappearance of visible labor in a country such as Germany.

In "Megacities" in particular, Glawogger does not allow these individual "stories" and "images" to follow each other in a simply paratactic way, instead he arranges them in an interlocking manner. For example, when a seamstress in Mumbai is shown (Fig. 3a), the rattling of her sewing machine and its speed are later associated with, as well as opposed to, a man with a bioscope who repairs his worn-out films by quietly and very slowly stitching them by hand (Fig. 3b/c). Now his machine, the bioscope, is rattling and its movies tell a lot about the inhabitants of Mumbai and their dreams (hence, here we find an example of Nichol's above mentioned "documentary of wish-fulfillment"). At the same time the scenes also function as a symbol of meta- or self-reference since the medium of Glawogger's documentary, the film, here addresses itself. Such self-referential move equally finds its way into the formal level, as the sequence's speed is accelerated and "Megacities" turns into a film within a film. Titled "Life in Loops", this sequence tells a story about the tailor Josely in Mumbai. In this context, the film narrates an episode that suddenly provides meaning for a previously shown scene where a raven is depicted as it picks food. While the viewer may previously have thought that this was just a documentary impression, s/he now understands it is actually pre-empting the film within in the film.

At the same time topics are overlapping, covering different countries. Thus, in one scene at the beginning, a young girl in Mumbai is shown carrying a chick. This can be related to a later scene in Mexico where a merchant lures children to buy chocolate by giving away a chick for free with each bargain. Glawogger then portrays some of these children the same way he has photographed the girl in Mumbai with her chick. But she might also refer to a later scene in Mumbai where chicken are slaughtered and processed in huge masses (the whole sequence appears somewhat as an anticipation of a similar scene with the Nigerian slaughter yard in "Working Man's Death").[9]

---

9 Spaich (2006, 191) compares Glawogger in this respect to the Italian documentary filmmaker Gualtiero Jacopetti who, in 1962 with his film "Mondo Cane", landed a huge suc-

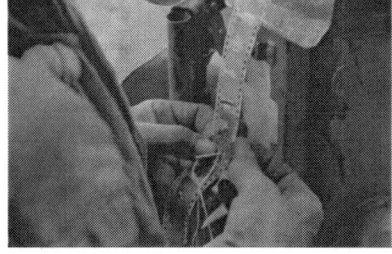

Fig. 3a–c: Screenshots from Michael
Glawogger, Megacities, 1998

(Source: From the DVD "Megacities", HOANZL,
2006/Lotus Film-GmbH, Wien/Fama-Film AG,
Zürich 1998)

At this point, the audience has already witnessed the process, based on the division of labor, of producing soup out of chicken feet.

That Glawogger obviously intends to hint at the globality of certain phenomena[10] and to raise the audience's awareness in this regard is equally made clear when at the end of the "film within in the film," the audience sees huge amounts of shirts being tailored in tailor Jocely's shop. These same shirts are later sold in New York, then worn in Mexico, before one of them is finally fished out of the trash back in New York towards the end of the film (Fig. 4a–c).

Closely associated with globalization, the phenomenon of garbage is a problem that ties together many different countries. Thus, apart from the scene depicting the shirt in New York, there are scenes in Mumbai where workers are fishing trash out of the river in order to sell these scraps, while workers in Mexico earn their living by collecting garbage and attending the waste dumps where people are sifting through the garbage, searching for still

---

cess in European cinemas, thanks also to shocking images of, for example, African people butchering pigs in a ritual of their tribe. However, as shown above, Glawogger just does not show these images (as Spaich maintains) in order to simply "ruin the appetite of the audience" or respectively to "test the resilience of the German cinemagoer", but rather in order to emphasize connections by confronting the viewer with images which he or she normally does not see.

10 See for this also Kösters (2008, 24–25) who, however, reads this motif rather formally as a means Glawogger uses in order to overlay the different episodes of his film.

Fig. 4a–c: Screenshots from Michael Glawogger, Megacities, 1998

(Source: From the DVD "Megacities", HOANZL, 2006/Lotus Film-GmbH, Wien/Fama-Film AG, Zürich 1998)

usable items,[11] while scenes in Moscow show a group of orphaned children who live in the sewer system.

At first sight it may seem as if these "Megacities", which are normally portrayed as industrial metropolises, are not shown as such and that instead, the focus is on the effects of industrialization (such as garbage and globalization), which in this case is contrasted with self-employed merchants and workers such as tailors and butchers. And indeed, we only see industrial large scale production in the scenes in Moscow that initially depict mass fabrication of light switches, followed by a female crane operator's work in a steel mill.

However, Glawogger's actual aim seems to be to emphasize the roots of the industrial city which are to be found in the large workshops: even the seemingly independent and self-employed merchants and workers are in a certain way already industrialized because they have to succumb to the rhythm and the velocity of the industry. Ultimately, there seems to be little difference between the full-scale production of the seamstress and the butcher in Mumbai and the workers who assemble light switches. Glawogger thus interlocks tradition and contrast: He refers to tradition inasmuch as industrialization emerges from such working processes which are increasingly

---

11 For Kösters (2008, 19), this relates even back to the above discussed scene with the bioscope-man who stitches together found film footage.

based on the division of labor that shape cities and their needs and which conversely also shape the guidelines for and demands towards self-employed merchants and workers.

Glawogger brings out contrast inasmuch as the un- or non-industrial ambience of the depicted self-employed workers such as sewers, butchers, cooks etc. might make them appear as less "estranged" at first sight than the workers in the light-switch-factory or the crane operator—Glawogger's film nevertheless poses the question if there actually is such a difference. This is also made clear by fact that he identifies their common aim as the attempt "to survive in the city", a purpose that is addressed in various ways throughout the film.

Even though the industrial city is only rarely depicted and if so, from a certain distance in "Megacities" (we then see the typical industrial skylines, for example those of Moscow and New York), it is nevertheless present in the actual individual existences of the portrayed people. Thus, in contrast to Sandberg and Coulthard who never show such individual cases and instead define the industrial city in a rather "top down" way as a phenomenon that overarches the individual, Glawogger follows a "bottom up"-strategy through which the industrial city is portrayed via its individuals. Other than Sandberg and Coulthard who, each in their own way, place the industrial city into a historical context that explains certain flaws and disadvantages of the industrial city, Glawogger works without such a historical perspective, thereby enhancing the drawbacks of the living conditions in the "Megacities" such as fraud, prostitution and alcoholism.

This crossing of tradition and contrast as a pattern in the filmmaking, as it has been analyzed above with respect to "Megacities", can also be observed in Glawogger's second documentary, "Working Man's Death". As in "Megacities", at first sight it seems as if the industrial city was absent here, too. Instead we see the Ukrainian workers in an abandoned coal-mine, we see the Indonesian sulfur miners, the Nigerian butchers and the Pakistani ship wreckers who—given that they work far away from industrial cities—appear as a contrast to the Chinese steel workers depicted in their plant, which is situated in the industrial city of Liáoníng. However (and this is also the topic of the epilogue in Duisburg), the industrial city is actually manifest in the other episodes due to its long-distance reach and exactly (and paradoxically) its absence: As the first episode, titled "Heroes" ("Helden"), shows, the Ukrainian coal miners are forced to work in the abandoned mine even though this is dangerous and illegal, because the large enterprises in the industrial cities

Fig. 5a–d: Screenshots from Michael Glawogger, Working Man's Death, 2005

(Source: From the DVD "Working Man's Death", filmladen Filmvereleih GmbH,
Wien/Lotus-Film GmbH, Wien/Quinte-Film, Freiburg/Arte G.E.I.E.)

have died. Glawogger stresses this crisis of the industrial city not only via the interviews with the coal miners, but also by contrasting the depressing present with the "glorious" past by showing the monuments in honor of Alexei Grigorjewitsch Stachanow (a proclaimed "hero of the work" role model for the coal miners who died in 1977 in the coal field of Donbass) which are now re-enacted by some of the workers (Fig. 5a–d) who later in the film also discuss in a critical and controversial way the so-called "Stachanow"-movement (a campaign aiming at the increase of productivity in the Soviet enterprises).

This first episode, set in the Ukraine, also works as a counterpart to the last episode. Entitled "Future" ("Zukunft"), this episode contrasts the coal miners' pessimism with the Chinese steel workers' optimism who not only applaud efficiency and power (two typical notions of the "Stachanow"-movement) and typical hero-virtues such as self-sacrifice, but also praise intelligence and knowledge and hope that their children will follow in their footsteps. They see history as proof of progress, exactly like some of their children who say that their city is a modern one. However, they contrast this modernity with the huge monument for the Chairman Mao, erected in 1969 as one of China's largest statues of Mao on the square Zhongshan in Shenyang during the Cultural Revolution. The adolescents consider the monument as old fashioned and rather "funny" which is why they some-

Fig. 6a–d: Screenshots from Michael Glawogger, Working Man's Death, 2005

(Source: From the DVD "Working Man's Death", filmladen Filmvereleih GmbH,
Wien/Lotus-Film GmbH, Wien/Quinte-Film, Freiburg/Arte G.E.I.E.)

times re-enact in a mocking way some of the poses of the monument's figures (in a way that parallels the re-enactment of the Stachanow-monuments
mentioned above). Thus, the adolescents see history and its "heroes" in a
very different light than their parents.

That this might not be a phenomenon exclusively found in China is addressed in the epilogue. Here, the city of Duisburg is shown, a city where the
industrial monuments are now populated by adolescents who prefer esthet-
ics and fun over an involvement with history—as with the Chinese youth, a
separation between the present and the past is discernible.

If one finally compares Glawogger's "Megacities" with "Working Man's
Death" an interesting intensification can be observed: in the first film the
director already uses a somewhat rather negative iconography with respect
to the depicted cities. In the second documentary this is even intensified
towards a typical iconography of the conditions of Hell as it can be encountered throughout art history. Hence, we find darkness, illuminated only by
fiery sparks as we see narrow, gloomy spaces deep below the earth, steam and
smoke, blood, destruction, death and wasteland (Fig. 6a–d). It might be a
sign of a somewhat timid optimism that the fire and the light in the Duis-
burg-epilogue are of a very different kind and that the "death" of this type of
worker as portrayed in this film via several examples is not to be automatical-

ly considered as something negative.

Glawogger's insistence on human pride also links these two films. Even under the most difficult and oppressing conditions, the human beings in "Megacities" and in "Working Man's Death" nevertheless maintain their pride throughout their fight for survival and hold on to certain values. However, at the same time

Fig. 7: Screenshot from Michael Glawogger, Working Man's Death, 2005

(*Source: From the DVD "Working Man's Death", filmladen Filmvereleih GmbH, Wien/Lotus-Film GmbH, Wien/Quinte-Film, Freiburg/Arte G.E.I.E.)*

some of these values hint at the fact that they are exactly the same values that fostered industrialization: While filming at the slaughter yard at Port Harcourt, Glawogger comes across two men, one a butcher, the other a meat-washer, both of whom boast that they might be the best among their ranks since they are the fastest and most efficient when it comes to killing and washing as many animals as possible (Fig. 7).

Conclusion: From Sandberg to Glawogger

Thus, we may have found something similar to the pride expressed by Sandberg concerning the "HOG Butcher for the World," only in these films, pride is being voiced by an individual and counterbalanced by images which show the particular working context of this individual as well as the consequences of his work in a very specific and almost tangible way. Glawogger thus, other than Sandberg and Coulthard with their "top down" processes, rather pursues a view which switches back and forth between the two positions of "bottom up" and "top down" in order to continuously tare and balance the view anew, keeping it in a state as mobile and dynamic as the modern Megacity and its working condition itself.

It would be interesting to see Sandberg's, Coulthard's and Glawogger's contributions concerning their views on the industrial city in the context of an exhaustive survey of the depiction of the industrial city in documentary film in order to better study changes and developments in the history of such depictions—an endeavor yet to be accomplished. But also when focusing on Sandburg and Coulthard on the one hand and on Glawogger on the other and when taking their contributions as ideal-typical representations of distinct perspectives on the industrial city, one can, as demonstrated here, distinguish shifts and changes in the relationship between the individual and the industrial city. While they are conceived as proudly mirroring (and thus re-enforcing) each other in Sandburg's and Coulthard's conceptions, in Glawogger's films the relationship between the single human being and the industrial city, partly due to the problems experienced in social and economic contexts over the past 40 years, has become much more refracted and complex, resulting in a representation of the relationship between the individual and the industrial city that is simultaneously optimistic as well as pessimistic. Moreover, it at the same time implies that for a Western audience it has actually become necessary to be faced with such a representation. As the industrial city in the global North is increasingly absent due to the effects of globalization and its implications in and for other countries, it should (still) nevertheless matter to us, too.

Works Cited

Deacon, D. (2005). "Films as foreign offices": transnationalism at Paramount in the twenties and early thirties. In A. Curthoys and M. Lake (eds.). *Connected Worlds. History in Transnational Perspective*, 139–156. Canberra: Australian National University Press.

Grierson, J. (1926). Moana. *New York Sun*, 2/8/1926.

Grierson, J. (1932). First Principles of Documentary. Here quoted after C. Fowler (ed.). (2002). *The European Cinema Reader*, 39–44. London: Routledge.

Hallwas, J. E. (1992). Introduction. In C. Sandburg (1916/1992). *Chicago Poems*. Ed. J. E. Hallwas, xiii–xxxi, Chicago: University of Illinois Press,

Hoffmann, K. (2012). Inszenierung im Dokumentarfilm. In K. Hoffmann, R. Kilborn and W. C. Barg (eds). *Spiel mit der Wirklichkeit. Zur Entwicklung dokufiktionaler Formate in Film und Fernsehen*, 21–39. Konstanz: UVK Verlagsgesellschaft.

Hoffmann, K., R. Kilborn, and W. C. Barg (eds). (2012). *Spiel mit der Wirklichkeit. Zur Entwicklung doku-fiktionaler Formate in Film und Fernsehen*. Konstanz: UVK Verlagsgesellschaft.

Hohenberger, E. (1998). Dokumentarfilmtheorie: Ein historischer Überblick über Ansätze und Probleme. In E. Hohenberger (ed.). *Bilder des Wirklichen: Texte zur Theorie des Dokumentarfilms,* 8–34. Berlin: Verlag Vorwerk.

Kösters, F. (2008). *Michael Glawoggers "Megacities—12 Geschichten vom Überleben."—Eine Dokumentarfilm-Analyse.* 4/16/2013, http://www.coderwelsh.de/texte/megacities_filmanalyse_public.pdf.

Lanzoni, R. F. (2002). *French Cinema: From its Beginnings to the Present.* New York: Continuum International Publishing.

Lipp, T. (2012). *Spielarten des Dokumentarischen. Einführung in die Geschichte und Theorie des Nonfiktionalen Films.* Marburg: Schüren.

Nichols, B. (2001). *Introduction to Documentary.* Indiana: Indiana University Press.

Pearson, R. (1996). Early Cinema. In G. Nowell-Smith (ed.). *The Oxford History of World Cinema,* 13–23. Oxford: Oxford University Press.

Sandburg, C. (1916/1992). *Chicago Poems.* Ed. J. E. Hallwas. Chicago: University of Illinois Press.

Spaich, H. (2006). Wie der Dokumentarfilm in die Kinos kommt. In P. Zimmermann and K. Hoffmann (eds.). *Dokumentarfilm im Umbruch. Kino—Fernsehen—Neue Medien,* 181–193. Konstanz: UVK Verlagsgesellschaft.

Taylor, I., K. Evans, and P. Fraser (1996). *A Tale Of Two Cities: Global Change, Local Feeling and Everday Life in the North of England. A Study in Manchester and Sheffield.* London: Routledge.

Notes on Contributors

Christoph Bernhardt is a senior researcher and head of Department for Historical Research at the Leibniz-Institute for Regional Development and Structural Planning in Erkner/Berlin. He is co-editor of the German Urban History Journal IMS (*Informationen zur modernen Stadtgeschichte*) and managing editor of the book series *Beiträge zur Stadtgeschichte und Urbanisierungsforschung*. He has extensively studied and published in the fields of European urban and environmental history.

Hans-Peter Dörrenbächer is Professor of Human Geography at the Saarland University in Saarbrücken. He received his Ph.D. in 1991 with a dissertation on corporate adaptation processes in the coal-mining sector of the Saarland. His research concentrates on regionalization processes with interest in the conceptualization of the interplay of various temporal, spatial and social levels, and recently on transboundary regions. His regional focus is on Western Europe and Canada.

Simon Gunn is Professor of Urban History at the University of Leicester, UK and co-editor of the journal *Urban History*. His books include *History and Cultural Theory* (2006) and *The Public Culture of the Victorian Middle Class* (2000). With Susan Townsend he is currently running a Leverhulme-funded project *Motor Cities: Automobility and the Urban Environment in Birmingham, England and Nagoya, Japan, 1955* and with Rebecca Madgin a JISC funded project *Manufacturing Pasts: Industrial Change in Twentieth-Century Britain*.

Christine Hannemann is Professor of Architecture and Housing at the University of Stuttgart. She received her Ph.D. at the Technical University Berlin in 1994 for her dissertation on the ideology and practice of industrialized building in the former GDR. Her second book was on *Marginalized Towns:*

Problems, Differentiations and Changes (2004). Her work focuses in particular on urban and regional developments. As co-editor she published since 2001 *Jahrbuch StadtRegion/Yearbook CityRegion*.

Martina Heßler is Professor of Modern Social and Economic History and the History of Technology at the Helmut-Schmidt University, Hamburg. Her research focuses on urban history, history of technology as well as on visual history. She did her Ph.D. at the Technical University Darmstadt in 2000. She is author of several books, including *Mrs. Modern Woman. Zur Geschichte der Haushaltstechnisierung* (2001) and *Kulturgeschichte der Technik* (2012). Currently she is President of the German Society for the History of Technology.

Martin Jemelka is Assistant Professor for social and economic history at the University of Technology Ostrava (Czech Republic) and research Fellow at the Economic and Social History Center, University of Ostrava. He got his Ph.D. in 2006. His areas of research are Modern economic and social history, Modern urban history, Oral history, Working-class history and Demography. He has published several books on the Everyday Life in Miners' Colonies (2007, 2008, 2009), Workers' Housing Schemes in Ostrava in the Czech Republic (2012, 2013) and co-edited a volume on the international Company Towns of the Bat'a Concern (2013).

Henry Keazor is Professor of Early Modern and Contemporary Art History at the University of Heidelberg. His research and publications are focusing on French and Italian painting of the 16th and 17th centuries and on contemporary media such as TV cartoons, music video, as well as the relation between film and art, including *Hitchcock und die Künste* (2013). Further publications deal with visual culture and contemporary architecture and its relation to modern media.

Robert Lewis is Professor of Geography at the University of Toronto and co-editor of Urban History. His research is focused on the industrial geography of Canadian and American metropolitan areas and on the social geography of colonial Bombay and Calcutta. He has written *Chicago Made: Factory Networks in the Industrial Metropolis* (2008) and *Manufacturing Montreal: The Making of an Industrial Landscape* (2000). He is presently working on a book that examines the military-industrial-state complex in Chicago between 1940 and 1950.

Timo Luks is Assistant Professor of Social and Economic History at the University of Technology Chemnitz. He received his Ph.D. in 2010 at the Carl von Ossietzky University Oldenburg. The same year, his dissertation on modernity, social engineering and industrial work was published (*Der Betrieb als Ort der Moderne*, Bielefeld: transcript). Currently he is working on a book about police history in the 19th century.

Rebecca Madgin is a Lecturer at the Centre for Urban History, University of Leicester. Her work focuses on the values of the historic environment in European cities. Her current work examines both the impact of de-industrialization on the urban environment in Italian and Scottish cities and the ways in which people working outside the formal planning system ascribe values to the historic environment. She is particularly interested in the ways in which the urban pasts inform the future development of the city.

Jörg Plöger is Senior Researcher at the Research institute for Regional and Urban development in Dortmund. He received his Ph.D. at the University of Kiel in 2006. His dissertation focused on recent urban transformation processes in Latin American metropolises, in particular on the appropriation of residential space. From 2006 to 2009 he worked on the *Weak Market Cities* project at the London School of Economics, analyzing the approaches of urban recovery in Western European cities (published 2010).

Richard Rodger is Professor of Economic and Social History at Edinburgh University. He has published widely on the urban history of Britain since 1800, and was editor of Urban History from 1987–2007. His book *The Transformation of Edinburgh: Land, Property and Trust in the 19th Century* was awarded the Frank Watson Prize for works on Scottish history. Other books include, *Scottish Housing in the 20th century, Housing in Urban Britain 1780-1914* and *Environmental and Social Justice in the City* (co-ed.).

Rolf Sachsse is Professor of Design History and Design Theory at the Hochschule der Bildenden Künste (University of art and design) in Saarbrücken. He received his Ph.D. at the University of Bonn in 1983 with a study on Photography as a medium of the interpretation of architecture. He curated numerous exhibitions on art and architecture. His books include *Bild und Bau: zur Nutzung technischer Medien beim Entwerfen von Architektur* (1997) and *Die Erziehung zum Wegsehen: Fotografie im NS-Staat* (2003).

Adelheid von Saldern is Emeritus Professor at the University of Hannover. She was vice-chairwoman at the Gesellschaft für Stadtgeschichte und Urbanisierungsforschung in 2000-2004. She received her Ph.D. in 1963 for her dissertation on Hermann Dietrich, a liberal politician of the Weimar republic. Her habilitation was about working-class people in a middle-seized city during the German empire. Her work emphasized in a large part on urban history, housing history, city representations and comparative media history.

Ondřej Ševeček is Research Fellow at the Institute of Philosophy, Academy of Sciences of the Czech Republic. His area of research is economic and social history of the 20th century, modern urban history and modern Czech Business History. He has published *The Birth of Bata's Industrial Metropolis: Factory, Urban Space and Society in the city of Zlín, 1900–1938* and co-edited a volume on the international company towns of the Bat'a concern (2013).

Judith Thissen is Associate Professor of Media History at Utrecht University. Her rescarch addresses the relationship between media culture and social history. She has published in numerous anthologies and in journals such as *Film History, Theatre Survey, KINtop* and *Tijdschrift voor Sociaal-Economische Geschiedenis*. With Kitty Zijlmans and Robert Zwijnenberg, she recently edited *Contemporary Culture: New Perspectives on Arts and Humanities Research* (Amsterdam University Press, 2013).

Clemens Zimmermann is Professor of Cultural- and Media History in Saarbrücken. He received his Ph.D. 1981 with a thesis on agrarian reform processes and his habilitation in Heidelberg 1990 with a study on housing policies in the German empire. He is co-editor of *Informationen zur modernen Stadtgeschichte*. He has published extensively on urban history, rural-urban relations and media developments in several European countries. His books include *Die Zeit der Metropolen* (1996, 2000, 2004, 2012).

Index